Memorand: That mr Edward Waterhouse and Edward
Collingwood Secretaries to the Companie for Virginia doe by theis
presentes, have examined and compared theis Bookes goeing beefore,
conteyninge one hundred sixteene leaves from Page 1. to Page 354.
with the originall Booke of Courtes &c. And doe finde theis Booke &c.
with the originall Booke of Courtes it self. And Doe finde theis Booke &c.
at twoe severall dayes of theis first originall Courtebooke. Beinge God
. . . the . . . from the first originall Courtebook. Beinge God
. . . . . meetinge from the second Court held the 28 of May 1620 .
beeinge . . . . the 22th bill as farre as theis bookes in theis Copie,
. . . . agree with the Originall itself. And to every Page
of Edward Collingwood . . . with my hand, and testifie the
to testifie as above Ego it is a true Copie /

Jan 26 1623 .

Edw: Waterhouse : Secr.

Ed: Collingwood : Secr.

THE RECORDS OF
THE VIRGINIA COMPANY OF
LONDON

———

THE COURT BOOK
VOLUME I

LIBRARY OF CONGRESS

The Records of
The Virginia Company of London

THE COURT BOOK, FROM THE MANUSCRIPT
IN THE LIBRARY OF CONGRESS

EDITED
WITH AN INTRODUCTION AND BIBLIOGRAPHY, BY
SUSAN MYRA KINGSBURY, A. M., Ph. D.
INSTRUCTOR IN HISTORY AND ECONOMICS
SIMMONS COLLEGE

PREFACE BY
HERBERT LEVI OSGOOD, A. M., Ph. D.
PROFESSOR OF AMERICAN HISTORY IN
COLUMBIA UNIVERSITY

VOLUME I

WASHINGTON
GOVERNMENT PRINTING OFFICE
1906

L. C. card, 6–35006

Facsimile Reprint
Published 1993 by
HERITAGE BOOKS, INC.
1540-E Pointer Ridge Place, Bowie, Maryland 20716
(301) 390-7709

ISBN 1-55613-874-1

Note

In my report for 1904 I gave the reasons in favor of the printing by the Library of this and of similar unpublished manuscript records in its possession. It would save excessive wear and tear upon the originals; it would enable the texts to be studied by investigators who can not come to Washington; and it would encourage that thorough, detailed, and continuing study of them which their value and interest and a proper understanding of American history require. These reasons apply with peculiar force to the Records of the Virginia Company, unique in themselves and unique of their kind, and an additional one, in their case influential; that publication would make them available to persons who would not master the difficult chirography of the original.

Their history is fully told in the Introduction by Miss Kingsbury, and their importance as a document emphasized in the Preface by Professor Osgood. Previous efforts to secure their publication *in extenso* had not been successful. The present one originated in a proposal by Professor Osgood in behalf of the Public Archives Commission of the American Historical Association to edit them as a contribution to one of the Annual Reports of the Association; and although the work as issued is an independent publication of the Library, it has had the benefit of his expert counsel. It was at his instance also that Miss Kingsbury, then a graduate student in his department at Columbia, began the undertaking which she has so well accomplished, and which has consisted (1) in a complete transcript of the text itself; (2) in a close study not merely of this but of the numerous collateral and subsidiary documents both here and abroad; (3) in the preparation of the Introduction, Notes, Bibliography, and Index; and (4) in aid upon the proof. The proof has also, however, been read word for word with the original text, and revised by the Chief of the Division of Manuscripts, with the excellent assistance of Miss Minnie V. Stinson of that Division.

HERBERT PUTNAM
Librarian of Congress

WORTHINGTON CHAUNCEY FORD
Chief, Division of Manuscripts

3

Preface

The records, and especially the Court Book, of the Virginia Company of London have long been regarded as among the most precious manuscript treasures which have found a lodgment within the United States. Not only is their inherent value as an historical source very great, as has been explained by the editor in her introduction, but a sentimental value also attaches to them. This has a twofold origin. It arises, in the first place, from the fact that they belong at once to the romantic period of our own beginnings and to the heroic period of England's great struggle against absolutism. The men who figure in the pages of this record were at the same time playing their parts, on the one side or the other, in the controversies which were then beginning with James I, and which were to broaden and deepen under his son till England was plunged into the agonies of the great civil war. They were contemporaries, and in not a few cases associates, of Coke and Eliot and Hampden, of Bacon and Wentworth and Buckingham. The names of Sandys and the Ferrars stand high on the roll of patriots by which the first generation of the Stuart period is distinguished. These same men also, together with a long list of the merchants and nobles of the time, were deeply interested in discovery and colonization. As successors of Gilbert and Raleigh they were planting a new England beyond the Atlantic. About this enterprise still clung some of the spirit and memories of the Elizabethan seamen and their early struggles with Spain. In the days when Smythe and Sandys were active the prosaic age of English colonization had not yet begun. The glamour of romance, of the heroic, attaches to the founding of Virginia and Plymouth, and makes them fit subjects for the poet. By the time when the other colonies were founded the glow and inspiration had grown faint or wholly disappeared. In the Records of the Virginia Company some reflection may be seen of this early zeal, of the plans and ideals to which it gave rise. Even their pages, cast in a style which is quite unusual in records of this nature, make one realize that he is in the company of noble and earnest spirits, men who were conscious that they were engaged in a great enterprise. The Court Book itself, now that it is printed in full, will be found to be a worthy monument of English speech, as it was used at the close of the Elizabethan epoch and by contemporaries of Shakespeare and Bacon.

The fate which probably befell the original of this record, and the unusual steps which it became necessary to take in order to secure and preserve a copy, were natural consequences of the struggles of the time, and add still further to the interest of the text as we now possess it. Miss Kingsbury, by her use of the Ferrar papers, has been able to establish by the clearest proof the connection of Nicholas Ferrar with the transcription, and in many other ways she has added definiteness to the accounts usually given of the origin and preservation of the record as we now possess it. The transfer of the copy of the Court Book to Virginia and its transmission from hand to hand till, through the medium of Thomas Jefferson's library, it finally passed into the possession of Congress fittingly concludes the remarkable history of the preservation of this manuscript.

The high estimate which has been placed on its value is evidenced not only by the use that has been made of it by historians, but by the long-continued efforts which have been made to secure its publication. In 1858 Mr. J. Wingate Thornton, in an article in the "Historical Magazine," explained the nature of the Court Book, told how it had been preserved, and insisted upon the importance of its being published. "As these volumes are of national rather than of local interest," said he, "reaching back to the very foundation of the English companies for colonizing America; as they have escaped the chances and mishaps of two centuries, on either side of the Atlantic, . . . and as Providence has now placed them in the keeping of our National Congress, is it not our national duty to have them appropriately edited and published?" The following year Mr. Thornton published a pamphlet in Boston, in which he outlined the history of the manuscript and again raised the question of its publication. But soon the Civil War came on, and plans of that kind, especially so far as they related to southern history, had to be postponed.

But in 1868, three years after the close of the war, Mr. Edward D. Neill presented a memorial to Congress, in which he dwelt on the neglect by historians of these most valuable manuscripts. He stated that, while preparing his book entitled "Terra Mariae," he had familiarized himself with the chirography of the records. He now offered to undertake their editing without compensation, if he might be furnished with two copyists for a limited time and be allowed a small sum for stationery and contingent expenses. But this offer met with no response, and Mr. Neill was forced to content himself with the publication of extracts from the manuscript in his "History of the Virginia Company of London" (Albany, 1869).

In March, 1877, Mr. Robert A. Brock, of the Virginia Historical Society, published in the "Richmond Daily Dispatch" a "Plea for the Publication of the Records of the Virginia Company." In 1881 Senator John W. Johnston, of Virginia, introduced into Congress a bill which was intended to provide for the publication of the records. This passed the Senate, but failed in the House.

During three successive sessions between the years 1885 and 1888 Dr. J. Franklin Jameson applied to the Library Committee of Congress for permission to edit and publish the records without expense to the Government. His plan was to obtain a sufficient number of subscribers to justify the issue of the volumes by a private firm and to meet the cost of the sale. Another suggestion which he also made was the appointment of a commission which should concern itself with the publishing of

historical material in the possession of Congress.   While occupied with this matter
Dr. Jameson explained the history and value of the records to the Rhode Island
Historical Society, and his address was reviewed in the "Magazine of American
History" (vol. 21, January–June, 1889, p. 82).

But meantime some progress had been made with the actual printing of the Court
Book.   Mr. Conway Robinson had made copious extracts from it, especially of the
documentary material which is contained in the second volume.   His extracts the
Virginia Historical Society published in 1889, under the editorship of Mr. R. A. Brock.
Until the present time this edition, in two volumes, has served the purpose of most
students.   But the requirements of historical study in this country have now reached
a point where more complete and critical editions of the sources are needed than have
been common in the past.   If this need was to be met, it became at once apparent
that no body of records was better adapted for a beginning than those which related
to the Virginia Company of London.   In date and subject matter they stand at the
very threshold of American history.   In character they form a distinct and unique
group of material.   By the issue of a definitive edition of these records the demand
which scholars have so long made for their publication would be met and satisfied.
It was under the influence of considerations like these that the present work was
undertaken.

In the preparation of this body of records for the press critical accuracy and
helpfulness have been sought in all possible ways.   The spelling of the original has
been carefully preserved throughout, for in editing a source of this character and
importance any attempt to modernize the text would be properly regarded as unjusti-
fiable.   Not only has the spelling been preserved, but also the signs and abbreviations which abound, the use of which the men of the period had inherited from still
earlier times.   So far as such a thing is possible in print, the text is exactly reproduced in these volumes, while an added element of reality is supplied by the photographs of specimen pages of the original manuscript.

Brief notes have been added where it was necessary to explain or call attention
to obscurities, omissions, or other irregularities in the text, the purpose being to
enable the reader to gain information of this kind from the printed page with the
same certainty as if he were using the manuscript.   In the notes, cross references
have also been given to the documents of the company and to its publications, when
they have been found to reproduce, or to illustrate and make more definite, the statements which are contained in the Court Book.   In citations of this kind the number
of each document is given as it appears in the List of Records in the Introduction.
In this way the unity of the records of the company as a whole receives illustration,
and the investigator will be aided in any effort which he may make to learn all which
they have to reveal in reference to any subject.   Finally, the index completes the
invaluable service which Miss Kingsbury has rendered in the editorship of the work.

HERBERT L. OSGOOD

COLUMBIA UNIVERSITY

Contents

Illustrations

1. The Character of the Company

The individual effort which had revealed itself at the close of the medieval period in other phases of the economic development and in the military history of the past quarter century was especially prominent in the movement in 1606 for a society of adventurers to trade in Virginia. The commercial advance had been due chiefly to private enterprise, and the naval expeditions into the West Indies against the Spanish had been fitted out and prosecuted by such adventurous spirits as Sir Francis Drake, while the zeal for exploration and for gold, which inspired John and Sebastian Cabot to search for a passage to Cathay and the East Indies in 1497, led Sir Humphrey Gilbert and Sir Walter Raleigh a century later to seek out the resources of the lands from Florida to Newfoundland. It is the same spirit of adventure which inspired the narratives of John Smith and Henry Spelman as they told of their relations with the Indians of America. But it is in the progress of both the commercial and the political life of England that the Virginia Company is important. For the plantation founded and nourished by a private concern as an enterprise purely for gain was the social cause from which developed the colony as a form of government. Its political organization is seen in its relations to the Crown, of which there were two distinct phases. During the first three years it was distinctly a creature of the King, the affairs of which were conducted by the King through a council created by himself and responsible to himself, while to the investors were left the privileges of raising the funds, furnishing the supplies, and sending out the expeditions. It was a modification of this form of management to which the government reverted after the dissolution of the Company in 1624, and again at the end of the century when royal colonies were substituted for proprietary and corporate forms throughout America. In the second phase the undertakers became distinctly proprietary, retaining the commercial responsibilities, but assuming governmental functions in place of the King.

A comparison between the royal grants for discovery in the sixteenth century and those of the Virginia Company shows that there was an increase in the direct territorial relations between King and subject, a limitation upon monopoly of trade, and a tendency on the part of the Crown to retain directly or indirectly the powers of government. Thus, in the letters patent to Richard Warde, Thomas Ashehurst, and associates in 1501,[a] to Sir Humphrey Gilbert in 1578, and to Sir Walter Raleigh in 1584,[b] the Crown conferred proprietorship of land with the right to grant it out in fee simple at will. But in 1606 the land was held by the undertakers, and again in 1609 by the adventurers and planters in free and common socage, as of the manor of Greenwich of the county of Kent. Under the first Virginia charter it was granted by the King to those approved by the council; under the second, by the members of the company to anyone who should have adventured a certain sum of money or his person. The fief, distinctly so called in the early charters, for which homage was to be rendered, with no service, however, save that of one-fifth of the gold and silver gained, had disappeared; and the only direct feudal relation with the King which remained arose from the requirement of a per cent of the precious metals. The monopoly of trade by which Warde, Gilbert, and Raleigh were allowed to seize and detain any one who trafficked within two hundred leagues of a settlement was altered in 1606 so that the planters had only the right of collecting a tax from such interlopers. The rights of government which had been surrendered absolutely to the grantees in the sixteenth century charters were reserved to the King by the letters patent of 1606 to be exercised through the council. In 1609 these powers were conferred on the company as an open body, it must be remembered, and thus differed from the earlier grants and from the later proprietary grants to Lord Baltimore or to William Penn.

Although the charter emphasizes the government of the plantation, the Virginia Company was purely a commercial enterprise conducted by a private concern, even before the charter of 1609, as is shown by the history of its early years. It was backed by the patronage of the King, but only for the purpose of advancing the trade of the Kingdom in foreign parts and saving the Crown from expense and responsibility, as had been the policy in regard to the other trading companies. Nevertheless, it was a step toward colonial expansion, for, as has well been said, "the explorer is potentially a colonizer," and the army of laborers on the plantation became in time an army of free tenants in a colony.[c] While in the spirit of its commercial life the company was closely allied to the efforts for exploration and search for gold, morally supported by Elizabeth in her feudal grants, in its organization, as well as in its purpose, it resembled the private companies for trade based on ancient charters, and in its development is to be understood only through a knowledge of both of these earlier movements.

[a] Biddle, *Cabot*, Appendix, pp. 312, 314, for this charter.
[b] Hakluyt, *Principal Navigations*, VIII, 17–23, 289–296.
[c] Osgood, H. L., *The American Colonies in the 17th Century*, I, 83.

Thus in order to protect trade, but not for exploration and settlement, the ancient charters granted to the Merchant Adventurers in 1407 and 1462, and particularly the one of 1564, incorporated that company into a "Body Politick." The words of the grant declared its purpose to be "for the good Government, Rule and Order of the * * * Fellowship of Merchants Adventurers * * *. As also of all and every other of the subject of our heirs * * * using the seate of Trade of the said Merchants Adventurers * * *."[a] This was also the object expressed in the charter to the East India Company,[b] although it contained an additional provision for the acquisition of lands by purchase. Monopoly of trade and powers of government over factors, masters, or others in the employ of the company were conferred, but the exemption from customs was to continue for only four years, and the only settlements provided for were to have the form of factories. It had been established as a regulated company, that is, one in which each individual invested his own capital subject to the rules of the company; but in 1612 by increasing the importance of the directors and investing sums for a limited period it became a joint stock company.[c]

As a prototype of the companies later incorporated both for discovery and trade, such as the Virginia Company, the Muscovy or Russian Company, known as the "Merchant Adventurers of England for the discoveries of lands and territories unknown," was established in 1555 with a joint stock of £6,000. Sebastian Cabot was appointed governor for life and with him was associated a board of directors of 4 consuls and 24 assistants. However, this company had also the rights of the companies for exploration—that is, those of conquest, of acquiring lands, and of seizing the ships of any who should infringe on their monopoly of trade.[d] In 1583 a committee from the Muscovy merchants drew up a set of resolutions concerning a conference with M. Carlile upon his "intended discoverie and attempt into the hithermost parts of America,"[e] which was not dissimilar to the plan of Sir Walter Raleigh, and hence foreshadowed companies of the seventeenth century. It proposed to send forth 100 men for one year, providing £4,000 for the adventure, in order to gain a "knowledge of the particular estate of the country and gather what commodity

[a] Lingelbach, *The Merchant Adventurers of England*, 218–236 for extracts from the charters. The first two are published in Rymer, *Foedera*, and Hakluyt.

[b] *East India Company, Charters.*

[c] Cunningham, W., *the Growth of English Industry and Commerce in Modern Times* (edition of 1903), Part I, ch. VI, sec. VII.

[d] See the patent in Hakluyt, II, 304–316. For full citation of the titles of printed works referred to in the notes, see the Bibliography, p. 212, *post.*

[e] See "Articles set down by the Committees appointed in behalfe of the Company of Muscovian Marchants to conferre with M. Carlile, upon his intended discoverie and attempt into the hithermost parts of America," printed in Hakluyt, VIII, 147–150.

may hereafter be looked for." Also, like the Virginia Company, it provided for a joint stock consisting of two groups, one of "adventurers" and one of "enterprisers," each to have one-half of the lands which should be divided among the members by the generality, but all trade was to belong to the adventurers and the corporation was to be closed after the first adventure. The scheme differed from the sixteenth century enterprises, which were especially intended for exploration, in that no question of government was considered, but it conformed to the ideas of Gilbert and Raleigh and of the trading companies, in that its rights over trade were to be purely monopolistic.

Apparently this plan of the Muscovy Company stands as a connecting link between the ideas of the explorer and those of the trader and the planter, a plan which may be said to have been carried out by the Virginia Company. It is significant that many of the members of the Virginia Company were men who had taken part in the expeditions of the late sixteenth century and had been interested in certain private voyages of exploration carried on during the five years preceding the receipt of its first charter, while most of the leaders of this company were at the same time stockholders and even officers in the Muscovy Company, the Company of Merchant Adventurers, the East India Company, and later of the Turkey, the Guinea, and the African companies.

It is unnecessary to cite the charters of other companies or to search the history of the trading corporations of the sixteenth century in order to show that the Virginia Company was similar in character. But, like the Muscovy Company and the East India Company, it was established to carry on trade in new and uninhabited lands, and hence had the additional features of a company whose purpose was exploration and plantation. The latter characteristic appears more especially in the charter, the former in the instructions and correspondence of the entire period of its life. The object of its first undertakers was doubtless to search for minerals and for a route to the southwest, and to secure for trade the materials which were native and peculiar to those regions. The plantation was a necessity for this purpose, and incidentally, because of the character of the country, it was forced to become a colony. To establish a settlement which should become a market for English goods, to advance the shipping, to spread the religion of the Kingdom were doubtless motives which aroused sympathy for the undertaking; but the arguments which brought investment were the opportunities for gain.

The position of the Virginia Company in the development of English exploration and trade was therefore important, and the study of its history is of value not only for the light which it throws on Virginia itself but for an understanding of the economic condition of England as well. Nor is this all. The few private records which remain of the Merchant Adventurers Company and those of the East India

Company correspond so closely in form and in subject-matter to the court book of the Virginia Company that the similarity in form of organization and methods of conducting business is established. The fact that the private records, the books from which the knowledge of the actual financial transactions could be obtained, are missing in most cases, may prove that their loss in the case of the early Virginia Company is not due to intentional destruction, but to the general opinion of the period that such material was valueless.

The only other enterprise of which there is sufficient material for anything like an exhaustive study is the East India Company, and hence its records combine with those of the Virginia Company to supply a source of information concerning all of these companies. The conclusion seems valid, therefore, that the great mass of minutes, orders, instructions, letters, and memoranda of the company for Virginia will aid in the interpretation of the comparatively few records of the earlier associations. The records of this company are necessary to enable one to comprehend the life of the other companies, as is its history to the understanding of their development.

It was during the life of the company that the plantation gradually assumed the aspects of a colony, that the settlement which was originally planned for exploration and the discovery of gold became a center for the development of the natural and agricultural resources of the surrounding country. The origin within the colony of the assembly, of local government, of private ownership of land, and of freedom of trade is to be found before the dissolution of the company by the Crown. Therefore the records of the company, as well as those of the colony, form the material through which the history of the beginnings of English colonies, viewed from the standpoint of the colonist, is to be gained.

Their value for the comprehension of the development of political institutions in England is not so patent. The growing correspondence between the Crown and the company and the interference in the acts of the company stand as evidence of the gradual increase of the interest of the Crown or its council in the undertaking. This interest was most apparent when the tobacco trade promised a revenue to the Crown, but the encouragement of the growth of other staple products, the spasmodic revival of acts touching English shipping and the balance of trade, and the maintenance of staple ports in England are all new activities appearing in the records of the company. Throughout, also, is apparent the readiness to allow the already uncertain economic policy to be altered or nullified by the political relations with Spain, or because of moral or whimsical views.

The gradual definition of policy on the part of the Stuarts, perhaps first apparent under Charles I, is closely connected with the leaders of the Virginia Company. The opinions expressed in the courts of the company by the adherents both of the Puritan party and of the party of the Crown, the correspondence between the Privy Council and the company, the letters and memoranda concerning the company and its policy, and the story of the formation of the Sandys and the Warwick factions, resulting in the dissolution of the company, furnish evidence of the gradual development of the despotic attitude of the Stuarts, especially in their reach for revenue and in their repression of the principles of freedom. The appointment of the commissions to investigate the affairs of the company and the condition of the colony, the creation of a commission for the control of the colony after the overthrow of the charter, the later appointment of a committee of the Privy Council for the same purpose are all steps in the growth of a colonial system and of a colonial policy. Although the maturity of this system and policy is not reached until after the Commonwealth, the influence of the associates of James I and of Charles I is apparent.

Every phase of colonial development, from the mixed system which existed under the patent of 1606 to the chartered proprietary company after 1609 and the royal province after 1624, is here illustrated. The transition from the chartered to the Royal Government in 1624, the prelude to "the most important transition in American history previous to the colonial revolt," is only to be understood from these records, since the tendency to self-government in the colony is one of the pretended reasons for the overthrow of the company. All the steps of the change are to be traced in the royal correspondence, in the memoranda of the royal party, and in the record of the suit under the writ of *quo warranto*. The significance of such material is best understood from the fact that "the constitutional law and practice of the old colonial system has not yet been attempted to be known," and as yet no book has been written concerning the forms or functions of the British Government as employed in colonial administration.

2. The Records of the Company under Sir Thomas Smythe

The Organization of the Company as in 1606

In the year preceding the grant of a charter to the Virginia Company there had been movements along two lines for establishing plantations in Virginia, one by private investment and the other by royal patronage. Examples of the private interests are the enterprise of the Earl of Southampton in 1605 and that of Lord Zouch as set forth in his contract[a] with Captain George Waymouth of October 30, 1605. In this Lord Zouch agreed to secure and provide two ships and 200 men of "arts suitable for a colony," and to pay £100 to Captain Waymouth for the transportation of the same. The interesting feature is the agreement, suggestive of feudal relations, that Lord Zouch should be the first officer and have the first choice of land, while Captain Waymouth as second officer should have second choice of land, which he was to hold from the former as lord paramount for himself, his heirs and assigns. At the same time Sir John Popham was busily engaged in the attempt to form royal colonies by obtaining charters from the Crown, whereby the territory from 34° to 45° north latitude should be taken under the protection of the King, and private settlements should thus be excluded.

The plan which obtained followed neither course, though it was bound to result in a modification of Popham's scheme. The motives of the grantees and the arguments which induced the King in 1606 to abandon the policy of Elizabeth and to give royal patronage to the undertaking, and even to assume royal control, are set forth in a petition presented to Parliament in 1606, entitled "Reasons for raising a publique stocke to be imploied in the discovering of such countries as may be found most convenient * * * ."[b] It is evident, however, that the unknown plan of investment in the adventure of 1606 is not here suggested, since there was no intimation of financial support by the King. The stock was apparently to be raised by a tax "Upon the emoderate gaines of those that contrary to lawe abuse the poore," and was not in any way to be "raised upon the sweat of the poore or the industrie of the

[a] Printed in full in Brown, *Genesis of the United States*, I, 33–35.
[b] Printed in full, Brown, *Genesis*, I, 36–42.

husbandmen, Artificer, or tradisman," but in such a way that nothing should "be demanded from anie man without presente assurance of gaine and hope of future profit * * * but in such sorte that the payer shall for every ij^d paied gaine iiij^d." To the Kingdom and to the Crown were to redound the greatest gain. Ten thousand pounds a year were to be added to His Majesty's receipts by an increase of many thousand pounds in the imposts and customs; and furthermore it "would savior too much of affectacon of a popular State to levie monies without imparting some convenient portion to his Majestie." But the value to shipping was emphasized perhaps more vigorously as developing a defence to the island, as furnishing a source for the necessities for ships—cordage, pitch, tar, and resin—and as protecting the shipping from decay. The desirability of a revival of the declining export trade, as well as that of establishing the importation of necessities from a part of the dominions, though distant, was urged, together with the importance of strengthening by settlement those countries already acquired by discovery. That such undertakings by private enterprise had been failures; that it was more honorable for the State to back an exploitation by public consent than by private monopoly; that public colonies were bound to be more obedient and industrious because of the greater confidence in the character of the control, were all reasons which had long before been set forth whereby to gain the support of the Crown.

CHARTER OF 1606.

The royal aid as finally obtained for a colonial enterprise came in a somewhat different form. The letters patent to Sir Thomas Gates and others for plantations to be made in Virginia[a] show that the investment was made solely by individuals, and that the joint stock was not public, although in the regulation of affairs in the colony the body of undertakers was to have little influence, even as far as its commercial interests in the plantation were concerned. The business management was left to the joint stock companies, and the magazine was controlled by a treasurer or cape merchant and by two clerks elected by the President and Council in the Colony. In fact, the only activity of the adventurers, so far as it is revealed in the extant documents, consisted in the choice in London of one or more groups of agents, called "companies," to manage the goods sent out and received and to look after the profits.[b] The undertakers were to have all lands with their resources

---

[a] For a reprint of the letters patent, see Brown, *Genesis*, I, 52–62, or Poore's *Constitutions*.

[b] *Articles, Instructions and Orders for the government of the Colonies*, November 20, 1606. Reprinted in Brown, *Genesis*, I, 64–75, from a manuscript record book in the register's office of Virginia. There is a manuscript copy in the Library of Congress, in the *Virginia Miscellaneous Records, 1606–1692*, pp. 25–33.

which lay within 50 miles of the plantation in any direction, together with the islands within 100 miles of the coast, and were privileged to inhabit and fortify the same according as the council for Virginia should direct. The right freely to transport subjects was granted the investors, while they were permitted customs free for seven years to export armor, provisions, and all necessities of life for the colonists. They could impose upon any subjects of the Crown, who were not adventurers, trafficking in those regions, a tax of 2½ per cent of the articles concerned, and upon foreigners twice that amount, and thus maintain a control of the trade for twenty-one years.

But the government of the colonies and of the territory of Virginia was reserved to the Crown through the council of thirteen for Virginia, which was to be appointed by the King and to reside in England. Instructions[a] were issued and signed by the royal hand, which outlined the form of administering affairs in the settlement and created a council of thirteen in the colony. They conferred upon it the right to coin money and to pass ordinances which should be valid till altered by the Crown, provided that they should be consonant with the laws of England. This council in Virginia was to choose its own president for one year. It could remove him or any member for just cause and fill the vacancies. All civil causes and all lesser criminal cases were to be decided by the president and council, the former having two votes in case of a tie. Cases of manslaughter and the more heinous crimes were to be tried before a jury and were punishable with death. To the president and council was reserved the right of pardon.

The council in England nominated to the Crown the persons to whom lands were to be granted by the King. It had, in fact, the supervision of affairs, appointed the first council in Virginia, issued orders for the conduct of the first expedition under Captain Newport,[b] and provided a paper of advice[c] as to the establishment of a fort and of a town.

It is in this latter document that the first indication of the real motive of the undertaking is found. The orders laid down were to "make choice" of the river "which bendeth most toward the North-West, for that way you shall soonest find the other sea," while the choice of a healthy location, wise intercourse with the natives, and the fortification and preparation of a single settlement were emphasized. The chief objects, however, were to plant in a place

---

[a] Printed in full, Brown, *Genesis*, I, 64–75.

[b] See *Certain Orders and Directions*, December 10, 1606. Manuscript in the Library of Congress, *Virginia Miscellaneous Records, 1606–1692*, pp. 19–23. Reprinted in Brown, *Genesis*, I, 75–79.

[c] See *Instructions by way of Advice*, December, 1606. Manuscript in the Library of Congress, *Virginia Miscellaneous Records, 1606–1692*, pp. 14–17. Reprinted in Brown, *Genesis*, I, 79–85.

which should be fitted "to receive the trade of all the countries about," to discover minerals, and to find the passage to the western sea.

The loss of the records, both of the council and of the "companies" for trade, covering this period, leaves, as the only source of information, both for affairs in England and in Virginia, the narratives of the early settlers. Of these the most important are the reports of Captain Newport, and the relations of John Smith, of Edward Maria Wingfield, and of George Percy.[a] The council had dispatched three expeditions, all under Captain Newport; one in December, 1606, in three ships with 120 emigrants; another in October, 1607, with two vessels and about the same number of passengers; and a third in August of 1608 with about 70 emigrants.

The reports of Newport, Percy, Wingfield, and Smith encouraged the managers of the enterprise to continue their efforts, but proved that a change in object as well as in policy would be necessary. From Newport came descriptions of the fruitfulness of the soil, of the quantities of fish and of timber, and of clay for making brick, and enumerations of the possible exports, comprising sturgeon, clapboard, wainscot, saxafrage, tobacco, dyes, furs, pitch, resin, turpentine, oils, wines, wood and soap ashes, iron, copper, pearls; but the reports as to the mines were vague. He declared that the country was rich in gold and copper, and took home with him earth to be assayed, while Smith, in *A True Relation*, states that he had been left to dig a rock which Captain Newport thought was a mine, but no mention of results is made.

The full description of the country by Newport and also by Captain John Smith gave the council a clear idea of its geography, as is indicated by the instructions to Sir Thomas Gates in 1609. But the expedition, which penetrated to a distance of 160 miles up the river, brought the explorers to hostile tribes and left the council still uncertain, though hopeful of the discovery of a passage to the south sea. Furthermore, Captain Newport positively stated that there could be no commerce with the Indians, and all evidence shows that the natives were to be a resource for the necessities of life rather than for the exchange of lucrative objects of trade. Hence it is that the broadside which was issued by the company in 1609,[b] as an incident of its

[a] See John Smith, *A True Relation*, 1608, reprinted in Arber, *Works of John Smith*, 1884; *Discourse of Virginia*, by Edward Maria Wingfield, printed in the *Archaeologia Americana*, IV, 77–103; *Observations gathered out of a Discourse of the Plantation * in Virginia * 1606*, by George Percy, printed in Brown, *Genesis*, I, 152–168; and the following documents probably written by Captain Archer: *A Relatyon of the Discovery of Our River, from James Forte into the maine: * * by Capt. Christopher Newport*, 1607, printed in *Archaeologia Americana*, IV, 40–58; *The Description of the now-discovered river and country of Virginia*, printed in the *Archaeologia Americana*, IV, 59–62; *A Brief Description of the People*, printed in *Archaeologia Americana*, IV, 63–65.

[b] *Nova Britannia*, printed February 18, 1609. This document is reprinted in Force's *Tracts*, I, No. 6.

attempt to secure capital for the undertaking in its new form, emphasized the richness of the soil and the resources of the country—which in later years would yield abundant return—the value of the settlement as a market for English cloths, and the advantage to shipping and shipbuilding which would come from colonization.

But the effort to develop the resources of the country and to found a settlement for such purposes rather than for exploration required larger investments and more men. Then, too, the regulation of the affairs of the colony without any control from the council in England meant continued jealousies and quarrels among such a small number of colonists and under such unsettled conditions. According to Wingfield the provisions for defense seem to have been insufficient, the magazine was mismanaged, and the relations with the Indians were strained. To John Smith must be attributed the wisdom of foreseeing the necessity of strong support from England and of the establishment of permanent colonial settlements and the development of the country for self-support.[a]

THE CHANGE IN CHARACTER FROM 1606 TO 1609

The fact that the source of authority before 1609 was in the Crown is nowhere so clearly evidenced as in the records themselves. The fundamental documents emanated from the King and his Council or from the council for Virginia representing the royal authority, all instructions to officers bore the sign manual and all letters and reports from Captain Newport, from Edward-Maria Wingfield, and from his associates were addressed to the council for Virginia. Furthermore, the president and council appeared in the name of the Crown as the plaintiffs in a suit by which an attempt was made to enforce the contract with the master of the "Guift of God" for supplying provisions to the passengers in a voyage to North Virginia.[b] The direct relations of the planters to the Crown are similarly emphasized by two heretofore unpublished documents, which are in the Library of Congress, consisting of the oaths administered to the colonists and to the secretary of the colony.[c]

The commercial status of the undertaking is more difficult to determine than the political. That the company was organized for the purpose of exploration and trade has been proved, but whether the control of trade was vested in the council or in companies or groups of undertakers is uncertain. The exact relation of the council to the plantation and of the Crown to the enterprise must have been stated in the

[a] For a history of the organization of the company and of the founding of the colony, see Osgood, I, Chs. i–iv.

[b] Bibliographical List of the Records of the Virginia Company, *post*, p. 121, No. 7.

[c] List of Records, p. 121, Nos. 5, 6.

court book, in which were kept the records of the acts of the council and perhaps of the companies for the administration of trade. This book, covering the period from the 28th of January, 1606, to the 14th of February, 1615, was in the possession of the company as late as 1623, but unfortunately no trace of the book has yet been discovered and even its existence has heretofore been unknown.[a]

Whatever may have been the source of control, the narrations of Captain Percy, Edward-Maria Wingfield, and Captain Newport indicate that the business of the company consisted chiefly in raising funds and equipping expeditions to be sent to Virginia under Captain Newport. This failure of the investment to bring in returns of gold and silver and of articles for trade, or to accomplish anything in the way of discovery of trade routes to the East Indies during the first three years, served to convince both King and undertakers that a change in method of control was essential. The document known as "Reasons against publishing the Kings title to Virginia. A justification for planting Virginia"[b] seems to show an agitation among the investors arising from fear lest the desire to placate Spain, or religious considerations, might lead the Crown to abandon the scheme. The arguments there adduced may well explain the readiness of the King to surrender not only the commercial and territorial control but also full rights of government to the corporate body of the Virginia company, and thus to avoid any rupture with Spain. Certain it is that the desire for more direct authority and for securing larger investments were the motives of the petitioners in asking for a new charter.

As a result of this movement the letters patent of 1609 were issued, transforming the undertakers into a body politic. In this case also the documents are especially characteristic of the organization. Whereas the Crown was formerly the source of all power, beginning with 1609 the council of the company, acting as a standing committee for the adventurers rather than in the name of the King, exercised the controlling authority. After the charter of 1612 had provided for more frequent meetings of the generality, the council was gradually superseded by special committees and the tendency arose to decide all matters of importance in the general quarter courts and to insist upon all communications being addressed to the company rather than to the council. The act of incorporation erected a commercial company and made it the overlord of a proprietary province. It at once strengthened its plantation as a center for traffic and established a system for joint management of land and trade to extend over a period of seven years, prom-

---

[a] When the Privy Council demanded the records of the company, a receipt bearing the date April 21, 1623, was given to the secretary of the company for the "several court books." This document was discovered by the Editor among the Ferrar papers, Magdalene College, Cambridge, in December, 1903. See List of Records, p. 171, No. 470.

[b] This document was recently found by the Editor in the Bodleian Library. *Ibid.*, p. 121, No. 1.

ising dividends to the adventurer and support to the planter. The records of the corporation reveal as clearly as do its broadsides and pamphlets that it was a business venture. These records may be grouped into seven classes.[a]

THE CLASSES OF RECORDS

I. The fundamental documents of the company were those by virtue of which it had its legal formation, and consisted of the letters patent, charters, and orders in council issued by the King and Privy Council.

II. The activity of the adventurers was recorded in the court books, which comprised the minutes of the transactions of the company. In those books were kept the discussions and decisions with regard to the plantation, the granting of land, and all financial policies and plans for developing the enterprise and increasing the income.

III. In carrying on its business the company gave commissions to the governors of the colony, issued regulations for the settlers, and, from time to time, sent instructions to the governor and council of the colony. It also granted lands and patents, entered into contracts, issued receipts, made pleas in court, and kept statements of accounts.

IV. From the colony itself came reports, declarations, letters, and complaints. They were an essential part of the records of the company and often determined its course of action.

V. To the public, for the purpose of inspiring confidence, securing adventurers, and maintaining the interest and support of its members, as well as of defending itself against the accusations of its enemies, the company issued advertisements, broadsides of its shipping investments, declarations, pamphlets, and sermons.

VI. A large part of the information which came to the company was derived from private correspondence between members of the company and individual planters. Furthermore, there was a gradual tendency to permit individuals or groups of individuals of the company to form stock companies for trade or plantation, and records of these transactions formed a valuable supplement to those of the company itself.

VII. To the student of history another group of supplementary material is of great value. It comes from the records of contemporary companies, corporations, and towns, as well as from the correspondence of officers of state or of other persons who were not directly concerned in the transactions of the Virginia Company.

[a] For the documents in these various classes, see the classifications by Roman numerals at the left of each entry under the "List of Records," *post*, pp. 121-205.

All of these records of the company for the period previous to 1616, so far as they were known to him, were collected and reprinted in full or cited, if already available in America, by Alexander Brown, in the year 1890.[a]

I.—FUNDAMENTAL DOCUMENTS

As far as appears from the evidence of the extant documents, when by the charters of 1609 and 1612, James I surrendered to the company full rights of trade, as well as territorial and governmental rights in Virginia he apparently lost all interest and part in the undertaking, and it was only when the plantation had developed into the colony, and when at the expiration of the privileges of free importation in 1619, the business of the corporation had become so good as to offer a prospect of revenue that the King in his council began to interfere in the affairs of the company.[b]   In 1613, under the administration of Sir Thomas Smythe, the adventurers were compelled to appeal to the Crown because of the complications with France which arose from the expedition of Sir Samuel Argall along the northern coasts of America,[c] while a similar relation was brought about by the controversy with Spain with regard to the attack on Spanish vessels by the ship *Treasurer* in 1619.[d]   In both instances the protection desired was granted.   When the financial stringency forced the adventurers to great efforts in 1614, and they appealed unsuccessfully to Parliament for aid, the Privy Council attempted to arouse confidence in the undertaking throughout the country.   It passed orders urging the city companies of London to invest sums in the Virginia lottery, and in the following year it addressed similar orders to the "Several Cityes and Townes of the Kingdome,"[e] with special letters to the lieutenants of County Surrey.[f]

But the aid thus secured was not such as to draw upon the resources of the Crown, and the attempt of members of the company to gain a monopoly of the tobacco trade in 1616 met with the same opposition as had similar efforts on the part of the merchant adventurers in previous years.   On the other hand the company was com-

---

[a] For the documents of the period from 1606–1609 not mentioned by Mr. Brown in his *Genesis of the United States*, most of which have recently been discovered, see List of the Records of the Virginia Company, *post*, pp. 121–125, Nos. 1–38.

[b] In March, 1619, Abraham and John Jacobs received a grant for the collection of customs or imports on tobacco. This became an important feature of the business of the company in its later procedure. See List of Records, pp. 127, 129, Nos. 53, 73.

[c] Brown, *Genesis*, II, 640–644.

[d] List of Records, p. 132, No. 102.

[e] Brown, *Genesis*, II, 676, 679, 685, 733, 760.

[f] List of Records, p. 126, No. 49.

pelled against its will to submit to the treatment of its plantation as a penal colony by James I in his spasmodic efforts to develop a policy which should save England from an overpopulation of vagabonds.[a]

With the exception of these unimportant relations with the Crown, the company seems to have conducted its business independently of royal aid or interference during the first decade of its existence as a corporate body.

II.—THE COURT BOOK

It is therefore in the court book of the company and in its instructions, correspondence, and other records suggested under the preceding classifications II and III, that its activity and methods must be found. That court books were kept under the administration of Sir Thomas Smythe is known from the receipt in the Ferrar papers, already referred to. The first book extended from January 28, 1606, to February 14, 1615, and with it were "other perticuler writings belonging to the company." The second included the period between January 31, 1615, and July 28, 1619. What these books contained can only be surmised from the scope of the two later volumes, dated April 28, 1619, to May 22, 1622, and May 20, 1622, to April 2, 1623, the contemporary copies of which are now extant and in the Library of Congress, at Washington.[b] The contents of the "other perticuler writings," none of which are now known to be extant, are suggested by a memorandum of Sir Nathaniel Rich in a document among the Manchester papers. In attempting to prove the good done during Sir Thomas Smythe's administration Rich cites certain records as authority. The first one mentioned was a "booke of perticulers" containing the "Public workes: done in Sr T. Smithes tyme", and showing "the plenty of Armes &c left in S^r Th. Smithes tyme"; the second was a "pticular already deliuered to the Com^{ra}." in which appeared the "Staple Comodityes raysed in Sr T. Smithes tyme"; while the third formed a "collec of the publiq$_h$ workes made by S^r Sa. Argall wch he [comenset]" and was entitled "The pticulars of the Boates". Rich mentions two documents contained in this volume. He states

---

[a] There is a series of 14 orders of the Privy Council for the transportation of prisoners to Virginia in the years 1617 and 1618 not hitherto noted. List of Records, pp. 121–131, Nos. 4, 41, 65, 90. The transportation thus effected is mentioned by Miss E. M. Leonard, *The Early History of the English Poor Relief*, pp. 229–230, n.

[b] This receipt covered these four volumes, "the other perticuler writings belonging to the company," and two volumes of the court book of the Somers Islands Company, December 3, 1613, to January 24, 1620, and February 7, 1620, to February 19, 1622. However, the second volume of the court book, which is now in the Library of Congress—the fourth volume here mentioned—was continued until June 19, 1624, after the return of the records to the company.

that pages "11, 12, 13, 14, 15, &c.," contain the "League of the Natiues," and that on pages 51 to 59 was "Sir T. Dales îre." In his notes for discussion Rich also refers to "The Courte Bookes," and further declares that "Wrott remembers 4 warrants" by which lotteries were erected under the hands of the "Counsell of Virginia". In connection with the lottery he cites "th' Accompts" of Gabnell and declares that "He kept Tables".[a] Thus the discovery by the Editor of these two documents in these two similar collections belonging to the hostile factions has proved that the company possessed record books; but a knowledge of their contents must be gained from other sources.

To supply the loss of these documents of the company, both during the control of the council and after that control had passed into the hands of the company by virtue of the charter of 1612, there is a considerable mass of material, which affords a fair outline of the transactions of the company and the life of the colony. But much of this information is lacking in the completeness and authenticity which would have been supplied by the court book and the other records. The greatest loss is perhaps that of definite knowledge concerning the financial status of the company. The sums adventured by individuals and corporations is preserved in two alphabetical lists; but, so far as is known, only one of these lists is official, and that includes the names of the particular adventure about the year 1610.[b] The other is an unpublished list apparently both incomplete and unofficial, and was probably made somewhat later than 1618 at the order of the court,[c] although the date 1618 has been assigned to it in the Manchester papers, where it is to be found.[d] From the records of the various London companies and from records of English towns, as also from adventures sealed to individuals by the Virginia Company, comes the most authentic information concerning the large sums invested during this decade. In a similar way the knowledge, otherwise to be found in the court book and "The pticulers of the Boates," concerning the ships dispatched and the sums expended for the equipment of planters, individuals, and companies, is scattering and indefinite. The broadsides issued are calls for adventurers, planters, and colonists, with the requirements or statements concerning the lottery schemes; but they do not furnish the wide information which is found in those of the later period. So far as revenue is concerned, there was probably little except that which came from new adventurers

---

[a] This paper is evidently a series of rough notes of heads and references to prove charges of mismanagement by the Sandys faction. It is in the handwriting of Sir N. Rich. *List of Records*, p. 167, No. 438.

[b] Brown, *Genesis*, I, 465–469.

[c] For an act providing for such a compilation see the record of the court, Dec. 15, 1619.

[d] *List of Records*, p. 127, No. 58.

and the lotteries, but we have no way of knowing even that resource, while our knowledge of the income from tobacco and commodities brought from Virginia is derived from three or four scattering receipts only, found mostly among the papers of the Earl of De La Warr and of Lord Sackville.[a]

Even our knowledge as to the economic condition of the colony is most indefinite and comes only from printed pamphlets issued by the company. Judging from the sources of information in the later period, this uncertainty is due to the disappearance of the letters themselves, since, after 1619, the published relations of individual planters, the declarations by the company, and even the records of the court books are all more general in character than the letters which were sent from the colony to the company. Furthermore, in the later period the daily acts of the colonists and their needs, as reported from time to time by returning ships, afforded the adventurers a body of information concerning the social condition of the colony which in form and accuracy left little to be desired. After the time of Captain John Smith not much was accurately known of the colony until the year 1617, when Captain John Rolfe and Ralph Hamor supplied statistics as to the numbers, condition, settlements, and resources of the colony as it then was.

The individual enterprises of this decade in the life of the company are altogether unknown, except from a few contracts for shipping found here and there. Such movements must at least have been noted in the court book. Of the first "hundred," established in 1618, nothing is recorded except the single report, heretofore unknown,[b] of a meeting of the committee for Smythes Hundred. But the greatest loss which we suffer through the disappearance of the court book is that of material which should throw light on the aims, motives, and unsuccessful efforts of the company and on the struggles and difficulties through which it passed. For example, there is a single reference to an attempt to found a college, but no information whatever on the subject. The factions which developed and which resulted finally in the dissolution of the company evidently existed in this period, for a letter from Chamberlain to Carleton, dated May 8, 1619,[c] in which he speaks of the failure to reelect Sir Thomas Smythe as treasurer of the Virginia Company as having been "somewhat bettered at a later meeting of the Summers Island Company by his choice as treasurer of that company," proves that the change was due to factional differences, although the extant court books open with the refusal of Sir Thomas Smythe to continue as treasurer. Similarly, the choice of officers for the company, the votes received by each candidate, the appointments to positions in the colony,

[a] List of Records, Nos. 59, 60. Also Brown, *Genesis*, II, 772.
[b] *Ibid.*, No. 76. This is among the Ferrar papers of Magdalene College, Cambridge.
[c] *Ibid.*, No. 108.

the petitions to the company and its action thereupon, and numerous other acts, revealing the relations and attitude of the individual members, are all unknown.[a]

III.—DOCUMENTS ISSUED BY THE COMPANY

Of the official documents issued by the company during the decade from 1609 to 1619 the most important have been unknown up to this time. They include the first instructions ever given to a governor of a colony by an English administrative body, and the records of the first suits entered by the company in chancery for the purpose of enforcing the payments of sums adventured in the company and of securing a part of the income from the lottery, which the company claimed had been withheld by the agent, William Leveson.[b]

The knowledge which the administrators of the affairs of the company had gained from the early settlers, and their grasp of the necessities for exploration, for trade, and for the conduct of affairs in the plantation, has hitherto been a matter of surmise based on the relations of the planters. From the "Instrucčons, orders, and constitučons to Sir Thomas Gates," [c] in May, 1609, and a similar document given to "Sir Thos. West Knight Lo:Lawarr" [d] in 1609 or 1610 comes a revelation of the motives of the adventurers, as well as of the policy adopted and of the methods outlined for the prosecution of their efforts. These instructions to Gates and De La Warr afforded the authority for the termination of the previous government in Virginia, the stated ideas of the company as to locations for settlements, forts, and magazines, and concerning journeys inland. It also included an interesting reference to Raleigh's colonists. The general policy in administering the affairs of the colonists and the detailed orders as to the relations with the Indians, as far as they concern guards, trade, and treaties, and the daily life of the inhabitants, indicate a definiteness in the control of the company which formerly was not understood. In such a revelation of the knowledge of the country and of the natives there is a

---

[a] Scattering information of such a character concerning this period appears in the discussions and quarrels recorded in the later court books.

[b] List of Records, pp. 123–124, Nos. 20, 21, 22, 24, 25, 26, 27, 28, 29, 31.

There are three cases recorded in the chancery proceedings in which the company attempted to enforce the payment of adventured sums. The bill of complaint is identical in each case, with the exception of the names of the defendant and the sums they underwrote. The bill, dated April 28, 1613, against Sir Henry Nevile, Sir Henry Carye, and eighteen others is printed in Brown's *Genesis of the United States*, II, pp. 623–631, from a copy found among the Smyth of Nibley papers. It differs slightly in orthography only from the original record. The five recorded answers supply even more valuable information than the bills of complaints.

[c] This manuscript is in the Bodleian Library, Oxford, *Ashmolean Manuscripts*, 1147, folios 175–190ᵃ. It was discovered by the Editor in October, 1903. See also List of Records, p. 122, No. 10.

[d] *Ashmolean Manuscripts*, 1147, folios 191–205ᵃ. See also List of Records, p. 122, No. 11.

basis for belief that the affairs of the company were managed and its records were kept in a systematic and businesslike way. [a]

The company had become convinced that the policy of John Smith was a wise one, and hence it ordered that a number of plantations should be settled and that efforts should be immediately directed to building healthful and sufficient houses and to planting widely enough for the self-support of the community. Here was the germ which was to develop into the colony, but the plan was as yet by no means so far-reaching. A common store, a common magazine, common refectories, labor by groups with a superintendent for each five or six persons, the prohibition of trade with the Indians except through the truck merchant were economic methods which looked to the gain of the adventurer in London rather than to the development of a colonial settlement. When the settlers had become self-supporting and capable of defense, then measures were to be taken to provide returns, so "that our fleetes come not home empty." Discovery of the seas and of royal mines, exchange of commodities, the exaction of tribute, and the development of the resources of the country for the purpose of securing "wines, pitche, Tarre, sope-ashes, Steele, Iron, Pipestaues, hempe, flaxe," silk grass, fishing for pearls, cod, and sturgeon were to be the sources of revenue. The instructions placed authority implicitly in the hands of the governor, who was expected to hear, but not necessarily to heed, the advice of the council and to judge according to "naturall right and equity then vppon the nicenes of the lawe."

The agents of the corporation—the governor and his council in Virginia—received their authorization for the exercise of judicial as well as legislative powers through a commission. The one issued to Sir Thomas Gates is lost, but doubtless is as similar to that given to Lord La Warr [b] as are his instructions. With the exception of a set of "Instructions for such things as are to be sente from Virginia, 1610," [c] these orders and commissions are the only documents which show anything of the direct authority exercised by the company over affairs in the plantation until the issue of the "Great Charter of privileges, orders, and Lawes" in November, 1618. [d]

Otherwise, the whole course of the activity of the company under Sir Thomas Smythe was in strong contrast with the work of Sir Edwin Sandys. It was a con-

[a] Care on the part of the company is also seen in the general instructions of 1609 to the lieutenant-governor of Virginia, which are known only through a copy of the sixth article, preserved in the papers of the Marquis of Lansdowne. *Ibid.*, No. 9.

[b] The commission bears the date February 28, 1610. It is printed in full in Brown, *Genesis*, I, 376–384.

[c] Printed in full in Brown, *Genesis*, I, 384–386.

[d] *Post*, p. 34. This set of instructions to Governor George Yeardley, although given late in 1618, belongs both in spirit and effect to the period of the Sandys-Southampton administration.

tinual struggle to arouse such interest in the scheme as would result in investment. The problem of marketing the products of the colony, which concerned the later company, did not arise until toward the close of the period, when a single unsuccessful effort was made to gain a monopoly of the sale of tobacco. In order to increase the capital stock, the company made personal appeals and issued printed statements and descriptions which it scattered broadly. The story is told in the lists of adventurers cited above, in the earnest endeavors to secure new planters and new adventures from individual town and guild, in the efforts to enforce the payment of sums already adventured, in a few receipts concerning tobacco, in the lottery schemes, which were legalized by the charter of 1612, and in printed broadsides and declarations. Thus the sums adventured by individuals, by the various London companies, and by the towns of England are given in a series of requests for adventure and in bills of adventure [a] issued by the company and found in the records of those companies and towns [b] as also in private collections. The chancery proceedings, in three suits, state that the company attempted to secure an adventure of £18,000 and the equipment of 600 men during the year 1611, and the failure to accomplish its purpose was set forth by the defendants as a reason for refusing to pay the sums adventured. Incidentally there was mentioned an income in the year 1613 of £8,000 from the lottery, of £2,000 from the sale of the Somers Islands, and of £600 or £800 from the disposal of the ship *De La Warr*.[c] However, with the exception of an unpublished letter from Sandys to the mayor of Sandwich [d] concerning the adventure by that town, in which he inclosed a list of the subscribers to that particular adventure, with the sums set down by each,[e] the official records reveal but little as to the sums which must have been received by the company.

In a similar manner there are unauthentic records of economic value concerning the lotteries and the importation of tobacco. Of the latter a few receipts and memoranda among the papers of Lord Sackville [f] and the Earl De La Warr [g] are positively

[a] For the text of these adventures, see Brown, *Genesis*, I, 238, 252–3, 308, 391–2 (has signature of secretary and seal of company), 452–3, 453–4, 461–2, 463–5; II, 496 (signature and seal), 555. For two not yet published see List of Records, pp. 122, 123, Nos. 16, 17, 23.

[b] For this series of about 30 records see Brown, *Genesis*, I, 254, 257, 257–8, 277, 277–8, 278, 280–2, 291, 292–3, 302–6, 306–7, 309–10, 388–9, 390, 344; II, 558–9, 560, 561, 592, 686–8, 690–1, 768–9, 757. Also List of Records, p. 122, No. 15.

[c] *Ibid.*, Nos. 21, 22, 25, 27, 31.

[d] Printed in Brown, *Genesis*, I, 461–2, 463–5.

[e] The list is printed in full in Brown, *Genesis*, I, 465–9.

[f] List of Records, p. 127, No. 59.

[g] *Ibid.*, No. 35, 60, and Brown, *Genesis*, II, 772. See also reference to payments for tobacco sent to Virginia in the List of Records, p. 122, No. 13.

all there is in existence relating to the origin of a trade which was estimated in 1619 to be worth £100,000. Of the former, there is a "Declaration for the Lottery," published in 1615 by the company, and an order of the Privy Council, together with letters urging the towns of the Kingdom to adventure in this the second great lottery of the company.[a] A letter from the governor of the Virginia Company to the mayor and aldermen of Ipswich [b] is to the same effect, but none of these documents tell of the income therefrom. The only record which will give an idea of the value of the first lottery is in the chancery proceedings, and relates to a suit of the company with William Leveson to secure moneys from the lottery,[c] in which the sum received in 1613 is here stated to have been £2,793 and 10 shillings. The answer of Leveson is of further interest in that it alone tells of the methods by which the business was conducted and of the house built for the lottery west of St. Paul's Church.

V.—PUBLICATIONS OF THE COMPANY[d]

The struggle for capital and for settlers before 1616 is most apparent from the advertisements that were issued. The broadsides of the years 1609, 1610, and 1611 are printed as official declarations of an intention on the part of the company to send voyages to Virginia, and contain the necessary information as to the classes of emigrants wanted—artificers only—and the conditions and rewards for emigration. The broadside of February, 1611, is of most value, in that the classes of emigrants with the numbers of each desired are specified, while that of 1610 is a defense against the slander of recently returned colonists, and emphasizes the former need of artificers as colonists.[e] The broadsides of 1613 and 1615 concern the drawing of the lotteries, the latter declaring in a general way the prosperous condition of the country and announcing the prizes and rewards, thus affording some conception of the sums received from such an enterprise.[f] The publications of the year 1616 disclose, as well as assert, the prosperity of the settlement and the assurance of its success, though giving no statistical information. That of April arranges for the first division of lands among old adventurers and promises the same to new adven-

---

[a] Brown, *Genesis*, II, 760–766. For unpublished letters, see List of Records, p. 124, Nos. 32, 33, 34.

[b] *Ibid.*, No. 71.

[c] *Ibid.*, No. 28.

[d] Because of the close relation of the publications of the company to the documents issued by the company, the discussion of Class V precedes that of Class IV.

[e] These are all reprinted in Brown, *Genesis*, I, (1) 248–249, (2) 354–356, (3) 439, (4) 445, (5) 469–470.

[f] Brown, *Genesis*, I, 608, 761–765.

turers, declaring the intention to send a new governor and surveyors to the colony for the purpose, while that of the winter of the same year announces that any settlers may return to England who will.[a]

In addition to the advertisements for investment and adventure, both of person and of money, the company put forth a series of publications, consisting of four sermons preached before the company at stated intervals, intended to arouse both interest and confidence in their undertaking. These afford but little if any definite information, but reveal the spirit of the times, as also the lines of criticism and resistance which the company had continually to meet.[b]

But of far greater importance to a comprehension of the attitude of the company, and especially of the progress of the plantation, are the declarations concerning the colony, which were published by the company.[c] They are nine in number, and bear the following titles and dates:

(1) *Nova Britannia.* London, 1609.

(2) *Virginia richly valued.* London, April 15, 1609.

(3) *A True and sincere declaration of the purpose and ends of the Plantation*, "by the authority of the Governor and Councellors of the Plantation." London, 1610. [December 14, 1609.]

(4) *Newes from Virginia*—a poem. 1610.

(5) *A True declaration of the estate of the colony of Virginia*, by the order of the "Councell of Virginia." London, 1610.

(6) *De La Warr's Relation.* London, July 6, 1611, with *Crashaw's Epistle Dedicatorie* as a preface.

(7) *The New life of Virginea—second part of Noua Britannia*, by "the Counsell of Virginea." London, May 1, 1612.

(8) *Good Newes from Virginia*, by Whittaker. London, 1613.

(9) *A booke called an narracon of the present State of Virginia by Ralph Hammer.* London, 1615.

The documents published in 1609 and also the poem of 1610 were efforts on the part of the company to defend itself against charges of failure in earlier years and to reveal the advantages which were promised under the new system of government. This is distinctly the tone and motive of the *Nova Britannia*, in which appear argu-

---

[a] Brown, *Genesis*, I, 774–779, 797–799.

[b] Brown, *Genesis*, I, (1) 282; (2) 293; (3) 312–316; (4) 360–373. A fourth sermon preached by Richard Crakanthorpe, March 24, 1608/9, on the anniversary of the accession of James I, has favorable references to the project. See Brown, *Genesis*, I, 255–256.

[c] Brown either reprints all of these or cites the reference. *Genesis*, I, (1) 241–243; (2) 279–280; (3) 337–353; (4) 420–426; (5) 427–428; (6) 477–478; II, (7) 558–559; (7) 577–588, 611–620; (9) 746–747.

ments in favor of the colony, and the statements of the plans, resources, and needs of the colony, together with an outline of the government which was now to be administered.

A True and sincere declaration further explains the unsatisfactory condition of the colony by reference to the incompetence of previous governors, furnishing perhaps the best historical narrative which was issued by the company during the first period of the plantation. It also holds out the promise of improved conditions under Gates and De La Warr, who are to be shortly sent to Virginia with a complete outfit of men and provisions. The second document describes the southern part of the country and cites the advantages of Florida as evidence of the opportunities in Virginia. After the time of De La Warr the published accounts of the plans, movements, and successes of the colonists became more complete. While the statements of De La Warr in his *Relation* are a bare outline of the conditions as he found them and the improvements in trade and discovery to which Captain Argall had contributed, together with his lordship's plans for the future, it is of value as forming, with Hamor's narrative four years later, a surprisingly accurate and satisfactory treatment of the development in the colony during those years.

Hamor gives a clear statement of the methods and success of Captain Dale in his relations with the Indians, of his organization and reform of the colony, and of his establishment of order therein, and reveals clearly the state of affairs on the arrival of Gates, the cause of the failure heretofore, and the details of the building of the successive towns, with descriptions and statistics for each. He gives also an historical narrative of the relations with the various Indian tribes and his knowledge and statements concerning the resources of the country are equally satisfactory. While Whittaker's *Good Newes from Virginia* and *The New Life of Virginea* are of value as corroborative evidence, they add but little to the knowledge of conditions or resources, and evidently were written more in the spirit of the poem of 1610, being intended to inspire confidence in the management of the colony, in the new system, and in the officers installed, as well as to arouse enthusiasm in the project.

It is evident that these publications are of more direct value in the study of the progress of the colony and tell at first hand but little more than the methods employed by the company to gain its end, but, together with the other reports from the colony which are preserved in manuscript form, they to an extent supply what has been lost by the disappearance of the court book. They prove that there was a gradual change in the motive and means of the company, due entirely to the exigencies of the case. The failure to discover precious metals forced the company to concern itself with the development of the resources of the country and with the production of staple articles which were needed in England. Then, too, the first written laws promulgated by Gates, De La Warr, and Dale in 1610–1612, martial in form and harsh in character, reveal the type of the plantation which the company now proposed;[a] the freedom of the individual was to be reduced to a minimum, all labor was to be regulated as if it were a military discipline and the produce was to belong to the common store. Thus the evils of the early settlement were to be avoided. But of necessity this plan was temporary. Argall, like Smith, was a good colonizer. The explorations of Smith and his trade with the Indians, together with the order and prosperity which were brought by Dale, resulted in the founding of various settlements, such as Henrico and others farther south, which became self-supporting and independent of the "supplies" from England. This meant that the company was to be forced to assume a different attitude toward the colony; that the common labor, common store, and common trade must be abandoned. By 1614 private lands had been given to a few inhabitants, every family had been assured of a house of four rooms, rent free, for one year, and women had been sent to the colony to aid in keeping the settlers contented and permanent.

Whether the company made any resistance to this development within the settlement, by which the adventurer in London must share the profit with the planter, will only be known when the court book shall have been discovered, but it is certain that by 1616 the point of view of the leaders of the company had changed. They had then come to realize that they were to be the middlemen for the marketing of the produce of the planters. This is proved by the movement in 1616 for the monopoly of the importation of the only lucrative staple, tobacco. Again, in 1619, when the time for free importation from the plantation had expired, they most eagerly sought an adjustment with the Crown, although, in 1614, Sir Edwin Sandys, by this time the leading spirit in the company, had been the chairman in the House committee which reported against monopolies.

To such an extent had the colony now grown that the instructions given to Sir George Yeardley in November, 1618, called "The Great Charter of privileges, orders, and Lawes," recognized the necessity for local government. They provided for two houses, the "Council of State," to be chosen by the company in its quarter court, and the general assembly, to consist "of the Council of State and two Burgesses

---

[a] *For the Colony of Virginea Britannia, Lawes Divine, Morall and Martiall, &c.*, entered for publication on December 13, 1611, is a code first established by Sir Thomas Gates, May 24, 1610, approved by the lord governor, June 12, 1610, and exemplified and enlarged by Sir Thomas Dale, June 22, 1611. They are reprinted in Force, *Tracts*, Vol. III.

chosen out of each Town Hundred or other particular Plantation."[a]   The great difference between this act of the company and that of nine years before, when the instructions to Gates were issued and the laws of Dale were approved, is apparent. Whether it was due entirely to the necessities arising from the changed conditions in the colony heretofore noted or to the abuse of power by Samuel Argall, from 1616 to 1619, is uncertain.[b]   Whether it was but a reflection of the growing popular sentiment within the company by which the generality exercised the powers of administration or whether it was due to the influence of the "opposition" in parliament can not be settled without fuller records than are at present extant.

IV.—LETTERS FROM THE PLANTERS AND RECORDS OF THE COLONY

The printed reports from the colonists and the printed declarations of the company were of course based on the letters from the planters and on those from the governor and council of Virginia to the Virginia Company.   There were also letters from individuals in the colony to officers of the company or to other adventurers in England. They may perhaps reveal more clearly the condition of affairs in the colony and the influences which moved the company in its change of policy, since they do not attempt to conceal, excuse, or palliate any of the circumstances.   Six of these narrate the story of the voyage of Gates and Somers, the misery in the plantation on the arrival of Gates and of De La Warr in 1610, and the steps that were taken to improve conditions.[c]   Through other letters from the colony the company gained its knowledge respecting voyages to Virginia, progress and order in the colony, and the building of Jamestown,[d] especially under Sir Thomas Dale, and as to the prosperity of the settlers. Dale in 1611, outlined his plans and his achievements, urged the sending of 2,000 men, and suggested that the difficulty of securing planters might be overcome by making the settlement a penal colony.   In 1615, 1616, and 1617 the company received reassurances from Dale, Hamor, and Rolfe of the prosperity of the colony; but the publications of the company and the letters from the colony from 1615 to 1618 were

---

[a] List of Records, p. 129, No. 72.

[b] There are extracts from two letters dealing with the alleged misappropriations and abuse of power by Captain Argall, deputy governor from May, 1617, to April 20, 1619.   One of these was addressed to Captain Argall and bears the date August 22, 1618; the other to Lord De La Warr, August 23, 1618. They are preserved in the court book of the company under the date of June 19, 1622.   See also *Ibid.*, Nos. 82, 83.

[c] These letters were from the governor and council, July 7, 1610; from John Radcliffe, October 4, 1609, Gabriel Archer, August 31, 1609, and from Captain Somers and Lord La Warr, August, 1610, to the Earl of Salisbury; and from William Strachey in *A True Repertory*, July 15, 1610.   They are reprinted in Brown, *Genesis*, I, 328–332, 400–402, 402–413, 416–417.

[d] See Strachey, *A True Repertory*, in *Purchas, His Pilgrimes*, IV, pp. 1734–1756.

either very few in number, or have not been preserved. These were the years of the excessive abuses in the colony under Sir Samuel Argall.[a]

The only evidence of records kept by the colonists is an abstract of "A Register book during the Goūm[t] of Sam[l] Argall Esq[r] admiral, and for y[e] time p[r]sent, prin-cipal Gou[r] of Virg[a]" in the year 1618. This abstract was probably made in 1730 under the direction of R. Hickman, deputy clerk of the general court of Virginia at that time, and has heretofore been unnoticed. From it comes a knowledge of correspondence between the governor and Bermuda Hundred and Kicoughtan, and between the governor and the company in London. A complaint of the largeness of privilege given to Captain Martin in his grant is significant because of the long con-test during later years, between the company and Captain Martin over this patent. There are, too, a number of commissions to officers for trade and for command, and several warrants, edicts, and proclamations. These are very similar in character to those issued by the governor and council in 1623, and reveal the fact that methods of government had not altered materially, though the source of authority had been changed by the great charter of 1618. The severity of penalty and the threats of reduction to slavery for offense are perhaps the features most characteristic of the period.[b]

VI.—PRIVATE PAPERS OF ADVENTURERS

While the company probably did not officially use the private correspondence received from the colony by individual adventurers, it doubtless profited by the information which it contained. Thus, the relation of John Rolfe,[c] addressed to Lord Rich and the King in 1616, ranked in value with the descriptions of Ralph Hamor, for it discussed the water supply of the colony, its food, clothing, houses, and government and gave statistical information as to the various towns, their location, the number of their inhabitants, and their officers. There are at least six other letters extant, similar in character, though of less value.[d]

But another series of private papers partakes most strongly of the nature of documents of the company. These are the contracts and correspondence relating

[a] For the log book of Argall and for these letters from Spelman, Dale, Argall, and Rolfe, see Brown, *Genesis*, I, 428–439, 483–488, 488–494, 501–508; II, 639–640: *Virginia Magazine of History*, IV, 28, 29; X, 134–138. Also noted in the List of Records *post*, p. 125, Nos. 39, 40.

[b] For full citation of these abstracts of about twenty documents, see *Ibid.*, Nos. 40, 42–48, 50–52, 55–57, 64, 65, 67, 74, 75.

[c] Reprinted in the *Virginia Historical Register*, I.

[d] (1) Sir Samuell Argall to Nicholas Hawes, June, 1613; (2) Whittaker to Crashaw, August 9, 1611; (3) Percy to Northumberland, August 17, 1611; (4) Dale to Winwood, June 3, 1616; (5) Dale to D. M., June 18, 1614; (6) Whittaker to Master G., June 18, 1614. See Brown, *Genesis*, I, (1) 640–644; (2) 497–500; (3) 500–501; II, (4) 780–782; (5) 747; (6) 747.

to individual adventures to Virginia or to groups of adventurers. They indicate a tendency in the company to grant private monopolies and to encourage private settlements—measures which indicate the growing importance of the undertaking and the development of individual trade. Only one series of documents relating to individual adventures is extant, those by which Lord Zouch's investment in Virginia was secured to him. His contracts were made in May, 1618, with John Bargrave and James Brett. There is also his warrant to John Fenner to pass to Virginia and trade with the colony and the savages in his pinnace *Silver Falcon*, in February, 1618/19.[a]

The other series of documents, which illustrate the legal forms and methods of the company, as also the way in which the first plantations were undertaken by private means, concern Smythe's Hundred and Berkeley Hundred. Among the Ferrar papers are the minutes of the meeting of the committee for Smythe's Hundred on May 8, 1618,[b] the first record concerning the hundred, which provides for the sending out and equipment of thirty-five men at an expense of £657 9s. 4d.

VII.—SUPPLEMENTARY CONTEMPORARY CORRESPONDENCE AND RECORDS

In addition to the documents which are either official records or similar to such records in character, there is a large amount of correspondence between officers of state in England and other individuals which by its reference throws light on the affairs of the company or gives additional or corroborative data. All of this which is earlier in date than 1616 has been published by Alexander Brown.

There are seven letters, the dates of which fall between 1616 and 1619, that are of the same character; but they add nothing in fact to the other documents, although two of them reveal the measures taken even at this early date to impress youths and maidens for Virginia and to send reprieved prisoners to the colony.[c] Of the documents of this character, which are given by Brown, perhaps the correspondence between the Spanish ambassador in London and the King of Spain is the most valuable, not in the trustworthiness of the data—though much of it confirms other sources—but in the revelation it contains of the part that Spanish relations played in the development of the company and especially in its decline during the following decade, while its reference to prevalent rumors, reports, and sentiment are extremely illuminating. There are thirty-seven of these documents in all, including the correspondence concerning the Spanish ship *Chaloner*. The Chamberlain-Carleton, Digby-Salisbury, Cottington-Salisbury, and Lee-Wilson correspondence add occa-

---

[a] For these documents see List of Records, p. 129, Nos. 77, 82, 98, 99.

[b] *Ibid.*, No. 76.

[c] *Ibid.*, Nos. 84, 85, 88, 89, 96.

sional data and serve to fix dates and facts which are known from other sources.[a] Of similar value are the chronicles of Howes, Abbot's Geography, Smith's Map of England and his General History, the Commons Journal, the writings of Sir Ferdinando Gorges, and other material which emanated from the Plymouth adventurers.[a]

[a]See Brown, *Genesis*, "Table of Contents."

3. The Collections of Documents, 1616-1624

The character of the documents of the company after 1619 is fundamentally the same as in the preceding decade. Virginia was still a proprietary province with a commercial company as an overlord, and therefore the company was still the immediate source of all government in the colony. To it came all appeals from colonial authorities; it exercised control over all commerce, both from and to Virginia; it granted all land and all privileges. Although the number of documents emanating from the Crown [a]—that is, of the first class—is large, they are rather an indication of the increasing wealth and importance of the company, than of royal interference. They concern the regulation of trade, complain of the abuse of power by the company, or provide for the investigation of its acts rather than assume any authority in the direct administration of its affairs. In them interference in the management is foreshadowed, but it is not until the dissolution of the company that the Crown again becomes the proprietor.

The mass of materials which form the records for this period is much greater than in the earlier decade. This is due on the one hand to their preservation in two or three collections, and on the other especially to the vast growth of business in the company and the rapid development from a colony for exploitation into a colony for settlement. Thus the minutes of the company, forming the second class of documents, show that it conducted a larger amount of business than any other proprietary company.[b] These minutes comprise two large volumes of the court book, and fill 741 manuscript pages.[c] In the third class there are nine letters from the company to the governor and council in the colony, and twelve from the latter body to the company, in addition to a large number of receipts, commissions, instructions, and laws.[d] A mass of material belonging distinctly to the plantation serves as a part of the records of the

[a] See documents under Class I in the List of Records.

[b] For this statement, as also for a full understanding of the character of the company, see Osgood, *The American Colonies in the Seventeenth Century*, I, 61.

[c] Grouped under Class II in the List of Records.

[d] *Ibid.*, Class III.

company and at the same time furnishes the story of the beginning of the political unity of the colony. This group consists of the "court booke" of the council of the colony during the last year of the authority of the company, covering about 65 pages; 54 commissions, orders, proclamations, and warrants to subordinates in the colony issued by the governor and council in Virginia, and 35 petitions to the same body from the members of the colony.[a] The publications of the company for this final period of its existence number 3 large broadsides, 11 declarations containing 168 printed pages, and 4 sermons and treatises made up of 150 pages.[b] The supplementary official material found in the correspondence between individuals of the company and of the colony or between members of the company in England, in addition to the records of the private companies within the larger body, includes many documents and memoranda.[c] Sixty-six of these are preserved in the Manchester papers, while 78 are from the Ferrar papers, which are now first made known and published. The unofficial material, consisting of records of other companies, of towns, and of correspondence touching on the affairs of the company or colony, numbers about 40 documents.[d]

The relative value of the various classes of the records for this period has been altered by the preservation of the court book which has made the other material supplementary, or even subsidiary, with the exception of the correspondence; for in it is either recorded or summarized the information which the company had received from all other sources, or which it imparted to individuals or to the public by other means. But the fact that the other records are supplementary does not decrease their value, for they often furnish the data which are the basis of the acts and conclusions of the company, while some of them also reveal the legal or political processes of the company, of the colony, of the courts, or of the sovereign authority, and others are of great value in the light which they throw on the dissenting party within the company.

The subject-matter of the court book, as well as the character and contents of the various documents, proves the changed condition which the increase of business had brought about, since a large proportion of the records deal with the founding and conducting of private enterprises, and many of them are really documents of a private nature. It is apparent that the company still looked upon the colony as a source of income for the investors, but that the ulterior object

---

[a] Grouped under Class IV in the List of Records.   These papers are all in the Library of Congress.

[b] *Ibid.*, Class V.

[c] *Ibid.*, Class VI.

[d] *Ibid.*, Class VII.

had become the development of the resources of Virginia instead of the production of wealth through mines and the opening of new trade routes. As a result of this change in commercial object had come the need of larger, more numerous, and more scattered settlements in the colony, and of greater co-operation on the part of the settlers, although it may well be claimed that the latter necessity had been urged upon the leaders by the mismanagement of Captain Argall during the three years previous to the change in administration. In order to increase the number of planters, concessions of privilege had been made to private parties or groups as early as 1618, since such investments were doubtless easier to secure when the adventure was under the immediate control of the undertaker. Similarly, for the purpose of stimulating capital and gaining the co-operation of the planters, the division of land, promised in 1609, was proclaimed in 1616. Free tenancy was now guaranteed to all individuals, even to indented servants, at the expiration of seven years. The organization of joint stock companies for the management of trade, which supplanted the magazine, was a movement toward private enterprize. Hence it is that these subjects, together with those which concern the importation and sale of tobacco, occupy the greater part of the court book, and must have consumed most of the attention of the corporation. The burden of discussion in the courts concerned the best means of marketing the products, whereas in the earlier decade it must have related to the increase of capital. The records of the colony were no longer simple reports to the company and instructions from the proprietor, but assumed the character of political documents, since liberty of land and trade, and the creation of numerous plantations and scattered settlements resulted in the growth of "political conditions and forces side by side with the commercial and economic." The minutes of the colonial legislative assembly, the records of the colonial court, the petitions to the governor and council, and the commissions and orders granted by that body are all distinctively new features in the records. Here is evidence of the creation of the colony, with its body of free citizens, out of the plantation, with its body of half-servile laborers.

THE JEFFERSON LIBRARY IN THE LIBRARY OF CONGRESS

The records of the company under the administration of Sir Edwin Sandys and the Earl of Southampton, or the copies of them so far as extant, are to-day scattered among many public and private collections both in England and in America. The Library of Congress at Washington possesses by far the largest and most important collection in this country. It contains the contemporary certified copy of the court book from 1619 to 1624, as well as a mass of original correspondence, or contemporary copies of the same, between the company and the council in Virginia.

It also includes many original records of the colony, many eighteenth century transcripts of the original commissions, patents, and other records, and many recent
transcripts and photographs of documents in the collections of England.

The eighteenth century transcripts and the original documents and contemporary
copies came to the Library of Congress from Thomas Jefferson's collection in two
different groups: the first in 1815, when his library, purchased "in a lump as
it stood on the catalogue," [a] was secured by Congress for the sum of $23,950; the
second was secured when the books of Mr. Jefferson were sold at auction subsequent
to his death in 1826. The catalogue of the auction sale classified those acquired
by the Library of Congress at the latter date under two numbers as follows: [b]

"No. 121. Records of the Virginia Company, 2 vols., fol. MS. (the authentic
copy mentioned in Stith's History).

"No. 122. Old Records of Virginia, 4 vols. fol. MS. viz:

"A. Letters, proclamations in 1622–23, and correspondence 1625.
(42) Transactions in council and assembly, their petition and his majesty's
answer.[c]

"B. (9). Orders from Feb. 1622 to Nov. 1627.[d]

"C. (32) A. Foreign business and Inquisitions from 1665 to 1676.
Transactions of the council from Dec. 9, 1698, to May 20, 1700."[e]

The volumes of Jefferson manuscripts relating to the company, which became
the property of the Government in 1815, were as follows:

(1) *First laws made by the Assembly in Va.   anno 1623.*[f]   (Used by Hening.)

(2) Journal of the Council and Assembly, 1626–1634.   (Used by Hening.) [g]

(3) Miscellaneous Records, 1606–1692, with a small quarto containing abstracts
of Rolls in the offices of State bound into the volume.   (Commonly known as the
Bland copy, because so cited by Hening.)

---

[a] Manuscript letters of Thomas Jefferson in the Library of Congress. In this letter to William
Hening, March 11, 1815, from Monticello, Mr. Jefferson stated that he could not retain a volume, since
Congress had purchased his library.

[b] The "Catalogue. President Jefferson's library .... (as arranged by himself,) .... to be sold
at auction, at the Long Room, Pennsylvania Avenue, Washington ...., 27th of February, 1829,
....," p. 4, is in the Library of Congress, *Miscellaneous Pamphlets*, Vol. 859, No. 14.

[c] This is classified as one folio manuscript in the catalogue of the Library of Congress, 1830, and
the latter is doubtless the manuscript covering the period from 1626–1634.

[d] This manuscript also contains loose papers to 1632.

[e] *Catalogue of the Library of Congress, 1830*, p. 167.

[f] *Catalogue of the Library of Congress, 1815*, p. 73.

[g] This is probably the same manuscript as that mentioned above under the Jefferson catalogue as
No. 122 (42). There is no other manuscript in the Library which corresponds to the title here given
or to the description above.

(4) *Miscellaneous Papers, 1606–1683. Instructions, Commiċons letters of Advice and admonitions and Public Speecħes, Proclamations &c. Collected, transcribed and diligently examined by the Originall Records, now extant, belonging to the Assemblie.*

The entire set in the first group, acquired in 1829, is composed either of original documents or of contemporary transcripts, while the second paper of the second group belongs to the same period. The Miscellaneous Papers, 1606–1683, are a seventeenth century transcript. The Laws of 1623 and the Miscellaneous Records, 1606–1692, are transcripts of the early eighteenth century and are attested by R. Hickman, who was clerk of the general court in 1722. The origin and identification of these various volumes, together with a later copy of the court book of the company, now in the library of the Virginia Historical Society and commonly known as the [John] Randolph [of Roanoke] copy, has been a subject of doubt and discussion, arising from the conflicting descriptions of the volumes by the early historians of Virginia, William Stith and John D. Burk, and by the editor of many of the documents in 1809, William Hening.

The following statements with regard to the first group made by Mr. Jefferson in a letter to Hugh P. Taylor, October 4, 1825,[a] will serve as a basis for the attempt to ascertain the history and authenticity of those manuscripts:

" The only manuscripts I now possess relating to the antiquities of our country are some folio volumes: Two of these are the proceeding[s] of the Virginia company in England; the remaining four are of the Records of the Council of Virginia, from 1622 to 1700. The account of the first two volumes, you will see in the preface to Stiths History of Virginia. They contain the records of the Virginia Company, copied from the originals, under the eye, if I recollect rightly, of the Earl of Southampton, a member of the company, bought at the sale of his library by Doctor Byrd, of Westover, and sold with that library to Isaac Zane. These volumes happened at the time of the sale, to have been borrowed by Col. R. Bland,[b] whose library I purchased, and with this they were sent to me. I gave notice of it to Mr. Zane, but he never reclaimed them.

" The other four volumes, I am confident, are the original office records of the council. My conjectures are, that when Sir John Randolph was about to begin the History of Virginia which he meant to write, he borrowed these volumes from the council office to collect from them materials for his work. He died before he had made any progress in that work, and they remained in his library, probably unobserved, during the whole life of the late Peyton Randolph, his son. From his executor, I purchased his library, in a lump, and these volumes were sent to me as a part of it. I found the leaves so rotten as often to crumble into dust on being handled; I bound them, therefore together, that they might not be unnecessarily opened; and have thus preserved them forty-seven years."

[a] From the *National Intelligencer*, October 19, 1825.   [b] Col. R. Bland died October 26, 1776.

CONTEMPORARY COPY OF THE COURT BOOK

The two volumes referred to by Mr. Jefferson as the "proceedings of the Virginia Company in England" are the contemporary copies of the court book which were secured by the Hon. William Byrd, of Westover, Virginia, from the estate of the Earl of Southampton, either at the time of his death in 1667 or later. Since Mr. Byrd was a boy of 15 living in London in 1667, it may have been when the Virginia estates were left him in 1671, or even in 1687 when he made a visit to England, that he made the purchase.[a] That the books remained in the possession of the descendants of Mr. Byrd for a century is proved by the fact that they are mentioned in a manuscript catalogue of the library of the third William Byrd, who died in 1777,[b] but these two volumes were not in the library of Colonel Byrd, when it was sold by his widow in Philadelphia to Isaac Zane. Mr. Jefferson's statement that he purchased them from Colonel Bland may be accepted,[c] but it would be difficult to prove whether he is equally reliable when he states that the volumes had been loaned to Colonel Bland and had not been returned by him to Colonel Byrd, or whether Mr. Deane is correct in saying that Colonel Bland, as an antiquary, had secured them. That Stith used these contemporary copies of the court book in his *History of Virginia* is apparent from his description of them, as also from his statement that they had been communicated to him by the "late worthy president of our council, the Hon. William Byrd, esq."[d]

MANUSCRIPT RECORDS OF THE COMPANY, VOLUME III

The other manuscript volumes, which the Library of Congress acquired from Mr. Jefferson and which are included under No. 122 of the Jefferson catalogue, belong to the early seventeenth century. They are the documents which Mr. Jefferson referred to in his letter to Mr. Taylor as having come from the library of the Hon. Peyton Randolph in such a fragile condition, and which in a letter to Mr. Wythe, of January 16, 1795, urging the necessity of publishing the laws of Virginia, he describes in a similar way.[e]

[a] William Byrd died December 4, 1704. See Byrd, *History of the Dividing Line.*

[b] "Catalogue of the Books in the Library at Westover belonging to William Byrd, Esqr.," p. 437, in *The Writings of Colonel William Byrd,* edited by J. S. Bassett.

[c] For a description of these volumes and the circumstances of their making, see the discussion, pp. 78–84, *post.*

[d] It is hardly possible that Mr. Jefferson's statement is incorrect and that, instead of having been acquired by Col. Richard Bland at that time, they passed from Stith to his brother-in-law, Peyton Randolph, and with the library of the latter to Jefferson. This is one of the solutions suggested by Justin Winsor. See *Narrative and Critical History of the United States,* III, 158.

[e] Hening, *Statutes at Large,* I, p. viii.

That these are the papers discussed by Stith is proved by comparing them with the Hickman (Bland) transcripts. In his preface, Stith confirms the description by Mr. Jefferson, but he apparently destroys the latter's theory that the papers had been in the possession of Peyton Randolph since the death of Sir John Randolph in 1736. Mr. Stith wrote his preface in 1746, and suggests that they were at that time in the possession of the House of Burgesses, although he does not make a positive statement to that effect. His assertions are worth recording, since they carry the history of the volumes back thirty years and also throw light on the Hickman transcripts.

"I must chiefly depend upon such of our Records, as are still extant. Many of them doubtless perished in the State-house at James-Town, and by other Accidents; and those, which have survived the Flames and Injuries of Time, have been so carelesly kept, are so broken, interrupted, and deficient, have been so mangled by Moths and Worms, and lie in such a confused and jumbled State (at least the most ancient of them) being huddled together in single Leaves and Sheets in Books out of the Binding, that I foresee, it will cost me infinite Pains and Labour, to reduce and digest them in any tolerable Order, so as to form from them a just and connected Narration. And some of them have been lost, even since Mr. Hickman was Clerk of the Secretary's Office. For I cannot find, among the Papers in our Offices, some old Rolls, to which he refers. I have therefore been obliged, in a few Points, to depend upon the Fidelity of that Gentleman's Extracts out of our oldest Records, made for the Use of Sir John Randolph. But these things were so far from discouraging and rebuffing me, that they were rather an additional Spur to my Industry. For I thought it highly necessary, before they were entirely lost and destroyed, to apply them to their proper Use, the forming a good History. But as the House of Burgesses in a late Session, upon my shewing their moldering and dangerous State to some of the Members, have justly taken them into their Consideration, and have ordered them to be reviewed and fairly transcribed, I doubt not, by their Assistance, and with the Help of the late Sir John Randolph's Papers, and such others, as are in the Hands of private Gentlemen in the Country, and will undoubtedly be readily communicated to further so noble and so useful a Design, to be able to collect and compose a tolerably regular and complete History of our Country." [a]

Hence, we are again left in a quandary. The papers may have come into Peyton Randolph's possession through the arrangement made by the burgesses for their transcription; but no transcript made directly from the documents as late as 1746 is known to us. Whether they were borrowed from the province by Mr. Stith or by Peyton Randolph, his brother-in-law, or by some other historian or antiquarian is not yet proved; and our only evidence that Jefferson secured them from Peyton Randolph's executor is his statement made twenty years after the date of the purchase.

[a] Stith, *History of Virginia*, preface, p. viii.

The papers, after almost a century in the Capitol, were in a still more deplorable condition in 1901 than that described by Mr. Stith, but the loose pages have now been carefully and skillfully repaired.   The order of contents of the volumes (while not chronologically arranged) may be known from the abstracts made under the direction of Hickman about 1722.   This agrees with an arrangement determined by the early pagination, the subject-matter, and the writing.   That these manuscripts are original records or contemporary copies is evidenced by the form of some of them, by the signatures of others, and by the autographs of the secretaries and clerks of the period.   The supposition is that they escaped destruction when the Province House was burned in Bacon's rebellion in 1678, during the administration of Gooch in 1698, and again during the Revolution, only to be lost to the State in the latter half of the eighteenth century.

The volume designated as 122, A, in the Jefferson catalogue, and there entitled "Letters, proclamations in 1622–23, and correspondence 1625," is evidently the one referred to by page in the Hickman abstract of the rolls as "the other side of No. A 42." [a]   This abstract is a quarto bound into the *Miscellaneous Records, 1606–1692*, called by Hening the "Bland copy."   In pages 1 to 14 a of this volume are eighteen letters from the colony to the King or to the company between 1621 and 1625, while pages 15 to 30 contain nine letters from the company to the colony between 1621 and August 6, 1623.   The first group are holographs, but of a secretary or clerk not yet identified.   The second are doubtless in the autograph of Edward Sharpless.[b]   Both are contemporary copies of the originals.[c]   The documents classed in the Jefferson catalogue as 122 (42) form the balance of this volume and also probably include the journal of the council and assembly, 1626–1634.   The latter was evidently used by Hening in compiling his statutes.

Presuming that this fragile document, which is the only one concerning the company and the colony while controlled by the company, formed one volume, its contents was as follows:

No. A 42:

      1. (*a*) Miscellaneous letters from the Privy Council to the governor and council in Virginia in 1623, pp. 1–3*a*.   An unknown holograph.

      (*b*) Declarations of the condition of the colony and answers thereto in 1623/4, pp. 3*a*–7*a*.   An unknown holograph.

[a] This volume of correspondence is cited in the List of Records as the "Manuscript Records of the Virginia Company of London, Vol. III, pt. ii," thus including in Vol. III all of this miscellaneous manuscript material of the company.

[b] Edward Sharpless had been a clerk of the secretary of the colony, Christopher Davison, and succeeded him upon his death in the winter of 1623/4.   He remained as acting secretary until his trial on May 20, 1624, for giving copies of the acts of the assembly to the commissioners of the King; John Sotherne then took up his duties.

[c] See Plates, *post*, Vol. II for illustrations of these holographs, and for evidence as to the autographs.

2. Fundamental orders, charters, ordinances, and instructions by the company in London and laws of the assembly in Virginia, pp. 8–21. Partly holographs as above.[a]

No. A 42. "The other side:"

1. (a) Letters from the colony to the King or to the company between 1621 and 1625. An unknown holograph.

(b) Letters from the company to the colony between 1621 and August 6, 1623. Holographs of Edward Sharpless.

2. Instructions, commissions, proclamations, orders, warrants, and letters of the governor and captain-general of Virginia and of the assembly, pp. 36–53. Partly the holograph of Edward Sharpless and partly perhaps of Christopher Davison, the secretary of the colony from November, 1621, until his death in the winter of 1623/4.[b]

4. Petitions to the governor and council in Virginia, pp. 58–63. Holographs as of the preceding.

5. A miscellaneous collection of letters between the Privy Council and the Commissioners for Virginia on the one hand and the governor and council in Virginia on the other, in 1625/6, pp. 68–70; a letter from the Virginia Company of London in 1626, p. 71, and a census of 1624, pp. 71–75. Unknown holographs similar to those in the first part of this end of the volume.[c]

The first part of the volume thus opens with the letters of the Privy Council to the colony on April 28, 1623, when the King first began the action looking toward the dissolution of the company, and with the first direct correspondence with the officers of the colony. The writing and the dates place the documents as consecutive through the entry of the acts of the assembly, March 5, 1623/4, when the assembly seems to have ceased. After that page, copies of scattered documents appear in a different writing, commencing on the back of the last assembly record. These are largely fundamental or constitutional, including the instructions of November 20, 1606, the charter of 1606, the order of 1607 enlarging the council, and the oaths administered to officials of the colony of the same period. The other part of the volume opens with the correspondence between the colony and the home government. After a hiatus of fifteen pages the documents of the governor and assembly begin as indicated under the second division above. The writing is that of Edward Sharpless and Christopher Davison, and remains the same throughout the petitions of the next group. The last group of miscellaneous documents agrees in subject with the

---

[a] This volume is cited in the List of Records, as "MSS. Records of the Virginia Company of London, Vol. III, pt. i."

[b] Christopher Davison was appointed at a quarter court, June 23, 1621. His commission was sealed November 28, 1621.

[c] Cited in the List of Records as "MSS. Records of the Virginia Company, Vol. III, pt. ii."

letters of the first part and in autograph with the first section of those letters. On a fly leaf among the loose papers is inscribed the following: "Records of W. Clay-bourne or Claiborne. / p Joseph [Jokeg] / Tho Farloue & / Vpton gent / Thos. Ba[u]rbag[e] / Clеr̄ Conc̄"./ This may belong to the records of the period after May 14, 1626, when William Claybourne was appointed secretary of the colony by Charles I, or it may have been placed in an earlier volume, or it may indicate that a part at least of the earlier volume was transcribed under his direction.

Section B (9) of No. 122 in the Jefferson catalogue, cited as orders from February, 1622, to November, 1627, and including loose pages as late as 1634, is the only octavo manuscript of these records and has been saved from its almost useless condition by repair. That this is the original blotter of the court book of the governor and council in Virginia, containing the original record of suits tried before that body and of orders issued by it, is proved by the hasty and brief entries, giving the volume an entirely different character from those of the carefully elaborated transcripts of the clerks. The records of twenty-three courts held as here given and of the cases considered during the era of the authority of the company, consisting of about forty-five pages of manuscript, are noted in the list of the records of the company, but are not printed in this collection since they may be included more properly in a publication of the "Records of the Colony."

THE TRANSCRIPTS OF THE VIRGINIA RECORDS

RANDOLPH COPY

It is now certain that at least two copies of the court book existed at the beginning of the nineteenth century, since the so-called John Randolph [of Roanoke] copy has recently come to light.[a] It bears every evidence of being an eighteenth century transcript made from the contemporary copy now in the Library of Congress; the manuscript is of the century following that of the contemporary copy; the order, paragraphing, form of insertion of documents, and material is identical; but the omissions and errors arise from illegibility in the earlier manuscript. The other differences lie in occasional carelessness by the copyist and in the fact that the abbreviations are expanded and the spelling and the capitalization are modernized.

The caption of the first volume of this eighteenth century copy is as follows: "The Ancient Records of this Colony under The Treasurer and Company." It opens with "A Quarter Court held for Virginia at Sir Thomas Smith's house in

[a] The three volumes are in the collection of the Virginia Historical Society in Richmond, but they are so closely associated with the Library of Congress MSS. that they are discussed here rather than under the MSS. of Richmond.

Philpott Lane, 28th of April 1619," and ends on page 535 with the court of July 3, 1622. The final statement is as follows: "The rest of the Company's Acts are contained in a Second Volume." Volume II begins with a court of July 17, 1622, and closes on page 491 with the proceedings of June 7, 1624. It bears the caption, "The Records of the Company of Virginia, Vol. 2^d." Pages 492 to 502 include a list of "The names of the Adventurers for Virginia, as they were in the Year 1620." On the inside of the board of this volume is written the name, "Sam'l Perkins of Cawson." There is a third volume of this series of transcripts which is described by Mr. Robinson thus: "The other volume begins with the first charter to the proprietors of Carolina dated the 24th of March, in the fifteenth year of Charles II, (1663) and ends page 543 with report of the petition of Philip Laudwell against the Lord Effingham made by the Lords Committees of Trade and Plantations, Dated at the Council Chamber 26th of April 1689." This document ends on page 530. The volume closes on page 544 with "A Memorial for obtaining a more perfect Rent Roll, & advancing Her Majesty's Quit Rents in Virginia". On the first cover is the date, "Sep 19th 1759."

Mr. Brown thinks that these copies were made for Colonel Richard Bland from Colonel Byrd's volumes and passed to Theodorick Bland of the family of Cawson, the grandfather of John Randolph of Roanoke, to whom they finally came. He adds that the Byrd volumes went to Mr. Jefferson with the Bland collection, which he bought about 1776, instead of the copies therefrom.[a] Mr. Jameson suggests that John Randolph of Roanoke may have inherited these transcripts from his great uncle, Sir John Randolph. In this case also they would have been made from Mr. Byrd's volumes, and perhaps should have gone to Mr. Jefferson with the Peyton Randolph library, but this would not account for the name "Cawson" in the second volume. Furthermore, according to Mr. Stanard, John Randolph of Roanoke was not an heir to Sir John Randolph, and the families were not even on friendly terms. Mr. Brown's supposition seems the more plausible, since Theodorick Bland, jr., of Cawson may have received the volumes from the son of Richard Bland by gift or purchase, though not by inheritance, and, as Theodorick Bland, jr., died without heirs in 1790, the books may have become the property of his sister's son, John Randolph of Roanoke.

The location of these volumes since the time of the death of John Randolph of Roanoke is known. According to Mr. Brown, John Randolph[b] in a codicil to

---

[a] See an account of "Two manuscript volumes now in the Library of Congress, at Washington, D. C.," in *The Magazine of American History*, New York, Vol. 29, April, 1893.

[b] Not to be confused with Sir John Randolph, father of the Peyton Randolph whose library Jefferson says he purchased in 1778.

his will in 1826 left his library to the master and fellows of Trinity College, Cambridge, but in 1831 so altered the will as to bequeath it to his niece, E. T. Bryan. Certain it is, however, that for ten years after his death on May 4, 1833, the volumes remained in his library in Roanoke, for Hon. Hugh Blair Grigsby examined them at that place on January 11, 1843. The library was sold in 1845, but it is evident from the statement of Judge William Leigh, the executor of the estate, that the Randolph copy of the court book remained in his hands.

The later history of this copy is told by Mr. Leigh Robinson, of Washington, D. C., as follows:

"A complete transcript of the Records of the Virginia Company had been in the possession of John Randolph of Roanoke, and by Mr. Randolph's executor, Judge William Leigh, was placed in the hands of my father, shortly after the termination of the war between the States. The Virginia Historical Society, having then no shelter of safety for such a work, my father placed it in the Vaults of one of the banks of Richmond, with a view to transferring it to the Society, as soon as it could be done with Safety. His death occurred before (in his opinion) this could be done. After his death, his family transferred to the Society the copy made by himself. It was some time before they were able to discover the place of deposit of the Randolph Copy. But they finally recovered it, and transferred this also to the Virginia Historical Society, where it now is."[a]

Mr. Conway Robinson, the father of Mr. Leigh Robinson, prepared for the press two volumes of abstracts from the court book, which were edited later by R. A. Brock for the Virginia Historical Society and entitled *Virginia Company, 1619-1624*. Robinson states that in the preparation of the volumes he had many transcripts made through Mr. Mehan from the copy in the Library of Congress, and also from the Randolph volumes which Judge Leigh had loaned to him.[b]

The third volume of this Randolph series, which is cited both by Burk and by Hening[c] as "Ancient Records, Volume III," was copied from the transcript attested by R. Hickman. This volume of Miscellaneous Records, 1606-1692, is the only volume which contains the substance found in the Randolph copy, and is of

[a] See a manuscript letter to Mr. Worthington C. Ford, Chief of the Division of Manuscripts in the Library of Congress, December 15, 1902. These volumes, and the third described by Mr. Robinson's father are now in the Virginia Historical Society collection in Richmond.

[b] A letter of Mr. Robinson to Mr. Deane, July 1, 1868. For the use of this letter, as also one from Mr. Deane to Mr. Robinson of July 6, 1868, the Editor is indebted to Mr. J. Franklin Jameson, professor of history in Chicago University. In a memorandum Mr. Deane states that he inspected these volumes in April, 1872, at which time they were at the house of Mr. S. A. Myers, the law partner of Mr. Conway Robinson.

[c] For the extracts from the "Ancient Records," Vol. III, so called, by Hening, see *Statutes at Large*, I, 76-113 (collated readings given), 113-120, 145, 146, 209, 223.

an earlier date, and, like the original rolls, is less chronological in arrangement. That the Randolph copy was not made from the original records is evidenced by the fact that the abstracts are identical with those of the Hickman or "Bland" copy.

That both Hening and Burk used the Randolph copies of the court book and also the third volume of that series is proved by their descriptions of the volumes, while the page references to "Ancient Records" cited by Hening coincide in each case with these three volumes. Mr. Hening speaks of three large folio volumes not in the orthography of the age of the events, and compiled without much regard to method for the purpose of forming material for a history of Virginia, and states that the first two volumes are minutes of the proceedings of the London Company, and the third an epitome of the legislative and judicial acts of authorities in Virginia, so far as then extant, which were regularly transmitted to England. These, he continues, were used by John Burk, who got them from John Randolph, and also by Skelton Jones, 1809, to complete Burk's History of Virginia.[a] Mr. Burk himself declares that there are two large volumes, instead of three, as stated by Hening, "containing the minutes of the London Company together with the proceedings of the Virginia Councils and Assembly, with little interruption to the middle of the reign of George II."[b]

JEFFERSON TRANSCRIPTS

The three volumes containing transcripts of the Virginia Records which came from the Jefferson Library in 1815 are unique, containing copies of records since destroyed. Two of them are attested by R. Hickman, the deputy clerk of the general court in 1722, and the third is the only seventeenth century transcript in our possession. Unlike the Randolph copies, the two large volumes include copies of records since destroyed.

Of this group the "First laws made by the assembly in Va. Anno 1623" bears on the back of the last page the following indorsement in Mr. Jefferson's hand: "This was found among the manuscript papers of Sr John Randolph and by the Hoñble. Peyton Randolph, esq. his son was given to Thos. Jefferson," and is attested as follows: "Copia Test R. Hickman D C G C." This early eighteenth century transcript was made by the same copyist as were the Miscellaneous Records, 1606–1692, and is the volume used by Hening and referred to in his first volume, pages 121–129. It must also be the subject of a letter from Thomas Jefferson to Hening, April 8, 1815, in which he states that the manuscript marked "A" contains laws of 1623–24, thirty-five acts, which was given him by Peyton Randolph from the materials used by Sir John Randolph, and which Mr. Jefferson declares to

---

[a] Hening, *Statutes at Large*, I, 76 n. (a).   [b] Burk, *History of Virginia*, I, ch. V; II, 7, 42, 67.

be the "Only copy extant of those laws!"[a]   In 1803 Mr. Jefferson had declined to lend to Mr. John D. Burk some of the printed laws of Virginia in his possession, since they were unique and could not be replaced.[b]   The internal evidence points to the fact that Hening also used the other volumes of this set, a fact corroborated by the following statement of Mr. Jefferson in a letter to Mr. George Watterson, May 7, 1815: "I gave to Mr. Milligan a note of those folio volumes of the Laws of Virginia belonging to the Library which being in known hands, will be recovered. One is a MS. volume from which a printed copy is now preparing for publication."[c]   Mr. Hening was doubtless using them in the preparation of his later volumes.   Certain it is that these documents form the basis for a part of his first volume, in which he cites the *Journal of the Council and Assembly, 1626–1634*, as belonging to Thomas Jefferson, and as having been "purchased by him with the library of Peyton Randolph, from his executors."   The third, the *Miscellaneous Records, 1606–1692*, he states was bought by Mr. Jefferson "from the executor of Richard Bland, dec'd."[d]

The seventeenth century volume, entitled *Instructions, Commiĉons letters of Advice and admonitions and Publique Speeches, Proclamations &c: Collected, transcribed and diligently examined by the Originall Records, now extant, belonging to the Assemblie*, is a vellum-covered book, with an embossed figure on the back cover, and with the following: "E / 1621 / Publiꝗ Letters / and Orders."   On the outside of the front cover upside down is: "E / John Bland / Richard Blan [d] / Alexander Morrison," / while on the half that remains of the first fly leaf is the name "Nelson."   On the fly leaf in the book in pencil is the statement: "date of MSS 1650–1695;" and on the front cover similarly is: "17" Century copie Bland." This presence of Richard Bland's name in the book shows that Mr. Jefferson secured it with the Bland Library.   The writing of the volume is similar to the early seventeenth century system in many of the abbreviations, the use of the double *f*, and the formation of some of the letters.   Evidently this is a collection of correspondence of the colony, transcribed from the court books and from the miscellaneous papers of the three volumes of the manuscript records of the company.[e]

The second volume of documents from 1606 to 1692 is in an eighteenth century hand, many of the documents bearing the attestation of R. Hickman.   The binding

---

[a] Jefferson Letters, in the Library of Congress.   This is an error, since a contemporary copy has been found among the "fragile papers" in Jefferson's own possession at the time.

[b] Thomas Jefferson to John D. Burk, Monticello, February 21, 1803.

[c] W. D. Johnston, *History of the Library of Congress*, I, 178.

[d] Hening, *Statutes at Large*, I, 147, 152, 224.   The first four volumes of this work were published in 1809.   By an act of the assembly in 1819 the work was completed.   In 1823 the first four volumes were reprinted.

[e] For the contents of this volume as late as 1624 see the List of Records.

is in calf and bears on the back the red label, "Vir/. Records." Bound into the back of this volume is a small quarto of twenty-five pages, containing outlines of documents in the Manuscript Records of the Company, which serves to identify the loose pages of the original records as Roll A. 42, and an abstract of Captain Argall's register during his government.[a] The documents in the folio volume are charters, instructions, commissions, letters from the Privy Council, and other documents emanating from the Crown, together with one or two from the company and from the council in Virginia.[b] That this volume is the one used by Hening in his *Statutes* and referred to as the "Bland copy"[c] is indicated by the contents as well as by the fact that it includes the quarto volume. His reason for citing it as the "Bland copy" can only be surmised, namely, that he had Mr. Jefferson's statement that it had been secured with the Bland library, an erroneous designation as is proved by Stith's statement in his preface, that R. Hickman made a copy of the Records for Sir John Randolph.[d] But the volume has been known for the past century as the "Bland copy," although its title as a "Hickman" or a "Randolph" volume would be more appropriate.

The conclusions which have been formed with regard to these original and contemporary manuscripts and the later transcripts disclose little concerning the circumstances under which they were made, or the original owners of the volumes. But the important facts to discover, in order to determine their authenticity, are the period of the transcript and the documents from which the copies were made, and these facts in each case have been ascertained.[e]

[a] The documents there referred to by page are noted in the "List of Records." The original register of Captain Argall has not been found.

[b] For the contents of this volume see the List of Records.

[c] Hening, *Statutes*, I, 223, 224–238.

[d] Stith, *History of Virginia*, Preface, which is dated December 10, 1746.

[e] For published statements and discussions of the history and identity of the volumes in the Library of Congress which concern the Virginia Company, as also of the Randolph copy, see:

Robert C. Howison, *History of Virginia*, I, 212 (footnote). 1843.

Fordyce M. Hubbard, Life of Sir Francis Wyatt in *Belknap's American Biography* (footnote). 1843.

Hugh Blair Grigsby in the *Southern Literary Messenger*, February, 1854.

J[ohn] W[ingate] T[hornton], in the *Historical Magazine*, February, 1858.

Charles Campbell, *History of Virginia*, p. 174. 1860.

William Green, in the *Southern Literary Messenger*, September, 1863.

Justin Winsor, *Narrative and Critical History of America*, III, 158. 1885.

E. D. Neill, *Virginia Company of London*. 1889.

J. Franklin Jameson, "The Records of the Virginia Company." An address delivered before the Rhode Island Historical Society, November 27, 1888. (The manuscript used by the Editor.) Reviewed in the *Magazine of American History with Notes and Queries*, Vol. XXI, January–June, 1889, p. 82.

Alexander Brown, in the *Magazine of American History*, April, 1893.

Lyon G. Tyler, in the *Report of the American Historical Association, 1901*, I, 545–550.

The Library of Congress has recently acquired a large number of transcripts of those manuscripts now in the libraries of Great Britain pertaining to the Virginia Company or to the colony under the authority of the company. It thus possesses reproductions of all of the Virginia material in the British Museum, the Privy Council office, the Bodleian Library, and the Magdalene College Library, Cambridge. In the Public Record Office all docquet notices on Virginia, all records of suits in chancery and the admiralty pertaining to Virginia, and the *quo warranto* in the King's Bench, by which the company was dissolved, as well as the most important documents and correspondence, have been transcribed or photographed for the Library of Congress, but the correspondence of the planters, the less important correspondence of the company, and mere memoranda are yet to be transcribed. The latter material is fairly outlined in the *Calendar of State Papers*, Colonial Series, 1574 to 1660, and in the Appendix of the eighth report of the *Royal Commission on Historical Manuscripts*, or is printed elsewhere in full.[a]

The collection of publications by the company belonging to the Library of Congress is fairly good. It contains twelve of those which were issued before 1616, but of the later books it has only three. The Declaration of 1620, the Declaration by Waterhouse in 1622, and John Donne's Sermon of the same year, in addition to Smith's General History, are the only ones of the eighteen now extant which are in the Library.

DOCUMENTS IN RICHMOND

The colonial records in Richmond, Virginia, relating to the period of the company are extremely few in number. Fortunately the original documents, which are in the Library of Congress, were borrowed or abstracted from the state house in time to save them from destruction during the Revolution or by fire in 1865.[b] There are, however, two volumes of original records in the Virginia State land office containing grants of land in 1623 and 1624, which were evidently entered by William Claybourne, at that time surveyor for the colony. The history of contemporary documents before 1625, which are located in the district of the old settlement, may thus be briefly told.

The valuable collections of the Virginia Historical Society in Richmond embrace the John Randolph of Roanoke transcripts described above, while the State library has three sets of transcripts and one set of abstracts from the British Public Record Office. Of the latter the De Jarnette papers, 1606–1691, include only

---

[a] All of these papers are included in the List of Records.

[b] William G. Stanard, "The Virginia Archives" in the *Report of the American Historical Association, 1903*, I, 645–664.

a few of the documents of interest; in the Macdonald and Winder papers are full and careful copies of several of the long and important documents, following generally the orthography of the originals; while the Sainsbury abstracts contain comparatively full outlines of those documents included in the *Calendar of State Papers*, Colonial Series.

MANUSCRIPTS IN THE NEW YORK PUBLIC LIBRARY

The New York Public Library is next in importance to the Library of Congress in manuscript material on the Virginia Company and second only to the John Carter Brown Library of Providence, Rhode Island, in publications. In the Lenox branch of the New York Library is to be found a unique set of documents relating to the settlement of Berkeley Hundred in 1619, known as the Smyth of Nibley papers which "are from the collection of Virginia manuscripts originally brought together by John Smyth (or Smith) of Nibley, the historian of the Berkeleys, who was born in 1567 and died in 1641. The collection comprises over sixty papers, original and contemporary transcripts, relating to the settlement of Virginia between 1613 and 1634. After passing into the hands of John Smyth the younger, and more recently into the Cholmondeley collection at Condover Hall, Shropshire, the manuscripts were offered for sale in January, 1888, by Mr. Bernard Quaritch, from whom they were lately bought and given to the New York Public Library by Mr. Alexander Maitland."[a] With the exception of the manuscripts in the Ferrar collection relating to Smythe's Hundred, these form the only extant records of the important movement for private plantations in Virginia under the régime of the company. Two other valuable documents are now in the possession of the Lenox Library,[b] the holographic letter of John Pory, secretary of the colony, dated September 30, 1619, and Commissioner John Harvey's declaration of the State of Virginia in 1624.

COLLECTIONS OF AMERICANA

The manuscripts in the Library of Congress, the Smyth of Nibley papers in the New York Public Library, and the patent books in Virginia are the only original records of the company or of the colony previous to 1625 now in America. But there are two public collections of Americana which are extremely valuable for this period: The John Carter Brown Library in Providence, Rhode Island, which contains only books on America published before the year 1800, and the New York Public Library.

[a] Quoted from the *New York Public Library Bulletin* (1897), I, 68, and (1899), III, 160.
[b] List of Records, Nos. 133 and 640.

In the John Carter Brown Library are two royal proclamations, which are the only documents of the character for the period in America; while a declaration of a division of land in 1616, which is a supplementary pamphlet in the *Declaration by the Company* of June 22, 1620, has no duplicate in existence, although there is an imperfect copy of the latter in the British Museum. The copy of the 1620 declaration in the Lenox Library is also unique, since it contains a different supplementary pamphlet of which there is but one other to be found, neither of which has heretofore been noted. [a] It is a declaration of November 15, 1620, concerning the dispatch of supplies, and proves by its date that this is a later edition of the declaration of June 22. The John Carter Brown Library also contains a unique treatise by John Brinsley, bearing the date 1622, the only other copy of which is in the Lenox Library. It has also two sermons, one by Patrick Copland, entitled *Virginia's God be Thanked,* [b] with duplicates in the possession of Edward E. Ayer, and of the Pequot Library, Southport, Connecticut, and one by John Donne, of which there are copies in the Lenox, the Ayer, and the Congressional libraries. In addition to these rare books, the Declaration of Edward Waterhouse of 1622, containing "The Inconveniences that have happened, 1622," and *Observations to be followed for making of fit roomes for silk worms,* 1620, including "A valuation of the commodities growing and to be had in Virginia; rated as they are worth," are to be found in the Providence collection, while the latter is also in the Harvard and the Lenox libraries. [c] In the same year a *Treatise on the art of making silk* was published by John Banoeil, containing a royal letter of encouragement to the Earl of Southampton, now to be found both in the Brown and the Lenox libraries.

The New York Public Library is second only in value to the John Carter Brown Library for this subject. In addition to the books noted above it contains two unique publications of the company, the first is a broadside of May 17, 1620, which is the only copy known to the Editor. A catalogue of Bernard Quaritch, in

---

[a] The other copy is in a private collection in New York. This library has also the first editions of the declaration of 1620; the treatise by Banoeil, reprinted in 1622, containing the letters of the King and of the council; Patrick Copland's *Virginia's God be Thanked,* and his *Declaration how the monies were disposed,* published in 1622; Edward Waterhouse's *Declaration of the State of the Colony,* 1622; John Donne's Sermon, 1622.

[b] There is a manuscript copy of this sermon in the Library of Congress.

[c] "*The Inconveniences*" was published separately as a broadside, and copies are to be found in the Lenox Library and in the collections of the Society of Antiquaries, London. A copy was in the Cholmondeley collection, which is probably the one mentioned in the Quaritch catalogue of May, 1887. This, as also a copy of the *Observations,* was sold to Mr. Kalbfleisch. The supposition that it was originally published as a part of the Declaration of Edward Waterhouse does not seem valid, since the John Carter Brown copy is the only one containing the broadside, and the page in that case has evidently been trimmed and inserted.

May, 1887, describes such a broadside, which is known to have been purchased by Mr. Kalbfleisch. The second is *A Note of the Shipping, etc., sent to Virginia in 1621.* The Cholmondeley copy of this also was sold by Mr. Quaritch to Mr. Kalbfleisch.[a] A third copy of the same is in the collection of printed broadsides of the Society of Antiquaries in London.

The volumes of printed material relating to the Virginia Company, which are in the Harvard Library, have been mentioned above.

Two private collections deserve mention for their comparatively large number of important publications of the company, the private collection in New York and that of Mr. Edward Ayer, in Chicago, Illinois.[b] In addition to twenty other rare publications of the company Mr. Ayer has a unique book entitled "Greevovs Grones for the Poore," 1621. It refers to the Virginia Company in its address only, and in the statement of the number of poor that had been sent to Virginia, but is of value for an understanding of that movement. The other private collection is of about the same size. It contains the duplicate of the 1620 declaration in the Lenox and the only known copy of a four-page tract entitled "Declaration how the monies were disposed (being) collections for the Grammar Schooles," by Patrick Copland.[c]

[a] In the catalogue of Bernard Quaritch for May, 1887, the broadside of May 17, 1620, and the Note of the Shipping, 1621, are both noted as being unique since each contains the final clause: "Whosoever transports himself or any other at his own charge unto Virginia, shall for each person so transported before mid-summer, 1625, have to him and his heirs forever 50 acres of land upon a first and 50 acres upon a second division." A copy of the Note of the Shipping, 1621, in the Cholmondeley collection is similarly described in the fifth report of the Historical Manuscripts Commission, page 341. The Quaritch copies were sold to Mr. Kalbfleisch, whose collection went to Mr. Lefferts, and finally through the dealers, Geo. H. Richmond or Dodd, Mead & Co., either to a private collection or to the Lenox Library. But the Lenox copies either do not correspond to these descriptions or were not purchased from Mr. Lefferts. The volumes of the Lefferts collection, which were not sold in America, were sent to Sotheby, England, but Mr. Eames of the New York Public Library states that no early Virginia material was allowed to return to England.

[b] The collection of Americana belonging to Mr. Ayer is open to the public through the Newberry Library. For the early Virginia material of the library see Index under "Ayer, Edward."

[c] This tract is described in the Appendix of the Fifth Report of the Historical Manuscripts Commission, as follows: "A Declaration how the monies, viz., 70^{li}, 8s. 6d., were disposed, which was gathered (by Mr. Patrick Copland, preacher in the Royal James) at the Cape of Good Hope (toward the building of a free schoole in Virginia) of the gentlemen and mariners in the said ship; a list of whose names are under specified, &c. 4to 7 pp. Imprinted at London by F. K. 1622."

TRANSCRIPTS IN THE NEW YORK PUBLIC LIBRARY

Other attempts have been made to secure resources for research in America. Not only is there the aggregation of excerpts from the English documents in Richmond, as described above, and the acquisition of transcripts in the Library of Congress within recent years, but half a century ago a similar interest was displayed by collectors and historians in New York City, forming three collections which are to-day in the Lenox Library.

William H. Aspinwall, a merchant, secured among other papers the Chalmers collection of letters and documents relating to Virginia from 1606 to 1775. They were in turn sold to Samuel Latham Mitchell Barlow, a lawyer and notable collector of New York City, from whom a part were purchased by the library, while others came to the Lenox with the Bancroft transcripts in 1893. Chalmers had been a clerk in the State paper office and seems to have taken these extracts, outlines, and sometimes full copies from the Plantation office papers, since he continually refers to them in his *Political Annals*.[a] They are modernized transcripts, failing to follow the early orthography, abbreviations, and capitalization. The writing is cramped and often almost illegible, while the table of contents is incomplete and useless. They comprise (1) a series of brief outlines of Privy Council orders; (2) extracts from the Dudley-Carleton papers; (3) outlines of additional Council orders; (4) a calendar of certain of the colonial State papers; (5) outlines of council orders dealing with other trading companies. All of the original documents are at present in the Public Record Office and are noted in the Bibliographical List of Records following.

The Bancroft papers relating to Virginia and the Simancas Archives are well bound, clear, and apparently careful, correct, and full copies of the documents included. The first two volumes of the Bancroft collection bearing on the Virginia Company are transcripts of many of the documents in the State paper office, probably made in 1852 by Noel Sainsbury, but the list is not complete. While the peculiar and characteristic signs of abbreviation are not followed, the orthography seems to be accurate throughout. Furthermore, the collection includes the document entire, unless otherwise indicated. The table of contents is carfeul and correct.[b] The "Simancas Archives" is a volume of transcripts of "Papers in the Simancas Archives relating to the History of Virginia and other portions

[a] See a statement by Victor H. Paltsits, April 14, 1896, inserted in the first volume of these papers now in the Lenox.

[b] The documents transcribed in both the Chalmers-Barlow and the Bancroft volumes are noted in the List of Records under "Remarks."

of America between 1608 and 1624, made for Alexander Brown and many of them used by him in his book, *The Genesis of the U. S.*" The only document relating to Virginia which is not reproduced in that collection is a repetition of the proclamation of the King of England concerning tobacco, bearing the date November 12, 1624.

COLLECTIONS IN ENGLAND

FERRAR PAPERS

The most unique collection in England for the study of the Virginia Company is that in the possession of Magdelene College, Cambridge. As the property of Nicholas and John Ferrar, who were second only to Sir Edwin Sandys in their activity in the company, it would be invaluable; but its importance is further enhanced by the fact that it contains the correspondence and papers of Sir Edwin Sandys himself. These seventy-eight papers, which are either records of the company or vitally concern it, cover the period of the Sandys-Southampton influence from 1617 to the summer of 1623. They were the property of Dr. Peckard, master of Magdalene College in 1790, and were bequeathed to the college upon his death. It is probable that the greater part of the collection came from the Ferrar family through Dr. Peckard's wife, Martha Ferrar, the great granddaugher of John Ferrar, since the Virginia papers form but one-third of the group. The remaining papers concern family affairs only, and date from 1601 to the middle of the eighteenth century. Some of them are doubtless those received from the Earl of Dorset by Dr. Peckard, when he was preparing his *Memoirs of Nicholas Ferrar.*[a]

The first knowledge of the Ferrar papers in later years was communicated to the Virginia Magazine of History by Michael Lloyd Ferrar, Little Gidding, Ealing, England. He sent a number of transcripts and photographs of letters to the magazine for publication, among which were some half dozen bearing on the affairs of the company, but the number which he was permitted to reproduce was limited by the college. While Mr. Ferrar was completing a history of the Ferrar family the entire collection was deposited at his home, and it was therefore in Ealing in the fall of 1903 that the Editor was first permitted by the authorities of the college to "see and note the contents" of the papers. Before the following summer Mr. Ferrar had died and the collection had been returned to Cambridge, where complete transcripts of all letters and photographs of all documents relating to the Virginia Company were made for the Library of Congress under the supervision of the Editor.

---

[a] In this work Dr. Peckard states that the Earl of Dorset had had his library searched and had sent him a few loose papers belonging to the Virginia Company.

These papers are loose, many of them being much damaged, and it is apparent that they are a part of a larger collection which must have been neglected while in the possession of the family. There are some envelopes without letters, many rough memoranda by both Nicholas and John Ferrar, some account books, and some rough drafts of petitions to the House of Commons and of discussions on the silkworm. The autographs which they furnish of both Nicholas and John Ferrar have been of no little interest, as well as value, for the identification of other papers in the Public Record Office, and in the Library of Congress. Furthermore, the proof that Nicholas Ferrar himself supervised the transcript of the court book is thus gained.

In this collection are twenty-three papers which are veritable records of the company.[a] Two documents give our only knowledge of the financial affairs of Smythe's Hundred, slight indeed, but from them comes additional information concerning the system of organization of the societies for private adventure. Sundry other unique though scattered documents are among these papers, such as receipts for money expended, showing the method of business, reports of committees, and of proceedings of the commissioners, revealing the bitterness of the factions, drafts or original records of certain courts, forming the only proof of the accuracy of the copies of the court books, and three new proceedings of the courts of the Somers Islands Company. One of the latter is evidently a blotter and reveals the methods used in keeping the court book. The *quo warranto* in English, which was served upon the treasurer and company, would have been of the greatest value had not the original record of the suit in the King's Bench just been discovered. Another document of great value is the receipt referred to above, which proves that a court book was regularly kept by the company from its very beginning. It reveals how much has been lost.

The series, consisting of twenty letters from Sir Edwin Sandys to John Ferrar, shows more clearly than any other documents we possess[b] who the real managers of the affairs were and what was the spirit of the Sandys faction. The absolute confidence which Sir Edwin Sandys had in John Ferrar and his great love for both of the brothers is significant. Moreover, the knowledge of the affairs of the company, the careful watch over every act and movement affecting the business, the deep and earnest plans for the advancement of its interests revealed in these letters prove that Sir Edwin Sandys was the keen financial manager of the undertaking. It was evidently he who determined what the policy should be; he was apparently the statesman

---

[a] List of Records, Nos. 76, 138, 164, 258, 259, 303, 304, 394, 421, 423, 470, 479, 539, 541, 543, and the *quo warranto*.

[b] For these letters see *Ibid.*, Nos. 120, 131, 135, 136, 171, 181, 191, 197, 211, 219, 271, 275, 282, 307, 315, 316, 317, 364, 368.

and the politician, directing the method of address to the lords of the council or the attitude to be assumed toward the Crown, controlling the courts so that he might be present when there was danger of faction, concealing the information received from the colony when he feared it would entail criticism. Much of the personal feeling and animosity that existed is here shown, and much also which reveals actual financial conditions.

The last group of these papers comprises thirty-five letters, all but one or two of which were written by planters or adventurers, resident in the colony, to Sir Edwin Sandys.[a] Of these, five came from Governor Yeardley, ten from either John Pory or George Thorpe, secretaries in the colony at different times, and two from the cape merchant; of the remainder, at least ten are from colonists whose opinions and reports have not reached us in any other way. These letters are as full of complaint with regard to the insufficient supplies sent with new planters, as are the letters in the Manchester papers which Sir Nathaniel Rich and the Earl of Warwick used as a basis of accusation against the management of the company, but they differ from the other complaints in that they are kindly in spirit. Mr. Pory's letters are full of definite information concerning the affairs, needs, and hopes of the colony, while Governor Yeardley also gives some valuable statements with regard to new settlers, the council, the relations with the Indians, and the government of the colony; both complain of the scant provisioning of the new settlers. The burden of the Yeardley letters, however, is the investigation of the affairs of Captain Argall and the consequent criticism drawn upon himself from Lord Rich. Unfortunately, comparatively few additional data are afforded concerning the Argall affair either by Pory or by Yeardley. The planters themselves tell much of their condition and of the districts in which they have settled, but the theme of their letters is most likely to be a demand for promised payments or a complaint as to the scarcity of provisions and clothes. The attitude toward Yeardley is generally favorable, John Rolfe alone supporting Argall and criticizing the governor. As from all correspondence of such a character, new ideas are gained, new points of view, and often additional knowledge of relations with the Indians and with one another. Many of these letters are annotated by John Ferrar, revealing the degree of importance which he attached to their various and often conflicting statements.

PUBLIC RECORD OFFICE—MANCHESTER PAPERS

A class of documents, very similar in character but of quite different spirit, is the Manchester papers, now in the Public Record Office, London. Robert, Earl of Warwick, and his cousin, Sir Nathaniel Rich, were both members of the company.

[a] For these letters, see List of Records, Nos. 93, 94, 115, 119, 134, 153, 156, 158, 166, 173, 179, 180, 235, 238, 239, 241, 243–250, 252–255, 285, 343, 466.

Sir Nathaniel was a leader in the Warwick faction, while Earl Robert, after the dissolution of the company in 1624, became a member of the council for Virginia. The third wife of the Earl was Eleanor, Countess of Sussex, daughter of Richard Wortley, and she, after the death of the Earl of Warwick, married, as her fourth husband, Edward Montague, second Earl of Manchester. Thus it is that the Kimbolton manuscripts, which are the records of the Duke of Manchester, contain a large collection of petitions, declarations, memoranda, letters, and lists which emanated from the Warwick faction of the Virginia Company.[a] Many of these are holographs of Nathaniel Rich and Alderman Johnson, prime movers in that conflict. Henry Montague, Viscount Mandeville and later Earl of Manchester, was at one time lord president of the Privy Council. Therefore many of the Manchester papers may have belonged to him. The autographs, however, identify those which concern the Virginia Company as having belonged to Nathaniel Rich.

The Manchester and the Ferrar papers therefore present the two sides of this conflict, not in open court or even in private contest, but in the private documents and memoranda of the leaders. The collections are of about the same size, there being sixty-six papers in the Manchester series, to seventy-eight in the Ferrar group. These, also, are unbound, but since the greater part are rough notes of documents, or drafts of propositions or speeches, they are much more difficult to decipher than the Ferrar papers. Indeed many of them are almost illegible, and not a few are unintelligible, having no connecting thought.

A dozen of these papers may be considered documentary; that is, rough copies of letters, petitions, and declarations, or of acts of the company, or of its members and officers in an official capacity. A few of these only are to be found among the other records of the company. Like the rest of the set, they, almost without exception, concern the accusations against the Sandys-Southampton management. Three of them are petitions or letters concerning the extent of the tobacco trade, but the rest are petitions to the King against one faction or the other, and answers to those petitions. Of these, one of the most important is a copy of the opinion of counsel concerning the powers conferred on the Virginia Company by the several letters patent.[b] Accusation and defense are set forth in these documents, but the headings of speeches, the drafts of propositions, and the notes from documents on which the arguments are based proclaim the motives and methods of the accusers. No proof could be clearer than these memoranda by Alderman Johnson and Nathaniel Rich that the company was to be overthrown by fair means or foul. In two or three papers are carefully prepared lists of alleged evil deeds of Sir

---

[a] These Manchester papers are calendared by the *Royal Commission on Historical Manuscripts,* Report VIII, Part 2.

[b] List of Records, p. 140, No. 170.

Edwin Sandys and catalogues of the faults and errors of the company, while the criticisms of the policy and of the management of the company are set down in order, based on letters from colonists, of which there are eleven in the collection. In these criticisms and drafts of propositions much information is afforded concerning the management, organization, and condition of the colony and company. Thus, various books kept by the company during Sir Thomas Smythe's time, and not otherwise known, are mentioned.[a] Five or six rough drafts of propositions concerning the tobacco and salary question are also to be found here, as well as numerous statements of sums adventured, of the number of men sent to the colony, lists of members favorable to one faction or the other and candidates for office from both parties. Many of the rough notes of both Johnson and Rich furnish the only source of information concerning the directions given to the commissioners appointed by the Crown to investigate the condition of the company and of the colony and their acts and reports, but a fact of greater significance is this, that the Warwick collection contains a dozen rough drafts of directions to those commissioners, of charges against the company to be sent to that body, of preliminary reports concerning the government of Virginia, and of projects for the settlement of the government and the colony. The source of the schism is here revealed, and the accusation by Sandys that accuser and judge were one is justified.[b]

COLONIAL AND DOMESTIC STATE PAPERS

The other large group of Virginia records, consisting of over one hundred and twenty separate documents, is found among the colonial and domestic papers deposited in the Public Record Office. The source of this collection is uncertain. Much of it came from the Plantation Office, and perhaps from the Privy Council Office. The consolidation of depositories took place in 1578, but the efforts of Dr. Thomas Wilson, the first clerk of the papers, to force the previous and incumbent magistrates to hand over all documents to the State, were evidently often unavailing, and hence it was that the creation of a State Paper Office was not really accomplished until the period of the company. After Sir Thomas Wilson succeeded his uncle during the reign of James I the aid of the King was much relied upon, and, though partially successful, the recent revelation of quasi-public documents in private collections shows that not only earlier but later officials considered papers of record private property.[c] Thus some of the Salis-

[a] List of Records, No. 438.

[b] A letter from Sir Edwin Sandys to John Ferrar, cited in the List of Records, No. 317.

[c] Scargill-Bird, *A Guide to the Documents in the Public Record Office*, Introduction, p. xxxvi. See also W. N. Sainsbury, "Calendar of Documents relating to the History of the State Paper Office to the year 1800," in the *Deputy Keepers Report*, No. 30, Appendix, No. 7, pp. 212–293.

bury papers, which Wilson failed to secure, are now at Hatfield House; and others have passed with the Lansdowne collection into the British Museum, where they are known as the Burghley papers. Similarly, the Cottonian papers in the Museum originally belonged to Sir Robert Cotton in the time of James I.

Among the State Papers deposited in the Record Office are the letters to John Ferrar, dated from Virginia in April, 1623, which may have been seized by the commission appointed on May 9, 1623, to investigate the affairs of the company. There, too, are found the attested copies of letters and records in the colony which concern the Harvey Commission, sent to the commission in England by Edward Sharpless. A few of these papers seem to have belonged to the company, such as the documents pertaining to the Walloons and dated 1621; Pory's report from Virginia, in the same year; and two copies of documents by Collingwood, dated the latter part of 1623. [a] All of these facts lead to the conclusion that a part of the records of the commissions, and a part of the confiscated records of the company are here deposited. If so, where are the remainder of these most valuable documents? [b]

The colonial papers and the domestic correspondence include about forty-eight which are records, and about nineteen which are documentary in character. The first group contains, among other papers, many of the petitions and letters addressed to the King and to the Privy Council, and many others of the council. It is thus apparent that the royal correspondence of the Privy Council and the Privy Council papers which should accompany the register are in this collection. To the second group belong those papers which contain projects presented by individuals and answers to such propositions, lists of adventures for the company, and also lists of men sent to the colony and of lands granted in Virginia. Among these papers are seven letters from colonists, in addition to about fifty which may be considered subsidiary correspondence in that they refer incidentally to the affairs of the company. Such are the Mandeville-Conway, Middlesex-Conway, Chamberlain-Carleton, Conway-Calvert, and Nethersole-Carleton letters.

RECORDS OF COURTS

In the libels of the admiralty court, instance and prize, are found records of suits in which the Virginia Company is plaintiff. As a part of the controversy in which William Wye appears as defendant is the suit of Yonge *vs.* Roberts; while the fragment of the record of the Earl of Warwick *vs.* Edward Bruister

---

[a] List of Records, pp. 145, ff., Nos. 227, 243, 444, 520, 579.

[b] For a discussion of the fate of the missing records and the probability as to their existence, see ch. V, *post.*

concerning the trouble over the ships *Neptune* and *Treasurer* completes the list of cases in that court which in any way affect the Virginia Company. The latter is so torn and defaced that but for an occasional date or fact, it affords no information of value. Among the other formal material of the suit against Wye are two valuable documents, namely, the commission given to Wye and a letter from the treasurer and council to Sir George Yeardley, dated June 21, 1619. In the latter are valuable references to Argall, and the complaints against Wye, though torn and illegible, reveal something of the loss estimated as resulting from the failure to settle the passengers in Virginia. These records of the admiralty court have not heretofore been published, although they were cited by R. G. Marsden in his discussion of those documents.[a] But the chancery files, which have furnished the records of suits by the Virginia Company, have only just been indexed, and hence the documents have not heretofore been known.

The record of the *quo warranto* suit by which the Virginia Company was overthrown has been erroneously declared to be not extant, a mistake due to a difference in view with regard to the court out of which such a writ would be issued and as to the court in which the writ would be returnable. Hence the search for the document has hitherto been conducted in the Petty Bag of the Chancery instead of in the coram rege roll of the King's Bench. It was in the latter roll that the full record of the writ, the pleadings, and the judgment were discovered by the Editor in the fall of 1903.[b] In *A Guide to the Documents in the Public Record Office* Mr. Bird gives the following explanation of the *placita de quo warranto:* They "consist of the pleadings and judgments on writs of 'quo warranto' in nature of writs of right on behalf of the King against those who claimed or usurped any office, franchise, or liberty. The pleadings and judgments on writs of 'quo warranto' or of 'quo titulo clamat' took place in the King's Bench or the Exchequer and are enrolled on the 'coram rege rolls' or the 'memoranda rolls' accordingly."[c] The statement in the court book of the company is that the "company had been served with process out of the King's Bench by virtue of a quo warranto." It was this clue and that from Mr. Scargill-Bird that led the Editor to conduct the search successfully in the coram rege roll.

In the Record Office are also the docquet books, which afford some knowledge of the grants of the King affecting the customs on tobacco, and the patent rolls,

[a] R. G. Marsden, "Records of the Admiralty Court" in the *Transactions of the Royal Historical Society*, new series, Vol. XVI, 90–96. Many parts of these records are undecipherable, and as a result the transcripts made for the Library of Congress are incomplete.

[b] For a discussion of the content of the document, see *post*, p. 103.

[c] P. 166.

which contain the letters patent of 1606, 1609, and 1612. In the colonial entry books and among the proclamations of the King are orders of the Privy Council and of the King, all of which are recorded in the Privy Council register.

Since the Privy Council took no direct part in the affairs of the company between 1617 and the summer of 1622, its orders related to those regulations which would enable the acts of the company to advance the interests of the kingdom, leaving absolute power to the company as the proprietor. Thus fully one-half of its thirty measures during those five years were reprieves of prisoners, with the warrants necessary to send them to Virginia or orders enabling children to be transferred from the cities of the kingdom to the colony. During this period the Crown commenced its attempts to secure a revenue from the tobacco trade, and a series of orders finally resulted in the approval of the contract with the company in February of 1622/3. In its foreign and external relations the company was of course subject to the action of the Privy Council, and hence the orders in council concerned the contest with Spain over the attack of the *Treasurer*. Furthermore, the disagreement with the northern colony concerning fishing privileges had to be adjusted by the council and resulted in the renewal of the patent to the northern colony and in regulations as to rights of fishing. It was in the summer of 1622 that the first movement was made which brought the difficulties between the factions into the open board. The petition of John Bargrave against Sir Thomas Smythe, Alderman Johnson, and others, in which they were accused of mismanagement, resulted in the defeat of Bargrave six months later, as was to have been expected from the hostility of the Crown to the party in Parliament led by Sir Edwin Sandys, of which Bargrave was evidently a member at that time. But the storm broke in the following April, when the commission was appointed to inquire into the true state of the Virginia and Somers Islands companies. From that date until the dissolution of the company in the summer of 1624 the council busied itself with the affairs of the company. No less than 31 orders are recorded which create commissions and empower them to investigate both the colony and the company and in the end to assume the functions of government in the name of the Crown, while seven of these documents pass directly between the council and the colony, and no other measures were considered except those which enabled the Warwick faction to tear down the work of the adventurers and to take into its own hands the control of the entire business. These forms of government, planned by the Crown and the commissions here recorded, by which the authority was vested in the commissioners and later in a committee of the Privy Council, stand for the beginning of royal control. Heretofore, with a few exceptions, these orders have been known only through the calendar of state papers, and even then not more than one-half have been included.

The Privy Council Office and its records are located in the treasury building, Whitehall, London; the registers of the council orders are kept in the clerk's office but all of the early registers are properly about to be transferred to the Public Record Office. These registers contain the orders of the council, and, after Charles I, also the petitions received and the letters issued by the council. In the earlier reigns such documents were not recorded; whether they were even preserved as public documents is not certain, although, as stated above, many of them have found their way to the Record Office and are there calendared among the colonial, domestic, or foreign papers. There is a collection of such original material, dating from the close of the seventeenth century, in the treasury building.[a]

BRITISH MUSEUM

The collection of manuscripts from which the most valuable returns might be expected is in the British Museum. The documents there deposited are small in number but they are of great value, and none of them have heretofore been printed. The originals of the precedents for patents of the Virginia Company, which are now noted for the first time, evidently formed a part of the records of the company, and it may be that they are some of the copies of the records made under the supervision of Nicholas Ferrar, or they may be the drafts of patents which were filed by the company according to an order of its court. Not only is the writing similar to much of that in the contemporary transcripts of the court book, but they are unsigned copies, and the headings of a number of them seem to be in the autograph of Edward Collingwood. The caption of the series shows that the copies were made for the sake of preserving the form, and reads as follows: "Presidents of Patents, Grants & Commissioners by the Virginia Company. 1621."[b] The company thus preserved the legal form of the various grants. Four of them are of value not only for the form but for the knowledge they furnish of the distinction made between the four classes of adventurers: those who paid money into the treasury and agreed to plant one hundred persons, those who established a private plantation, those who were private planters, and those whose "shares exceedinge 50 ac͠r are exempted from payinge any Rent to y͠e Company for the persons they transporte." In addition certain knowledge is afforded concerning the grants. Two out of the other nine documents are commissions granted to owners and masters of ships for voyages to Virginia, by

[a] The clerk's office is entered from Downing street, but the library containing the original documents must be reached through the main entrance on Whitehall.

[b] "List of Records," pp. 149 ff., Nos. 256, 257, 267, 276-278, 298, 299, 323-325. The volume is catalogued as *Additional MSS., 14285.*

which they are to transport passengers to Virginia. Another is a covenant by the company to pay for the victualing and transporting of passengers, while still another is for the transporting of goods only. Other forms are those used for granting rights of fishing on the coast of America, for voyages to Virginia, and free fishing along the shores, and others still for discovery, fishing, and trading in furs in Virginia. The covenant signed by William Ewens in which he agreed to fit out the ship *George* reveals the form of contract required of the masters of ships by the company.

These papers form the last group in a volume which contains "A Catalogue of the Nobility of England in the time of King James the first," 1626, and "A list of all the Officers belonging to Courts of Justice the Kings household & Reuenue wth their seuerall fees." There are several signs for identification, but none which indicate the original owner of the volume. It is a small quarto in leather, bearing the signature, "H Cowle A. 29," on the inner cover, and also the arms of James Bindley with the motto, "unus et idem." At the bottom of the same cover is written the following: "Purchased at the sale of W. Berwicks library at Sotheby's, 27 Apr. 1863. (Lot 427)," while on the second fly leaf in the upper right-hand corner is the inscription: "The gift of Mr Danl Prince, Bookseller. Oxford—July 23^{d} 1776." Farther than this the history of the papers is unknown.

Another set of documents in the Museum is also unique. One of these supplies all that is known outside of the court book and a single reference in Argall's register book regarding the controversy over the grant of land to John Martin in Virginia. The other letters from Martin to his brother-in-law, Sir Julius Cæsar, written in December, 1622, give startling suggestions with regard to an ideal policy for the colony. "The manner howe to bringe in the Indians into subiection wth out makinge an utter extirpation of them . . ." is the heading of the paper in which Martin proposes to disable the main body of the enemy by cutting them off from their sources of supply at home and by destroying their trade. He would thus require two hundred soldiers "Contynuallie harrowinge and burneinge all their Townes in wynter." By this means and by gaining a store of grain for two years' supply, he plans for the recovery from the massacre. In order to secure the entire territory from the Indians, in a second letter he propounds a scheme by which the Crown or the company can make a "Royall plantation for gods glory his Matie: and Royall progenyes euer happines and the Companies exceedinge good." The responsibility and control was to be thrown upon the shires of England. The fact that the Martin letters have not heretofore been generally known may be due to an error in the catalogue. They appear under the name "Tho. Martin" instead of "Jho. Martin." [a]

[a] List of Records, Nos. 378, 384, 385.

Two other projects for the advancement of the colony are in the same collection of papers; one by Captain Bargrave, brother of the Dean of Canterbury, is dated December 8, 1623, and the other a year later. The latter relates to the division of income from tobacco between the King, the planter, and the grower, with a reward to those endeavoring to preserve the plantation, but approves the Ditchfield offer. The Ditchfield offer itself is also in this collection.[a] Captain Bargrave's proposition for the government of the colony stands midway between absolute royal control and full autonomy of the planters, and holds an important place in the development of the plans from the proprietary to the royal colony. Furthermore, it is rather significant that in the collection of Sir Julius Cæsar are to be found the propositions of Martin, of Bargrave, and the document by which the commission was finally appointed in 1624, to establish the government in Virginia under royal control. Sir Julius Cæsar, having been a judge of admiralty under Elizabeth and chancellor of the exchequer in the reign of James I, became master of the rolls on January 16, 1610/11, and one of the keepers of the great seal on May 3, 1621. His position evidently enabled him to secure a large collection of valuable drafts of documents. This was sold at auction in 1757. One-third of the collection was purchased by the Earl of Shelburne (Lord Lansdowne) from Webb and came to the Museum among the Lansdowne papers.

Two collections of printed material of the company are to be found in England, the British Museum and the Society of Antiquaries. While the British Museum has a large number of the earlier publications, it possesses only the declaration of June 22, 1620, and also the unique note of shipping of 1620, the only other copy of which is owned by the Society of Antiquaries. The collection of that society is rich in royal proclamations, besides possessing a copy of the Note of Shipping, 1621, and of the *Inconveniences* of 1622. The scattering documents to be found in private collections throughout England are often valuable, but nowhere else is to be found any considerable number of papers or any that are of great importance.[b]

[a] List of Records, Nos. 604 and 733.

[b] For those documents in private collections, see the List of Records. In the concluding section of this "Introduction" will be found a discussion of the collections which have been searched in vain for material relating to the Virginia Company. Furthermore, a statement will there be found of those families in whose possession we should expect to find Virginia records, because of their connection with the men prominent in the company or in the commissions which supplanted the company. A very helpful article, entitled "The Stuart Papers," is published by Mrs. S. C. Lomas, in the *Transactions of the Royal Historical Society*, new series, XVI, 97–132.

4. The Records of the Company under the Sandys-Southampton Administration

Organization of the Company

In order to comprehend what the records of the company were and what their value, it is necessary to gain an understanding of the system which the corporation worked out in order to further its purposes. The forms and usages of the company after 1619 were determined by the charters granted by the King and by the "Orders and Constitutions" which it adopted in 1619 and printed in June, 1620,[a] although the latter were altered or newly interpreted from time to time by action of its courts.

The membership of the company was unlimited and was granted by the courts to anyone who had "adventured" £12 10s. for a share of stock or to whom the company had awarded a share of stock for services.[b] The distinction between a member who was free of the company and an owner of land in Virginia was brought out in a controversy on February 19, 1622/3, in which a proposition to limit the adventurers to those approved by the generality met with opposition on the ground that land in Virginia was held in free and common socage and could not be forbidden to any man. But Sir John Brooke, the legal authority in the company, declared that such exclusion was agreeable to the law since it was a question of a vote in a court and not a question of ownership of land. The argument was based on the power to withhold the privilege of voting from Samuel Wroth, who was under censure, and similarly on the power to exclude any man who had purchased land from a member who was indebted to the company until the debts were paid. This discussion also revealed that no oath of fidelity was required in the Virginia Company as in the Muscovy and other corporations. At a later date the King proposed that no member should be free of the courts who had not sent men to the colony as planters, claiming that less than thirty of the adventurers could meet the requirement.[c] The power to disfranchise an unworthy member was reserved to the company.

[a] List of Records, No 183.
[b] MS. Records of the Virginia Company of London, *Court Book*, Vol. I, Nov. 15, 1619.
[c] *Ibid.*, II, Feb. 19, 1622/3; I, Nov. 3, 1619.

The members met in four great or quarter courts, held on the last Wednesday except one of each law term. On the Monday preceding they assembled in a preparative court and on every Wednesday fortnight thereafter in a common or ordinary court, as required by the charter of 1612; and they might also be summoned to an extraordinary court by the treasurer or deputy. The meetings were held in the private houses of various members of the company [a] until the time of the tobacco contract, when a company house was established.

In the quarter court the adventurers elected all councilors and principal officers of the company and colony, made all laws and ordinances, confirmed all grants of land, settled all questions of trade, and passed all measures which should bind the company for a term of years. Their action with regard to questions of a new charter and of investment for the colony was legal only when transacted in a quarter court, but they might transfer to other courts actions which concerned correspondence with the lord treasurer or similar business. Fifteen of the generality and five of the council formed a quorum for the ordinary courts, and in those they signed warrants, ordered the payment of bills passed by the auditors, and sealed bills of adventure. In that meeting also were perfected commissions for transportation of men and provisions and for trade and barter. Special officers and committees were appointed in this court, and even actions of great importance, such as the dissolution of the magazine or the extension of freedom of the company to honorary members, were consummated. [b]

The officers chosen by the company were a council, a treasurer, a deputy, auditors, a general committee of sixteen, a secretary, a bookkeeper, a husband, and a beadle. The adventurers looked to the treasurer or governor not only as the president and moderator, but as the manager of their business interests, and expected him to be responsible for the policy of the company in its relations with the government and to formulate and present plans for the development of the plantation and the profit of the adventurers. To him was entrusted the supervision of the treasury and the collection of moneys.

The care of the court books was given to the deputy. It was his duty to attend to the engrossing of the orders and resolutions of the courts, the registration of letters to and from the company, and the formulation of statements to be given to the public. He also kept the court of the committees and supervised the issue of warrants.

The council was a body, gradually increasing in size, elected for life, and was sworn by the lord chancellor or by the lord chamberlain. In the earlier years it was the most important committee of the generality of the company, but after 1621 its

---

[a] MS. Records of the Virginia Company of London, *Court Book*, Vol. II, May 24, 1623.

[b] *Ibid.*, I, Dec. 15, 1619; Dec. 3, 1619; Jan. 12, 1619/20; Feb. 16, 1619/20; Feb. 22, 1619/20.

duties seem oftentimes to have been assigned to the auditors or to special committees. According to the "Orders and Constitutions" its chief care was the preparation of laws for the company and for the colony, the issue of instructions to the governor and council of the colony, and the formation of a preliminary court for the trial of the officers of the company or of the colony. But the practice in the courts was to refer to it those difficult duties for which its titled and distinguished personnel made it especially fit. To it was referred, as a final resort, the examination of the claims of John Martin, the attempts to gain a statement of accounts from the old magazine, and the settlement or arbitration of both the Bargrave and the Argall cases. *a*

A body called the "committees" was at first composed of twelve members, six being chosen annually, but later the number was increased to sixteen, four being elected anew each year.*b* Its duties were chiefly to attend to the buying and selling of the commodities of the company, and to the furnishing of ships departing for Virginia.

The auditors formed the other important standing committee, composed of seven members, elected annually. The chief duty assigned to them by the "Orders and Constitutions" was that of reducing to a book the receipts and expenditures. The court book discloses the fact that the company imposed upon them the burden of examining all claims against the company, as well as all claims of the company, of investigating the accounts of the lottery and of the magazine, of determining the awards of land or of shares for service or for adventure, of perfecting all patents and grants, and even of investigating controversies, such as the Bargrave and Martin cases and the dispute as to the seal and coat of arms.*c*

The other officers performed such duties as usually pertain to those who hold the corresponding titles.*d*

As the business of the company increased additional officers were chosen, as those for the control and execution of the lotteries and of the tobacco contract; while the custom of referring important matters to special committees grew rapidly, until in the later years many duties were transferred to them from the council, and even from the auditors. In this way such affairs as the securing of men to send to the

---

a MS. Records of the Virginia Company of London, *Court Book*, Vol. I, Nov. 17, 1619; Nov. 3, 1619; June 28, 1620.

b Ibid., I, May 2, 1621.

c Ibid, I, June 24, 1619; Dec. 15, 1619; Feb. 2, 1619/20; Feb. 16, 1619/20; May 23, 1620. For a discussion of the seal of the company, see Cooke, "Clayborne the Rebel," in the *Magazine of American History*, New York, Vol. X (1883); and also Baxter, "Great Seal of the Council for New England" in *Ibid.*, Vol. XI (1884).

d A report of the committee appointed to describe the "particular duties" of the several officers is among the Manchester papers. It is incorporated in the published "Laws and Orders." List of Records, No. 105.

colony, the provisioning of ships, the hearing of petitions, the investigating of claims, the sending of maids to the colony, the planning for new settlements and industries, the representing of the interests of the company in Parliament, the defending of the company in the suit of the *quo warranto* were intrusted to special committees.[a]

METHODS OF PROCEDURE

In order to secure legality of action, the "Orders and Constitutions" were read at one quarter court each year, since in those meetings the measures of great importance were determined.[b] That the forms and usages followed in other commercial companies, in other corporate bodies, and in Parliament greatly influenced the decisions of the company is seen in the following illustrations: The question as to the entry in the minutes of the names of dissenters or of reasons disallowed by the court except by special order was thus settled according to the practice in Parliament; to prove that individual adventurers would not be liable for the debts of the company in the management of the tobacco magazine, decisions were cited both in a case involving the corporation of Norwich, and in the insolvency of the Muscovy Company; when the question arose as to salaries in the tobacco business involving £100,000, the precedent furnished by all joint stocks of no greater capital than £7,000 was brought forward; the custom of private corporations as well as of judicial bodies of imposing a fine upon any man who spoke against the judge or the court was urged by Lord Brooke as a proper action to be taken against Samuel Wroth.[c] Elections were conducted by ballot, except for the council, in which case, as in all other matters, the will of the court was determined by an "erection of hands."

The reward for services rendered by the officers was determined by the court and set down in the Orders and Constitutions. The annual payment to the secretary was £20, to the beadle £40, to the husband £50, and to the bookkeeper £50. Although the chief officials and committees received no salary, at the expiration of the year's term of office it was customary to award 20 acres of land in Virginia to each individual, with the provision that such land should not be sold. The company similarly rewarded individuals who had rendered great service, but sometimes it granted shares of stock instead, or agreed to transport for the individual a certain number of men free of charge. Shares thus given could not be sold below par value of £12 10s.[d] Each share carried with it the privilege of a vote in

[a] *Court Book*, July 13, December 15, 1619; March 2, 1619/20; June 26, July 7, 12, November 15, December 13, 1620; July 3, October 7, November 6, 1622.

[b] *Ibid.*, I, Jan. 31, 1619/20.

[c] *Ibid.*, II, Dec. 11, 1622; Jan. 14, 1623; Feb. 4, 1622/23; Dec. 11, 1622.

[d] *Ibid.*, I, June 28, 1620; November 15, 1620; May 2, 1621.

the courts and the receipt of 100 acres of land in Virginia on the first division, with a similar amount on the second division providing the first section had been peopled. In addition, the sending of a man to the plantation before midsummer of 1625 entitled the adventurer to 50 acres of land on each division. If a planter had adventured his person only, after three years' residence in the colony the company gave him one share of stock; or if a resident in England had sent a man to the colony who had remained there three years, the one who bore the charge was similarly rewarded. Through reward or by purchase an individual might thus own land and not possess stock, but he might secure the latter within three years by "planting" or peopling his land. The result was that there were five classes of individuals connected with the company.

(1) The old adventurer who had paid at least £12 10s. for a share of stock, and who thus owned, rent free, at least 100 acres of land after the first division which took place in 1616.

(2) The new adventurer who had exactly the same privileges, except that after seven years he must pay 12d. to the company for each 50 acres gained by trans portation of settlers.

(3) The adventurer who received a share of stock for service or for adventure of person and who would have the privileges of an old or of a new adventurer according to whether he received the award before or after 1619.

(4) The individual who had received a grant of land for service or who had purchased land and had not yet gained the grant of shares of stock by adventure of his person or by sending out planters.

(5) The individual who had purchased land of a debtor of the company and could not become free of the courts until the debts were paid.

It will thus be seen that ownership of land and possession of freedom of the company were not always coexistent, but that each involved the possibility of the other.[a] No assessments were ever levied upon the shareholders, the first suggestion of such a course coming from the Privy Council in July, 1623.[b]

RECORDS PROVIDED FOR BY THE COMPANY

The company was thus a body of adventurers, who had gained the freedom of the company by payment of money, by rendering a service, or by settlement of land in Virginia. It was presided over by a treasurer chosen by itself at will, and conducted all of its business through its regularly elected officers or committees, or by special committees. According to the "Orders and Constitutions" it kept

[a] "Orders and Constitutions:" List of Records, No. 183. *Court Book*, I, May 2, 1621; June 28, 1620; Nov. 15, 1620.

[b] *Ibid.*, II, July 9, 1623.

a complete record of its actions in the courts and compelled its officers and committees to do the same. Provision was thus made for six books which were to contain the following records:

(1) Copies of the letters patents, and also of all letters, orders, and directions from the King and his council, as well as the replies of the company.

(2) The laws and standing orders passed in quarter courts for the company and for the colony.

(3) A register of all patents, charters, and indentures of validity granted by the company, of all instructions issued by the council, and of all public letters sent to or received from Virginia.

(4) The acts of the general courts.

(5) The acts of the committees; invoices of provisions sent to Virginia by the company; the certificates of the receipts to be returned from Virginia; invoices of goods sent from Virginia with the husband's certificate of receipt or defect.

(6) The names of adventurers, by payment of money or by rendering service, to whom shares of land had been given, together with the number of shares belonging to each person; the lawful transfers of shares from one to another; the names of His Majesty's council for Virginia.

(6a) The names of all planters in Virginia on the public and on the private plantations separately, based on the certificates from the governor and council in Virginia and from the heads of each plantation.[a]

All of these books were in the custody of the Secretary, and were to be kept in the company's chest, together with the originals of the letters patents and all other papers. In his custody also were the husband's books of accounts of every voyage to Virginia, all accounts approved by the auditors, the canceled and uncanceled charter parties, and all bonds issued to the company.

The proof of the care with which the company kept its records is found in the contemporary copy of the court book, and in a few scattering originals and copies of originals which are preserved among the Ferrar and Manchester papers and in the British Museum. That all of the books required by the orders and constitutions were really kept can not be proved, since not a page nor a copy of a page of many of them is known to be extant; but the copy of the court book serves as an evidence that the laws were as carefully obeyed in this respect as in others. The references in the minutes to many of these records, the insertion of many of them in the copy of the court book, and the continual provision for supplementary records all go to show that the "Orders and Constitutions" furnish a reliable outline of the records kept by the company.

[a] A note of such a list of men sent to Virginia during the time of Sir Thos. Smythe is among the Manchester papers. List of Records, No. 443.

The books which the courts added to the list of records from time to time reveal an increasing effort to conduct the business in an orderly manner. Immediately upon assuming his duties as treasurer, Sir Edwin Sandys instituted an investigation of the accounts of Sir Thomas Smythe. In this connection four books and four rolls were prepared containing the subscriptions, which had been made for carrying on the business, and a list of the adventurers with the sums invested during the previous years. The treasurer made a similar request of the deputy, John Ferrar, on September 18, 1620, in which he asked that the secretary and Mr. Carter should make three catalogues of the adventurers indebted to the company in order that they might be given to a solicitor for collection. He throws light upon the customary carelessness by urging that the lists should be made "from the company's books and not from memory," lest many a £12 10s should be lost.[a]

On May 17, 1620, three books of the deputy were audited. The first contained an account of the money disbursed for provisions,[b] the second, a catalogue of the provisions sent to the colony, and the third, a list of the names of the persons dispatched to the plantation with the trade of each. Because of the erection of private plantations in later years it was necessary that these records should be supplemented. Hence an order of court provided that the names of all persons transported to Virginia should be reported to the company and that a bookkeeper should be appointed to be at the house of the court to register the names before the departure of every ship. This record was to consist of the name, age, country, profession, and kindred of each individual and was to state at whose charge the transportation was effected. Contrary to custom each person was required to pay a fee for registration. A duplicate of the register was to be sent to the Governor of Virginia, but the names of those departing were not to be made public until after the ship had sailed.[c]

Provision was made in 1620 for keeping duplicates of all patents issued. A part of this series is now deposited in the British Museum, from which the various kinds of patents and the terms for each may be discovered.[d] A registration of all shares passed from one member of the company to another was ordered on November 19, 1621, and such a book was to be used as evidence of the right to be admitted to courts. Other records added from time to time were a book containing the rates of commodities,[e] a register of all petitions to the court,

---

[a] List of Records, No. 211.

[b] Two warrants are preserved among the Ferrar papers, one addressed to the Earl of Southampton and one to Deputy John Ferrar. List of Records, p. 149, Nos. 258, 259.

[c] *Court Book*, II, Nov. 18, 1622.

[d] *Ante*, p. 67. "Order of Court," I, June 26, 1620.

[e] *Court Book*, I, Dec. 13, 1620; Jan. 31, 1620/21.

with the action thereupon,[a] and a record of all covenants between adventurers and indentured servants, a copy of which was to be sent to the governor of Virginia.[b] The rolls signed by adventurers must have been numerous. Nine are mentioned in the court book on July 24, 1621, in addition to others cited at various times.[c]

With the increase in trade and the establishment of the company magazines new measures were adopted for controlling the business. These often consisted of separate documents rather than books. A statement was thus required of the deputy certifying that the freight had been paid before any goods should be delivered, and invoices were also demanded of the cape merchant.[d] Copies of such certificates, as also of the accounts of the treasurer of the various joint stock investments for the glass works and for the fur trade, were kept in the company's chest.[e]

THE EXTANT RECORDS—THE COURT BOOK

HISTORY OF THE CONTEMPORARY COPY

The paucity of the actual extant documents of the company has made the circumstances of the transcription of the court book the more interesting and its authenticity the more important.

As the growing controversy between the two factions of the company resulted in serious accusations of mismanagement by sundry adventurers and planters, the Crown soon appointed a commission to investigate the affairs of the company, with a consequent sequestering of all of the company's court books in May, 1623.[f] The clear mind of Nicholas Ferrar immediately foresaw the danger of a seizure of the documents of the company, and appreciating full well the value of the "court books, registers and writings, instructions, letters, etc.," as political papers and also as evidences of the possession of land and investment of capital, upon their return by the Privy Council, he "did fairly copy out all the court books, etc. (which cost 50^{li}) and carried them to the noble Earle of Southampton."[g]

[a] *Court Book*, II, Oct. 23, 1622.

[b] *Ibid.*, II, Nov. 18, 1622; Nov. 20, 1622.

[c] *Ibid.*, I, May 8, 1622; II, July 4, 1623.

[d] *Ibid.*, I, Apr. 3, 1620.

[e] *Ibid.*, I, Jan. 16, 1621–22; Feb. 27, 1621–22.

[f] *Court Book*, II, May 14, 1623.

[g] "Some directions for the collecting materiall for the writing the life of Nich: Ferrar," a manuscript in the Cambridge University Library, Mm. 1.46 (Baker 35), pp. 389–432, especially p. 392.

During the following year the activities of Nicholas Ferrar, as well as the attention of other members of the company, must have been under great strain. The time not taken in attendance "twice or thrice a week"[a] upon the Privy Council, and in the attempts to defend the company against the charges of "abuse of its privileges," was evidently devoted to supervising the transcript of the company's records. The attestation at the end of each volume shows that the first was completed January 28, 1623/4, and the second June 19, 1624.[b] This was none too soon, for just a week later the Privy Council ordered Deputy Ferrar to bring to the council chamber all patents, books of accounts, invoices of the company, and lists of settlers in the colony, to be retained by the Privy Council chest until further notice.[c] A commission had been appointed two days before to take into their hands all "charters, letters patent, grantes and instructions, bookes, orders, letters, advices and other writings concerning the company."[d] The company urged in these words that the council should permit the books to remain inviolate: "So by this meanes [that is, by the transcripts] have the Original Court bookes yet escaped purging: And wth all duety wee humbly beseech yor Lop^s that they may hereafter be protected from it: And that howsover yor Lop^s shall please for the future to dispose of the Companie, that the records of their past Actions may not be corrupted & falsified." Further, when the council demanded that the Earl of Southampton should surrender to the commissioners his copies of the records, before he sailed for the Netherlands in August, he sent them word, "that he would as soon part wth the evidences of his Land, as wth the said copies, being the evidence of his honour in that Service."[e]

How these transcripts were made, and especially what became of them at that time, and where they remained for the following half century can be a matter of

[a] Peckard, *Memoirs of the Life of Mr. Nicholas Ferrar*, pp. 89–167.

[b] According to the attestation two full courts were omitted, May 30, 1620, and June 1, 1622, and also a part of May 20, 1620. The Robinson abstracts comprise a little more than about one-half of the original records and are much more complete for the later years when the controversy with the King over the tobacco contract and the abuses of the company was being carried on. The part of the court book which reveals most with regard to internal organization, commercial activity, and inner life of the company is not included in these abstracts. Thus such data as that which concerns the trouble with Spain over the *Treasurer*, the suit with William Wye, the accusations against Samuel Argall, the old magazine, the Pierce patent, and many other private grants are not included. Moreover, a comparison of the publication with the original manuscript shows that the John Randolph of Roanoke copy was used almost exclusively, and many inaccuracies have resulted.

[c] Order of the Privy Council, June 26, 1624: List of Records, No. 689.

[d] The commission was sealed July 15, 1624: *Ibid.*, No. 701.

[e] For these quotations see *Discourse of the Old Company of Virginia addressed to the Lords of the Privy Council*, April, 1625. List of Records, No. 759.

conjecture only, based on the divers statements of contemporary authorities.   These
are three in number:

> (1) *The Discourse of the Old Company of Virginia addressed to the Privy
> Council, May, 1625.*
>
> (2) *The Memoirs of the Life of Nicholas Ferrar by Dr. Peckard in 1790.*
>
> (3) *A Short Collection of the Most Remarkable Passages from the originall
> to the dissolution of the Virginia Company*, by Arthur Woodnoth, written
> between 1635 and 1645, and printed in 1651 by Richard Cotes.[a]

The *Discourse of the Old Company* gives much the same history of the
records as does Dr. Peckard.   The facts set forth by the latter were taken from
the "Memoirs of Nicholas Ferrar" by his brother John, about 1654, and therefore
this work may be considered as based on contemporary authority.   According to
Dr. Peckard, Nicholas Ferrar, knowing that malice was at work, procured a
clerk to copy out all the court books and other writings and caused them to be
carefully collated with the original.   It cost him the sum of £50, which he thought
was the best service he could render the company.   After the seizure of all the
muniments of the company, and after Lord Treasurer Middlesex had procured
sentence against the company, Mr. Ferrar informed Sir Edward Sandys and others
of what he had done.   These men were greatly rejoiced and advised that the copies
be taken to the Earl of Southampton, who was so overcome that he is said to have
embraced Mr. Ferrar and to have declared that he valued them as an evidence of his
honor more than as evidences of his land.   John Ferrar is quoted as having stated
that the Earl of Southampton was advised not to keep these records in his house
and so delivered them to Sir Robert Killigrew, who left them on his death to Sir
Edward Sackville, the Earl of Dorset.   Mr. Ferrar continues that the Earl of Dorset died in 1652, but he hopes the records are still in the possession of the Earl's
family.[b]

Certain it is that Dr. Peckard had a large collection of manuscripts which
concerned the Virginia Company, some of which must be considered a part of the
records of the company, for such were the Ferrar papers described above which
Dr. Peckard bequeathed to Magdalene College, Cambridge.   That some of them, at
least, came from the Earl of Dorset's family is to be concluded from the statement
of Dr. Peckard that the "Duke had had his library searched and found a few loose
papers, which he sent to him."[c]   Some of them doubtless belonged to Dr. Peckard's

---

[a] This pamphlet is in the volume entitled: *Copy of a Petition from The Governor and Company of the
Sommer Islands, with Annexed Papers, presented to the Right Honorable The Council of State July the 19th,
1651.*   London, Printed for Edward Husband, 1651.

[b] Peckard, pp. 155–156.

[c] See discussion of the Ferrar papers, pp. 59 ff., *ante*.

wife, Martha Ferrar. But the story of the purchase of the two volumes from the estate of the Duke of Southampton by Colonel William Byrd in 1673 or 1688 for 60 guineas has firm credence through statements of Mr. Byrd himself; and there is no evidence that they came from the Earl of Dorset's family. That they were sent to Tichfield by the Earl of Southampton before he sailed for the Netherlands and there remained until his son's library was sold after his death in 1667 seems probable. Perhaps some of the other records went to Sir Robert Killigrew, as stated by John Ferrar, and even some from which these copies were made.

The statement by Woodnoth, who was a nephew of Nicholas Ferrar, that Sir John Danvers had the transcripts of the records made in order to keep out of the way an indigent man who had been employed by the company as a copyist and who might be persuaded to say something ill of Sandys and of Southampton, does not bear the stamp of truth or even of probability. There may have been a copy made by Danvers, but the internal evidence reveals that the existing volumes in the Library of Congress were not transcribed by any one man, and that the work was accomplished under the personal direction of Nicholas Ferrar.[a]

DESCRIPTION OF THE CONTEMPORARY COPY

The contemporary copies of the court books, which are now in the Library of Congress and which may well be called the Ferrar copies, consist of two volumes of large quarto size well bound in rough calf. About 1898 the books were boxed, that is, repaired with new backs without disturbing the sewing. The old labels were pasted on the new backs and bear the title in gold letters on red leather: Record / of the Virgin: / Compan:/, while gold letters on black leather indicate the volume: Vol. / I. / and Vol. / II. / . In the first volume manila strips are pasted from the inner cover to the first and to the last fly leaf in order to strengthen the binding. The paper is of the seventeenth century type, hand-made and uneven in texture. In the first volume there are three hundred and fifty-four pages, with five fly leaves in the front and seven in the back, while the second contains three hundred and eighty-seven pages preceded by three fly leaves and followed by four, with two extra manila pages in both the front and back. The pencil entries on the first leaf of the first volume are as follows: "Records of the / Virginia Company / of London./ Vol I. April 28, 1619 to May 8, 1622. / Vol 2. May 20, 1622 to June 7, 1627./ The above title in hand of / Mr. A. R. Spofford / Sig.: H. F[riedenwald][b]

[a] *A Short Collection of the Most Remarkable Passages from the originall to the dissolution of the Virginia Company*, pp. 17-18. The description here given of Southampton's attitude on receiving the books is similar to that given by Dr. Peckard.

[b] Mr. Spofford was the Librarian of Congress from 1864 to 1897. Mr. Friedenwald was in charge of the Division of Manuscripts from 1897 to 1900.

Oct. 11 / 97./ ". On the inside of the front cover of the second volume in an unknown modern autograph is: " p. 366 cf with p. 71 v 3," [a] and on the first manila leaf: "May 20, 1622 / to / June 7, 1624."

The discovery of the Ferrar papers has made it possible to make a final statement both as to the method of the transcription of the documents and as to its accuracy, for the autographs there found of Nicholas Ferrar and also of his clerk or business agent in his private accounts prove indisputably that these two men supervised and carried on the copying of the volumes.[b] Particularly in the second volume, where there are many entries of reports of committees, projects, objections, letters, petitions, declarations, and relations by the company or by individuals, the headings, the initial words, even the first line of each document, and sometimes entire documents are in the autograph of Nicholas Ferrar. The rest of the insertion is usually by his assistant, who was perhaps Thomas Collett, his nephew. All of the insertions in the first volume and about twenty in the second are entirely in the so-called Collett autograph, numbering about the same as those superintended by the deputy himself. The way in which these insertions are often crowded in, is evidence that they were copied from the original documents in spaces left for the purpose by the hired copyist.[c]

As to the identity of the other three or four distinct autographs, in which the remaining part of the volumes appear, nothing has been determined. The first and third copyists are distinctly different in style, while what appears as the writing of a fourth and a sixth clerk may possibly be identical with that of the first. With the exception of the autograph of Nicholas Ferrar, the whole is clearly, carefully, and legibly written in the characteristic running hand of the period, resembling the chancery hand. The spelling, capitalization, and abbreviations are distinctive and characteristic of each copyist. The use of curved lines to complete blank spaces at the end of the line, and often at the bottom and top of the page, shows the labor expended to make the transcript accurate and complete. The memoranda at the end of the volumes declare that the transcript had been carefully collated with the original "courte booke" and with the authentic documents by the secretaries, Edward Waterhouse and Edward Collingwood, in the first volume, and by Thomas Collett and Edward Collingwood in the second. That the insertions were copied from the original documents is shown by the statement

[a] The letter on page 366 is identical with that on page 71 of the fragile seventeenth century papers referred to above as Vol. III, pt. ii, of the *Records of the Virginia Company.*

[b] For examples of the autograph of Nicholas Ferrar and of that of his assistant, Thomas Collett (?), see the plates in this volume.

[c] For the documents thus inserted in the Court Book see List of Records under "Reference." For an illustration of the insertion of the documents see the plates in this volume.

in the memorandum of volume II that in two instances the letters had been missing for purpose of collation. Many pages reveal the corrections of errors or omissions of the copyist. In most instances this was done by Edward Collingwood himself, though sometimes by Thomas Collett.[a] At the bottom of each page is the signature "Conc Collingwood," the abbreviation standing for concordat, as is shown by the word appearing as "Concord:" on page three hundred and fifteen of the first volume.[b]

In addition to this internal evidence of accuracy, further proof of the care with which the books were transcribed is found among the Ferrar papers. The records of four courts were there discovered, which are almost identical with those of the same date in the Library of Congress volumes.[c] The only differences, and these are not numerous, are those which would naturally result from the fallibility of the copyist, and the apparent custom of the time to ignore the orthography of the original. One is led to believe that these loose pages of courts form a part of the book from which the copy was made. This is shown by the use of larger letters to emphasize certain words, and by Edward Collingwood's corrections of the Library of Congress copy to make it conform to these drafts. Even the omission of one or two lines in the Ferrar copy, later corrected, can be accounted for by reference to these sheets, since in each case it has resulted from the same word occurring in the same place on two successive lines. Furthermore, the directions in the margin of these courts as to where certain documents were to be entered were followed in the transcript and seem to point to these as a part of the original minutes. The autograph of the court held on June 25 is identical with that of the first copyist of the transcript, while the courts of July 4 and July 9 were apparently written by the sixth copyist of the transcript. Among the Ferrar papers are two drafts of a resolution concerning the "Lo Tfer speach touching Mr Alderm. Johnson," which was entered in the court book. One is a rough draft written, altered, and corrected by Edward Collingwood, and bearing the above indorsement by the writer and a similar indorsement by John Ferrar. The other draft is in the autograph of the sixth copyist of the court book, following the above, and is attested by Edward Collingwood. The transcript in the court book is identical with the latter, but the vote is omitted; the substance, however, is given after the discussion follow-

[a] For the evidence that the corrections are by Edward Collingwood, compare the autographs as shown in the plates of Vol. II, *post*.

[b] Signatures of Edward Collingwood may also be found in the Public Record Office among the *State Papers Colonial*, II, Nos. 10–11, 13, 19 (II, III). His signature is reproduced from the first Plymouth Patent, June 1, 1621, in the *Massachusetts Historical Collections*, Series 4, Vol. II, p. 163.

[c] Compare the plates in Vol. II, *post*. These courts are dated March 7, 1622/3, July 4, 1623, July 9, 1623, January 25, 1623/4.

ing the presentation of the resolution. Thus they seem rather to have been drafts of a resolution which had been presented than of one prepared to be offered. Comparison between these records of courts and a draft of a Somers Islands court, in the same collection, leads to the conclusion that they do not form a part of the blotter or blurred book from which the original book was made, since the latter are much corrected and altered and then canceled diagonally from corner to corner;[a] but are rather a part of the original book itself. The reliability of the Library of Congress transcripts is also confirmed by collating them with the original documents, or with other copies of the documents, which are inserted in the court book, and these careful comparisons have shown how accurately Edward Collingwood and his assistants conducted the work for Nicholas Ferrar.[b]

THE SYSTEM OF KEEPING THE COURT BOOK

The system by which the minutes of the courts were kept is thus outlined in the minutes; the court book was first drawn up by the secretary, was approved by the deputy, and later accepted or corrected by the court.[c] That there must have existed a "Blurr booke" in addition to the various reports or other documents offered in any court is proved by an extract from a memorandum by Sir Nathaniel Rich, which is a warrant requiring all records of the court to be brought to the commissioners on Virginia, and includes the "Court Bookes w[ch] should warrant the ſd Record[s], and the Blurr bookes w[ch] should warrant the Court Booke and is the first ground of the Record[s]; that it may [be] discouered whether there be any difference betweene them."[d] The entries in the court book are the minutes of all the various courts, of several meetings of the Somers Islands Company, and of one meeting of the committees.

Introducing each court is a list of the adventurers in attendance. A comparison of the number with the number of votes cast as recorded shows that these are quite complete for the quarter courts, but in the ordinary courts either the attendance was very small or the entry was incomplete, since the list is often terminated with the expression "and divers others." It was sometimes entered later than the transcript of the body of the text, as though from a book of attendance, but no mention of a roll book is found among the records. This part of the book alone furnishes a valuable comment upon the social classes interested in the undertaking and from it may be gained a knowledge of the faithfulness

[a] *Post*, Plates in Vol. II.
[b] For any variations of importance, see footnotes to documents in the "Court Book," *post*, I, II.
[c] *Court Book*, I, Dec. 11, 1622.
[d] List of Records, No. 465.

of the members and especially of the factions which developed toward the close of its history.

The order of business does not seem to have been regular. The approval of the previous court is usually recorded first, although many times this is deferred until the quarter court; then follows the report of the treasurer, through which the important matters to be determined are presented to the court, and the hearing of petitions, passing of shares, and grants of land appear at the end of the session.

In the ordinary courts were propounded all of those matters which did not require action in the general court and often many measures for preliminary discussion which were postponed for final action to the fuller court. Thus the records of the common courts and also of the preparative courts usually contain the full reports and discussions of the various subjects, while the statements in the quarter courts are brief and perfunctory, embodying the decisions reached in the lesser courts. The reports of officers, from which so much concerning the financial status is to be learned, are entered in the minutes of the general court. To trace the course of any question necessitates a search through all of the courts, but in the quarter courts will be found the elections and the final action on all laws and ordinances, on the patents for private plantations or monopolies, or, in short, on all measures by which the company would be bound for a term of years.

CONTENTS OF THE COURT BOOK

The business recorded during the first two years of the Sandys administration concerned the establishment of laws and orders in the company and in the colony, the systematizing of methods, the formation of joint stock companies for the erection of new industries in Virginia, and the opening up of new adventures. But after the massacre early in the year 1622, the whole tone of the book changes. Personal feuds and quarrels, complaints, and accusations fill the pages. Whether the friction was due to the extreme distress brought about by the attack of the Indians or whether it was but the excuse for open opposition by the party of the Crown, which had been rapidly developing, is difficult to determine. From the spring of 1622 until February, 1622/3, the burden of the record concerns the tobacco contract with the Crown. It resulted in the discussion of salaries for the officers and the quarrel with Samuel Wroth, which occupied the attention of the company for three months. Then followed the Butler and Johnson accusations, the investigation by the Crown, and the dissolution of the company. It is literally true that, after June, 1622, no new measures for trade, for industry, or for commerce are entered in the court book. There was the usual transferring of shares and hearing of petitions and claims, but the business activity was evidently destroyed. That the colony could survive the massacre and continue its development with so little encouragement from the proprietor is evidence of the strong foundation laid during the governorship of Sir George Yeardley.

From the court book it would be possible to reconstruct a part or the whole of some of the other records. A list of all of the ships departing or arriving with the names of the masters could thus be drawn up, but the terms of the charter party could not be determined.[a] A full statement of the shares of stock granted or transferred, of the land assigned for adventure or for service, and of the private plantations erected could be given. Even a partial financial account could be rendered, though not an itemized statement. The larger sums invested or received from the various sources are usually given in the treasurer's plans and the officers' reports, although unfortunately only those of the treasurer and deputy are entered in full. But from scattered statements in plans, reports, and discussions, from grants, patents, suits, letters, petitions, and claims will come much that will illuminate the financial situation when these are gathered together.

The full record of all documents for which record was not provided elsewhere was made in the court book. Plans, reports of committees, and reports of chief officers seem to have been entered in full, but letters to and from the colony, and to and from the privy council, petitions with the action thereupon, charter parties, grants for monopolies, lists of departing planters, expenditures and receipts of the magazines, and rolls of adventure, were all recorded in the other books provided by the "Orders and Constitutions" or in the books created later. A single illustration will suffice. Of the twenty-seven letters sent to the colony and received from the colony, copies of many of which have been found among the papers in Virginia, but fifteen are mentioned in the court book, and only a few are spread in full upon the minutes. A great many more documents are entered in the court book during the later years, due evidently to the desire to keep a record of the controversy which might serve as a defense against the accusations of the malcontents. That many of these were not entered in the original court book is revealed by the marginal notes in the extant court minutes of the Ferrar papers, which read as follows: "Enter the quietus est," "Enter the resolution," and other similar directions.

The court book is not only a source of information, but it also serves as a guide to the other records of the company. That all of the twenty-one documents mentioned but not entered in the court book have been found in other collections is most important and interesting. These include some of the publications of the company, most of the correspondence of the company with the King and with the

[a] The terms in general are given in the *Presidents for Patents* in the British Museum. List of Records, Nos. 256, 257, 266, 267, 268, 276, 277, and 278.

colony, many of the orders of the Privy Council, the Admiralty suits of the company, the laws passed in the colony, the charter granted to the colony, and the forms for patents used by the company. There are thirteen documents entered in the court book which are on record elsewhere, consisting of declarations or reports which were published by the company, petitions and letters to the King, and orders of the King's council. But thirty most valuable documents are spread upon the minutes which have not yet been discovered among other papers. These include a few petitions to the King, many petitions received by the company, a number of letters from and to the colony, the propositions brought forward in the attempt to form a tobacco contract with the King, the plans propounded by the treasurer for the advancement of the enterprise, and the declarations of the state of the affairs of the company and of the colony by the same officer. [a]

THE EXTANT SUPPLEMENTARY RECORDS

DOCUMENTS OUTLINING THE ACTIVITY OF THE COMPANY

The organization and the method of procedure of the company have been outlined, in order to enable the reader to comprehend the nature of the records, and through them the machinery by which it conducted its internal affairs; but there is a wider and more important field to consider. The real interest in the company comes from its activity in carrying on trade and in developing the resources and government of the colony. Again, the starting point must be the court book, not only as a guide to the records which it kept in executing its purposes, but in discovering what activities are to be traced. Two kinds of documents afford the clearest outline of the subject; in one are the reports which the treasurer offered to the company and which are spread upon the minutes; in the other are the printed declarations and broadsides which the company issued for the purpose of securing interest, confidence, and investment in the undertaking. With the same motive it reprinted treatises and published sermons which had been delivered before the company.

The first report of Sir Edwin Sandys after he became treasurer was offered on November 3, 1619, in which he thus defined his policy: The resources of the company were to be augmented by settling and developing the company's land and by increasing the number of industries to be established, an action which must advance the plantation from a colony for exploitation into a colony for settlement. The report begins with a statement of the number of men which had been transported

[a] All of these documents, whether entered in the court book or not, are cited in the List of Records, and are also referred to by foot notes in this edition of the court book.

by the company for the college land and for the public land during the summer and continues with propositions to the same effect, by which 300 additional persons should be sent to the colony, 100 of whom were to be maids for wives and 100 to be apprentices or servants from the city. The other measures discussed are indicative of the development which rapidly took place. First of these was the effort to establish other commodities in Virginia and restrain the excessive production of tobacco; the second was the encouragement of a spirit of local patriotism in the colony. The treasurer urges that men should be sent from the low countries to raise fortifications for the colony, stating that the colonists were willing to bear the charges of the work since they had recently been encouraged by the charters and grants of liberties. The dependence of the company upon the lotteries for an income and the care to arrange for an economical transportation of the men are indications of the financial policy and status of the colony. The income of the lottery is estimated at £3,500, and the total expense of perfecting the plan submitted is placed at £4,000 or £5,000.

Six months later the treasurer made his annual report, which revealed to what extent his plans had been executed. It was issued as a broadside under the date of the court in which it was delivered and describes the state of the colony from April, 1618, to April, 1619, taken from a general letter to the company, and then proceeds to outline the successful activity of the colony during the succeeding year. It emphasizes the erection of private plantations, the number of men sent to the company's land, the commodities provided for—there being ten instead of two as in the former year—the interest in the care of religion and education in the colony, and the stable financial condition of the company. The general receipts amounted to £9,831 14s 11d and the disbursements were £10,431 14s 07d, but the surplus in the college fund more than exceeded this deficiency, the receipts from that source being £2,043 02s 11½d and the expenditures £1,477 15s 5d. The lottery was reported to have an increase in stock over the previous year of £1,200. Although not re-elected treasurer, the financial management remained in the hands of Sir Edwin Sandys, as is proved by the entries of his plans in the court book and by his private letters to John Ferrar. A scheme outlined in the court of July 7, 1620, is practically the measure put forth in the printed declaration of June 22, 1620, and proposes a continuation of the policy stated above.

The printed documents of 1619 and 1620 add but little to the plans revealed in the treasurer's reports concerning the activity of the company, although the measures taken to advance the comfort of the planters and of the tenants upon arrival in Virginia, the establishment of many private plantations, and the encouragement given to the self-government of the colony are brought out more clearly. After the note of the shipping in 1621, so far as is known, there were no propositions issued by the company. This was due to the massacre which paralyzed the efforts of the company for a time and forced upon it publications of defense and excuse or directions of warning. While the company was torn by dissension, after 1622 the colony slowly but steadily advanced. The proprietor was no longer active, and the center of interest is therefore transferred from the courts in London in which the plans had been conceived to the settlement in which they were maturing.

The various publications of the company afford not only an understanding of the measures proposed, but also of their execution. They were in themselves a means of carrying out its schemes. Before 1622 five of these advertisements were issued by the company. The broadside bearing the date May 17, 1620, is a full statement of the prosperous condition in the colony, setting forth the ability of the colony to receive newcomers in its guest houses, newly built in each of the four ancient boroughs and in the other plantations, and describing the measures provided to sustain ministers in each borough. It states the number of men who had been sent to the public land, with the provisions allowed, and describes fully the efforts which had been made to establish six industries in the colony.[a]

A book of great importance was issued by the company in June of the same year containing a series of declarations.[b] There were at least two editions in the year 1620, having variations in the title page; in the first edition the pages are numbered according to each pamphlet and the imprint is "T. S.," while in the second the pagination is consecutive from 1 to 92 and the imprint is that of Thomas Snodham. The latter varies also in the orthography of the word "colony" in the title. The former was probably the first edition and was composed of pamphlets, each of which may have been issued separately, and seems to have been reissued, with an additional pamphlet concerning a division of land in Virginia,[c] in which the signature is consecutive. Copies of the first issue of the first edition of the "Declarations" are in the Harvard Library and in the New York Public Library ("No. 1"), but the only copy of the second issue is in the John Carter Brown Library (copy "A"). The copies in the British Museum, the Cambridge University Library,[d] the Library of Congress, the John Carter Brown Library (copy "B"), and the New York Public Library (Thomas Addison Emmet Collection, "No. 2") are identical and are evidently the first issue of the second edition. The copies in the New York Public Library and in a private collection in New York are probably a second issue of the second edition, having four additional pages and containing a

[a] List of Records, No. 174.

[b] *Ibid.*, No. 183.

[c] The pamphlet must have been printed in 1616. An imperfect copy is in the British Museum.

[d] This copy is evidently imperfect, since it lacks pages 91 and 92.

declaration, "By his Maiesties Councell for Virginia," dated November 15, 1620.[a]
The pagination and the signature are consecutive but the style of type is changed.

The pamphlets included in all editions are as follows:

(1) "By his Maiesties Counseil for Virginia." This is a declaration of the industries which have been established, of the good government which has been formed in the colony so that it "begins to have the face and fashion of an orderly State," and of the purpose of the company in the division of land.

(2) "A Note of the Shipping, Men and Prouisions sent to Virginia, by the Treasurer and Company in the yeere 1619."

(3) "A Declaration of the Supplies intended to be sent to Virginia in this yeare 1620. 18 Julij, 1620."

(4) "The Names of the Aduenturers, with their seuerall summes aduentured * * * paid to Sir Thos. Smith," to "Sir Baptist Hicks," and to "Sir Edwin Sandys."

(5) "Orders And Constitutions, * * * for the better gouerning * * * of the said Companie * * * Anno 1619, and 1620."

Some light is thrown upon these publications by the court book, in which provision for four similar pamphlets was made between November, 1619, and June, 1620, as follows:

(1) An advertisement for laborers, approved to be published on November 17, 1619.

(2) A publication which should confute the slander as to the barrenness of the soil in Virginia, ordered November 22.

(3) A list of the names of adventurers with the sums adventured, ordered to be drawn up by the treasurer and Dr. Winstone, December 15.[b]

(4) An apology for Virginia, ordered to be printed June 23, 1620. On June 26 and 28 it was provided that the standing orders should be printed and annexed to the book to be given to all members by order of the council.

The conclusion seems valid that these pamphlets are the ones included in the book and that they first appeared at various times, but that finally in June, 1620, they were collected, the fourth one added, and the volume published under the date of the latter.

The publication of this declaration in four different issues during the year 1620 indicates the interest which Sir Edwin Sandys had aroused in the measure, as well as

[a] This is copy No. 3 in the New York Public Library. The copy in the private library is evidently the Smyth of Nibley volume, secured from the Cholmondely papers through Bernard Quaritch.

[b] Such a list of adventurers is among the Manchester papers. List of Records, No. 58.

the virility of the company, while reference to the book in much of the correspondence of the day reveals the same attitude toward the venture. In order to promote the silk industry a pamphlet entitled "*Observations to be followed for making of fit roomes for silk wormes*," written by Banoeil, was translated under the patronage of the company toward the end of the year 1620.[a] It contains a pamphlet called "A Valuation of the Commodities growing and to be had in Virginia: rated as they are worth," in which is presented the astonishing list of 49 articles. The natural commodities which did not require especial cultivation, such as various kinds of fish, furs, woods, shrubs and berries, were of course included. But this proof of rapid development in the industrial habits and occupations of the colonists is most important, and the note of the shipping of the same year and the one in 1621 are confirmatory. In the former is the statement of the number of men sent for each of four industries, and in the latter a similar declaration. The rapid transportation of settlers and the development of private plantations in these two years is as surprising. Thus in 1620 six ships with 600 persons were sent to the colony, and 400 more settlers were to be sent at once, of whom 500 were destined for the company's land. The next year the number of ships dispatched increased to twenty-one and the number of persons to 1,300, while the number of patents for private plantations grew from six to twenty-six.

During the year 1622 the books printed by the company were much less valuable, although more numerous, there being seven in all. *The Declaration of the state of the Colony of Virginia with the Relation of the Massacre of the English, by the Natiue Infidells with the names of those that were Massacred*, by Edward Waterhouse, was more concerned with the disaster than with the previous development of the plantation.[b] A broadside is inserted in the copy of this declaration in the John Carter Brown Library, entitled "Virginia Inconveniences,"[c] which was published separately and was a set of directions with regard to the provisions which each person should have before sailing for the colony. This included apparel, victuals, household implements, arms, sugar, spice, and fruit for consumption at sea, and nets, hooks, lines, and a tent for large numbers. The declaration was made that for its own tenants the Virginia Company followed the proportionate provision as set forth in this broadside. It is at once an advertisement for new tenants and a warning against the dangers which had wrought dissatisfaction and brought complaints to the company. Two sermons and two treatises were published in the same year; one of the

[a] This translation was ordered in an ordinary court on November 15, 1620, and was reported ready for the press on December 13. In the same courts there is a discussion of the prices of commodities produced in Virginia. List of Records, p. 138, Nos. 150, 151.

[b] List of Records, p. 152, No. 293.

[c] *Ibid.*, No. 292.

latter was a reprint of Banoeil's book on silk worms, including a letter of encouragement from the King and one of advice from the treasurer, which were intended to promote the industry of silk as opposed to that of tobacco;[a] the other treatise was by John Brinsley and was an encouragement for the advancement of learning and the foundation of schools.[b] Of the same character was a four-page pamphlet, which was published in the same year, declaring the sums which had been collected "towards the building of a free schoole in Virginia."[c]

A number of general works were approved by the company in the courts or were accepted and rewarded. Thus the proposition by Smith to write a history of Virginia on April 12, 1621, seems to have been acceptable to the adventurers, while George Rugh, who had rendered service to the Virginia council by writing a treatise on government, was publicly eulogized upon his bequeathing £100 to the company for the education of infidels' children.[d] Edward Bennett was admitted to the company as a reward for a treatise against the importation of tobacco from Spain, and the chronicler, Howes, was granted 12 pounds of tobacco as a yearly payment for his references to Virginia.[e]

A number of works were suggested in the courts of which we have no trace or which can not be identified as appearing under other titles. To what the company referred when it petitioned the Archbishop of Canterbury for permission to publish the book which he had prohibited is unknown.[f] The printed book proposed by Sir Edwin Sandys on November 4, 1620, in which he wished to defend the lotteries and to hasten the dispatch of persons to Virginia, may have been the declaration of the shipping in 1620, but it is not mentioned again in the court book. In 1621 three other proposed publications failed to be executed, so far as is known, the first of which was a treatise on the government of Virginia by Thomas Bargrave.[g] The second was a defense of the company, and concerned the health, trade, and manners of the colony, and the third considered the defects and remedies of Virginia and discussed the food,

---

[a] The first suggestion of a reprint of this book came in a court of October 31, 1621, but it was not until September 5 of the year following that the book was ordered to be printed, including the two letters. List of Records, No. 347. The sermons were *Virginia's God be Thanked*, by Patrick Copland, 1622, and one by John Donne. See List of Records, Nos. 312, 375.

[b] An order of court, December 19, 1621, provided for an expression of gratitude to John Brinsley and an appointment of a committee to peruse and report upon his work. On January 16 the committee was granted additional time, and Patrick Copland was asked to review the book and report to the company. List of Records, No. 291.

[c] List of Records, No. 289.

[d] *Court Book*, II, November 20, 1622.

[e] *Ibid.*, I, April 12, 1621.

[f] *Ibid.*, I, July 18, 1620.

[g] *Ibid.*, I, February 22, 1620/21.

health, fortifications, wealth, and religion of the colony.[a]   In the following year an attempt was made to collect the "binding laws which had been ratified in courts" and to add them to the printed books, but it seems to have failed, since no trace of such a publication has been found, and no final action is recorded in the court book.[b]

DOCUMENTS REVEALING THE MOVEMENTS FOR TRADE AND INDUSTRY

The printed advertisements between 1619 and 1621 were successful in securing the capital with which to carry on the enterprise.   It now remains to discover how the trade was conducted and controlled, how the plantation was developed and governed, and how the business was finally destroyed.

The income which enabled the company to provide for new industries in 1619 and 1620 was derived from the £12 10s. paid by each new adventurer for each new share of stock, and from the lotteries.   Special collections and particular gifts for the advancement of religion and of education in the colony were frequent, and thus the account and management of the college land became important.   Before the introduction of freedom of trade into the colony, and the dissolution of the old magazine on January 12, 1619/20, the company had some profit from that monopoly,[c] but the ease with which returns came from the lotteries had doubtless led the company to abolish the monopoly of trade which had become so difficult to maintain.   That the company depended on the lotteries is indicated by the following statements in the court book: On December 1, 1619, the lotteries were continued until summer because there was no other means of securing money, and the plan put forth for the development of the colony on July 7, 1620, provided that the estimated expense of £17,800 should be met by the income from the lotteries, which would amount to £18,000. Information concerning the organization for conducting the lottery is wanting. Books and rolls and catalogues of prizes are referred to but have not been found.[d] Thus the only documents which throw light on the system outside of the court book are the records of the suit of the Virginia Company against William Leveson, an agent for the lottery in 1613, which discloses that books and rolls had been kept, and that a house for the lottery had been erected and furnished "at the west end of St. Paules Church;" a proclamation by the King for the overthrow of the lottery on March 8, 1620/21; and a few letters soliciting investments.[e]

The investments by the company during the period of the lotteries followed three lines—the old magazine, the planting of the public and the college lands in

[a] *Court Book,* I, April 12, June 11, 13, 1621.

[b] *Ibid.,* I, November 19, 21, 1621; March 13, 1621/22.

[c] *Ibid.,* I, July 7, 1619.

[d] *Ibid.,* I, June 24, 1619; January 12, 1619/20.

[e] List of Records, Nos. 28, 29, 71, 78.

Virginia, and the erection of industries for the production of certain commodities. The court book is the only source of information with regard to the old magazine, in which the company through its general stock of the company had invested more than twice as much as any other adventurer.   Hence, during the last half of the year 1619, it made every effort to gain an account and secure a settlement of that adventure. The discussion, which resulted in the adoption of free trade to the colony, reveals the system used for the control of the magazine, indicates to a slight degree the income which the company had had from that joint stock, and incidentally shows that it had some returns from the public lands in Virginia.[a]   The numbers of men sent to the company's land and their equipment are given in the printed declarations, in the reports of the treasurer spread on the minutes, and in the discussions recorded in the court book, and although the sums invested for the purpose are not recorded, the statement was made by Sir Edwin Sandys that 800 men were sent through the income from the lottery.   The transportation of dissolute persons in the year 1619 to meet the command of the King, and the settlement of boys and girls on the company's land previous to 1622, were other means used to people the public and college lands.[b]

Five commodities enumerated in the broadside of May 17, 1620, were established by action of the court.   No record is extant of the exact nature of the investment, but it appears from the court book to have been chiefly an investment from the general stock.   The movement for monopoly of certain industries rather than a monopoly of all trade began during the latter part of the year 1620, and as a result the records deal extensively with plans for the sole importation of tobacco, by which a joint stock of £15,000 was to be raised to carry out what is known as the "Somerscales plan."

The overthrow of the lotteries carried consternation to the company.   An income was essential with which to send out settlers to develop the soil or to create new industries, but the general stock was so low that the company could not even carry out its plans for glassworks.   Finally, after several months of discussion, recourse was had to special adventure or new joint stock companies for special undertakings, controlled by a treasurer who should be elected by the adventurers in the scheme.   Thus followed the creation of a series of magazines for the erection of a glass furnace, for the establishment of a fur trade, for sending maids for wives, and for supplying a magazine for apparel.   The records of these ventures are to be found only in the court book, and the data there given is very insufficient.   This, of course, meant no advantage to the general stock, and the company was forced to discover means for securing returns from the general investment and an income with

a *Court Book*, I, June 24, 28, July 7, 13, November 3, December 15, 1619.

b *Ibid.*, December 23, 1619; January 12, February 2, 1619/20; July 3, 1622.

which to develop the company's land. Hence, private plantations were organized, and private patents and monopolies for the industry of pitch and tar, for ironworks, for new discoveries were granted, while special commissions for trade along the coast and for fishing added to the revenue. With the exception of the movement for private plantations and for the sole importation of tobacco, but few records exist outside of the court book to reveal these vigorous endeavors to reap the results of the great investments in the earlier years.[a] The grants for private plantations to individuals or groups of individuals, called hundreds, commenced as early as 1616, but increased rapidly during and after 1621, there being entries in the court book of over fifty patents granted in four years, which provide for the transportation of at least 100 men each and often for four times as many. The system by which each hundred in Virginia and the adventurers for the hundred in England was organized is to be found in the court book and in the extant records of the companies. The minutes of one meeting for Martin's Hundred and one for Smythe's Hundred, and the forms for patents deposited in the British Museum, in addition to about seventy papers of Berkeley Hundred, afford a very satisfactory reconstruction of the terms of agreement, the expenses, the provisioning, the form of government, the instructions issued to the captain or governor of the hundred, and the terms of settlement with tenants and servants. The adventures of Lord Zouch and Lord La Warr in 1617 and 1618, and of the Walloons and French in 1621, complete the series of which any record exists.[b]

But the private grants did not promise sufficient income to meet the great demands for supplies from the general stock which the massacre of 1622 brought about. As a result the company turned to the income from tobacco, regardless of its high purposes and its endeavors to enforce the production of other commodities. This feeling of the importance of a contract for the sole importation of tobacco took such a strong hold upon the company that from May, 1622, until its dissolution, just a year later, nothing else worth mentioning is recorded in the court book, while the quarrel concerning the salaries to be paid for the management of the £100,000 to be invested in this project monopolized the attention of several courts. In addition to the record of an entire year in the court book, numerous memoranda of various estimates of the value of the tobacco monopoly to the Crown and to the company are deposited among the Manchester papers

[a] The discussions in the *Court Book* with regard to the magazine, the development of commodities, and private plantations will be found through the Index under those headings.

[b] For the documents on Berkeley Hundred see the Smyth of Nibley Papers in the New York Public Library, which are cited in the List of Records. See also Nos. 71, 72, 76, 77, 82, 227, 264, 735. These are really records of the private companies and fall under class VI in the List of Records. Among the forms for patents in the British Museum is that granted to Martin's Hundred: List of Records, No. 323.

in the Public Record Office. The communications with the Privy Council on the subject are spread on the company's minutes, and are also to be found among the Colonial State papers. This series includes the proclamations of the King in 1624, and the new propositions and measures for tobacco importation of the same year. The economic condition of the planter, the necessity of a revenue to the company, the amount of the importation and of the customs value to the King, the relations with Spain, and the economic values in England are all brought out in the estimates, discussions, and arguments.[a]

DOCUMENTS DISCLOSING THE RELATIONS WITH THE COLONY

The study of the relations of the company to the colony and the development within the colony may be based on a greater variety of documents than any other phase of the subject, especially with regard to the political conditions. The court book furnishes an understanding of the attitude and motives of the company and often serves to connect the data gathered from letters, instructions, commissions, patents, and grants. Thus the emphasis on the custom of martial law in the colony and the severity of penalty imposed is revealed both in the court book and in the extracts from Governor Argall's register.[b] The additional forms of government required by the development of the colony are recorded in the court book, by which the company created the offices of deputies to the governor for the college and for the public land, secretary, treasurer, chancellor, and surveyor, and provided for the compensation of officers by grants of land, by transportation of tenants, by the income of the company's land, and by allowance of fees.[c] The requests for the appointment of a council of State and for laws and orders, urgently repeated by Governor Yeardley, as recorded in the court book in 1619, give evidence that the source of such development was in the colony. But the fundamental law for the government of the colony is recorded in three documents, the instructions to Governor Yeardley, November 8, 1618, which created the land system, the instructions to Governor Wyatt, July 24, 1621, which emphasized the industrial development, and "An Ordinance and Constitution * * * for a Councill of State and Generall Assembly" in Virginia, which confirmed the political forms.

These documents provided for the creation of two councils. The council of state, composed of the governor and council, was to form an executive and

---

[a] List of Records, 60, 102, 147, 184, 185, 59, 263, 287, 448, 392, 396, 410, 413, 411, 414, 424, 425, 431, 482, 676, 678, 680, 681, 682, 691, 692, 693, 695, 696, 703, 705, 712, 724, 729, 733, 737, 744, 747, 756. See also the index of the Court Book, *post*, Vol. II, under "Tobacco."

[b] List of Records, No. 40, ff.

[c] *Court Book*, I, April 3, May 15, 17, 1620. See also Bruce, *Economic History of Virginia*.

judicial body, and the assembly, composed of the council and two burgesses from each town or borough, was to be purely a legislative body.[a] The approval of a quarter court of the company, which was necessary for legalizing the acts of the assembly, is referred to in the court book in three places only.[b] The constitution and the provisions for division of the country into cities and boroughs, recorded both in the instructions and in the patents by which the government of the private plantations was delegated to a private body, form the basis for a study of the local systems. The records of Smythe's, Martin's, and Berkeley Hundred referred to above, the correspondence of Samuel Argall with Bermuda Hundred, and the commissions for government issued by Governor Argall and later by the council of state complete the sources on this subject.[c] The precedents for patents are valuable in the information which they afford with regard to the position of the following classes of colonists: The old adventurer not subject to rent; the adventurer paying money for his shares and agreeing to transport 100 persons; the adventurer settling a private plantation; the individual planter.[d] These documents also throw light on the liberty of the individual, his exemption from taxation without his consent by the colony or by the private plantation, and his submission to a government almost military in character.

The strict supervision which the company exercised over the economic, industrial, and social conditions of the colony is to be seen in the measures enacted in the courts and in the correspondence between the company and the colony, supplemented by a large number of private letters to the officers of the company. Four letters to the colony are mentioned in the court book, of which two have not been found, but eight others not mentioned are extant. It is more difficult to determine what letters came from the colony, due to the usually brief reports of the letters in the court book, to the omission of the date from the copies of the letters, and from the uncertainty of the date of the receipt of the letters as noted in the court book. Seven letters seem to have been received by the company of which no trace has been found, while only four of the ten extant are mentioned in the court book. It is apparent therefore that only a part of the official correspondence is in existence. The directions to the colony disclose the care and earnestness of the company, and emphasize the endeavors to establish the various commodities, while the descriptions given by the colonists are extremely valuable in the picture they present of their efforts, ambitions, and attainments. The pri-

[a] List of Records, Nos. 72, 260, 261.

[b] *Court Book*, I, April 3, May 15, 1620.

[c] The patents, the Argall correspondence, and the records of the Hundreds are new material and will aid much in an understanding of the local conditions and government.

[d] List of Records, Nos. 299, 323, 324, 325.

vate correspondence proves that the official letters were likely to give but one phase of the conditions.

About thirty-five letters addressed to Sir Edwin Sandys during the years 1619 to 1621 have been found among the Ferrar papers, which are full of complaint because of the scarcity of provisions. Apparently Sir Edwin's policy to develop the plantation, and especially the company's land as a source of revenue, was overdone, and he was not as wise in carrying out his plan as he had been in forming it, since the colony was unable to provide for the large numbers sent out. These complaints are casually mentioned in the court book, but the Sandys-Ferrar correspondence shows that it was the desire of the administration to conceal the difficulties and distress of the colony not only from the public but also from the hostile faction. The Manchester papers preserve letters, or copies of them, which came to the company or to individuals in 1622 and 1623 complaining of similar deprivations in the colony.[a]

The company was not only interested in the economic and industrial development and the necessary political forms of the colony, but, as Sir Edwin Sandys declared, it had a higher purpose than the Muscovy or the other commercial corporations. This high ideal is proved by the attention which is devoted to plans for the college, by the appointment of ministers, by the collections in the churches, and by the gifts received,[b] but the theory that the chief motive of the enterprise was religious is not supported either by the spirit or by the data of the records.

RECORDS KEPT BY THE OFFICERS IN THE COLONY

The acts of the administration in Virginia are recorded in the volume of contemporary records of the company kept by the colony which are described above. They consist of a series of nine orders and proclamations by the governor and council and of twenty-one orders, proclamations, commissions, and warrants issued by the governor as the executive officer of the council for the regulation of affairs in the colony. They cover the years 1621, 1622, and 1623, and concern the collection of taxes, the designation of laborers for public works, the regulation of prices of commodities, the restraint of relations with the Indians, and the control of the morals of the citizens. In addition to these documents issued by the governor is a series of twenty-four commissions and warrants issued to individuals to act as commanders of cities and hundreds, to carry on trade with the Indians, to make discoveries, to wage war upon the Indians, and to collect moneys. Another group of documents in the same collection consists of thirty-six petitions to the governor and council between 1622 and 1624. They are

[a] For a citation of these letters in the List of Records, see the Index under "Letters."
[b] *Post*, Vol. II, Index under "College," "Education," "Ministers."

claims for wages and for moneys due, demands for fulfillment of contracts, requests for pardon and for justification in personal quarrels, demands for lands, and petitions to be allowed to return to deserted plantations and to England.[a]

The only extant record of the council for 1619 is an account of the "putting out of the Tenants that came over in the B[ona] N[ova] wth other orders of the Councell," found among the Ferrar papers.[b]

The "courte booke," or original record of the meetings of the governor and council, in which these petitions were heard and orders issued, is extant from 1624 to 1632, with a record of one court in 1622 and of one in 1623. These are mostly the actions of the council sitting in a judicial capacity and concern controversies over property, probate matters, and criminal charges. The punishments seem extreme. Two actions of the court are particularly interesting, one affecting Edward Sharpless for sending copies of the colonial records to England, and the other consisting of accusations against Captain John Martin of slanderous and false utterances. A few additional orders and warrants are preserved among the Colonial State papers,[c] together with a report of the proceedings of the assembly in 1619, written by John Pory and sent to England, the only other account of which was sent to Sir Edwin Sandys by John Rolfe, and is among the Ferrar papers.[d] The acts of the assembly for March 5, 1623/24 are the only measures of that body during the life of the company which are extant, with the exception of the letters and petitions addressed to the company and to the King, and of a few orders.

DOCUMENTS CONCERNING THE DEVELOPMENT OF FACTIONS AND THE DISSOLUTION OF THE COMPANY

A series of documents remains which does not bear directly on the organization of the company or the expression of its activity in trade and in colonial enterprise, but is invaluable for a study of the history of the company, since it concerns the relations of the individual members to one another, reveals the inner life and motive of the company as a whole and of the various groups, and explains the conditions which resulted from the interference of the King and the overthrow of the corporation. The entire movement centers about the growth of factions in the company. The movement begins in the years just preceding the accession of Sir Edwin Sandys to the position of treasurer, and seems to have had its origin in the trouble over

[a] For citation of these documents in the List of Records, see the Index under "Warrants," "Commissions," "Proclamations," "Orders."

[b] List of Records, Nos. 138, 139.

[c] *Ibid.*, Nos. 240, 521, 645.

[d] *Ibid.*, Nos. 116, 154.

Sir Samuel Argall and the appointment of Sir George Yeardley as governor of the colony. It finally involved many of the personal complaints and difficulties which presented themselves to the company, and therefore requires a study of those problems before it can be understood.

The measures which thus arose with regard to individuals are to be found chiefly in the court book. They supply much information which can not be obtained elsewhere with regard to the methods of procedure of the company, and afford scattered data of great importance in addition to the light they throw on the disputes of the factions. The subjects discussed include such problems as the relations with the northern colony, the conflict with Spain concerning the ship *Treasurer*, the suit against William Wye for failing to land settlers in Virginia, and various accusations against Governor Yeardley and Captain Argall for misgovernment in the colony. The accounts of Sir Thomas Smythe, the settlement of Alderman Robert Johnson's accounts for the magazine, and the illegality of Captain John Martin's patent for a plantation, were also questions which were of vital importance to the financial affairs of the company and took the attention of numerous courts; but neither the accounts of Sir Thomas Smythe nor of the magazine were ever adjusted.

The claims against the company presented by William Tracey, by William Welden, the deputy of the college land who was superseded by George Thorpe, and by the heirs of Sir George Somers for a compensation for the Somers Islands are but illustrations of the many demands made upon the company. The court sat as a judiciary body to settle numerous personal quarrels, including the Brewster-Argall, the Argall-Smythe, the Bargrave-Smythe, and the Johnson-Southampton cases. Disputes which arose within the courts and resulted in slander and counter accusations took much of the time and attention of the company, the trouble between the council and Samuel Wroth over the question of salaries thus consuming the entire time of the courts for three months, from December to February, 1622/3. In the various collections in London are about a dozen papers which give additional information on the Argall-Rich troubles, the censure of Alderman Johnson, the Martin patent, the accounts of Sir Thomas Smythe, and the suits against William Wye.[a]

The documents which bear directly on the factional differences in the company are among the Manchester and the Ferrar papers. From them comes the insight into the very motives and thoughts of the opposing parties, and the proof that

---

[a] For the history of these cases as given in the court book, see the citations in the Index, *Post*, Vol. II, under the names suggested. References to the documents in the List of Records, may also be found in the Index.

the accusations of the Warwick party are well founded, in so far as they relate to concealment of the sufferings and dissatisfactions in the colony, comes as a surprise.[a] For a history of the factions the student must first review the reports of the personal conflicts referred to above and then turn to the numerous documents which include the accusations against the company, the defense of the colony and of the company, and the memoranda and letters upon the charges.

When the quarrels had finally been carried to the Privy Council, the matter was taken up officially by the company, and the second volume of the court book after the spring of 1623 is composed entirely of documents spread upon the minutes which concern the action of the company. In fact, all of the papers after that time are of the same character except the records of the governor and council in Virginia. Since they number upward of two hundred, it will be impossible to discuss them separately, but it must be remembered that in them is to be found an outline of the history of the company reaching back into the time of Sir Thomas Smythe, presented first by one faction and then by the other. The most important of these reviews are the charges of Captain Butler, of Alderman Johnson, and of Captain Bargrave, with replies to each; the complaints of the adventurers and of the planters against the Sandys administration, and a declaration by the "ancient planters" comparing the two administrations in the colony. Finally, the "Discourse of the Old Company" is the last review of the whole situation. Another most important group of papers is a series of projects for readjusting the government of the colony and the administration of the company. The projects of Martin, Bargrave, Ditchfield, and Rich thus afford an opportunity to study the beginnings of royal control.

The relations between the Crown and the company assume three different phases during the Sandys-Southampton administration—the first before the discussion over the tobacco contract in 1622, the second concerning that contract, and the third relating to the abuses in the company and the dissolution of the corporation. The court book shows a readiness and a desire on the part of the company before 1622 to refer to the Privy Council such matters as the magazine accounts which seemed beyond their control, but it also contains declarations to the effect that an interference with the patent rights is not to be tolerated. The questions arising in those years concern the transportation of dissolute persons to the colony, the right of the King to nominate men from whom the treasurer should be chosen, the restriction on trade to other countries, the refusal of a new charter to the company, and the dissolution of the lotteries. Supplementary to these records in the court book are the orders of the Privy Council affecting all of these

---

[a] Citation of these documents in the List of Records may be found by reference to the Index under the Sandys-Ferrar letters, the Rich and Johnson memoranda, and the letters in the Manchester papers.

problems. One of the most important documents, however, has not been found, since the efforts for a new patent can not be traced beyond the statements in the court book. It was first proposed November 15, 1620, and was ordered to be continued and to be confirmed by Parliament on January 31, 1620/21. On the 22d of the following month the Lords were appointed to secure the seal, and on April 12 the objections of the attorney-general, to whom the King had referred the patent, were discussed. That it never went into effect is certain, since no record is to be found among the sign manual warrants in the record office or in the signet docquet book. Furthermore, it is not enrolled in the chancery files, and it is not entered on the patent rolls, while in the suit of the *quo warranto* the only letters patent cited are those already known of 1606, 1609, and 1612.[a]

Unless the documents have been lost or the date of the entry has been mistaken the conclusion must be reached that after the surrender of the draft of the new charter to the solicitor-general it disappeared from sight. During the year 1622 the communications between the King and the company concerned the tobacco contract and its final acceptance at the command of the King, and revealed the maturity of the policy of interference which had been developing during the previous years. The number of accusations against the company increased during the year, and the records of the early part of 1623 abound in letters of complaint and charges of mismanagement from the colony. The memoranda of the Warwick party, found among the Manchester papers, are also essential to the understanding of the movements toward the overthrow of the company. Many of the forty communications between the King and the company are spread on the court book, while all of them are found in the Privy Council register. These include the commissions to the board chosen to investigate the affairs of the company,[b] and the

---

[a] The Editor searched the following documents in the Public Record Office for a record or citation of this charter:

Sign Manual Warrants, Nos. 11, 13–17.

Exchequer, 19 James I. (1621.)

Docquet of the Signet Office.

Chancery Privy Seal, 19 James I, January–August. (1621.)

The suggestion that a charter was reissued at a later date led to a similar fruitless search in the Chancery of the Privy Seal as follows:

22 James I. July, August. (1624.)

7 Charles I. February, March, October–December. (1631.)

9 Charles I. August. (1633.)

14 Charles I. August, September. (1638.)

16 Charles I. April. (1640.)

[b] A record of the grand committee appointed to defend the company before the commissioners and a record of a meeting of the commissioners are among the Ferrar papers. List of Records, Nos. 394, 543.

directions to the commissioners sent to Virginia. The correspondence between the King and the colony during those months of struggle concerned the latter commission and established the royal authority, but the letters from the colony were addressed to the company as late as the close of the year, six months after the judgment was rendered in the *quo warranto* suit.

The record of this suit is found in the *coram rege roll* of the Kings Bench. In the entry the usual writ served upon the company is followed by the information read by Edward Offley, the attorney for the company, citing the letters patent of 1606 and especially of 1609. It enumerates the rights granted to the corporation, and claims that other privileges were never used. The third document is the reply of Attorney-General Coventry in which he prays for the conviction of the accused on account of the usurpation of privileges, and cites those mentioned in the information, claiming that there had not been sufficient answer in any point. The answer of Nicholas Ferrar and others states that the company is ready to verify its rights as quoted. The judgment was rendered on the morrow of Holy Trinity, and declares that Nicholas Ferrar and the others are convicted of the usurpation of privileges and that the "said privileges are taken and seized into the hand of the King and the said Nicholas Ferrar and others shall not intermeddle but shall be excluded from the usurpation of liberties, privileges, and franchises of the same so taken from the King, and that they are to satisfy to the King his fine for the usurpation of said privileges." The writ of *quo warranto* was issued out of the Kings Bench on the Tuesday next after the morrow of All Souls (November 4, 1623). The suit was opened on the Friday after the quindecim of St. Martin's (November 28), and was then postponed until the eighth of Hillary (January 20). It was postponed a second time to the quindecim of Easter (April 11), and judgment was finally rendered on the morrow of Trinity (May 24, 1624).

VALUE OF THE VIRGINIA RECORDS

It has been the purpose of this paper to give to the reader a knowledge of what records the Virginia Company kept and to afford a guide to the extant records, as well as to indicate the character and importance of the various collections of records and of the various classes of documents. The value of this series of papers is threefold—it discloses the organization and activity of the company; it aids in an understanding of the various problems, policies, and conditions of the State under the early Stuarts; and it is of great importance in a study of the entire movement of the earlier and of the later century for exploration, for trade, and especially for colonization.

The object of the previous discussion has been to show that an intimate knowledge of the mechanism of the company, of the methods of other corporations and business houses, of the policies of the company toward the plantation, of the growth of the colony, and of the change in the attitude of the Crown may be gained from the various documents. Thus the value of the records in revealing the methods employed by the company in conducting its courts, in keeping its books, in securing capital, and in finding investment which would result in immediate returns and enable the company to transport men to the colony, has been pointed out. The evidence of the change of the plantation from a colony for exploitation to a colony for settlement, and the consequent effort of the company to stimulate exploration, settlement, and the development of resources, as well as the proof of the liberality of the proprietors in advancing self-government, has been outlined.

The indication in the records of the colony that the control changed from absolute authority centralized in the governor to local management and government through a representative legislative assembly, and that the social conditions developed from life in a few compact settlements to plantation life has been suggested. Moreover, the documents which show the efforts of the joint-stock companies to gain protection and become privileged monopolies, on the one hand, and the tendency of the Crown, on the other, to utilize the company to relieve the country of its undesirable population, to secure a share in the revenue, and finally to assume the full proprietorship of the colony has been cited.

The court book and other records of the company have another value in that they incidentally aid in an understanding of many problems of the government. Thus the attitude of the King toward the company was much influenced by his desire for marriage relations with Spanish royalty. Various questions of policy were often discussed in the meetings of the company, such as the freedom of trade and of fishing, monopolies, customs, and shipping, while the financial aid given to colonization by Spain is cited in contrast to the action of England, and the favor to the Spanish colonies by the State in allowing the sole importation of certain products was dwelt upon. The desire to cement the colony to the State and the necessity of avoiding separation was much emphasized, but the wisdom of allowing self-government to the colony was never once forgotten. In fact, the argument that democracy was unavoidable, since the planter had the privilege of the adventurer, was urged in opposition to the accusations of the King that the company favored democratic forms. This spirit in the company is also seen in the tendency to address Parliament whenever possible, as illustrated in the movement for a new patent and in the settlement of the tobacco question.

The economic and industrial situation in England is perhaps better revealed than any other phase of affairs. Thus the commodities which were in demand and not produced in England, the rates of such commodities, the prices of necessities, and the system of vending goods were all matters of great importance to the company, and appear again and again in the various documents. The poverty of skilled labor is shown in the necessity the company was under to go to the Continent for men to superintend and carry on every industry which it attempted to establish in the colony. Dutchmen, Swedes, Poles, and Frenchmen were thus imported for conducting sawmills, cultivating silkworms, and making potash, clapboards, salt, wines, and glass. When engineers for constructing fortifications were desired, General Cecil declared that he had not men for the purpose, but hoped he might be able to recommend some Frenchmen of ability. The papers which concern the transportation of vagabonds and of boys and girls furnish a comment on a special phase of social life, while the spirit of the entire records reveals the demand for an outlet for activity and an opportunity for investment.

Throughout, the minutes of the courts and the correspondence and references to the other trading companies emphasize the strong similarity between their organization and that of the Virginia corporation. Illustrations of this fact are seen in the citation of the precedent from other joint-stock companies of employing a deputy and a director, of the salaries paid in the East India Company, and of the liberty of trade enjoyed by the Muscovy Company; while among the Ferrar papers are drafts of petitions from the Commons to the King in the writing of Nicholas Ferrar on behalf of the Turkey merchants and of the "Ginny and Binny" company, showing the intimate relations between the different movements.

Perhaps the most important result of a study of the Virginia Company comes from the knowledge which may be gained of the whole movement which had as its object exploration, trade, and settlement before and since the time of the company in all of the colonies. In its records are to be found one of the earliest sources of information concerning colonial experience from the English standpoint, and hence through them may be gained an understanding of the way in which proprietary colonies were established; of the development of the plantation into a colony of settlement; and of the consequent relation between the settlers and the proprietor. These steps as well as those by which the Crown was led to resume the authority and to establish a royal proprietorship in place of that of a company or of an individual, and the consequent development of the freedom of the settler were repeated in the history of all of the proprietary colonies of America.

5. The Fate of the Original Records [a]

It was in July, 1622, that the controversy between the factions in the company was first brought before the Privy Council, and, strangely enough, the plaintiff was John Bargrave, who later championed those whom he now accused. The complainant declared that he had lost 6,600 pounds through the "unjust practices and miscarriage of government" on the part of Sir Thomas Smythe and Alderman Robert Johnson. The matter was referred to a committee composed of Lord Viscount Grandison, Lord Brook, the master of the rolls, Lord Keeper Coventry, and Secretary Conway, but the affair dragged on in the council until it was finally settled on January 22, 1622/3, by its ordering Bargrave to forbear troubling Sir Thomas Smythe.[b] From that time the battle between the factions in the company had begun. The tobacco contract between the lord treasurer as representative of the King on the one hand and the company on the other, which had occupied so much of the time of the courts, was allowed by the Privy Council on the 2d of February.[c] But the spirit of conflict was seen in the entire correspondence, and during the few succeeding months bitter complaints concerning the mismanagement of affairs in the colony were made by Nathaniel Butler in his *Unmasking of the Colony of Virginia* and by Alderman Johnson in his *Declaration.*[d] That both of these originated in the Warwick faction has been revealed by the Manchester papers.

On April 17 a committee headed by Lord Cavendish was summoned before the Privy Council to defend the Virginia Company against the "grievances of Planters and Adventurers." As a result, the first blow was struck at the liberty

[a] That the Virginia Company had a large number of records which are not now extant has been revealed by a study of the existing documents. In addition to the original court books and the five other records provided for by the "Orders and Constitutions" there were the books created at a later date, the duplicates of patents and grants, the petitions, and all of the account books of the various magazines and joint stock companies. If the papers of the private plantations and hundreds which are represented by the Smyth of Nibley papers, were added to these, the volume of missing records would become very great. A discussion therefore of what resources have been searched, though in vain, seems desirable, in order to aid further investigation.

[b] List of Records, Nos. 351, 401.

[c] *Ibid.*, No. 401.

[d] *Ibid.*, Nos. 388, 395.

of the company when the Privy Council announced that it was the King's intention that a commission should be appointed to inquire into the state of the Virginia and Somers Islands plantations.[a] From that time the affairs of the company were under surveillance, and the correspondence, the trade, and even the personal liberty of its officers were subject to restraint. The company was immediately forbidden to receive any private letters except on its own business, while on the 28th of the same month its letters were disallowed by the Privy Council because they failed to "certify the King's grace to the Colonies." Already the court books and other writings had been required of the secretary of the company, as is shown by a receipt for the same, dated April 21, among the Ferrar papers. This receipt was given to Edward Collingwood by the clerk of the council. As a concomitant the council dissolved the tobacco contract and reduced the former customs on tobacco from twelve to nine pence per pound. It allowed the companies the sole importation of tobacco, but it required that the whole crop should be brought into England.[b]

There were other acts which partook of the same spirit as the interference with the correspondence and business of the company. On May 13 the Privy Council ordered that Lord Cavendish, Sir Edwin Sandys, and Nicholas and John Ferrar should be confined to their houses, a punishment inflicted for a contempt of an order of the council table against the use of bitter invectives, and brought about by the complaint of the Earl of Warwick. Lord Cavendish was in restraint five days and the others eight days. The release came as a result of their "acknowledgment of offence and expression of sorrow."[c] The threat of the King was carried out, and the declaration of war was made on May 9 by the appointment of a commission to investigate the disputes in the Virginia Company and to report upon their method of procedure.

The danger of confiscation of the company's records was fully realized for the the first time on May 22, 1623, when the Privy Council enforced a previous order to surrender "all Charters Books, (and by name the blurred Book or Books), Letters, Petitions, Lists of Names and Provisions, Invoyces of Goods, and all other writing whatsoever, and Transcripts of them, belonging to them." The new order declared that the "Blurred Book or Books" had been kept back. The documents were to be surrendered to the clerk of the council, but the custody of the records was given to the commissioners. Each party was to have free use of them "in such sort as to ye Commissioners shall seem good." Furthermore "all Boxes & Packages of Letters which hereafter shall be brought over from Virginia or ye Summer Islands during this Commission" were to be "immediately delivered to ye Commissioners by them

[a] List of Records, No. 467.   Printed in full in Le Froy, I, 289–290.

[b] List of Records, Nos. 476 and 478.

[c] See Orders in Council, cited in *Ibid.*, Nos. 506 and 510.

to be broken open, perused or otherwise disposed [of] as they shall find cause."[a] The records were in the possession of the clerk of the council from the date of this order, or earlier, until November 7, 1623, as is shown by a warrant bearing the latter date, in which the commissioners of May 9 required of the council a "trunk of writings" locked up under the custody of the Privy Council to be delivered to the "bearer."[b]

A careful search for the missing papers must commence at this point. Although the records, or at least the court books, were later returned to the company, some of them may have been retained by the commissioners or by individuals thereof. Therefore, hidden away in the collections of the heirs of these men, it might be supposed, would be found the much sought-for documents. The members of this commission, created April 17, were Sir William Jones, Sir Nicholas Fortescue, Sir Francis Gofton, Sir Richard Sutton, Sir William Pitt, Sir Henry Bouchier, and Sir Henry Spiller.[c] But, as far as can be determined from personal investigation, from the report of the Royal Commission on Historical Manuscripts, from conversation with Sir Henry Maxwell Lyte, of that body, or from other men conversant with the private and public depositories in England, none of the papers did remain in the possession of those commissioners.

A committee of the Privy Council may have had access to these papers, for on July 22 Lords Grandison, Carew, and Chichester were appointed to take into consideration the reports on the colony and to present to the council orders most fit for the regulation of the government of Virginia.[d] Another group of men intrusted with the investigation of affairs at that time, and into whose hands and private possession might have come papers belonging to the company, were John Harvey, John Pory, Abraham Percy, Samuell Matthews, and John Jefferson. This commission was sent to Virginia for the purpose of investigating conditions, and many of the documents bearing on their relations with the colony are among the colonial State papers.

The documents remained in the custody of the commission until November 21, and were then returned to the secretary of the company. An order in council declared that all the "Books and writings, whether remayneing in the hands of the Com[rs] or elswher, shalbe fwthw[th] deliuered by Inventorie vnto the said Company." The complaint had been made by the treasurer that they could not make answer to the *quo warranto* which had been issued out of the King's Bench against the company without the use of their records.[e] Therefore, from November, 1623, until June,

[a] List of Records, No. 513.

[b] *Ibid.*, No 580.

[c] For the order in council creating this commission, see *Ibid.*, No. 499.

[d] *Ibid.*, No. 547.

[e] *Ibid.*, No. 593.

1624, the company was in possession of its documents, and it was during that period that Nicholas Ferrar was busily engaged in having them transcribed.

The last order which concerned these records from December 30, 1623, until the company was finally overthrown, in June of the following year—when the organization, according to Nethersole, became a company for trade and not for government—was a letter of the council to "Nicholas Ferrar, Deputie," to bring to them unopened all letters which had come in a ship lately arrived from Virginia.*a* That the King in the meantime was concerned in the preservation of all papers relating to Virginia is seen in a letter from Secretary Conway to Sir Thomas Merry, in which he was requested to preserve all papers in the possession of "his late cousin," John Puntis, vice-admiral of Virginia, and any others which concerned the business.*b*

Following up the recall of the charter, the Privy Council declared that it was the King's intention to renew the charter of the company without the imperfections of the former grant. A committee was therefore appointed on June 24 to resolve on the well settling of the colony, to give the orders therefor, and to report to the King for further directions. This body consisted of Lord President Mandeville, Lord Paget, Lord Chichester, the lord treasurer, the comptroller, the principal secretaries of state, the chancellor of the exchequer, the chancellor of the duchy, the attorney-general, the solicitor-general, Sir Robert Killigrew, Sir Thomas Smythe, Francis Gofton, John Wolstenholme, and Alderman Johnson.*c*

Two days later an order in council was issued instructing Mr. Ferrar, deputy of the company, to bring to the council chamber all patents, books of accounts, and invoices of the late corporation and all lists of people in the colony, to be retained by the keeper of the council chest till further order.*d* Thus was ended the control of the government by the old organization, if not of the affairs of the company and its colony, and thus the records passed into the charge of the clerk of the Privy Council.

A commission to establish a government in Virginia is to be found in the chancery privy seals under July of the twenty-second year of James I, countersigned to pass by immediate warrant. The patent roll of the period records this commission, dated July 15, 1624, by which the Virginia Company was to be supplanted and the first royal province in America was to be established.*e* The records of the old company, however, are not lost to sight till three days later. On July 15 the commissioners met at Sir Thomas Smythe's house and determined that the charters, seals, and writings of the company were to be brought to Sir Thomas Smythe's house and

---

a For the order in council creating this commission, see List of Records, No. 608.

b List of Records, No. 683.

c *Ibid.*, No. 687.

d *Ibid.*, No. 689.

e *Ibid.*, No. 701.

kept in charge of the clerk of the commissioners, H. Fotherby, to be used by the commissioners at pleasure.[a]

In the Privy Council register, under date of June 26, 1624, there is an order for Mr. Ferrar to deposit in the council chamber the papers of the late corporation, and in the margin is a note which gives the last glimpse of those records. It reads as follows: "Nd: All theis Patents bookes of accounts &c were delivered to Henry Fotherby clarke to the Comissioners, by order from the Lords the 19 of July 1624."[b]

That these members of the Privy Council and others of the commissioners for Virginia had all of the original records of the company in their possession at that date is thus proved. What became of them later can be a matter only of speculation. That they had been so carefully preserved and were deposited "for use by the members of the commissioners," seems to indicate that the theory of their destruction by the Crown is not tenable. There are two theories which seem much more likely. It may be that they passed finally into the possession of the Privy Council, which evidently soon assumed the burden of the control of the affairs of the province; for, on May 13, 1625, a royal proclamation arranged for a council which was to be subordinate to the Privy Council.[c] The papers may thus have remained with the King's Council until the creation of the commission for Virginia in 1631, which in turn was supplanted by the Board of Commissioners for Foreign Plantations in 1634.[d] The commission created in July of 1624 was composed of the lords of the council and "certain others," and the council register seems to indicate that it was usually the council sitting as a commission. After 1624 the papers, letters, and instructions were all issued by the council, the commissions to the councillors and to

[a] List of Records, No. 702.

[b] *Ibid.*, No. 689.

[c] A letter to the Earl of Warwick dated November 16, 1624, bears the signatures of the council for Virginia as follows: Sir Thomas Smith, Ferdinando Gorges, John Wolstenholme, Samuel Argall, Thomas Gibbs, Samuel Wrot, and John Pory. There had been some question concerning the addition of names to the commission, but whether this is a portion only of the council of July 15 or a new organization is uncertain. *Ibid.*, No. 738.

[d] The members of the commission for Virginia appointed June 17, 1631, were: Edward Earl of Dorset, Henry Earl of Danby, Dudley Viscount Dorchester, Secretary Sir John Coke, Sir John Danvers, Sir Robert Killigrew, Sir Thomas Rowe, Sir Robert Heath, Mr. Recorder [Heneage Finch], Sir Dudley Diggs, Sir John Wolstenholme, Sir Francis Wiatt, Sir John Brooke, Sir Kenelm Digby, Sir John Zouch, John Bankes, Thos. Gibb, Nath. Rott [Wrote?], Mr. Sands, John Wolstenholme, Nicholas Ferrar, Mr. Barber, and John Ferrar. See *Colonial Papers*, Vol. VI, No. 14.

The commissioners for plantations appointed April 28, 1634, were: William Laud, Archbishop of Canterbury; Thomas Lord Coventry, lord keeper; Richard Neile, Archbishop of York; Richard Earl of Portland, lord high treasurer; Henry Earl of Manchester; and seven other officers of state.

governors of the colony passed the privy seal and were engrossed on the patent roll, and the letters or papers from the colony were addressed to the council.

Another theory as to the fate of the records is that they were at first in charge of Henry Fotherby, clerk of the commissioners, but that they were gradually scattered among the members of the commission most interested in the career of the company as the authority of the commission became purely that of government. The members of the commission, created July 15, 1624, in whose families such papers might be found, are as follows: Henry Viscount Mandeville, Lord President of the Council, Wm. Lord Paget, Anthony Lord Chichester, Sir Thomas Edmonds, Sir John Suckling, Sir Geo. Calvert, Sir Edward Conway, Sir Richard Western, Sir Julius Caesar, Sir Humphrey May, Sir Saville Hicks, Sir Thomas Smith, Sir Henry Mildmay, Sir Thomas Coventry, Sir Robert Heath, Sir Ferdinando Gorges, Sir Robert Killigrew, Sir Charles Montague, Sir Philip Carew, Sir Francis Goston [Gofton], Sir Thomas Wroth, Sir John Wolstenholme, Sir Nathaniel Rich, Sir Samuel Argall, Sir Humphrey Handford, Mathew Sutcliff, Dean of Exeter, Francis White, Dean of Carlisle, Thomas Tamshaw, Alderman Robert Johnson, James Cambell, Ralph Freeman, Morris Abbott, Nathaniel Butler, George Wilmore, William Hackwell, John Mildmay, Philip Germayne, Edward Johnson, Thomas Gibbes, Samuel Wrote, John Porey (?), Michael Hawes, Edward Palavacine, Robert Bateman, Martin Bond, Thomas Styles, Nicholas Leate, Robert Butt, Abraham Cartwright, Richard Edwards, John Dyke, Anthony Aldy, William Palmer, Edward Ditchfield, George Mole, and Richard Morer.[a]

Had not the receipt from the Privy Council to the secretary of the company revealed the existence of the early records in 1623, and had not the memoranda of Sir Nathaniel Rich confirmed the fact,[b] the theory might be put forth that the papers of the early period were burned in the destruction of Sir Thomas Smythe's house at Deptford on February 6, 1618/19. The fire at Whitehall on the 16th of January, 1618/19, at which the privy seal, signet, and council records are supposed to have been destroyed, is sometimes suggested as the cause of the disappearance of the Virginia records. But the facts given above, in addition to the statement of Sir Thomas Wilson to the King that there had been but little loss of papers since they had been transferred to the new office refutes that theory.[c]

It remains for the future enquirer to examine the collections which are known to contain papers belonging to the families indicated by the names of the various commissioners and of the Privy Councillors for that period. Such investigations are made difficult by the transfer of papers from one branch of a family to another, necessitating

[a] *Virginia Magazine of History*, VII, 40.

[b] *Ante*, pp. 25, 63.

[c] *Documents relating to the History of the Public Record Office*, in the Record Office.

a knowledge of the genealogy of the various families represented. Having found the heirs of the families in question, the search may then be conducted through the reports of the Royal Commission on Historical Manuscripts. But this is not sufficient. Since trace of the family is often lost, or no evidence can be found of collections of documents, it becomes necessary to search through every section of those reports of the commission for stray sets of papers. The greatest confusion also results from the sale of libraries, and while the catalogues of Quaritch or Sotheby may afford a clue to the offer of such material for sale, often in small lots, the name of the purchaser is not usually to be discovered. The result is that the student must wait in patience until the papers have drifted into some great depository—such as the British Museum and the Bodleian Library—or until they have been made known to the public through the Manuscripts Commission or by private enterprise.[a]

Another difficulty, which can not be overcome by the individual student, is the insufficiency of the catalogues of early date. This is gradually being met by the re-issue of catalogues and calendars in the British Museum, and the Bodleian, although the new catalogue of the latter is only "summary." The Ashmolean and Rawlinson papers in the Bodleian may afford many surprises. Furthermore, the early reports of the Manuscripts Commission were often incomplete and too general in character. However, the more recent volumes are full calendars, and the older volumes may be republished in time.

In the great collections of the British Museum are brought together the papers or portions of the papers of a few of the men with whom we are concerned. In the Lansdowne collection are about one-third of the papers of Sir Julius Caesar, master of the rolls, which were sold at auction in 1757. Among these have been found the valuable letters of John Martin and the draft of the commission of 1624. In the Harleian collection, brought together by Robert Harley, Earl of Oxford, at the close of the seventeenth century, and among the papers of Sir John Cotton, who was a noted antiquarian of the time of James I, are a few important documents.

The valuable collection of the Marquis of Bath, containing the Cecil papers, has been recatalogued and found to contain nothing which concerns the company after 1616, and nothing of the earlier period not known to Alexander Brown.

Two other collections, imperfectly calendared by the Manuscripts Commission, are those of Lord Sackville, of Knole, Seven Oaks, Kent, and of the Earl of Coventry, Croome Court, Severn Stoke, Worcestershire. Since the statement was made by John Ferrar, in the later years of his life, that Sir Robert Killigrew had left the Virginia papers to Sir Edward Sackville, the Earl of Dorset, our interest in

[a] The search for the records has not only been conducted along these lines, but the collections belonging to the families of the officers of State under James I, and Charles I, have been investigated.

this collection is intensified.   Both Sir Robert Killigrew and Richard Sackville, Earl of Dorset, are seen to have been vitally connected with the company and the settlement of its affairs.   Two other connections of this family may have brought together collections which might contain Virginia papers.   Richard Sackville, Earl of Dorset, married Frances, the daughter of Lionel Cranfield, the first Earl of Middlesex, and he himself became heir to the Cranfield house and title as third earl.   The first Earl of Middlesex was the lord treasurer during the régime of the company and figures prominently as the individual who conducted the *quo warranto* suit against the Virginia Company.   Furthermore, Lionel Sackville West is the direct descendant of Lord De La Warr, of Virginia fame.   The combination of the four houses of Killigrew, Sackville, Middlesex, and De La Warr, which were of so great importance in Virginia affairs, leads to the hope of a valuable collection of manuscripts.   Four documents are mentioned in the report of the commission, and these refer to the tobacco trade, but an inquiry of Lord Sackville as to other material in his possession elicited the reply from Lionel Sackville West that Lord Sackville knew of "no other papers at Knole relating to the colony of Virginia than those mentioned in the report of the commissioners."   It may be, however, that a more careful calendar of this collection will disclose papers of great importance.

From March 14, 1616, to January 11, 1620, Thomas Coventry was solicitor-general; later, during the Sandys-Southampton administration of the Virginia Company, he held the position of attorney-general.   On November 1, 1625, he became lord keeper, and remained in that office during the period coinciding with the organization of the colonial administration.   Hence it was that, when it was found from the report of the Manuscripts Commission that many of Lord Keeper Coventry's papers had not been investigated, the Editor addressed a letter to the Earl of Coventry, Croome Court.   This resulted in a confirmation of the statement, and a promise to search the papers which are now in the "strong room here."   In a letter to Ambassador Choate, July 27, 1904, the Earl of Coventry made the following statement: "In company with a son I went through the boxes containing papers of the Lord Keeper Coventry in which I thought it likely I might find the documents referring to the Virginia Company of London, some time ago, but I could discover nothing relating to the company."   The letter goes on to say that the "papers are in bad condition and very difficult to decipher."   Hence the conclusion may be reached that this most likely hiding place for Virginia records is not to reveal new material.

The collections at Thirlestaine House, Cheltenham, and at Hatfield House, are extremely valuable, but T. Fitzroy Fenwick, esq., the present owner of the former, states that there is no material in that collection relating to the early history of Virginia, and a manuscript catalogue, kindly loaned to the writer by Lord Salisbury, indicates that the papers at Hatfield House, now being calendared, have no bearing on the subject in hand.

By tracing the family connections of the descendants of Sir Thomas Smythe and the Earl of Southampton intermarriages are found which might result in the location of valuable papers in many of the large depositories. All of these have been investigated by the Manuscripts Commission. Thus, from Sir Thomas Smythe the documents might have been inherited by the first or the second Earl of Leicester; by Sir Sydney Stafford Smythe, baron of the exchequer in 1772 and last of the descendants of the male line; by the eighth Viscount Strangford, vice-president of the Royal Geographical Society, with whose death in 1869 the senior branch of the family was terminated; and by the present Duke of Marlborough through the second marriage of Lady Dorothy Sydney Smythe, daughter of Robert, second Earl of Leicester. The Wriothesley family is to-day represented in the houses of the Duke of Bedford and of the Duke of Portland, the former having inherited the London property of Robert, third Earl of Southampton, and the latter the Tichfield estate.

The large number of documents among the Smyth of Nibley papers[a] suggests that in private collections may be many records which concern the private enterprises or companies formed within the corporation for setting out plantations and carrying on trade. Other groups of manuscripts and early books have seemed to offer opportunities for the discovery of the missing records. But the Lambeth Palace Library, the college libraries both of Oxford and of Cambridge have proved valueless, with the exception of that most important group in Magdelene College, Cambridge. Every one of the college libraries, has been searched or investigated, but to no avail. All Souls College, Oxford, contains a collection of manuscripts which may afford a few papers on the subject when it has been more carefully catalogued.

The fact that the original records of the company before 1619, and a comparatively small portion after that date have not been discovered has led generally to the conclusion that the party of the Crown destroyed the evidences of the mismanagement during the first decade and of the comparatively prosperous condition in the second. That they failed to take into account the records in the colony and the Ferrar transcripts of the court book is the good fortune of posterity. But the destruction of the records can not properly be considered as proved until the public collections have been more carefully calendared and the private collections have been more thoroughly investigated. The absolute lack of evidence that the Crown and its supporters held such an attitude and the knowledge that the commissioners took the records into their charge "for use" encourages the hope that a faithful endeavor to discover their location may yet be rewarded by success.

[a]*Ante*, p. 55.

LIST OF RECORDS

List of Records

THE VIRGINIA COMPANY OF LONDON

EXPLANATORY NOTE

This list includes all documents, letters, publications, or other records of the Virginia Company, or relating to the company between 1616 and 1625, which the Editor has been able to discover, and also those previous to 1616 which are not published or cited by Alexander Brown in the *Genesis of the United States*. The object in compiling the list has been to give to the student of history the necessary information concerning each document in as convenient form as possible in order to aid him in finding or in identifying the papers. The documents have been arranged in chronological order, but with the provision that whenever the day of the month is uncertain the document has been placed at the beginning of the month, and when the month is not known it has been placed at the beginning of the year. Thus, at the first of each year and of each month will be found the undated papers, or those to which it has been impossible to assign dates. The subject-matter, as well as the title and the name of the author has been given rather for identification than to serve as a calendar, since it is the aim of this series to publish all material except that which is purely supplementary. The documents which it is intended to publish in this series, if the privilege can be secured, have been indicated by an asterisk. The title has been quoted wherever possible, and the orthography of proper names has been made to conform to that of the document. The location, indicated by abbreviated forms, and the reference, following the abbreviation, *Ref.*, of every edition, contemporary copy, or later transcript has been given, but the description of the document is either in the introduction or will be found in connection with its publication in the succeeding volumes. Wherever the paper has been published or calendared the reference has been cited after the abbreviation, *Pub.* The material has been classified with regard to source or authorship and the classes have been indicated by Roman numerals, placed to the left of the "reference." The bibliographies have been included in the index in the second volume of the series. It has been found necessary either to abbreviate or to use symbols for the names of the libraries or collections in which documents are found, and those abbreviations have been placed at the extreme right hand of the page.

CLASSES OF DOCUMENTS

I. Fundamental documents, emanating from the Crown.
II. The court book of the company.
III. Documents issued by the company: instructions, commissions, grants, receipts, official corre- ⋅ spondence.
IV. Records of the colony: court book, orders, reports, letters.
V. Publications of the company.
VI. Private papers of individual adventurers.
VII. Supplementary correspondence and records of nonmembers of the company.

Symbols Indicating Location of Documents

ANT.	Society of Antiquaries, London.
BEL.	Collection of the Earl of Rutland, Belvoir Castle.
BM.	British Museum, England.
BOD.	Bodleian Library, Oxford.
CAMB.	Cambridge University Library, England.
CHILD.	Collection of J. Eliot Hodgkin, Childwell, Richmond, Surrey.
DOV.	Borough of Dover, England.
DROP.	Collection of Hon. G. M. Fortescue, Dropmore, Maidenhead, England.
HARV.	Harvard Library, Cambridge, Massachusetts.
HL.	Repository of the House of Lords, London.
IPS.	Ipswich, England.
JCB.	John Carter Brown Library, Providence, R. I.
KP.	Collection of Lord Sackville, Knole Park, County Kent.
LAMB.	Lambeth Palace Library, London.
LEI.	Leicester, England.
LC.	Library of Congress, Washington, D. C.
[LC]	Transcript in Library of Congress, Washington, D. C.
MC.	Magdalene College, Cambridge, England.
MONT.	Montague House, London.

NEWB.	Library of Ed. E. Ayer in the Newberry Library, Chicago.
NY.	New York Public Library.
[NY]	Transcript in New York Public Library.
P.	Imperial Library, Paris.
PC.	Privy Council, London.
PEQ.	Pequot Library, Connecticut.
PET.	Collection of Lord Leconfield, Petworth House, County Sussex.
PRIV.	Private library in New York City.
PRO.	Public Record Office, London.
Q.	Queens College, Oxford.
R.	Archives of Jesus, Rome.
READ.	Borough of Reading, England
SHER.	Sherbourne Castle, County Dorset.
SUF.	Collection of W. W. Molyneux, Suffolk County, England.
SYON.	Collection of Duke of Northumberland, Syon House, England.
VHS.	Virginia Historical Society, Richmond, Virginia.
WELB.	Collection of Duke of Portland, Welbeck Abbey.
WOD.	Collection of Edmund R. Wodehouse, esq., England.
WYC.	Borough of Wycombe, England.
YAR.	Yarmouth, England.

GENERAL ABBREVIATIONS

A. L. S.	Autograph letter signed.
Bull.	Bulletin.
Col.	Collections.
Com.	Commission.
Co.	Company.
D. S.	Document signed.
Hist.	Historical, History.
Lib.	Library.
L. S.	Letter signed.

Mag.	Magazine.
MS.	Manuscript.
Misc.	Miscellaneous.
Pub.	Public.
Rec.	Records.
Rept.	Report.
Soc.	Society.
*Document will be published in this series.	

1600

1.* **Reasons** against publishing the King's title to Virginia. A justification for planting Virginia.
     VI.   *Ref:* Tanner MSS., XCIII, fo. 200 (old fo. 352).   BOD. [LC]

1606 (?)

2.* "**A plaine** declaracon, how greatlie the ffarmours of the Tobacco impost have bene endam-
    aged by that ffarme, and what proffitt and benefitt their labour & travell have brought
    to his Matie."   BM. [LC]
     VI.   *Ref:* Lansdowne, Caesar Papers, 156, fo. 58.

> The date is in the index in the writing of the century. The names mentioned in the docu-
> ment prove that it was as early as 1612, the date when tobacco was first planted in Virginia.

1606/7

3. **Payments** for apparel and tobacco for Mr. George Percy sent to him in Virginia.   SYON.
     VI.   *Ref:* Rolls of the Duke of Northumberland.
          Pub: Calendar: Hist. MSS. Com., *Sixth Report*, 229a.

1607/8

4. **Payments** for Mr. Geo. Percy for necessities for building a house in Virginia and for trinkets.
     VI.   *Ref:* Rolls of the Duke of Northumberland.   SYON.
          Pub: Calendar: Hist. MSS. Com., *Sixth Report*, 229a.

1607

5.* **King and Privy Council.** Oaths of supremacy and allegiance administered to colonists.
     I.   *Ref:* MS. Rec. Virginia Co., Vol. III, pt. i, pp. 20, 20^a.   LC.
6.* ———. Oath of the Secretary of the Colony administered by Governor and Council in Virginia.
     I.   *Ref:* MS. Rec. Virginia Co., Vol. III, pt. i, p. 21.   LC.

1608

7.* **Popham con Havercombe.** The President and Council of the Virginia Company *v.* the
    master of the "Guift of God," for not sufficiently providing the passengers. Complaint,
    answer, and judgment.   PRO. [LC]
     III.   *Ref:* Admiralty, Instance and Prize, Libels 73, Nos. 274, 279.
          This suit concerns the northern colony for Virginia.

8. **Ralph, Lord Eure.** A letter to Sir Robert Harley, stating that Captain Newport has brought
    over Captain Wingfield, accused of some treachery, but not yet tried.   WELB.
     VII.   *Ref:* MSS. of the Duke of Portland.
          Pub: Calendar: Hist. MSS. Com., *Fourteenth Report*, pt. 2, p. 5.

---

        * Reproduced in the present publication.
        [LC] Transcript in the Library of Congress.
        I, II, III, etc., represent the class of document.

1609

9.* **Virginia Council** (?).   General instructions to the lieutenant governor of Virginia.   Copy of
   the sixth article.   BM.
    III.   *Ref:* MSS. of the Marquis of Lansdowne, Vol. 58.
           Pub: Calendar: Hist. MSS. Com., *Fifth Report*, 226.

MAY

10.* **Virginia Council.**   "Instrucc̃ons, orders, and constituc̃ons . . . to Sr Thomas Gates knight
   Governo^r of Virginia . . . by vs his Maiesties Councell for [Virginia.]"   BOD.   [LC]
    III.   *Ref:* Ashmolean MSS., 1147, fos. 175–190a.
        A contemporary copy.

1609 (?)/10

11.* **Virginia Council.**   "Instructions, orders, and constituc̃ons . . . to Sr Thomas West knight
   Lo: La Warr, . . . by vs his Mat^les Councell for the Companie of adventurers . . .
   [for Virginia]."   BOD.   [LC]
    III.   *Ref:* Ashmolean MSS., 1147, fos. 191–205a.
        A contemporary copy.

1609–12 (?)

12.* **G[eorge] P[ercy].**   "A trew relation of the proceedings and occurents of momente which
   have happened in Virginia from Sr Thomas Gates—1609 to my departure, A. D. 1602
   [1612]."   PET.
    IV.   *Ref:* MSS. of Lord Leconfield, No. 81, 4th to 17th century, vellum, p. 1.
         Pub: Catalogue: Hist. MSS. Com., *Sixth Report*, 307.

1609/10

1609/10, FEBRUARY 7–1610/11, FEBRUARY 6

13.   **Payments** for tobacco for the Earl and Lord Percy and for George Percy in Virginia.
    VI.   *Ref:* MSS. of the Duke of Northumberland.   SYON.
         Pub: Calendar: Hist. MSS. Com., *Sixth Report*, 229b.

1610

NOVEMBER 18

14.* **George Yeardley.**   A letter to Sr Henry Peyton, stating that the country needs only "round
   and free support of men and money."   BOD.   [LC]
    VI.   *Ref:* Eng. Hist. MSS., c. 4, new No., MS. 29724, fo. 3.

1610/11

MARCH 4

15.   **Town of Ipswich.**   Order for "adventuring out of the towne treasure one hundred pounds
   . . .   in the voyage to Virginia."   IPS.
    VII.   *Ref:* Ext. from General Court Books, 4 March, 8 James I.
         Pub: Calendar: Hist. MSS. Com., *Ninth Report*, pt. 1, p. 256.

1611 (?)

16.   **Virginia Council.**   A letter "to Sr Raphe Winwood, Ambassador," requesting adventurers
   in the Netherlands, and telling of the prosperous condition of the Colony.   MONT.
    III.   *Ref:* Duke of Buccleuch and Queensberry MSS., Winwood Papers.
         Pub: Full calendar: Hist. MSS. Com., *Report* on above, Vol. I (1899), p. 103.

1611

APRIL

17. **Sir Thomas Smythe.** A letter to Sr Raphe Winwood, Ambassador, acknowledging £72 from above request, and sending the bills of adventure. MONT.

  III. *Ref:* Duke of Buccleuch and Queensberry MSS., Winwood Papers.

    Pub: Full calendar: Hist. MSS. Com., *Report* on above, Vol. I (1899), p. 99.

1611/12

MARCH 10

18. ———— **Bruz.** A letter to the Earl of Rutland concerning Dale's departure with three hundred men at expense of £8,000. BEL.

  VII. *Ref:* Earl of Rutland Papers.

    Pub: Calendar: Hist. MSS. Com., *Twelfth Report*, pt. 4, p. 429.

1612

APRIL 28

19. **Sir John Digby.** A letter to W. Trumbull concerning the Spanish attitude toward the Virginia plantation, and other letters of similar character. SHER.

  VII. *Ref:* George Wingfield Digby MSS., Register of Letters.

    Pub: Calendar: Hist. MSS. Com., *Tenth Report*, pt. 1, pp. 576, 583, 600, 608, 609.

NOVEMBER 25

20.* **Virginia Company.** Virginia Company con Sir Thomas Mildmaye, James Bryarley, and Matthew de Quester. The bill of complaint addressed to Thos. Lord Ellesmere, Lord Chancellor, with regard to the payment of certain sums adventured. PRO. [LC]

  III. *Ref:* Chancery Proceedings, James I, Bundle U, No. 2/27.

DECEMBER 11

21.* **Sir Thomas Mildmaye.** The answer of Sir Thomas Mildmaye to the bill of complaint of the Virginia Company. PRO. [LC]

  III. *Ref:* Chancery Proceedings, James I, Bundle U, No. 2/27.

1612/13

JANUARY 11

22.* **James Bryarley and Mathewe de Quester.** The answer of James Bryarley and Mathewe de Quester to the bill of complaint of the Virginia Company. PRO. [LC]

  III. *Ref:* Chancery Proceedings, James I, Bundle U, No. 2/27.

JANUARY 26

23. **John Wheeler.** John Wheeler to Sir Raphe Winwood requesting adventures in the lottery for himself and others. MONT.

  III. *Ref:* Duke of Buccleuch and Queensberry MSS., Winwood Papers.

    Pub: Calendar: Hist. MSS. Com., *Report* on above, Vol. I (1899), pp. 122–123.

1613

APRIL 28

24.* **Virginia Company.** Virginia Company con Sir H. Neville, Sir Geo. Huntleye, Wm. Hall, et al., regarding the payment of sums adventured. The bill of complaint. PRO. [LC]

  III. *Ref:* Chancery Proceedings, James I, Bundle U, No. 4/17.

MAY 18

25.* Sir George Huntley. The answer of Sir Geo. Huntley to the bill of complaint of the Virginia
Company.   PRO.   [LC]
    III.   *Ref:* Chancery Proceedings, James I, Bundle U, No. 4/17.

OCTOBER 8

26.* Virginia Company. Virginia Company con Sir Edmond Boyd, Sir John Sammes, et al.,
regarding the payment of sums adventured.   The bill of complaint.   PRO.   [LC]
    III.   *Ref:* Chancery Proceedings, James I, Bundle U, No. 2/69.

NOVEMBER 1

27.* Sir John Sammes. The answer of Sir John Sammes to the bill of complaint of the Virginia
Company.   PRO.   [LC]
    III.   *Ref:* Chancery Proceedings, James I, Bundle U, No. 2/69.

NOVEMBER 15

28.* Virginia Company. Virginia Company con William Leveson, regarding the payment of
certain sums collected in the lottery and not surrendered.   The bill of complaint.
    III.   *Ref:* Chancery Proceedings, James I, Bundle U, Nos. 2/55.   PRO.   [LC]

NOVEMBER 30

29.* William Leveson. The answer of William Leveson to the bill of complaint of the Virginia
Company.   PRO.   [LC]
    III.   *Ref:* Chancery Proceedings, James I, Bundle U, Nos. 2/55.

1613/14

[1613, DECEMBER 29]–1614 [JANUARY 8]

30. J. Luntius. Letters to Sir Raphe Winwood, ambassador, concerning the rumor of a Spanish
attack on the Virginia Colony.   MONT.
    VII.   *Ref:* Duke of Buccleuch and Queensberry MSS. Winwood Papers.
          Pub: Calendar: Hist. MSS. Com., *Report* on above, Vol. I (1899), pp. 122–123.

FEBRUARY 16

31.* William Hall, Esq. The answer of William Hall to the bill of complaint of the Virginia
Company.   PRO.   [LC]
    III.   *Ref:* Chancery Proceedings, James I, Bundle U, No. 4/17.

1614/15

FEBRUARY 22

32. Privy Council. Order of Privy Council to Lord Howard Effingham, Sir Geo. More, Sir Ed.
Howard, and others, requesting cooperation in the lottery and sending books for
adventurers' sums.   WOD.
    I.   *Ref:* (1) MSS. of E. R. Wodehouse. (2) MSS. of W. W. Molyneux, Esq.
        Pub: (1) Calendar: Hist. MSS. Com., *Thirteenth Report*, pt. 4, p. 437.

MARCH 8

33. Consideration of the "Letters from Lordes of the Counsell concerninge the Lottery for the
helpe of the Englishe in Virginia."   READ.
    VII.   *Ref:* Corporation of Reading Records, MS. XLVIII, a.
        Pub: Calendar: Hist. MSS. Com., *Eleventh Report*, pt. 7, p. 211.

1615

APRIL 18

34. Action of the assembly. Every alderman to urge inhabitants to adventure in the Virginia lottery.   **YAR.**

     VII.   *Ref:* Corporation of Great Yarmouth. Records, 40 Elizabeth to 12 James I, Assembly Book. D (j).

         Pub: Calendar: Hist. MSS. Com., *Ninth Report*, pt. 1, p. 319.

1615/16

FEBRUARY 10

35. Certificate for 104 lbs. of midding tobacco from Virginia.   **KP.**

     III.   *Ref:* MSS. of the Earl De La Warr.

         Pub: Calendar: Hist. MSS. Com., *Fourth Report*, 314.

1615/16, MARCH 6-1623, JUNE 9

36.* Shareholders in the Virginia Company from 1615–1623.   **PRO.**   **[NY]**

     VI.   *Ref:* State Papers, Colonial, James I, Vol. II, No. 33.

         Pub: Virginia Magazine of History and Biography, IV, 299–310.

           Transcript in the N. Y. Public Library, Bancroft, I, 203–205.

1616

DECEMBER 19

37. Virginia Company. A letter to the mayor of Salisbury concerning a college for Virginia.

     III.   *Pub: New England Historical and Genealogical Register*.

1616/17

38.* Virginia Council. A proclamation by His Majesty's Council for Virginia giving license to any in Virginia to return, by obtaining permission from the governor.   **NY.**

     III.   *Ref:* Smyth of Nibley Papers.

         Pub: Brown, *Genesis of the United States*, II, 797–798.

1617

JUNE 7

39.* Governor Argall. A letter and proclamations or edicts as to sale of goods and banishment of John Hudson.   (1) LC.   (2) VHS.

     IV.   *Ref:* (1) Misc. Papers, 1606–1683, quarto. (Abstract only.)   (2) MS. Coll. Va. Hist. Soc., John Randolph MSS., III, 91.

         Pub: Va. Mag. of Hist., IV, 28–29.

           Cited from "No. 41A Register book during the Goum'. of Sam' Argall Esq' admiral, & for y' time p'sent, principal Gou'. of Virg'.," a record not now known to be in existence.

JUNE 8

40.* John Rolfe. Letter to Sir Edwin Sandys, giving the story of the journey from Plymouth and the good condition of the colony, though in need of clothing.   **MC.**

     IV.   *Ref:* Ferrar Papers.

         Pub: Va. Mag. of Hist., X, 134–138.

           A. L. S. Endorsed by Sir Edwin Sandys.

41.* Privy Council. Orders for transportation of prisoners, mentioned by name, to Virginia.
    I.   *Ref:* Privy Council Register, James I, Vol. III, 91, 121.   PC. [NY]
        Pub: Mass. Hist. Soc. Coll., ser. 4, Vol. IX, pp. 1–4.
        Transcript in N. Y. Pub. Lib., Barlow Papers, Virginia, Vol. I.

42.* Governor Argall. Pardon to George White for running away to the Indians with arms and ammunition; also to Arthur Edwards and to Henry Potter.   (1) LC. (2) VHS.
    IV.   *Ref:* (1) Misc. Papers, 1606–1683, quarto. (Abstract only.) (2) MS., Coll. Va. Hist. Soc., John Randolph MSS., III, 91.
        See No. 40, Remarks.

43.* ———. Commission to trade to north parts of Virginia and for commanders of the several hundreds.   (1) LC. (2) VHS.
    IV.   *Ref:* See under No. 40.
        See No. 40, Remarks.

44.* ———. Appointment of William Powell, captain of guards belonging to the governor and lieutenant-governor and commander of James Town.   (1) LC. (2) VHS.
    IV.   *Ref:* See under No. 40.
        See No. 40, Remarks.

45.* ———. Commission to trade in south parts and in the bay.   (1) LC. (2) VHS.
    IV.   *Ref:* See under No. 40.
        See No. 40, Remarks.

46.* ———. Commission to Captain Nathaniel Pool to be serjeant major general.
    IV.   *Ref:* See under No. 40.   (1) LC. (2) VHS.
        See No. 40, Remarks.

47.* ———. Commission to Francis West, master of ordinance, during life.   (1) LC. (2) VHS.
    IV.   *Ref:* See under No. 40.
        See No. 40, Remarks.

48.* ———. Commission to Nathaniel West, to be captain of the Lord General's company.
    IV.   *Ref:* See under No. 40.   (1) LC. (2) VHS.
        See No. 40, Remarks.

49. Sir Edwin Sandys. A letter to the Puritans.
    III.   *Pub:* Neill, *Virginia Company of London*, 124–125.

50.* Governor Argall. Confirmations as to cattle.   (1) LC. (2) VHS.
    IV.   *Ref:* See under No. 40.
        See No. 40, Remarks.

51.* Citizens of Bermuda Hundred. A letter signed by the recorder and nine other citizens claiming West and Shirley hundreds as belonging to them.   (1) LC. (2) VHS.
    IV.   *Ref:* See under No. 40.
        See No. 40, Remarks.

NOVEMBER 30

52.* **Governor Argall.** Letter to citizens of Bermuda Hundred that he will not infringe their rights but begs that colony servants may remain there this year.   (1) LC.   (2) VHS.

     IV.   *Ref:* See under No. 40.

See No. 40, Remarks.

DECEMBER 4

53.* **Privy Council.** Order that the Virginia Company should be custom free for goods returned from the Colony until expiration of the grant.   PC.   [NY]

     I.   *Ref:* Privy Council Register, James I, Vol. III, p. 201.

Transcript, New York Public Library, Barlow Papers, Virginia, Vol. I.

DECEMBER 27

54.* **Lord De La Warr.** Lord De La Warr's covenant to Lord Zouch for his adventure to Virginia.

     VII.   *Ref:* State Papers, Colonial, James I, Vol. I, No. 36.   PC.   [NY]

          Pub: Sainsbury, *Calendar of State Papers, Colonial*, p. 18.

Transcript, New York Public Library, Bancroft Collection, Virginia Papers, Vol. I, pp. 199-201.

1617/18

55.* **Governor Argall.** "Certain Reasons touching ye most convenient times & seasons of ye year for ye magazine ship to set forth for Engl^d towards Virg.^{a}"   (1) LC.   (2) VHS.

     IV.   *Ref:* See under No. 40.

See No. 40, Remarks.

56.* ——. Letter to the Council for Virginia, wishing to be relieved as governor, complaining because they have joined the cape merchant with him in equal trust.

     IV.   *Ref:* See under No. 40.   (1) LC.   (2) VHS.

See No. 40, Remarks.

57.* ——. Four warrants as to trade and relations with the Indians.   (1) LC.   (2) VHS.

     IV.   *Ref:* See under No. 40.

See No. 40, Remarks.

[1618 ?]

58.* **A complete** list in alphabetical order of the "Adventurers to Virginia," with the several amounts of their holding.   PRO.

     III.   *Ref:* Manchester Papers, No. 241.

          Pub: Calendar: Hist. MSS. Com., *Eighth Report*, pt. 2, p. 33.

The date may be 1619. See an order of the Virginia Company Court Book, Dec. 15, 1619, and June 23, 1620.

59.* **Defalcation** made to the farmers of the customs for the subsidy of goods from and to Virginia, 1613–18.   KP.

     III.   *Ref:* MSS. collection of Lord Sackville.

          Pub: Calendar: Hist. MSS. Com., *Eighth Report*, 251.

60.* **Abraham Jacob.** Receipt of tobacco from Lady-day to Michaelmas; Michaelmas to January 23. Total of £5,646 18s. 6d.   KP.

     III.   *Ref:* MSS. collection of Lord Sackville.

          Pub: Calendar: Hist. MSS. Com., *Fourth Report*, 314.

1617/18

JANUARY 18

61. John Chamberlain. A letter to Sir Dudley Carleton concerning the death of Pocahontas.
  VII.   *Ref:* State Papers, Domestic, James I, Vol. 40, No. 25.   PRO.
            Pub: Sainsbury, *Calendar of State Papers, Colonial*, p. 18.

JANUARY 27

62. John Robinson and William Bruster (Puritans). Letter to Sir John Wolstenholme.
  VI.   *Pub:* Neill, E., *Virginia Co. of Lond.*, 125–126.

JANUARY 31

63. John Chamberlain. A letter to Sir Dudley Carleton concerning the departure of Lord
            La Warr for Virginia.   PRO.
  VII.   *Ref:* State Papers, Domestic, James I, Vol. 45, No. 27.
            Pub: Sainsbury, *Calendar of State Papers, Colonial*, p. 19.

FEBRUARY 3

64.* Governor Argall. Order addressed to the commander of Kiquotan not to permit landing
            of sailors on arrival of vessels.   LC.
  IV.   *Ref:* Misc. Papers, 1606-1683, quarto.   (Abstract only.)
            See No. 40, Remarks.

FEBRUARY 20

65.* Governor Argall. Commission to William Cradock to be provost marshal of Bermuda City
            and Hundred.   LC.
  IV.   *Ref:* Misc. Papers, 1606–1683, quarto, pp. 92-93.   (Abstract only.)
            See No. 40, Remarks.

MARCH 5

66.* Privy Council. Letter to Lord De La Ware stating that Henry Sherley, an escaped debtor is
            not to be harbored in Virginia.   PC.
  I.   *Ref:* (1) Privy Council Register, James I, Vol. III, p. 295.   (2) State Papers, Domes-
            tic, James I, Vol. 46, p. 527.

MARCH 10

67.* Governor Argall. Letter to the Virginia Company describing the ruinous condition in which
            he found the colony and the improvements he had made.   LC.
  IV.   *Ref:* Misc. Papers, 1606–1683, quarto.   (Abstract only.)
            See No. 40, Remarks.

MARCH 16

68. John Chamberlain. A letter to Sir Dudley Carleton, concerning the departure of Lord La
            Warr for Virginia.   PRO.
  VII.   *Ref:* State Papers, Domestic, James I, Vol. 45, No. 63.
            Pub: Sainsbury, *Calendar of State Papers, Colonial*, p. 19.

MARCH 20

69.* Privy Council. Orders for transportation of prisoners, mentioned by name, to Virginia.
  I.   *Ref:* Privy Council Register, James I, Vol. III, p. 319.   PC.

1618

MARCH 29

70. Virginia Company. A letter to the mayor of Salisbury concerning a college for Virginia.
    III.   *Pub: New England Hist. and Geneal. Register.*

MAY 2.

71.* Governors of the Virginia Company. Letter to the mayor and aldermen of Leicester, soliciting countenance of the lottery for the furtherance of the endeavor of the said company.   LEI.
    III.   *Ref:* Corporation of Leicester, 6th vol. of Hall Papers. VIII.
          Pub: Calendar: Hist. MSS. Com., *Eighth Report*, pt. 1, p. 435.

MAY 3

72.* Lord Admiral Nottingham's pass for the "Edwin" of London, returned from Virginia.
    VI.   *Ref:* State Papers, Domestic, James I, Vol. XCVII, No. 56.   PRO.
          Pub: Sainsbury, *Calendar of State Papers, Colonial*, p. 538.

MAY 4

73.* John Bargrave and James Brett. John Bargrave, owner, and James Brett, master of "Edwin;" bond for £100 to indemnify Lord Zouch for delivering the ship to them.
    VI.   *Ref:* State Papers, Domestic, James I, Vol. XCVII, No. 56.   PRO.
          Pub: Sainsbury, *Calendar of State Papers, Colonial*, p. 538.

MAY 10

74.* Governor Argall. Proclamations or edicts relating to attendance at church.   LC.
    IV.   *Ref:* Misc. Papers, 1606–1683, quarto. (Abstract only.)
            See No. 40, Remarks.

MAY 18

75.* Governor Argall. Proclamations or edicts regulating acts of colonists as to trade.   LC.
    IV.   *Ref:* Misc. Papers, 1606–1683, quarto. (Abstract only.)
            See No. 40, Remarks.

76.* Sir E. Sandys, H. Timbertake, J. Ferrar. Meeting of a committee for Smythes Hundred to provide for transportation and furnishing of 35 men to be sent to the Colony, giving method of Hundreds.   MC. [LC]
    IV.   *Ref:* Ferrar Papers.
                Photograph and transcript in Library of Congress. Corrections by Nicholas Ferrar and address and notes by J. Ferrar.

JUNE 11

77.* Lord Zouch. Letter to Captain Ward concerning the venture of a pinnace to Virginia with John Bargrave.   PRO.
    VI.   *Ref:* State Papers, Domestic, James I, Vol. CIII, No. 44.
          Pub: Sainsbury, *Calendar of State Papers, Colonial*, p. 19.

JUNE 12

78.* Governors of the Virginia Company. Letter to the mayor and aldermen of Leicester Account of drawings of lottery, June 12, 1618.   LEI.
    III.   *Ref:* See under No. 75.
          Pub: See under No. 75.

79.* Privy Council. Order for the transportation of prisoners to Virginia.   PC.
    I.   *Ref:* See under No. 41.
        Pub: See under No. 41.

80. Virginia Company. Letter to Capt. Samuel Argoll sent by the "William and Thomas"
      concerning his abuse of the company's property.   LC.
    III.   *Ref:* MS. Court Book, Virginia Co., II, 23.
        Pub: (1) Kingsbury, *Records Virginia Co.*, II.   (2) Brock, *Virginia Company*, II, 31–33.

81. Virginia Company. An extract from a copy of a letter sent to Lord De La Warr, by
      "Wililam and Thomas," touching Capt. Samuel Argoll.   LC.
    III.   *Ref:* MS. Court Book, Virginia Co., II, 29.
        Pub: (1) Kingsbury, *Records Virginia Co.*, II.   (2) Brock, *Virginia Company*, II, 33–35.

82.* Captain Andrews. A letter to Lord Zouch, concerning his intended voyage to Virginia
      with Jacob Braems.   PRO. [NY]
    VII.   *Ref:* State Papers, Domestic, James I, Vol. CIII, No. 33.
        Pub: Sainsbury, *Calendar of State Papers, Colonial*, p. 19.

          Transcript in N. Y. Public Library, Bancroft Collection, Virginia Papers, I, p. 227–233.

83. John Chamberlain. A letter announcing the death of Lord La Warr and the shipping of
      100 boys and girls to Virginia by "City."   PRO.
    VI.   *Ref:* State Papers, Domestic, James I, Vol. CIII, No. 33.
        Pub: *Calendar, State Papers, Domestic,* James I, 1611–1618, p. 548.

84. Sir Ed. Hext. A letter from the justice of peace of Somersetshire, to the Privy Council,
      concerning the impressment of maidens to be sent to Virginia.   PRO.
    VII.   *Ref:* State Papers, Domestic, James I, Vol. CIII, No. 42.
        Pub: (1) *Va. Mag. of Hist.*, VI, 228–230. (2) Sainsbury, *Calendar of State Papers,*
          Colonial, 19.

85.* John Pory. A letter to Sir Dudley Carleton, concerning the appointment of Sir Geo.
      Yeardley as governor of Virginia.   PRO.
    VII.   *Ref:* State Papers, Domestic, James I, Vol. CIII, No. 46.
        Pub: Sainsbury, *Calendar of State Papers, Colonial*, pp. 19–20.

86. Virginia Company. The form of a patent of land.
    III.   *Pub:* Brown, *First Republic*, 605–606, note.

87.* Virginia Council. Proprietary instructions to George Yeardley, governor of Virginia.
                                    (1) LC. (2) VHS.
    III.   *Ref:* (1) Misc. Records 1606–1692, pp. 72–83. (2) Randolph MSS., III, 44–160.
        Pub: *Virginia Magazine of History and Biography*, II, 154–165.

NOVEMBER 28

88.* John Pory. A letter to Sir Dudley Carleton, concerning Pory's appointment as secretary of Virginia.   PRO.

    VII.   *Ref:* State Papers, Domestic, James I, Vol. CIII, No. 111.

          Pub: Calendar, State Papers, Domestic, James I, 1611–1618, p. 598.

89.* John Chamberlain. A letter stating that Yeardley, "a mean fellow," goes to Virginia as governor, knighted by King, and flaunts the same.   PRO.

    VII.   *Ref:* State Papers, Domestic, James I, Vol. CIII, No. 110.

          Pub: Sainsbury, *Calendar of State Papers, Colonial,* p. 20.

NOVEMBER 30

90.* Privy Council. A warrant to send James Stringer, a reprieved prisoner, from Newgate to Virginia.   PC.

    I.   *Ref:* Privy Council Register, James I, Vol. IV, 53.

1619

91.* Ferdinando Yate. "The voyage . . . to verginia," a story of the journey.   NY.

    VI.   *Ref:* Smyth of Nibley Papers, 13.

          Pub: N. Y. Pub. Lib. Bull., I 70–72.

              Autograph document. The voyage was probably in September, and the account written in January.

92.* Virginia Company. "Anote of the shipping, men, and Provisions, sent to Virginia by the Treasurer and Company, in the yeere 1619." Printed: 1619.   (1) NY.   (2) KP.

    III.   *Ref:* (1) Broadside. (2) MSS. in the Collection of Earl De La Warr.

          Pub: (1) Force, *Tracts,* III, No. V. (2) *Va. Mag. of Hist.,* VI, 231–2.

              This broadside is usually included in the Declaration of the State of Virginia, 1620. See *post,* No. 183.

[1619]

93.* [John] Delbridge [Yeardley]. A letter to Sir Edwin Sandys, concerning Captain Argoll and the specific affairs of the colony upon his arrival.   MC. [LC]

    IV.   *Ref:* Ferrar Papers.

              An indorsement in a later hand gives letter as from Delbridge. Autograph is Sr Geo. Yeardley's. Written soon after April 29, 1619. [Photographic reproduction of part, and transcript in the Library of Congress.]

94.* Sir Geo. Yeardley. A letter to [Sir Edwin Sandys] concerning the seating of old settlers, Captain Argoll, tobacco sent to Flushing, and relations with Opochancono.   MC. [LC]

    IV.   *Ref:* Ferrar Papers.

          A. L.

95.* Sale of ship "New Year's Gift," to Robert, Earl of Warwick, by Roger Dunster and John Thompson.   PRO.

    VII.   *Ref:* Manchester Papers, No. 248.

          Pub: Calendar: Hist. MSS. Com., *Eighth Report,* pt. 2, p. 33.

1618/19

FEBRUARY 3

96. Lord Russell. A letter to Sir Clement Edwardes, concerning a prisoner to be sent to Virginia.

    VII.   *Ref:* State Papers, Domestic, James I, Vol. CV, No. 75.   PRO.

          Pub: Calendar, State Papers, Domestic.

97.* Indenture between Sir Wm. Throckmorton and the Virginia Company et al., for a plantation in Virginia.   NY.
  III. *Ref:* Smyth of Nibley Papers, Smyth 3 (4), pp. 53–58.
    Pub: N. Y. Pub. Lib. Bull., 1899, III, 161–164.
     A contemporary copy.

FEBRUARY 4

98. Wm. Ward. A letter to Lord Zouch, warden of Cinque Ports, concerning Mr. Upton as captain of a pinnace to Virginia.   CHILD.
  VI. *Ref:* MS. collection of J. Eliot Hodgkin, esq., F. S. A.
    Pub: Calendar: Hist. MSS. Com., *Fifteenth Report*, pt. 2, p. 279.

FEBRUARY 15

99.* Lord Zouch. A warrant for John Fenner, captain of "Silver Falcon," and Henry Bacon, master, to pass to Virginia, and trade with colony and savages.   PRO. [NY]
  VI. *Ref:* State Papers, Colonial, James I, Vol. I, No. 44.
    Pub: Sainsbury, *Calendar of State Papers, Colonial*, p. 21.
     Transcript, New York Public Library, Bancroft Papers, I, pp. 235–237.

FEBRUARY 18

100.* Sir Wm. Throckmorton and others. A letter to Sir Geo. Yeardley, concerning a patent for their Virginia plantation.   NY.
  VI. *Ref:* Smyth of Nibley Papers, 4.
    Pub: Calendar: *N. Y. Pub. Lib. Bull.*, 1899, Vol. III, p. 165; I, p. 187.
     A contemporary copy.

FEBRUARY 25

101.* Privy Council. An order concerning the ship "Treasurer," and its offence against Spaniards.
  I. *Ref:* Privy Council Register, James I, Vol. IV, 433.   PC.
    Pub: Brown: *First Republic*, 358.

MARCH

102.* Grant to Abraham and John Jacobb, collector of customs or imposts on tobacco imported into England and Wales. Yearly fee £150.   PRO.
  I. *Ref:* Docquet Book, Signet Office.

1619

APRIL 10

103.* Sir Wm. Throckmorton. A letter to John Smyth, concerning the plantation in Virginia.
  VI. *Ref:* Smyth of Nibley Papers, Smyth, 6.   NY.
    Pub: Calendar: *N. Y. Pub. Lib. Bull.*, I, 187.
     A. L. S. with seal.

APRIL 18

104.* Richard Berkeley. A letter to John Smyth, of Nibley, concerning the plantation in Virginia.   NY.
  VI. *Ref:* Smyth of Nibley Papers, Smyth, 5.
    Pub: Calendar: *N. Y. Pub. Lib. Bull.*, I, 187.
     A. L. S. with seal.

105.* Sandys, Harwood, Wolsenhan, Rich, Johnson. Draft of a report of a committee describing the " particular duties " of the several officers of the Virginia Company.

    III.   *Ref:* Manchester Papers, No. 245.   PRO.

        Pub: (1) Brown, *First Republic*, 301–305. (2) Calendar: Hist. MSS. Com., *Eighth Report*, pt. 2, p. 33.

106.* Virginia Company. The Court Book of the Virginia Company of London; the minutes of the extraordinary, preparative, and general quarter courts from 1619, April 28, to 1624, June 7, except May 20, and the first part of May 22, 1620, which are missing.   LC.

    II.   *Ref:* MS. Rec. Virginia Co., Vols. I, II.

        Pub: (1) Kingsbury, *Records Virginia Co.*, Vols. I, II. (2) Brock, *Virginia Company*, Vols. I, II. (Extracts.)

        A contemporary copy, attested by the secretary of the company, Edward Collingwood.

107.* Notes made from the Court Books [of the Virginia Company] "concerning the manner of levying public charges," etc., 1619, April 28–July 21.   PRO.

    II.   *Ref:* Manchester Papers, No. 246.

        Pub: Calendar: Hist. MSS. Com., *Eighth Report*, pt. 2, p. 33.

108. John Chamberlain. A letter to Sir Dudley Carleton, concerning election of Sir Edwin Sandys, treasurer of the Virginia Company.   PRO.

    VII.   *Ref:* State Papers, Domestic, James I, Vol. CIX, No. 18.

        Pub: Calendar, *State Papers, Domestic*, p. 44.

109. Governor Argoll. An enactment fixing the limits of Jamestown, Virginia.   LC.

    IV.   *Ref:* MS. Court Book, Virginia Co., II.

        Pub: (1) Kingsbury, *Rec. Virginia Co.*, II, Index. (2) Brock, *Virginia Company*, II, 37.

110.* Treasurer and Council for Virginia. (1) A commission to Wye. (2) A letter to Sir Geo. Yeardley, expressing pleasure at reforms enacted and outlining policy toward the Indians.

    III.   *Ref:* Admiralty Court, Instance and Prize, Libels 80, No. 123.   PRO.

        In the records of the suit of the Virginia Company with Wye, 1620. See *post*, No. 148.

111.* Geo. Thorpe. A letter to John Smithe, of Nibley, concerning the expenses of a voyage to Virginia.   NY.

    VI.   *Ref:* Smyth of Nibley Papers, Smyth, 7.

        Pub: Calendar: *N. Y. Pub. Lib. Bull.*, I, 187.

        A. L. S. with seal.

112.* "The Counsell of Virginia." Copy of minutes relating to the censure passed on Alderman Johnson by a committee of the Council of Virginia.   PRO.

    III.   *Ref:* Manchester Papers, No. 250.

        Pub: Calendar: Hist. MSS. Com., *Eighth Report*, pt. 2, p. 33.

113.* **A short** draft of censure against Alderman Johnson abandoned in favor of "the preceding."
    III.   *Ref:* Manchester Papers, No. 251.   PRO.
        Pub: Calendar: Hist. MSS. Com., *Eighth Report*, pt. 2, p. 34.

JULY 20

114.* **Geo. Thorpe.** A letter to John Smyth, concerning Partridge's misbehavior.   NY.
    VI.   *Ref:* Smyth of Nibley Papers, Smyth, 8.
        Pub: Calendar: *N. Y. Pub. Lib. Bull.*, I, 187.
            A. L. S. with seal.

115.* **Sir Geo. Yeardley.** A letter concerning Argoll's letters from Lord Ritch.
    IV.   *Ref:* Ferrar Papers.   MC. [LC]
        A. L. S.

JULY 30, 31; AUGUST 2, 3, 4

116.* **Mr. Pory.** "A Reporte of the manner of Proceeding in the General Assembly convented at James City." In the autograph of John Pory indorsed by Sir Dudley Carleton.
    IV.   *Ref:* State Papers, Domestic, James I, Vol. I, No. 45.   PRO. [NY]
        Pub: (1) Wynne and Gilman, *Colonial Records of Virginia.* (State Senate Document, extra) Richmond, 1874, pp. 1–32. (2) New York Hist. Soc., 2d ser., III, 335. (3) Sainsbury, *Calendar of State Papers*, p. 22.
            Transcript in N. Y. Public Library, Barlow Papers; Bancroft Papers, I, 251–343.

JULY, AUGUST, AND SEPTEMBER

117.* **The cost** of furnishing the "Margaret." Payment for things bought in London by Mr. Thorpe in July, August, and September, 1619.   NY.
    VI.   *Ref:* Smyth of Nibley Papers, Smyth, 3 (13)–(16), pp. 79–93.
        Pub: *N. Y. Pub. Lib. Bull.*, III, 213–223.

AUGUST 3

118.* **Sir Ed. Sandys.** A letter to Sir George Yeardley, commending to him the care of Berkeley Hundred.   NY.
    VI.   *Ref:* Smyth of Nibley Papers, Smyth 3 (12), p. 78.
        Pub: Catalogue: *N. Y. Pub. Lib. Bull.*, I, 186.

AUGUST 11

119.* **Gabriel Barbor.** A letter to Sir Ed. Sandys, recommending Mr. Newland.   MC.
    VI.   *Ref:* Ferrar Papers.
        A. L. S. written from Exeter.

AUGUST 16

120.* **Sir Ed. Sandys.** A letter to John Ferrar, concerning the factions in the company and concerning Smith's Hundred.   MC. [LC.]
    VI.   *Ref:* Ferrar Papers.
        A. L. S.

AUGUST 18

121.* **Charter** party with Mr. Williams, of Bristol, for the hire of his ship "Margaret."   NY.
    VI.   *Ref:* Smyth of Nibley Papers, Smyth, 3 (17), pp. 94–96.
        Pub: (1) *N. Y. Pub. Lib. Bull.*, III, 165–167. (2) Calendar: Hist. MSS. Com., *Fifth Report*, pt. 1, p. 341.

122.* Remembrances for Captain Woodleefe against the return of the ship.   NY.
    VI.   *Ref:* Smyth of Nibley Papers, Smyth, 3 (8), pp. 71–72.
        Pub: Catalogue: *N. Y. Pub. Lib. Bull.*, I, 186.

123.* "**A lyst** of the men nowe sent for plantacon vnder Captayne Woodleefe governor."   NY.
    VI.   *Ref:* Smyth of Nibley Papers, Smyth, 3 (9), pp. 73–75.
        Pub: N. Y. Pub. Lib. Bull., III, 210–212.

124.* Sir Wm. Throckmorton et al. A commission to Capt. John Woodleefe as governor of the
        town of Barkley in Virginia, and to act as chief merchant for them.   NY.
    VI.   *Ref:* Smyth of Nibley Papers, Smyth, 3 (5), pp. 59–60.
        Pub: Catalogue: *N. Y. Pub. Lib. Bull.*, I, 186.

125.* An agreement between Sir Wm. Throckmorton, Richard Berkeley, Geo. Thorpe, John Smyth,
        and Capt. John Woodleaf, giving the terms.   NY.
    VI.   *Ref:* Smyth of Nibley Papers, Smyth, 9, also 3 (7), pp. 64–70.
        Pub: N. Y. Pub. Lib. Bull., III, 167–171.

126.* Wm. Throckmorton, Rich. Bearkley, et al. "Ordinances direccions and Instructions to
        Captaine John Woodlefe for the goverment of o^r men & servants in the Towne and
        hundered of Bearkley in Virginia."   NY.
    VI.   *Ref:* Smyth of Nibley Papers, Smyth, 10, also 3 (6), pp. 61–63.
        Pub: N. Y. Pub. Lib. Bull., III, 208–210.

127.* Indenture between the four adventurers of Berkeley Hundred and Robert Coopy of North
        Nibley.   NY.
    VI.   *Ref:* Smyth of Nibley Papers, Smyth, 11.
        Pub: Calendar: *N. Y. Pub. Lib. Bull.*, I, 187.
        Original document with seals affixed.

128.* Sir William Throckmorton and his three associates. Letter dated at Bristol to Sir George
        Yeardley, asking him to join in the project.   NY.
    VI.   *Ref:* Smyth of Nibley Papers, Smyth, 3 (11), p. 77.
        Pub: Catalogue: *N. Y. Pub. Lib. Bull.*, I, 186.

129.* The Certificate of John Lwye, the mayor of Bristol, relating to the men shipped under Capt.
        John Woodleefe.   NY.
    VI.   *Ref:* Smyth of Nibley Papers, 3 (10), p. 76.

1619–20

130.* Account of A. B. of the expenses of the last voyage, from September 16, 1619, to September
        16, 1620.   NY.
    VI.   *Ref:* Smyth of Nibley Papers, Smyth, 3 (32), pp. 140–141.
        Pub: Catalogue: *N. Y. Pub. Lib. Bull.*, I, 186.

1619

SEPTEMBER 20

131.* Sir Edwin Sandys. A letter to John Ferrar, urging a steadfast policy and the securing of
warrants.   MC. [LC]

  VI. *Ref:* Ferrar Papers.
    A. L. S.

SEPTEMBER 29

132.* Sir Edwin Sandys (?). A letter to the [Earl of Southampton], concerning plans for planters
and Yeardley's resignation.   MC. [LC]

  VI. *Ref:* Ferrar Papers.
    A rough draft in Sandys' autograph.

SEPTEMBER 30

133.* John Pory. A letter to "the Right Honble and my singular good lorde" from James city in
Virginia, concerning the expedition of Captain Argall to the West Indies; the need of
the English plough, vines, and cattle in the colony; the success of some of the colonists
in acquiring wealth.   NY.

  IV. *Ref:* Barlow Collection, 2270.
    A. L. S.

OCTOBER 2

134.* Gabriel Barbor. A letter to Sir Edwin Sandys, concerning the ease with which money was
collected for the lottery.   MC. [LC]

  VI. *Ref:* Ferrar Papers.
    A. L. S.

OCTOBER 4

135.* Sir Edwin Sandys. A letter to John Ferrar, concerning entries in the Court Book.
  VI. *Ref:* Ferrar Papers.   MC. [LC]

OCTOBER 16

136.* Sir Edwin Sandys. A letter to John Ferrar, concerning factions in the company and his own
finances.   MC. [LC]

  VI. *Ref:* Ferrar Papers.
    Pub: Virginia Mag. Hist. and Biog., X, 416–417.
    A. L. S.

NOVEMBER 6

137.* Privy Council. A letter to Abraham Jacobs to release the tobacco to the Virginia Company.
  I. *Ref:* Privy Council Register, James I, Vol. IV, p 358.   PC.

NOVEMBER 11

138.* Council in Virginia. "The putting out of the Tenants that came over in the B. N. wth other
orders of the Councell."   MC. [LC]

  III. *Ref:* Ferrar Papers.
    Indorsement and marginal notes in John Ferrar's handwriting. Photographic reproduction
    and transcript in the Library of Congress.

NOVEMBER 12

139.* Governor and Council in Virginia. An order appointing tasters of tobacco.   MC. [LC]
  III. *Ref:* Ferrar Papers.
    Photographic reproduction and transcript in the Library of Congress.

140.* **Sir George Yeardley.** Certificate with regard to the arrival of the "Margaret" in Virginia, with the names of passengers.   NY.

       IV.   *Ref:* Smyth of Nibley Papers, Smyth, 3 (18), p. 97.

             Pub: Catalogue: *N. Y. Pub. Lib. Bull.*, I, 186.

141.* **James I.** Printed proclamation to restrain the planting of tobacco in England and Wales.

                          (1) PRO.   (2) KP.   (3) ANT.   (4) Q.

       I.   *Ref:* (1) Proclamations, James I, No. 74.   (2) Earl DeLaWarr Collection.   (3) Antiquaries.   (4) Collections of proclamations.

             Pub: Calendar: Hist. MSS. Com., *Fourth Report*, pt. 1, p. 299.

[1620] (?)

142.* **Adventurers and Planters.** Copy of a petition to the "Lds & rest of the body politic for the state of his Maj's Colony in Virginia," from "many of 1″ person, adventurers & planters willing and ready to prepare thither."   PRO.

       III.   *Ref:* Manchester Papers, No. 247.

             Pub: Calendar: Hist. MSS. Com., *Eighth Report*, pt. 2, p. 33.

143.* **Sir Nathaniel Rich (?).** Statement, possibly intended for a speech before Virginia Company in defense of the Earl of Warwick.   PRO.

       III.   *Ref:* Manchester Papers, No. 279.

             Pub: Calendar: Hist. MSS. Com., *Eighth Report*, pt. 2, pp. 35–36.

144.* —— Rough notes for his defense before the council of the Virginia Company on the charge of having altered an order of the council, which he had been requested to draw up.

       III.   *Ref:* Manchester Papers, No. 280.   PRO.

             Pub: Calendar: Hist. MSS. Com., *Eighth Report*, pt. 2, p. 36.

145.* **Rough** draft of proposition affecting the Virginia Company, viz, that matters in dispute between them and Captain Argall be referred to arbitration, etc.   PRO.

       III.   *Ref:* Manchester Papers, No. 281.

             Pub: Calendar: Hist. MSS. Com., *Eighth Report*, pt. 2, p. 36.

146.* **List** of names of His Majesty's council for Virginia, given in the three patents and since.   PRO.

       III.   *Ref:* Manchester Papers, No. 288.

             Pub: Calendar: Hist. MSS. Com., *Eighth Report*, pt. 2, p. 37.

147.* **Governor Nath. Butler.** A letter to [Sir Nath. Rich] (?) from the Summer Island colony, referring to the "Treasurer."   PRO.

       IV.   *Ref:* Manchester Papers, Nos. 269–270.

             Pub: Calendar: Hist. MSS. Com., *Eighth Report*, pt. 2, p. 35.

1620–22

148. **Capt. Nath. Butler.** History of the Bermudas.   BM.

       VII.   *Ref:* Sloane MSS., 750.

             Pub: LeFroy, *The Historye of the Bermudoes.*

1620

149.* **Virginia** Company con Wye. Complaint and accompanying documents.   PRO.

       III.   *Ref:* Admiralty court, Instance & Prize, Libels 80, Nos. 121–124.

          See *ante* No. 110.

1620

150. Banoeil. "Observations to be followed, for the making of fit roomes, to keepe Silk-wormes in: as also, for the best manner of planting Mulbery trees to feed them." Printed.
V.   (1) JCB.   (2) NY.

> Quarto. 21 pages. Imprinted Felix Kingston. Pages 25-27 missing, evidently misnumbered. This work contains *post* No. 151, pp. 25-28. Reprinted, 1622. See *post* No. 347.

151. *Virginia Company. "A Valuation of the Commodities growing and to be had in Virginia (?) rated as they are worth."   Printed.   (1) PRO.   (2) BOD.   (3) JCB.   (4) NY.
V.   *Ref:* (1) State Papers, Colonial, James I, Vol. I, No. 24 (MSS.).   (2) MSS. No. 50ᵇ, 14.
> Included in the printed book, cited above, No. 150.

152.* Virginia Company. "A note of Shipping, Men, and Provisions, sent and Prouided for Virginia." Printed.   (1) BM.   (2) ANT.   (3) PRO.
V.   *Ref:* (2) Printed broadsides, James I, No. 180.   (3) Manchester Papers, No. 291.

1619/20

JANUARY

153.* John Peirse. John Peirse to Sir Edwin Sandys by the "George."   MC.   [LC]
IV.   *Ref:* Ferrar Papers.
> A. L. S.

JANUARY

154.* John Rolfe. A letter to Sir Ed. Sandys, concerning the first meeting of the Assembly and other details of the Colony.   MC.   [LC]
IV.   *Ref:* Ferrar Papers.

JANUARY 10

155.* Sir Geo. Yeardley. "Sʳ. Geo: Yardles l'r 10. Jan: 1619: of the Place assigned for our Berkely."   NY.
VI.   *Ref:* Smyth of Nibley Papers, Smyth, 14.
       Pub: N. Y. Pub. Lib. Bull., I, 72.
> A. S.

JANUARY 13

156.* John Pory. A letter to [Sir Ed. Sandys] by the "George," concerning Samuel Argall.
IV.   *Ref:* Ferrar Papers.   MC.   [LC]
> [Photographic reproduction of part and transcript in the Library of Congress.] A. L. S.

JANUARY 14

157. John Pory. A letter to Sir Edwin Sandys, concerning the arrival and location of men.   MC.
IV.   *Ref:* Ferrar Papers.
       Pub: Va. Mag. of Hist., X, 289-290.
> [Photograph of beginning and of end, Vol. X, pp. 416-417.] A. L. S.

JANUARY 16

158.* John Pory. A letter to Sir Edwin Sandys, concerning Gov. Yeardley and also various commodities.   MC.   [LC]
IV.   *Ref:* Ferrar Papers.
> L. S.

JANUARY 21

159. Council in Virginia. Letter from colony to company concerning tobacco.   LC.
IV.   *Ref:* MS. Court Book, Virginia Co., II, 220.
       Pub: (1) Kingsbury, *Records Virginia Co., post*, II; (2) Brock, *Virginia Company*, II, 116.

160. Sir Edwin Sandys. A letter to Sir Robt. Naunton, concerning the poor children to be sent
to Virginia.   PRO.
    III. *Ref:* State Papers, Domestic, James I, Vol. 112, No. 49.
        Pub: Va. Mag. of Hist., VI, p. 232; Sainsbury, *Calendar of State Papers, Colonial*, p. 23.

161.* Privy Council. Order giving authority for 100 children to be sent to Virginia.   PC.
    I. *Ref:* Privy Council Register, James I, Vol. IV, p. 400.

162.* Charges incurred in obtaining for the plantation new supplies sent with Governor Thorpe.
    VI. *Ref:* Smyth of Nibley Papers, Smyth, 3 (19), pp. 98–99.   NY.
        Pub: Catalogue: N. Y. Pub. Lib. Bull., I, p. 186.

163. Sir John Danvers. A letter to the Marquis of Buckingham, concerning a proposition for his
Majesty's profit.   DROP.
    VII. *Ref:* MSS. of Hon. G. M. Fortescue.
        Pub: Calendar: Hist. MSS. Com., *Second Report*, p. 57.

164.* Jas. Berblocke. Order to Mr. Ferrar to pay £32 to Thomas Stevens for Smith's Hundred.
    VI. *Ref:* Ferrar Papers.   MC. [LC]
        [Photographic reproduction of the end in the Library of Congress.]

165.* Privy Council. An order concerning the offence of the "Treasurer" against the Spaniards.
    I. *Ref:* Privy Council Register, James I, Vol. IV, p. 433.   PC.
        Pub: Brown, *First Republic*, 358.

166.* Wm. Weldon. A letter to Sir Ed. Sandys, complaining at provisions sent and reporting on
College Land.   MC. [LC]
    IV. *Ref:* Ferrar Papers.
        [Photographic reproduction of part in the Library of Congress.]

1620

167.* Sir Thomas Rowe, Mr. Leate, Mr. Caning, et al. (1) Petition to the Privy Council for a
patent for the sole import of tobacco for 7 years.   (2) A project for the same.
                                  (1) PC.   (2) BM. [LC].
    I. *Ref:* (1) Privy Council Register, James I, Vol. IV, p. 475.   (2) Lansdowne MSS.,
162, fo. 159.

168.* Privy Council. An order allowing the sole importation of tobacco as above.   PC.
    I. *Ref:* Privy Council Register, James I, Vol. IV, p. 475.

169.* William Tracy. A letter to John Smyth, concerning endeavors for men for the plantation.
    VI. *Ref:* Smyth of Nibley Papers, Smyth, 16.   NY.
        Pub: N. Y. Pub. Lib. Bull., III, 248.
          A. L. S.

MAY (?)

170.* **Copy** of opinion of counsel upon the patents of the [Virginia] Company with special reference
    to the power of removing Sir Thomas Smith from office of treasurer.   PRO.   [LC]
    III.   *Ref:* Manchester Papers, No. 271.

MAY 1

171.* **Sir Edwin Sandys.**   A letter to John Ferrar, concerning the examination of the acts of the
    Assembly in Virginia and also their accounts.   MC.   [LC]
    VI.   *Ref:* Ferrar Papers.
            A. L. S.   [Transcript and photographic reproduction of part in the Library of Congress.]

MAY 7

172.* **Indenture** assigning Sir Wm. Throckmorton's share of Berkeley Hundred to Wm. Tracy.
    VI.   *Ref:* Smyth of Nibley Papers, Smyth, 3 (20), pp. 100–102.   NY.
            Pub: N. Y. Pub. Lib. Bull., III, 248–250.

MAY 16

173.* **Alderman Johnson.**   A letter to Sir Edwin Sandys, concerning the sale of tobacco.
    III.   *Ref:* Ferrar Papers.   MC.   [LC]
            A. L. S.   [Transcript and photographic reproduction in the Library of Congress.]

MAY 17

174.* **Treasurer, Council, and Company for Virginia.**   A Broadside concerning the condition
    of the colony and especially the commodities there produced.   Printed.   NY.
    V.
            Indorsement in autograph of John Smith of Nibley (?).

[JUNE]

175.* **Wm. Tracy.**   Two letters to John Smyth "at ye blew lion in Chauserilane this," asking aid
    for raising a company.   NY.
    VI.   *Ref:* Smyth of Nibley Papers, Smyth, 19.
            Pub: N. Y. Pub. Lib. Bull., III, 253.
                A. L. S.

176.* **Wm. Tracy.**   A letter to John Smyth, concerning accounts.   NY.
    VI.   *Ref:* Smyth of Nibley Papers, Smyth, 18.
            Pub: N. Y. Pub. Lib. Bull., III, 252.
                A. L. S.

JUNE 1

177.* **John Smyth.**   "Copy of my lettre to Mr Berkeley. 1. Junii. 1620 about our accompts for the
    Virginia ship then returned".   NY.
    VI.   *Ref:* Smyth of Nibley Papers, Smyth, 15.
            Pub: N. Y. Pub. Lib. Bull., III, 250–251.
                Indorsed by John Smyth.

JUNE 7

178.* **Sir Edwin Sandys.**   A letter to Marquis of Buckingham, justifying his exposures of Sir Thos.
    Smyth.   PRO.   [NY]
    VI.   *Ref:* State Papers, Colonial, I, No. 51.
            A. L. S.   Transcript, New York Public Library, Bancroft Papers, I, 345–353.

179.* **Sir Geo. Yeardley.**   A letter to [Sir Ed. Sandys], complaining at the lack of provisions sent.
    IV.   *Ref:* Ferrar Papers.   MC.   [LC]
            A. L. S.   Indorsed by Sir Ed. Sandys.

180.* **John Pory.** A letter to Sir Edwin Sandys, giving an elaborate description concerning the condition of the colony. MC. [LC]

    IV.   *Ref:* Ferrar Papers.

> L. S. Marginal note in John Ferrar's autograph. Photographic reproduction and transcript in the Library of Congress.

181.* **Sir Edwin Sandys.** A letter to John Ferrar, concerning letters from Virginia. MC. [LC]

    VI.   *Ref:* Ferrar Papers.

> A. L. S.

182.* **William Tracy.** A letter to John Smyth, "about his dispatch into Virgynia, June 1620."

    VI.   *Ref:* Smyth of Nibley Papers, Smyth, 17. NY.

        Pub: *N. Y. Pub. Lib. Bull.*, III, 151–152.

> A. L. S.

183.* **"Counseil for Virginia".** "A Declaration of the State of the Colony and Affaires in Virginia". Printed. Including also the following:

> "A Note of the Shipping, 1619";
>
> "The Names of the Adventurers" with the sums adventured;
>
> A Declaration of the Supplies to be sent, July 18, 1620;
>
> "The Orders and Constitutions . . . for the better gouerning of the Actions and affaires of the [Virginia] Companie";
>
> Also in different editions are found A Declaration of the division of land, 1616;
>
> And A Declaration of November 15, 1620.   (1) BM.   (2) CAMB.
>
>   (3) HARV.   (4) JCB.   (5) LC.   (6) NEWB.   (7) NY.

    V.   *Pub:* Force, *Tracts*, III, Nos. V, VI.

> For a discussion of the difference between the editions and the different supplementary "Declarations" added after the "Orders and Constitutions," see *ante*, pp. 89–90. See also List of Records, Nos. 92, 220.

184.* **James I.** Printed proclamation for the restraint of the disordered trading for tobacco.

    I.   *Ref:* Proclamations, James I, No. 82. PRO.

185.* **[Privy Council.]** Commission to the Lord Treasurer to contract with Sir Thomas Rowe, Abraham Jacob, and Hurdman, Budd, et al. for the importation of tobacco. PRO.

    I.   *Ref:* Docquet Book, Signet Office.

186.* **Mr. Russell.** "Mr. Russell's proiect touching artificiall wyne in Virginia." NY.

    IV.   *Ref:* Smyth of Nibley Papers, Smyth, 30.

        Pub: *N. Y. Pub. Lib. Bull.*, III, 255–256.

> A. S.

187.* **William Tracy.** A letter to John Smyth, concerning "my cousin barkli". NY.

    VI.   *Ref:* Smyth of Nibley Papers, Smyth, 20.

        Pub: *N. Y. Pub. Lib. Bull.*, III, 253.

> A. L. S.

188. **John Chamberlain.** A letter to Sir Dudley Carleton, from London, concerning the election of the Earl of Southampton as treasurer of the Virginia Company. PRO.

    VII.   *Ref:* State Papers, Domestic, James I, Vol. CXVI, No. 13.

        Pub: Calendar: *State Papers, Domestic*, Vol. CXVI, p. 162.

189. Virginia Company.   "A Commission graunted vnto Willm Tracy Esq for a voyag intended
          to Virginia ".   NY.
     III.   *Ref:* Smyth of Nibley Papers, Smyth, 3 (22), p. 123.
              Pub: N. Y. Pub. Lib. Bull., III, 254–255.
                A copy.

190.* Wm. Tracy.   Two letters to John Smyth.   NY.
     VI.   *Ref:* Smyth of Nibley Papers, Smyth, 21, 22.
              Pub: N. Y. Pub. Lib. Bull., III, 253–254.
                A. L. S.

191.* Sir Edwin Sandys.   A letter to John Ferrar, concerning personal and financial affairs.   MC.
     III.   *Ref:* Ferrar Papers.   [LC]
                A. L. S.

192.* Privy Council.   Order to the Sollicitor General to prepare a patent for North Colony of
          Virginia.   PC.
     I.   *Ref:* Privy Council Register, James I, Vol. IV, 574.

193.* Virginia Council.   Extract from a letter affecting Capt. Argall.   PRO.   [LC]
     III.   *Ref:* Manchester Papers, No. 272.

194.* Wm. Tracy.   A letter to John Smyth, concerning Berkeley Hundred.   NY.
     VI.   *Ref:* Smyth of Nibley Papers, Smyth, 23.
              Pub: N. Y. Pub. Lib. Bull., III, 256.
                A. L. S.

195.* Wm. Tracy.   A letter to John Smyth, concerning Berkeley Hundred.   NY.
     VI.   *Ref:* Smyth of Nibley Papers, Smyth, 24.
              Pub: N. Y. Pub. Lib. Bull., III, 257.
                A. L. S.

196.* Throkmorton, Berkeley, Thorpe & Smyth.   Revocation of Capt. John Woodleaf's com-
          mission.   NY.
     VI.   *Ref:* Smyth of Nibley Papers, Smyth, 3 (23), p. 124, also 31.
              Pub: N. Y. Pub. Lib. Bull., III, 257–258.
                    3 (23), copy.
                    31, "Vera copia exᵗ p. Rob: Maundey."

197.* Sir Edwin Sandys.   A letter to John Ferrar, concerning demands from Huddleston.
     III.   *Ref:* Ferrar Papers.   MC.   [LC]
                A. L. S.

198.* "**Covenants** and agreements between Richard Berkeley of Stoke . . . Geo᷈ge Thorpe . . .
          Willm Tracy of Gayles" . . . and . . . "John Smyth of Northimbly" . . .   NY.
     VI.   *Ref:* Smyth of Nibley Papers, Smyth, 3, also 3 (25), pp. 127–129.
              Pub: N. Y. Pub. Lib. Bull., III, 276–278.
                Copy.

199.* Commission to George Thorpe & Wm. Tracy as governors of the plantation in Virginia. NY.
    VI.   *Ref:* Smyth of Nibley Papers, Smyth, 3 (24), pp. 125–126.
        Pub: Catalogue: *N. Y. Pub. Lib. Bull.*, I, 186.
           Copy.

AUGUST 31

200.* Charter party with Wm. Ewins for the ship "Supply" in which Wm. Tracy went to Virginia.
    III.   *Ref:* Smyth of Nibley Papers, Smyth, 3 (29), pp. 134–136.   NY.
        Pub: Catalogue: *N. Y. Pub. Lib. Bull.*, I, 186.
           Copy.

SEPTEMBER

201.* An account with Ed. Williams for hire of the first ship, and the wages of Toby Felgate, pilot
    in the first voyage.   NY.
    VI.   *Ref:* Smyth of Nibley Papers, Smyth, 3 (33), p. 142.
        Pub: Catalogue: *N. Y. Pub. Lib. Bull.*, I, 187.

202.* The cost of furnishing the "Supply" sent from Bristol.   NY.
    VI.   *Ref:* Smyth of Nibley Papers, Smyth, 3, pp. 143–150.
        Pub: *N. Y. Pub. Lib. Bull.*, III, 283–290.

SEPTEMBER 1

203.* Berkeley, Thorpe, Tracy, and Smyth. Agreement to supply Richard Smyth and wife,
    Anthony and Wm., their sons, Robt. Bisaker and wife, and Richard Hopkins with land
    for cultivation in Virginia.   NY.
    VI.   *Ref:* Smyth of Nibley Papers, Smyth, 3 (27), pp. 132–133.
        Pub: Catalogue: *N. Y. Pub. Lib. Bull.*, I, 186.

204.* Wm. Tracy. A letter to John Smyth concerning Berkeley Hundred.   NY.
    VI.   *Ref:* Smyth of Nibley Papers, Smyth, 25.
        Pub: *N. Y. Pub. Lib. Bull.*, III, 278.
          A. L. S.

SEPTEMBER 3

205.* List of Settlers. "A list of men nowe sent for plantačon in Virginia."   NY.
    VI.   *Ref:* Smyth of Nibley Papers, Smyth, 3 (31), pp. 138–139.
        Pub: *N. Y. Pub. Lib. Bull.*, III, 290–292.
        The day of month not given in MSS.

SEPTEMBER 10

206.* Richard Berkeley and John Smyth. Instructions and advice to Geo. Thorpe.   NY.
    VI.   *Ref:* Smyth of Nibley Papers, Smyth, 3 (26), pp. 129–131.
        Pub: *N. Y. Pub. Lib. Bull.*, III, 278–280.

SEPTEMBER 15

207.* Wm. Tracy. A letter to John Smyth. Personal affairs of the plantation, otherwise unim-
    portant.   NY.
    VI.   *Ref:* Smyth of Nibley Papers, Smyth, 26.
        Pub: Calendar: *N. Y. Pub. Lib. Bull.*, I, 188.
          A. L. S.

208.* Agreement between Richard Berkeley, George Thorpe et al., and Robert Pawlett to go to
    Virginia as preacher, surgeon, and physician.   NY.
    VI.   *Ref:* Smyth of Nibley Papers, Smyth, 3 (28), p. 133.
        Pub: Catalogue: *N. Y. Pub. Lib. Bull.*, I, 186.

1620-22

1620, SEPTEMBER 18-1622, MICHAELMAS

209.* **Account** of money expended since Wm. Tracie's departure, September 18, 1620, until Michaelmas, 1622.   NY.

     VI.   *Ref:* Smyth of Nibley Papers, Smyth, 3 (35), pp. 151-152.

         Pub: Catalogue: *N. Y. Pub. Lib. Bull.*, I, 187.

1620

SEPTEMBER 18

210.* **Thomas Parker.** Certificate of the mayor of Bristol to sailing of "Supply," with names of passengers.   NY.

     VI.   *Ref:* Smyth of Nibley Papers, Smyth, 3 (30), p. 137.

         Pub: Catalogue: *N. Y. Pub. Lib. Bull.*, I, 186.

211.* **Sir Edwin Sandys.** A letter to John Ferrar, urging Mr. Carter to make three catalogues of indebted adventurers.   MC. [LC]

     VI.   *Ref:* Ferrar Papers.

         A. L. S.

SEPTEMBER 20

212.* **John Smyth.** Account of expenses for Virginia plantation.   NY.

     VI.   *Ref:* Smyth of Nibley Papers, Smyth, 32.

         Pub: Calendar: *N. Y. Pub. Lib. Bull.*, I, 189.

             Autograph of John Smyth.

SEPTEMBER 22

213.* **Timothy Gate.** A letter to his "cosyn Mʳ Williā Tracy att Bristol".   NY.

     VI.   *Ref:* Smyth of Nibley Papers, Smyth, 45.

         Pub: *N. Y. Pub. Lib. Bull.*, III, 281.

SEPTEMBER 23

214.* **John Bridges.** A letter to John Smyth concerning the incarceration of Tracy.   NY.

     VI.   *Ref:* Smyth of Nibley Papers, Smyth, 29.

         Pub: *N. Y. Pub. Lib. Bull.*, III, 281-282.

           A. L. S. with seal.

SEPTEMBER 24

215.* **Wm. Tracy.** A letter to John Smyth concerning the journey.   NY.

     VI.   *Ref:* Smyth of Nibley Papers, Smyth, 27.

         Pub: *N. Y. Pub. Lib. Bull.*, III, 282.

         A. L. S.

SEPTEMBER 25

216.* **William Tracy.** A letter to John Smyth concerning his imprisonment.   NY.

     VI.   *Ref:* Smyth of Nibley Papers, Smyth, 28.

         Pub: *N. Y. Pub. Lib. Bull.*, III, 282-283.

         A. L. S.

SEPTEMBER 30

217.* **Indenture** between George Thorpe on one part and Robert Oldesworth and John Smyth on the other.   NY.

     VI.   *Ref:* Smyth of Nibley Papers, Smyth, 12.

         Pub: Calendar: *N. Y. Pub. Lib. Bull.*, I, 187.

218.* Capt. Butler. Captain Butler to Nathaniel Rich, stating difference between the 2 earls [Southampton and Warwick]. PRO.

    VI.   *Ref:* Manchester Papers, No. 284.

219.* Sir Edwin Sandys. A letter to John Ferrar, with a reference to Lord Chamberlain.

    VI.   *Ref:* Ferrar Papers. MC. [LC].

    A. L. S.

220.* Councell for Virginia. Declaration in addition to that of July 18 of ships and supplies to be sent to Virginia, and soliciting planters and money. Printed. NY.

    V.   *Ref:* In "Declaration of the State of the Colony and Affaires in Virginia."

        See *ante*, No. 183; also *ante*, p. 89-90.

221.* Geo. Thorpe. A letter to John Smyth from "Southampton Hundred." NY.

    VI.   *Ref:* Smyth of Nibley Papers, Smyth, 33.

        Pub: N. Y. Pub. Lib. Bull., III, 292-293.

        A. L. S.

222. "Greevovs Grones for the Poore," dedicated to the "Company of the Virginian and Sommer Iland Plantations." Printed. NEWB.

    VII.   *Ref:* Collection of Ed. E. Ayer.

        Printed for Michael Sparke.

1621

223.* Virginia Company. "A note of the shipping, men, and prouisions . . . prouided for Virginia by . . . Southampton, and the Company . . ." Printed.

    V.   *Ref:* (2) Collection of Broadsides, James I, No. 194.   (1) NY.   (2) ANT.

224. Henry Fleet. Henry Fleet's Journal of Voyage in the "Warwick" to Virginia. LAMB.

    IV.   *Pub:* Neill, *The English Colonization of America.*

225.* Virginia Company. "A Comission granted by the Treasuror Counsell and Company for Virginia to Sʳ Thomas Smith for the free fishinge on the coast of America." BM. [LC]

    III.   *Ref:* Additional MSS., 14285, fols. 73-74.

226.* Earl of Warwick with Edward Bruster concerning the ships "Treasurer" and "Neptune."

    III.   *Ref:* Admiralty Court, Instance and Prize, Libel 81, No. 6.   PRO.   [LC]

1621(?)

227.* "Wallons and French." Promise of certain "Wallons and French" to emigrate to Virginia. PRO.

    III.   *Ref:* State Papers, Colonial, I, No. 45.

        Pub: Sainsbury, *Calendar of State Papers, Colonial,* p. 498.

1620/21

228.* Sir Geo. Yeardley. Certificate to Council and Company of Virginia of the arrival at Berkeley of 50 persons, with list of names. NY.

    IV.   *Ref:* Smyth of Nibley Papers. Smyth, 34.

        Pub: Calendar: *N. Y. Pub. Lib. Bull.* I, 189.

        A. S. of George Yeardley and Jo: Pory, Secr. Seal and stamp: double rose.

229.* **Sir Geo. Yeardley** & the Council in Virginia. Copy of a letter to Earl of Southampton and Council and Company for Virginia, forwarding a petition of colonists vs. the King's proclamation forbidding importation of tobacco. PRO.
    IV.   *Ref:* Manchester Papers, No. 290.
        Pub: Calendar: Hist. MSS. Com., *Eighth Report*, pt. 2, p. 37.
          Certified by John Pory.

230.* **House of Lords.** Act for repressing odious . . . sin of drunkenness and restraint . . . of excess price of beer and ale. ⅓ of penalties to go to the Virginia Company. HL.
    I.   *Pub:* Calendar: Hist. MSS. Com., *Third Report*, p. 18.

231.* **Privy Council.** Order upon the complaint of Parliament of great abuse of lotteries for raising monies towards the advancement of the plantation in Virginia, & relief of distresses there, suspending the same. PC. [NY]
    I.   *Ref:* (1) Privy Council Register, James I, Vol. V, p. 11. (2) Colonial Entry Book, Vol. 79, p. 201.
        Pub: Sainsbury, *Calendar of State Papers, Colonial*, p. 25.
          Transcript, N. Y. Pub. Lib., Bancroft Papers, I, fo. 357.

232.* **Sir George Yeardley.** Grant by Sir Geo. Yeardley, Governor of Virginia. to Geo. Harrison . . . of 200 acres of land . . . PRO. [NY]
    IV.   *Ref:* State Papers, Colonial, James I, Vol. I, No. 53.
        Pub: Sainsbury, *Calendar of State Papers, Colonial*, p. 25.
          Original document with autograph signatures, indorsed by John Pory. Transcript. N. Y
          Pub. Lib. Bancroft, I, 361–5.

233.* **James I.** Proclamation by the King commanding Virginia Company to forbear license for keeping and continuing any lottery. (1) Q. (2) ANT. (3) PRO. (4) JCB.
    I.   *Ref:* (3) Proclamation. James I, No. 89.
        Pub: Sainsbury, *Calendar of State Papers, Colonial*, p. 25.

234.* **Geo. Thorpe.** "A note ffor Mʳ Ffelgate to receaue his ffraight" NY.
    VI.   *Ref:* Smyth of Nibley Papers, Smyth, 35.
        Pub: Calendar: *N. Y. Pub. Lib. Bull.*, I, 189.
        D. S.

235. **A** true relation of a sea fight between two great well-appointed Spanish men of war and the "Margaret and John."
    VI.   *Pub:* (1) *Purchas, His Pilgrimes*, IV, bk. ix, ch. 14. (2) Brown, *First Republic*, 415–416.

1621

236.* **Wm. Powell.** A letter to Sir Edwin Sandys concerning a difference with Yeardley.
    IV.   *Ref:* Ferrar Papers. MC. [LC]
        A. L. S.
        [Transcript and photographic reproduction in the Library of Congress.]

APRIL 17

237.* House of Lords. Draft of "An Act for the freer liberty of fishing and fishing voyages to be made and performed in . . . the sea coasts . . . Virginia, New England . . . and parts of America."   HL.

    I.   *Ref:* Commons Journal, I, 578.

         Pub: Calendar: Hist. MSS. Com., *Third Report*, p. 21.

MAY

238.* Whittaker. A letter to Sir Edwin Sandys, by "Bona Nova", concerning reception of new men.   MC. [LC]

    IV.   *Ref:* Ferrar Papers.

         A. L. S. Outlined in Nicholas Ferrar's Autograph.

         [Transcript and photographic reproduction of part in the Library of Congress.]

MAY 3

239.* Richard Bucke. A letter to Sir Edwin Sandys, requesting payment of the sums due.

    IV.   *Ref:* Ferrar Papers.   MC. [LC]

         A. L. S., with seal.

240.* Council of Virginia. Warrant by Council for Lieutenant Saunders to have custody of cattle left in Virginia by Captain Martin.   PRO.

    IV.   *Ref:* State Papers, Colonial, James I, Vol. III, No. 36, III.

         Pub: Virginia Mag. of Hist., VII, 146.

MAY 9

241.* Geo. Thorpe and Mr. John Pory. A letter to Sir E. Sandys. Complaints against Powell and Madison.   MC. [LC]

    IV.   *Ref:* Ferrar Papers.

MAY 13

242.* Governor and Council of Virginia. Warrant concerning Capt. John Martin.

    IV.   *Pub:* Brown, *First Republic*, 414.

MAY 15 AND 16

243.* Geo. Thorpe and John Pory. A letter to Sir Edwin Sandys concerning Indians, commodities, and perplexities of government.   MC. [LC]

    IV.   *Ref:* Ferrar Papers.

MAY 15

244.* George Thorpe and John Pory. A letter to Sir Edwin Sandys, concerning the commodities and need of clothes, etc.   MC. [LC]

    IV.   *Ref:* Ferrar Papers.

         Autograph letter, with an indorsed summary by John Ferrar.

         [Transcript and photographic reproduction of part in the Library of Congress.]

MAY 16

245.* Sir Geo. Y[eardley (?)]. Copy of a letter to the New Magazine Company by the Bona Nova, concerning personals.   MC. [LC]

    IV.   *Ref:* Ferrar Papers.

246.* ———. Copy by John Pory of a letter to Sir Edwin Sandys in answer to that of Nicholas Hyde.   MC. [LC]

    IV.   *Ref:* Ferrar Papers.

247.* Sir Geo. Y[eardley. A letter to Sir Edwin Sandys, concerning his acts in the colony and
his desire to return home. MC. [LC]

    IV.   *Ref:* Ferrar Papers.

        Pub: Virginia Mag. of Hist., X, 286–289 (photograph of signature).

           A. L. S. Indorsement by John Ferrar.

MAY 24

248.* Abraham Piersey. Two letters to Sr Edwin Sandys, concerning a fishing voyage to New
Foundland from James City, and concerning tobacco trade. MC. [LC]

    IV.   *Ref:* Ferrar Papers.

        Pub: Virginia Mag. of Hist., X, 418.

           A. L. S. With seal.

           [Transcript and photographic reproduction in the Library of Congress.]

MAY 27

249.* Capt. Nuce. A letter to Sir Edwin Sandys, concerning the commodities and lack of provisions.

    IV.   *Ref:* Ferrar Papers. MC. [LC]

           In handwriting of a clerk.

           [Transcript and photographic reproduction of part in the Library of Congress.]

JUNE 9

250.* Francis Smith. A letter to Sir Edwin Sandys. Unimportant. MC. [LC]

    VI.   *Ref:* Ferrar Papers.

           A. L. S.

           [Transcript and photographic reproduction of part in the Library of Congress.]

JUNE 18

251.* Privy Council. Order concerning North and South Colonies and their fishing relations.

    I.   *Ref:* Privy Council Register, James I, Vol. V, p. 58. PC. [LC]

JUNE 22

252.* Richard Bucke. A letter to Sir Edwin Sandys, complaining that agreements are not kept by
the company. MC. [LC]

    IV.   *Ref:* Ferrar Papers.

           A. L. S.

           [Transcript and photographic reproduction of part in the Library of Congress.]

JUNE 27

253.* George Thorpe. A letter to Sir Edwin Sandys, concerning matters of small importance.

    IV.   *Ref:* Ferrar Papers. MC. [LC]

           A. L. S.

254.* Sir George Yeardley. A letter to Sir Edwin Sandys, concerning the election of a successor
and new arrivals in the colony. MC.

    IV.   *Ref:* Ferrar Papers.

        Pub: Virginia Mag. of Hist., X, 288–289, (photograph of signature).

           A. L. S.

JULY

255.* John Rowe. A letter to Sir Edwin Sandys. MC. [LC]

    IV.   *Ref:* Ferrar Papers.

           A. L. S.

           [Transcript and photographic reproduction of a part in the Library of Congress.]

256.* **William Ewens.** Covenant on part of Wm. Ewens for 480ᶦᶦ to see that the Ship George 150 tuñ is staunch and strong and fitted out with furniture and with marriners and seamen, to take on passenges and goods and to bring back tobacco from the plantation, with forfeit of 1000ᶦᶦ.   BM. [LC]

    III.   *Ref:* Additional MSS., 14285, fos. 78a–79a.

257.* **Wm. Ewens.** Covenant by Wm. Ewens to fit out the Ship Charles, 80 tuñ and take same with fraight and passengers to Virginia for certain [blank] sum. Forfeit of 1000ᶦᶦ for not returning ship with freight.   BM. [LC]

    III.   *Ref:* Additional MSS., 14285, fos. 80–81.

JULY 6

258.* **Nicholas Ferrar and others.** Warrant to pay Geo. S[andys] £20, addressed to the Earl of Southampton, signed by Nicholas Ferrar, Benett, Blaney, Wyseman.   MC. [LC]

    III.   *Ref:* Ferrar Papers.

<blockquote>Autograph signatures; indorsement by John Ferrar.
[Photographic reproduction in the Library of Congress.]</blockquote>

JULY 24

259.* **J. Barnard and others.** Warrant to Deputy J[ohn] F[errar] for £6 to Joseph Fitch; signed— J. Barnard, N. Rich, Bull, Richard Caswell, John Blande.   MC. [LC]

    III.   *Ref:* Ferrar Papers.

<blockquote>[Photographic reproduction in the Library of Congress.]</blockquote>

260.* **Virginia Company.** "Instructions to the Governor for the time being, and Counsell of State in Virginia."   LC.

    III.   *Ref:* (1) MS. Records, Virginia Co., III, pt. ii, pp. 11–14.   (2) Instructions, commiĉons, and letters, 1606–1683, 1–19.

        Pub: Outline: Hening, *Virginia Statutes at Large,* I, p. 114.   Outline: Stith, *Virginia,* pp. 194–196.

261.* **Treasurer and Company.** An Ordinance and Constitution of the Treasurer and Company in England for Council and Assembly in Virginia.   LC.

    III.   *Ref:* (1) MS. Rec., Virginia Co., III.   (2) Instructions, commiĉons, etc., 1606–1683, 21–23.

        Pub: (1) Hazard, *Hist. Coll. of State Papers,* I, 131–133.   (2) Hening, *Virginia Statutes at Large,* I, 110.   (3) Stith, *Virginia,* app. 4.   Outline, p. 196.

JULY 25

262.* **Treasurer and Company.** Letter to Governor and Council in Virginia concerning Wyatt as governor.   LC.

    III.   *Ref:* (1) MS. Rec. Virginia Co., III, ii, 15, 16.   (2) Instructions, commiĉons, etc., 1606–1683, pp. 68–75.

        Pub: Neill, *Virginia Company of London,* 223–233.

JULY 30

263.* **Privy Council.** Copy of a Council order that Lord Treasurer may make warrants of assistance for suppressing the importation and sale of tobacco.   KP.

    I.   *Ref:* MSS. of Earl De La Warr.

        Pub: Calendar: Hist. MSS. Com., *Fourth Report,* 313.

AUGUST 11

264.* **Virginia Company.** Answer to the request of the Walloons and French to plant in Virginia, signed by John Ferrar, deputy.   PRO. [NY]

    III.   *Ref:* State Papers, Colonial, James I, Vol. I, No. 55.

        Pub: Sainsbury, *Calendar of State Papers, Colonial,* p. 26.

<blockquote>Transcript: N. Y. Pub. Lib., Bancroft Papers, I, fos. 369–371.</blockquote>

AUGUST 12

265.* Virginia Company.   Letter concerning the sending of maids; Capt. Norton and the Italians, making beads; Mr. Gookin; the French men and families to sail.   LC.

     III.   *Ref:* (1) MS. Rec. Virginia Co., III, pt. ii, pp. 17–18a.   (2) Instructions, Commiĉons, etc., 1606–1683, pp. 76–83.

          Pub: Neill, *Virginia Company of London,* pp. 233–239.

AUGUST 24

266.* Virginia Company.   "A Coñ̃iission graunted by vs the Trer Counsell and Company for Virginia vnto our louinge freinds Capt Arthur Guy and Nicholas Norburnes for a Voyage intended to Virginia."   BM. [LC]

     III.   *Ref:* Additional MSS., 14285, fos. 70–70a.

267.* Treasurer and Company of Virginia.   Covenant to pay Capt. Arthur Guy, Robert Toakley, and John Packesall 300ˡⁱ more for victuall and transportation of said 100 persons.

     III.   *Ref:* Additional MSS., 14285, fos. 71–71a.   BM. [LC]

268.* ————.   Covenant to pay to Capt. Arthur Guy et al. 3ˡⁱ for each tun of goods, provisions, and commodities here put aboard and there delivered.   BM. [LC]

     III.   *Ref:* Additional MSS., 14285, fos. 72–72a.

SEPTEMBER 11

269.* Virginia Council and Company.   Letter to Governor and Council in Virginia, concerning the failure of the old magazine and dissatisfaction with the new.   LC.

     III.   *Ref:* (1) MS. Records Virginia Co., III, pt. ii, pp. 19–20.   (2) Instructions, commiĉons, etc., 1606–1683, pp. 84–92.

          Pub: Neill, *Virginia Company of London,* pp. 241–250.

SEPTEMBER 19

270.* Ed. Blayney.   A letter to Sir Ed. Sandys concerning an East India ship.   MC. [LC]

     VI.   *Ref:* Ferrar Papers.

        A. L. S.

OCTOBER 1

271.* Sir Edwin Sandys.   A letter to John Ferrar, or to N. Ferrar, concerning personal matters.

     VI.   *Ref:* Ferrar Papers.   MC. [LC]

OCTOBER 24

272.* Privy Council.   Order that the Virginia Company is not to have a foreign house for importation of their goods; tobacco to be first landed in England, with respite for four months.

                                             (1) PC.   (2) PRO.   [NY]

     I.   *Ref:* (1) Privy Council Register, James I, Vol. V, p. 173 (new number).   (2) Colonial Entry Book, Vol. 79, pp. 201–202.

          Pub: Sainsbury, *Calendar of State Papers, Colonial,* p. 26.

               Transcript, New York Public Library, Bancroft Papers, II, fos. 373–375.

OCTOBER 20

273.* John Stratford.   "Mʳ Tho: Dawson note for all my tobacco sold by him, for mee wᵗʰ much labor at this poare rate."   NY.

     VI.   *Ref:* Smyth of Nibley Papers, Smyth, 39.

          Pub: Calendar: *N. Y. Pub. Lib. Bull.,* I, 189.

274.* Sir Thomas Smith and Alderman Johnson. Reply of Sir Thomas Smith and Alderman Johnson to the petition of John Bargrave. PRO.

    III.   *Ref:* State Papers, Colonial, James I, Vol. III, No. 12.

        Pub: (1) *Virginia Mag. of Hist.*, VI, 378-381. (2) Sainsbury, *Calendar of State Papers, Colonial*, p. 60.

NOVEMBER 5

275.* Sir Edwin Sandys. A letter to John Ferrar, concerning his debts, and also Southampton Hundred. MC. [LC]

    VI.   *Ref:* Ferrar Papers.

        [Transcript and photographic reproduction in the Library of Congress.]

NOVEMBER 21

276.* Virginia Company. Grant to Daniel Gats to be master of "Darling," and a permit to fish on the coast of Virginia between 33° and 45° N. lat. BM. [LC]

    III.   *Ref:* Additional MSS., 14285, fos. 74a-75.

277.* Council and Company for Virginia. "A Comission Graunted . . . to John Huddleston for a Voyadge to Virginia and for a free fishinge on the Coast of America." BM. [LC]

    III.   *Ref:* Additional MSS., 14285, fos. 75a-76a.

278.* —— "A Comission Granted . . . to Captaine Tho: Jones M^r of the Discouery, for the free fishinge on the Coast of America, Tradinge for furs in Virginia." BM. [LC]

    III.   *Ref:* Additional MSS., 14285, fos. 77-78a.

NOVEMBER 26

279.* Virginia Company. A letter to the governor and council in Virginia, concerning the sending of maids and the trading for furs. LC.

    III.   *Ref:* (1) MS. Records Virginia Co., III, pt. ii, p. 20, 20^a. (2) Instructions, Commiĉons, etc., 1606-1683, pp. 93-95.

        Pub: Neill, Edward, *Virginia Company of London*, pp. 263-266.

NOVEMBER 30

280.* Governor and Council in Virginia. Proclamation warning persons from going aboard ships. LC.

    IV.   *Ref:* MS. Records Virginia Co., III, pt. ii, p. 45^a.

DECEMBER

281.* Nicholas Ferrar. Receipt to John Smyth of Nibley of £6 13^s 4^d for subscription in the "Roule" for trade of furs and for the "Roule" for building of boats and houses. NY.

    III.   *Ref:* Smyth of Nibley Papers, Smyth, 36.

        Pub: Calendar: *N. Y. Pub. Lib. Bull.*, I, 189.

        Signature of Nicholas Farrar.

DECEMBER 3

282.* Sir Edwin Sandys. A letter to John Ferrar, concerning his enemies in the Company.

    VI.   *Ref:* Ferrar Papers. MC. [LC]

        A. L. S.

DECEMBER 5

283.* Virginia Company. Letter to the governor and council in Virginia concerning trade and discovery. LC.

    III.   *Ref:* (1) MS. Rec. Virginia Co., III, pt. ii, p. 21. (2) Instructions, commiĉons, etc., 1606-1683, pp. 96-101.

        Pub: Neill, *Virginia Company of London*, 267-273.

DECEMBER 15

284.* Privy Council. A letter to Sir Dudley Carleton, ambassador at States of United Province, against Dutch settling in North Colony of Virginia (called New England).   **PC.**
    I.   *Ref:* Privy Council Register, James I, Vol. V, p. 209.

285.* Peter Arundell. A letter to Sir Edwin Sandys, complaining at the neglect of the Company, but promising to hide defects.   **MC. [LC]**
    IV.   *Ref:* Ferrar papers.
                A. L. S. Transcript and photographic reproduction of part in the Library of Congress.

DECEMBER 23

286.* Governor in Virginia. Commission by the governor and captain-general of Virginia to Dan'l Tucker to trade with the Indians.   **LC.**
    IV.   *Ref:* MS. Rec. Virginia Co., III, pt. ii, p. 36.

1622

287.* Draft of a letter to see that grant of the King to the Company of the importation of tobacco for seven years from Virginia and Bermuda is consigned to them.   **KP.**
    VI.   *Ref:* MSS. of Lord Sackville.
           Pub: Calendar: Hist. MSS. Com., *Seventh Report*, p. 259b.

288.* Mr. Wroth. Notes from lists showing total number of emigrants to Virginia, and making total loss 3,000 and survivors 1,700, 1619–1622.   **PRO.**
    VI.   *Ref:* Manchester Papers, No. 298.
           Pub: Calendar: Hist. MSS. Com., *Eighth Report*, pt. 2, p. 38.

289.* Patrick Copland. A Declaration how the monies viz., 70£ 8ˢ 6ᵈ were disposed, which were gathered by Mr. Patrick Copland, towards the building of a free schoole in Virginia. Printed.   **PR.**
    V.   *Pub:* Calendar: Hist. MSS. Com., *Third Report*, p. 66.

290. Bermuda Company. Laws of Bermuda Company on the selection and settlement of "Land in Virginia." XXX, in "Orders and Constitutions" for the Summer Islands. Printed.
                                           (1) LC.   (2) NY.
    V.   *Pub:* Le Froy, *Memorial of the Bermudas*, I, 228.
                An order of court, Feb. 6, 1621/2. Imprint, Felix Kingston.

291. John Brinsley. "A Consolation for ovr Grammar Schooles: more especially for all those of an inferiovr sort, and all ruder countries and places, namely . . . Virginia with the Sommer Ilands." Printed.   **(1) JCB.   (2) NY.**
    V.
              84 pages, quarto. Printed by Richard Field for Thomas Man. 1622.

292.* [Virginia Company.] "The Inconveinencies that have happened to some Persons which have transported themselves from England to Virginia, without prouisions necessary to sustaine themselves: For Preuention of like disorders hereafter,—is published this short declaration—of necessaries—." Printed.   **(1) NY.   (2) ANT.   (3) JCB.**
    V.   *Ref:* (2) Collection of Broadsides, James I, No. 195.
           Pub: Reprinted in *Purchas, His Pilgrimes*, IV, Bk. IX, ch. 15, sec. IV.
               Imprinted by Felix Kingston. Broadside. For discussion of edition, see *ante*, p. 91.

293.* Edward Waterhouse. "Declaration of the state of the Colony of Virginia with the Relation of the Massacre" and the names of those massacred.
    V.   **(1) LC.   (2) JCB.   (3) HARV.   (4) NEWB.   (5) PRIV.**
               Copies (1) and (2) include "The Inconveniences." See *ante* No. 292.

1622 (?)

294.* **Francis West, Wm. Claiborne et al.** Petition to the King on behalf of the distressed
subjects, relating chiefly to tobacco.   PRO.

     IV.   *Ref:* State Papers, Colonial, James I, Vol. II, No. 15.

         Pub: (1) *Virginia Mag. of Hist.*, VI, 233. (2) Sainsbury, *Calendar of State Papers*, p. 35.

1621/22

JANUARY

295.* **Virginia Council.** Letter to Virginia Company of London, describing the conditions and
needs of the colony in detail.   LC.

     IV.   *Ref:* MS. Rec. Virginia Co., III, pt. ii, pp. 1–2a.

         Pub: Neill, *Virginia Company of London*, 274–286.

296.* **Peter Arundle.** Fragment of a letter to John Smyth of Nibley concerning opportunities of
Virginia.   NY.

     VI.   *Ref:* Smyth of Nibley Papers, Smyth, 37.

         Pub: Calendar: *N. Y. Pub. Lib. Bull.*, I, 189.

           A. L.

JANUARY 14

297.* **Virginia Council.** Settlement of the wages of tradesmen in Virginia.   LC.

     IV.   *Ref:* MS. Rec. Virginia Co., III, pt. ii, p. 46.

JANUARY 16

298.* **"A Commission** granted by vs the Treᵵ Counsell and Companies for Virginia vnto our louinge
frend Theodore Wadsworth for a Voyage intended to Virginia."   BM.   [LC]

     III.   *Ref:* Additional MSS., 14285, fos. 69–69a.

JANUARY 30

299.* **Virginia Company.** The forme of a Patent to such Aduenᵗˢ whose shares exceedinge 50ˢᵒʳ:
are exempted from payinge any Rent to yᵉ Company for the persons they transporte.

     III.   *Ref:* Additional MSS. 14285, fos. 58–64a.   BM.   [LC]

1622, FEBRUARY 4 AND 1623, DECEMBER 11 TO 1624, NOVEMBER 27

300.   **Council in Virginia.** The Courte Booke. The original minutes of the Courts of the Council
in Virginia, held about once a month, to decide controversies, to hold trials of accused
persons, to hear petitions, and to pass orders concerning the affairs of the Colony.

     IV.   *Ref:* MS. Rec. Virginia Colony.   LC.

1621/2

FEBRUARY 12

301.* **Mayor of Plymouth.** Request to Lord Treasurer of the fulfilment of the promise that they
be not interrupted in a fishing voyage for Virginia as threatened by Sir Ferdinand
Gorges.   PRO.

     VI.   *Ref:* State Papers, Domestic, James I, Vol. cxxvii, No. 92.

         Pub: *Calendar of State Papers, Domestic*, James I, 1619–1623, p. 344.

302.* **State** of case and decision between John Bargrave, plaintiff, and Sir Thomas Smythe et al., defendants, with reference to losses of Bargrave by being prohibited free trade in Virginia, according to his patent.   PRO. [NY]

    III.   *Ref:* State Papers, Colonial, James I, Vol. II, No. 4, II.

           Pub: Sainsbury, *Calendar of State Papers, Colonial*, p. 29.

                Transcript, New York Public Library, Bancroft Papers, I. Fos. 437-453.

303.* **Somers Islands Company.** Court for Somers Islands. Committee to consider planting land granted by Virginia Company has not met, and is commanded to meet hereafter: also names of committee.   MC. [LC]

    II.   *Ref:* Ferrar Papers.

             [Photographic reproduction in the Library of Congress.]

304.* **Somers Islands Company.** Court for Somers Islands. To investigate the government and laws for Somers Islands touching the sending of youths to Virginia.   MC. [LC]

    II.   *Ref:* Ferrar Papers.

             [Photographic reproductions in the Library of Congress.]

1622

305.* **Virginia** Company con. Wye. Defense of Wye.   PRO. [LC]

    III.   *Ref:* Admiralty Court, Instance and Prize, Libels 81, No. 216.

306.* **Colony in Virginia.** Letter to Virginia Company of London, describing the massacre and the needs of the Colony.   LC.

    IV.   *Ref:* MS. Rec. Virginia Co., III, pt. ii, p. 3, 3ᵃ.

307.* **Sir Edwin Sandys.** A brief letter to John Ferrar requesting frequent letters.   MC. [LC]

    VI.   *Ref:* Ferrar Papers.

308.* **John Bargrave.** Charges against the former government of Virginia.   PRO. [NY]

    VI.   *Ref:* State Papers, Colonial, James I, Vol. II, No. 4, I.

           Pub: (1) *Va. Mag. of Hist.*, VI, 225-228.   (2) Sainsbury, *Calendar of State Papers*, p. 28.

                Transcript, New York Public Library, Bancroft Papers, I, fos. 465-475.

309.* ———. Petition to the Privy Council, complaining against the company and asking that his new plan of government be considered.   PRO. [NY]

    VI.   *Ref:* State Papers, Colonial, James I, Vol. II, No. 4.

           Pub: Sainsbury, *Calendar of State Papers, Colonial*, pp. 28-29.

                Transcript, New York Public Library, Bancroft Papers, I, fos. 425-427.

310.* **Governor in Virginia.** Commission by Governor and Captain-General of Virginia to Capt. Roger Smith to command Charles City.   LC.

    IV.   *Ref:* MS. Records Virginia Co., III, pt. ii, p. 37.

311.* **Governor in Virginia.** Commission by governor and captain-general of Virginia to Capt. Ralph Hamer for trading.   LC.

    IV.   *Ref:* MS. Rec. Virginia Co., III, pt. ii, p. 37.

APRIL 18

312.   **Patrick Copland.**   "Virginia's God be Thanked, or a Sermon of Thanksgiving for the Happie success of the affayres in Virginia this last yeare."   Printed by order of the company.

                     (1) JCB   (2) NY   (3) NEWB.   (4) PRIV.

     V.   *Pub:* Neill, E., *Memoir of Rev. Patrick Copland*, Ch. III.

         Dedicated May 22.   Printed by J. D. for William Shefford and John Bellamie.

APRIL 19

313.*   **Governor in Virginia.**   Order "By the Governor and Captaine generall of Virginia" to Ralph Hamor to bring the people from Wariscoyack.   LC.

     IV.   *Ref:* MS. Rec. Virginia Co., III, pt. ii, p. 50ª.

APRIL 20

314.*   **Governor in Virginia.**   Commission by the governor and captain-general of Virginia to Captain Smith to remove the people of Henrico Ileand and Coxendale.   LC.

     IV.   *Ref:* MS. Rec. Virginia Co., III, pt. ii, p. 37.

APRIL 22

315.*   **Sir Edwin Sandys.**   A letter to John Ferrar, alleging that petitions to the King emanate from Sir Thos. Smith, and discussing Spanish accusations.   MC.   [LC]

     III.   *Ref:* Ferrar Papers.

APRIL 25

316.*   **Sir Edwin Sandys.**   A letter to John Ferrar concerning value of Peirse in the factional differences.   MC.   [LC]

     VI.   *Ref:* Ferrar Papers.

         A. L. S.

APRIL 30

317.*   **Sir Edwin Sandys.**   A letter to John Ferrar, urging use of "form" in State affairs and approving Capt. Each's proposition with regard to fortifications.   MC.   [LC]

     III.   *Ref:* Ferrar Papers.

MAY

318.   **Sir Francis Wiat.**   Letter from Sir Francis Wiat, governor of Virginia, describing the massacre.

     IV.   *Pub:* Outline: *Purchas, His Pilgrimes*, Vol. IV, Bk. IX, Ch. 15, Sec. III.

319.*   "**Accompt** of the charge of the . 4 . servants sent into Virginia in the Ship furtherance."

     VI.   *Ref:* Smyth of Nibley Papers, Smyth, 3 (36), p. 153.   NY.

MAY 2

320.*   **Privy Council.**   Daniell Frank, William and John Ireland, prisoners . . . to be delivered to the "Governor of the Company of Virginia."   PC.

     I.   *Ref:* Privy Council Register, James I, Vol. V, p. 342.

MAY 7

321.*   **Governor in Virginia.**   Commission by governor and captain-general of Virginia to Capt. Ralph Hamer for trade.   LC.

     IV.   *Ref:* MS. Rec. Virginia Co., III, pt. ii, p. 37ª.

MAY 18

322.*   **Governor in Virginia.**   Commission by governor and captain-general of Virginia to Captain Smith to command "Pasbehay."   LC.

     IV.   *Ref:* MS. Rec. Virginia Co., III, pt. ii, p. 37.

323.* Virginia Company. "The Forme of a Patent for such as are Aduenturers by payinge money into the Treasury of yᵉ Company vndertaking to transp: and plant 100: persons."

    III.   *Ref:* Additional MSS., 14285, fos. 49–53.   BM. [LC]

324.* ———. "The forme of a Patent for a Planter only." An indenture between the Virginia Company and Sir Bowyer Worsly.   BM. [LC]

    III.   *Ref:* Additional MSS., 14285, fos. 54–57.

325.* ———. A grant for a private Plantation to Johnn Bounall, a Frenchman.   BM. [LC]

    III.   *Ref:* Additional MSS., 14285, fos. 65–68.

326.* Capt. John Bargrave. The answer of Capt. John Bargrave to his own aspersions against the present management.   PRO. [NY]

    III.   *Ref:* State Papers, Colonial, James I, Vol. II, No. 7, I.

           Pub: Sainsbury *Calendar of State Papers, Colonial*, p. 30.

                Transcript, New York Public Library, Bancroft Papers, I, fos. 429–433.

327.* Capt. John Bargrave. Petition to Privy Council, declaring he had stated the present government good because pressed by the Council for Virginia to do so.   PRO. [NY]

    III.   *Ref:* State Papers, Colonial, James I, Vol. II, No. 8.

           Pub: Sainsbury, *Calendar of State Papers, Colonial*, p. 30.

                Transcript, New York Public Library, Bancroft Papers, I, fos. 461–463.

328.* Virginia Company. Letter to Governor and Council in Virginia, desiring some commodities sent, and especially silk for the King.   LC.

    III.   *Ref:* MS. Rec. Virginia Co., III, pt. ii, pp. 22, 23.

329.* John Pountis. Petitions "To Sʳ Francis Wyate Knight Governor and Captaine Generall of Virginia and to the rest of his Maᵗⁱᵉˢ Counsell in Virginia."   LC.

    IV.   *Ref:* MS. Rec. Virginia Co., III, pt. ii, p. 58.

330.* The King. "A copy of the King's letter to the 11s. touching the mainteining of the decree in Chäcery for Sʳ Tho. Smith against Mr. Bargrave."   BM. PRO. [LC]

    I.   *Ref:* (1) Additional MSS., 12496, fo. 450. Caesar Papers. (2) State Papers, Domestic, James I, Vol. 131, No. 38.

        Pub: Sainsbury, *Calendar of State Papers, Colonial*, pp. 31–32.

331.* Governor in Virginia. Commission by governor and captain general of Virginia to Captain Maddison to assist the Potomacks in war.   LC.

    IV.   *Ref:* MS. Rec. Virginia Co., III, pt. ii, p. 37ᵃ, 38.

332. John Martin, Robert Haswell. Petition to King to take certain forest land in Virginia into his own hands.   LC.

    II.   *Ref:* MS. Court Book, Virginia Co., II, 20.

        Pub: Kingsbury, *Rec. Virginia Co.*, II.

        Court of this date.

333. Virginia Company. Answer of the counsell and company to the petition of John Martin and Hassell. LC.
    II.   *Ref:* MS. Court Book, Virginia Co., II, 21.
          Pub: (1) Kingsbury, *Rec. Virginia Co.,* II.   (2) Brock, *Virginia Company,* II, 21.
          (3) Neill, E., *Virginia Company of London,* 312–313.

334. Adam Dixon. Petition to King concerning the possession of land in Virginia. LC.
    II.   *Ref:* MS. Court Book, Virginia Co., II, 22.
          Pub: (1) Kingsbury, *Rec. Virginia Co.,* II.   (2) Brock, *Virginia Company,* I, 188–189.
          Court of this date.

335. Virginia Company. Answer of the Virginia Company to the petition of Adam Dixon. LC.
    II.   *Ref:* MS. Court Book, Virginia Co., II, 23.
          Pub: (1) Kingsbury, *Rec. Virginia Co.,* II.   (2) Brock, *Virginia Company,* I, 189.

336. William Kemp. The grievances of the inhabitants of Kikatan (Elizabeth City) by the testimony of William Kemp. LC.
    II.   *Ref:* MS. Court Book, Virginia Co., II, 23.
          Pub: (1) Kingsbury, *Rec. Virginia Co.,* II.   (2) Brock, *Virginia Company,* I, 190–191.
          Court of this date.

337. Virginia Company. Answer of the Virginia Company to the grievances of William Kemp.
    II.   *Ref:* MS. Court Book, Virginia Co., II, 23. LC.
          Pub: (1) Kingsbury, *Rec. Virginia Co.,* II.   (2) Brock, *Virginia Company,* I, 191.

338. Capt. Mathew Somers. Petition in the Kings Bench to the King concerning the discovery and right to the Somers Islands. LC.
    II.   *Ref:* MS. Court Book, Virginia Co., II, p. 24.
          Pub: (1) Kingsbury, *Rec. Virginia Co.,* II.   (2) Brock, *Virginia Company,* I, 192–193.
          Court of this date.

339. Virginia Company. Answer of the Virginia Company to the petition of Mathew Somers.
    II.   *Ref:* MS. Court Book, Virginia Co., II, 25. LC.
          Pub: (1) Kingsbury, *Rec. Virginia Co.,* II.   (2) Brock, *Virginia Company,* I, 193–195.

340. ———. Letter to Captain Argoll. LC.
    II.   *Ref:* MS. Court Book, Virginia Co., II, 27–28.
          Pub: Kingsbury, *Rec. Virginia Co.,* II.

JUNE 20

341.* Sir Francis Wyatt. Commission to Sir George Yardley to command on an expedition upon the coasts from 33° to 40° to make new discoveries for another settlement. LC.
    IV.   *Ref:* MS. Rec. Virginia Co., III, pt. ii, p. 38.

JUNE 21

342.* ———. Proclamation against drunkenness, swearing, stealing boats. LC.
    IV.   *Ref:* MS. Rec. Virginia Co., III, pt. ii, p. 46ᵃ.

JUNE 27

343.* Robert Newland. A letter to Nicholas Ferrar, concerning preparation to sail for Virginia.
    III.   *Ref:* Ferrar Papers. MC. [LC]
        A. L. S.

JUNE 29

344. Virginia Company. Propositions to the lord high treasurer concerning the tobacco contract. LC.
    II.   *Ref:* MS. Court Book, Virginia Co., II, 31.
          Pub: (1) Kingsbury, *Rec. Virginia Co.,* II.   (2) Brock, *Virginia Company,* I, 196–198.

345. Virginia Company. Propositions to the lord high treasurer concerning the tobacco contract. LC.

    II.   *Ref:* MS. Court Book, Virginia Co., II, 50–51.

            Pub: (1) Kingsbury, *Rec. Virginia Co.*, II. (2) Brock, *Virginia Company*, I, 215–218.

346. Mo(u)rninge Virginia. Printed. (Mentioned in Register of London Company of Stationers, 1562–1638.)

    V.   *Pub:* Cited: Report of Amer. Hist. Assoc., 1896, Vol. I, pp. 1251–1261.

347.* John Bonoeil. Reprint of the treatise on the culture of silk worms, including:

    (1) **The King.** Letter to treasurer, deputy, and others of the Virginia Company, recommending the setting up of silk works.

    (2) **Virginia Council and Company.** Letter to the governor and council in Virginia, endorsing the King's letter. Printed.   (1) HARV. (2) JCB. (3) NY. (4) PRIV.

    V.   *Pub:* Sainsbury, *Calendar of State Papers, Colonial*, pp. 31, 41 (King's letter).

              Imprinted Felix Kingston. King's letter is mentioned in Docquet Book, James I. See *ante*, No. 150.

348.* Privy Council. Order concerning the Spanish vessel wrecked on coast of Bermudas, of which Virginia Company had made restitution.

    I.   *Ref:* (1) Privy Council Register, James I, Vol. V, p. 431. (2) Colonial Entry Book, Vol. 79, p. 202.

        Pub: Sainsbury, *Calendar of State Papers, Colonial*, p. 31.

349. John Chamberlain. A letter to Sir Dudley Carleton, concerning a ship arrived from Virginia with news that savages have by surprise slain 350 (circum) of the English.   PRO.

    VII.   *Ref:* State Papers, Domestic, James I, Vol. 132, No. 38.

         Pub: Sainsbury, *Calendar of State Papers, Colonial*, p. 31.

350. Sir Thomas Wilson. Indians have killed in Virginia 300–400 English, and but for accident man, mother, and child had all been slain.   PRO.

    VII.   *Ref:* State Papers, Domestic, James I, Vol. 132, No. 41.

         Pub: Sainsbury, *Calendar of State Papers, Colonial*, p. 31.

351.* Privy Council. Order for a report on petition of John Bargrave against Sir Thomas Smythe, Alderman Johnson, and others for unjust practices and miscarriage of government of the Virginia plantation.   PC. [NY]

    I.   *Ref:* Privy Council Register, James I, Vol. V, p. 439.

        Pub: Sainsbury, *Calendar of State Papers, Colonial*, p. 31.

           Transcript: New York Public Library, Bancroft, I, fo. 477.

352.* Governor in Virginia. Commission from governor and captain-general of Virginia to Daniel Tucker to command a plantation.   LC.

    IV.   *Ref:* MS. Rec. Virginia Co., III, pt. ii, p. 36ᵃ.

353.* Note of articles ready or to be provided for exportation by Virginia Company.   BM. [LC]

    III.   *Ref:* Cotton MSS., Otho, E. X., fo. 121.

354. * **Note** of arms in the Tower for which the Virginia Company are suitors. To be delivered to them. PRO.

   I.   *Ref:* State Papers, Colonial, James I, Vol. II, No. 9.
        Pub: Sainsbury, *Calendar of State Papers, Colonial*, p. 32.

355. * **Privy Council.** Order of Privy Council that old cast arms in Tower, unfit for modern use, be delivered to Virginia Company for use against Indians. (1) PC. (2) PRO. [NY]

   I.   *Ref:* (1) Privy Council Register, James I, Vol. V, p. 449. (2) Colonial Entry Book, Vol. 79, p. 202.
        Pub: Sainsbury, *Calendar of State Papers, Colonial*, p. 32.
          Transcript: New York Public Library, Bancroft Papers, I, fos. 481–483.

356. * **Treasurer and Council for Virginia.** Letter to governor and council in Virginia, concerning protection from Indians and sole importation of tobacco. LC.

   III.   *Ref:* (1) MS. Rec. Virginia Co., III, pt. ii, pp. 23ᵃ–25. (2) Instructions, Commissions, and Letters, 1606–1683, pp. 102–107.
        Pub: Neill, *Virginia Company of London*, pp. 322–333.

357. * **John Smyth.** A list of servants remaining in Virginia. NY.

   VI.   *Ref:* Smyth of Nibley Papers, Smyth 3 (37), pp. 153–154.
        Pub: *N. Y. Pub. Lib. Bull.*, Vol. III, pp. 293–294. Catalogue: *Ibid.*, I, p. 187.
          Autograph of John Smith.

358. * **Privy Council.** A warrant staying the execution of Jas. Wharton and an order sending him to Virginia. PC.

   I.   *Ref:* Privy Council Register, James I, Vol. V, p. 465.

359. * **John Carter.** Petition to the Privy Council of a poor distressed prisoner to be recommended for transportation to Virginia. PRO.

   III.   *Ref:* State Papers, Colonial, James I, Vol. II, No. 12. State Papers, Domestic, James I, Vol. 133, No. 10.
        Pub: Sainsbury, *Calendar of State Papers, Colonial*, p. 33.

360. * "**A warrant** to the lord Trēr, to give order . . . for . . . delivery vnto the Company for the Virginia Plantaçon of 1000. browne bills." PRO.

   I.   *Ref:* Docquet Book, Signet Office, Vol. 7.

361. * **Sir Edwin Sandys.** A letter to Mr. John Ferrar, concerning the discouragements in the Virginia business, the ill effects of the bad news from Lady Wyatt, and his plans for Virginia. MC.

   III.   *Ref:* Ferrar Papers.
        Pub: *Virginia Mag. of Hist.*, X, 417–418.
        A. L.

362. * **Governor in Virginia.** Commission by governor and captain-general of Virginia to Sir George Yeardley to make war on the Indians; also for his voyage to Pamunkey. LC.

   IV.   *Ref:* MS. Rec. Virginia Co., III, pt. ii, pp. 38ᵃ, 39.

363.   "**The Late** Massacre in Virginia."   "A Poem."   PRO
     V.   *Ref:* Manchester Papers.
          Pub: Cited: *Amer. Hist. Assoc. Rpt.*, 1896, I, pp. 1251–1261.

364.*   Sir Edwin Sandys. Letter to John Ferrar, concerning books and letters to be sent to
          Colony by "Abigail."   MC. [LC]
     III.   *Ref:* Ferrar Papers.
          A. L. S.

1622/3

365.*   Thomasin Woodshawe. Petition to the governor of Virginia.   LC.
     IV.   *Ref:* MS. Rec. Virginia Co., III, pt. ii, p. 58.
366.*   Richard Pace. Petition to governor and council in Virginia.   LC.
     IV.   *Ref:* MS. Rec. Virginia Co., III, pt. ii, p. 58.

1622

367.*   Virginia Company. A letter to the governor and council in Virginia, concerning further
          advice about destroying the Indians.   LC.
     III.   *Ref:* MS. Rec. Virginia Co., III, pt. ii, p. 25a–27.
          Pub: Neill, *Virginia Company of London*, pp. 347–359.

368.*   Sir Edwin Sandys. A letter to John Ferrar, concerning "Ferrar's remembrances."   Grieves
          at desperate condition of Colony.   MC. [LC]
     VI.   *Ref:* Ferrar Papers.
          A. L. S.

369.*   Thomas Hamour. Petition to governor and council in Virginia.   LC.
     IV.   *Ref:* MS. Rec. Virginia Co., III, pt ii, p. 58.

370.*   Governor of Virginia. Commission to Capt. Ralph Hamer to force a trade with the Indians
          for provisions for the Colony.   LC.
     IV.   *Ref:* MS. Rec. Virginia Co., III, pt. ii, p. 39.

371.*   Governor of Virginia. Commission to Capt. William Eden, alias Sampson, to trade for
          corn, etc., between the lat. 33° and 40°.   LC.
     IV.   *Ref:* MS. Rec. Virginia Co., III, pt. ii, p. 39a.

372.*   Privy Council. Order that, on Thursday A. M., Nov. 14 [1622], the parties on both sides
          bring witnesses before the Łłds, and the Cape Merchant of the Virginia Company be
          present.   PC.
     I.   *Ref:* Privy Council Register, James I, Vol. V, p. 509.

373.* George Sandis. Petition to governor and council in Virginia concerning the transfer of servants of William Nuce, lately deceased, to his estates in lieu of £50 indebtedness.
    IV.   *Ref:* MS. Rec. Virginia Co., III, pt. ii, p. 39.   LC.

374.* Governor of Virginia. Commission to Captain Isaak Maddison and Robert Bennet to trade for corn between the lat. 33° and 40°.   LC.
    IV.   *Ref:* MS. Rec. Virginia Co., III, pt. ii, p. 39*a*.

375. John Donne. A sermon preached to the Honorable Companie of the Virginia Plantacon by John Dun (i. e. Donne) deane of St. Pauls, London. Printed.
    V.   (1) JCB. (2) NY. (3) PR IV. (4) MHS. (5) NEWB.
        Imprinted London: A. Neat: for Thomas Jones, 1622.

376. John Chamberlain. A letter to Sir Dudley Carleton concerning the sermon by the Dean of Pauls.   PRO.
    VII.   *Ref:* State Papers, Domestic, James I, Vol. 134, No. 15.
        Pub: Calendar: *State Papers, Domestic,* Vol. 134.

377.* Privy Council. A warrant to deliver John Carter to Lord Sackville to be sent to Virginia.
    I.   *Ref:* Privy Council Register, James I, Vol. V, p. 516.   PC.

378.* Privy Council. Order to Capt. John Bargrave *vs.* Sir Thomas Smyth to deliver his complaint in writing.   PC.
    I.   *Ref:* Privy Council Register, James I, Vol. V, p. 518.

379.* Henry Marten. Decree in case of the Virginia Company with Wye, absolving Wye.
    III.   *Ref:* Admiralty Court, Instance and Prize, Libels 81, No. 216.   PRO. [LC]
380.* Younge *vs.* Roberts, on ground that Wye, master of ship Garland, expelled Younge on aspersions of Roberts.   PRO.
    III.   *Ref:* Admiralty Court, Instance and Prize, Libels 81, No. 256.

381. Doctor Donne. A letter to Sir Thos. Roe, giving particulars concerning his sermon before the King and Virginia Company.   PRO.
    VII.   *Ref:* State Papers, Domestic, James I, Vol. 134, No. 59.

382.* John Marten. "The Requests of my brother John Marten to the Virginia Cõpany: his offer touch. that Cõpany."   BM. [LC]
    III.   *Ref:* Additional MSS., 12496, fo. 452. (Caesar Papers.)

383.* Governor and Council in Virginia. Proclamation of governor and council in Virginia against engrossing commodities.   LC.
    IV.   *Ref:* MS. Rec. Virginia Co., III, pt. ii, p. 47.

DECEMBER 15

384.* Jhδ. [John] Martin. "The manner howe to bringe the Indians into subiection wthout makinge an utter extirpation of them together wth the reasons."   BM. [LC]
VI.   *Ref:* Additional MSS., 12496, fos. 459–460. (Caesar Papers.)

385.* —— "The manner howe Virginia may be made a Royall plantation——."   BM. [LC]
VI.   *Ref:* Additional MSS., 12496, fos. 456–457. (Caesar Papers.)

DECEMBER 17

386. Council for New England. Letter to be written to the treasurer of Virginia Company against Jones for robbing natives of New England of their furs and taking some prisoners.
VI.   *Ref:* State Papers, Colonial, James I, Vol. II, pp. 24–25.   PRO.
         Pub: Sainsbury, *Calendar of State Papers, Colonial*, p. 35.

DECEMBER 18

387. Sir Thomas Coventry. Sir Thomas Coventry (attorney general) to the Earl of Middlesex, returning the Proclamation for Tobacco, corrected.   KP.
VII.   *Ref:* MSS. of Earl De La Warr.
         Pub: Calendar: Hist. MSS. Com., *Fourth Report*, p. 315.

[WINTER]

388. Captain Butler. Captain Butler's Dismasking of Virginia.   (1) LC. (2) PRO. [NY]
IV.   *Ref:* (1) MS. Court Book, Virginia Co., II, 271–2. (2) State Papers, Colonial, James I, Vol. II, No. 20.
         Pub: (1) Kingsbury *Rec. Virginia Co.*, II. (2) Brock, *Virginia Company*, II, 171–173. (3) Sainsbury, *Calendar of State Papers*, p. 39.

1623

389.* Governor and Council of Virginia. Petition to the King for the grant of the sole importation of tobacco to them and to Somers Island.   PRO.
III.   *Ref:* State Papers, Colonial, James I, Vol. I, p 5.
         Pub: Sainsbury, *Calendar of State Papers*, p. 56.

[1622/3]

390. Paper touching the discussion of salaries in the Summer Islands company.   PRO.
II.   *Ref:* Manchester Papers, No. 300.
         Pub: Hist. MSS. Com., *Eighth Report*, pt. 2, p. 38.

1623 (?)

391.* Proportion of the charge to furnish and transport six men to Virginia, estimated at £114 19^s. 6^d.
III.   *Ref:* State Papers, Colonial, James I, Vol. II, No. 54.   PRO. [NY]
         Pub: Sainsbury, *Calendar of State Papers, Colonial*, p. 56.
         Transcript New York Public Library, Bancroft, II, fos. 5–7.

1623

392.* Petition for a warrant by the late Undertakers for the importation of Tobacco. At council it was agreed that the Undertakers should receive 3 d. per pound on 28000 pounds.
III.   *Ref:* MSS. of Earl De La Warr.   KP.
         Pub: Calendar: Hist. MSS. Comm., *Fourth Report*, p. 283.

1623 (?) OR 1617

393.* The King. Order to Archbishops of Canterbury and York, requiring them to arrange for the collection of liberal contributions, so that the Undertakers of the Virginia plantation may erect churches and schools.   PRO.

    I.   *Ref:* State Papers, Colonial, James I, Vol. II, No. 37.

        Pub: (1) Anderson, *History of the Church of England in the Colonies*, pp. 315–316.   (2) Sainsbury, *Calendar of State Papers, Colonial*, p. 49.

          Date in Sainsbury, 1623, but given by Alexander Brown, 1617.

1623 (?)

EARLY

394.* Mr. Gibbs. To Sir E. Sa[nd]. Notes of proceedings before Lords Commissioners concerning Captain Butler's unmasking of Virginia, Thomas Smith's records, the "black box," etc.

    I.   *Ref:* Ferrar Papers.   MC. [LC]

        Indorsement in the autograph of John Ferrar. Photographic reproduction in the Library of Congress.

395.* Alderman Johnson. "Alderman Johnsons Declaratione of the Prosperous estate of the Colony duringe Sr Th. Smiths tyme of Gouerment."   (1) LC.   (2) PRO.   [LC]

    III.   *Ref:* (1) MS. Rec. Virginia Co., III, pt. 1, p. 4. (2) Manchester Papers, Nos. 344–346.

        The Manchester paper gives the conclusion.

1622/3 (?)

396.* Statement of advantages to Virginia and Summer Island companies of a contract in force compared with a previous period from 1619.   PRO.

      Ref: Manchester Papers, No. 311.

      Pub: Calendar: Hist. MSS. Com., *Eighth Report*, pt. 2, p. 38.

        Autograph of Edward Collingwood (?).

1622/3

BETWEEN JANUARY AND APRIL

397.* John Robinson's son. Petition to Governor Wyatt.   LC.

    IV.   *Ref:* MS. Rec. Virginia Co., III, pt. ii, p. 58.[a]

JANUARY 3

398.* Governor in Virginia. Instructions by governor and captain general of Virginia to Tucker concerning trade.   LC.

    IV.   *Ref:* MS. Rec. Virginia Co., III, pt. ii, p. 36.

JANUARY 4

399.* Charles Harmoun. Petition to Governor Wyatt.   LC.

    IV.   *Ref:* MS. Rec. Virginia Co., III, pt. ii, p. 38.

JANUARY 20

400.* Virginia Council. Letter from Council in Virginia to Virginia Company of London, acknowledging arms sent, and defending colonists for acts in massacre.   LC.

    IV.   *Ref:* MS. Rec. Virginia Co., III, pt. ii, pp. 4–5.[a]

        Pub: Neill, *Virginia Company of London*, pp. 363–376.

401.* **Privy Council.**   Order that John Bargrave forbear troubling Sir Thomas Smith.   PC.
    I.   *Ref:* Privy Council Register, James I, Vol. V, p. 564.

402.* **George Harrison.**   Letter to his brother, John Harrison.   Accounts with Mr. Bennett.   PRO.
    VI.   *Ref:* State Papers, Colonial, James I, Vol. II, No. 17.
           Pub: Sainsbury, *Calendar of State Papers, Colonial*, p. 36.

403.* **The Governor,** Council, and Assembly of Virginia to the King, representing Capt. Nathan
       Butler's information entitled "The Unmasking of Virginia."   PRO.   [NY]
    IV.   *Ref:* State Papers, Colonial, James I, Vol. II, No. 20.
           Pub: Sainsbury, *Calendar of State Papers, Colonial*, p. 38.
              A. S.   Transcript.   New York Public Library.   Bancroft Papers, I, Fos. 497–527.

404.* **[Sir Nathan. Rich.]**   Rough notes touching the affairs of the Virginia and Summer Island
       Companies, especially the salary. (fragment).   PRO.
    VI.   *Ref:* Manchester Papers, No. 304.
           Pub: Calendar: Hist. MSS. Com., *Eighth Report*, pt. 2, p. 38.

405.* **Papers** touching discussion of salaries in the Summer Island Company, on Feb. 17, 1622/3,
       June 10, 1618.   PRO.
    II.   *Ref:* Manchester Papers, No. 309.
           Pub: Calendar: Hist. MSS. Com., *Eighth Report*, pt. 2, p. 38.

406.* **Privy Council.**   Order for a contract between the Lord Treasurer on behalf of King and the
       Virginia Company touching the importation of tobacco.   (1) PC.   (2) PRO.
    I.   *Ref:* (1) Privy Council Register, James I, Vol. V, p. 583.   (2) Colonial Entry Book,
              Vol. 79, p. 203.
           Pub: Sainsbury, *Calendar of State Papers, Colonial*, p. 37.

407.   **Mr. Wrote.**   Mr. Wrote's Project concerning salaries.   LC.
    II.   *Ref:* MS. Court Book, Virginia Co., II, 136.
           Pub: Kingsbury, *Rec. Virginia Co.*, II.

408.   **Objections** against the salaries.   LC.
    II.   *Ref:* MS. Court Book, Virginia Co., II, 168–169.
           Pub: Kingsbury, *Rec. Virginia Co.*, II.

409.* **Governor of Virginia.**   Order or warrant demanding sassafras, 60,000 pounds, to be sent
       home.   LC.
    IV.   *Ref:* MS. Rec. Virginia Co., III, pt. ii, p. 51ᵃ.

410.   **Proposition** agreed on by the Lord High Treasurer of England and the Company of Virginia
       and the Summer Islands touching the sole importation of tobacco.   KP.
    III.   *Ref:* Duke of Dorset Collection.
           Pub: Peckard, *Memoirs of Nicholas Ferrar.*

411.* **[Sir Nathan. Rich.]** First Rough Draft of a proposition for the advancement of His Majesty's profit, and the good of Virginia and the Summer Islands by settling the trade of tobacco.
$\qquad$ PRO.
    III.   *Ref:* Manchester Papers, Nos. 312, 313.
            Pub: Calendar: Hist. MSS. Com., *Eighth Report*, pt. 2, p. 38.

412. **Paper** touching the discussion of salaries in the Summer Islands Company.$\qquad$PRO.
    VII.   *Ref:* Manchester Papers, No. 310.
            Pub: Calendar: Hist. MSS. Com., *Eighth Report*, pt. 2, p. 38.

1622/3, MARCH, TO 1624, JULY

413.* **Rough** notes of an estimate of the value to the King for a year of the proposed preemption of tobacco and pepper.$\qquad$PRO.
    III.   *Ref:* Manchester Papers, No. 314.
            Pub: Calendar: Hist. MSS. Com., *Eighth Report*, pt. 2, p. 38.

[MARCH]

414.* **[Sir Nathan. Rich.]** Notes on the Tobacco Contract.$\qquad$PRO.
    III.   *Ref:* Manchester Papers, No. 316.
             Pub: Calendar: Hist. MSS. Com., *Eighth Report*, pt. 2, p. 39.

MARCH

415.* **G. S.[andys]?** A letter to Mr. Farrer by the "Hopewell."$\qquad$PRO.
    IV.   *Ref:* Manchester Papers, No. 318.
            Pub: Hist. MSS. Com., *Eighth Report*, pt. 2, p. 39.
               A. L. S. Photograph of autograph in the Library of Congress.

MARCH 4

416. **Privy Council.** Order concerning the importation of goods from colony to enforce order of October 21, 1621.$\qquad$(1) LC. (2) PRO. (3) PC. [NY]
    II.   *Ref:* (1) MS. Court Book, Virginia Co., II, 232–233. (2) Colonial Entry Book, Vol. 79, p. 203. (3) Privy Council Register, James I, Vol. V, p. 618.
           Pub: (1) Kingsbury, *Rec. Virginia Co.*, Vol. II. (2) Brock, *Virginia Company*, II, 126–127. (3) Sainsbury, *Calendar of State Papers, Colonial*, p. 40.

417.* **Governor in Virginia.** Order of the governor and captain-general of Virginia to keep the 22d of March holy, forever after. Date of the massacre.$\qquad$LC.
    IV.   *Ref:* MS. Rec. Virginia Co., III, pt. ii, p. 51ª.

MARCH 5

418. **Virginia Colony.** Petition to King concerning the tobacco trade.$\qquad$LC.
    II.   *Ref:* MS. Court Book, Virginia Co., II, 221.
           Pub: (1) Kingsbury, *Rec. Virginia Co.*, Vol. II. (2) Brock, *Virginia Company*, II, 221.

MARCH 5

419.* **Frethorne.** Copy of a letter from Frethorne to Bateman, describing the distress of the colony due to the massacre.$\qquad$PRO.
    VI.   *Ref:* Manchester Papers, No. 317.

MARCH 7

420. **Virginia Company.** Answer to Privy Council, concerning importation of goods and tobacco from colony.$\qquad$LC.
    II.   *Ref:* MS. Court Book, Virginia Co., II, 236–237.
           Pub: (1) Kingsbury, *Rec. Virginia Co.*, II. (2) Brock, *Virginia Company*, II, 130–131.

421. * **Order** of court for Virginia and Summer Island, concerning Lord Cavendish's ommission of a part of Lord Treasurer's Speech at Counsell Table touching Alderman Johnson.

    II.   *Ref:* Ferrar Papers.   MC. [LC]

        Photographic reproduction in Library of Congress.
        Signed by Ed. Collingwood. Indorsed in autograph of Collingwood.

422. * **A rough** draft of above.   MC. LC.

    II.   *Ref:* Ferrar Papers.

        Indorsed in Collingwood's and John Ferrar's writing.
        Holograph of Ed. Collingwood.

MARCH 17

423. * **Extraordinary** court of Sumer Island, concerning the grievances of inhabitants of Summer Island. Part of the blurred book (?).   MC. [LC]

    II.   *Ref:* Ferrar Papers.

        Photographic reproduction and transcript in the Library of Congress.
        Marginal entries in autograph of John Ferrar.

MARCH 20

424. * **Reasons** offered to Privy Council against Sir Edwin Sandys's contract and joint stock for the Virginia and Summer Island tobacco, and against monopoly of tobacco.   PRO. [NY]

    III.   *Ref:* State Papers, Colonial, James I, Vol. III, No. 10.

        Pub: Sainsbury, *Calendar of State Papers, Colonial*, p. 59.

        Transcript: New York Public Library, Bancroft Papers, II, 413–429.
        Date in Sainsbury, March 20, 1623/4. On MS. in contemporary writing, March 20, 1622/3.

MARCH 24

425. **Virginia Company.** Petition to the Privy Council concerning importation of tobacco. LC.

    III.   *Ref:* MS. Court Book, Virginia Co., II, 244–248.

        Pub: (1) Kingsbury, *Rec. Virginia Co.*, Vol. II. (2) Brock, *Virginia Company*, II, 137–143.

MARCH 27

426. * **[Lord Treasurer Middlesex.]** Copy of a letter to officers and farmers of customs, and to Abraham and John Jacob, the collectors who had delayed the passing of the tobacco in a ship from the Bermudas.   PRO.

    I.   *Ref:* Manchester Papers, No. 293.

        Pub: Calendar: Hist. MSS. Com., *Eighth Report*, pt. 2, p. 37.

1623

MARCH 28

427. * **George Sandys.** Letter from George Sandys to Samuel Wrote.   PRO.

    IV.   *Ref:* Manchester Papers, No. 319.

        Pub: Neill, E., *Virginia Vetusta*, pp. 122–127. Calendar: Hist., MSS. Com., *Eighth Report*, pt. 2, p. 39.

        Holograph.

428. **Samuel Matthews.** A letter concerning the property of Thomas Sheffield, and his son, who was tongue-tied.   PRO.

    III.   *Ref:* Admiralty Court, Instance and Prize, Libels 80, No. 118.

MARCH 30

429.* **George Sandys.** A letter to his brother, Sir Samuel Sandys, imputing the cause of "theyr ill proceedings to ye directions from hence." PRO.

    IV.   *Ref:* Manchester Papers, No. 320.

          Pub: Calendar: Hist. MSS. Com., *Eighth Report*, pt. 2, p. 39.

430.* —— A letter to his brother, Sir Miles Sandys, complaining that the colony would have been strong had they settled close together. PRO.

    IV.   *Ref:* Manchester Papers, No. 321.

          Pub: Calendar: Hist. MSS. Com., *Eighth Report*, pt. 2, p. 39.

431.* **Virginia Council.** Virginia Council to Lord Treasurer Mandeville, concerning tobacco.

    III.   *Ref:* State Papers, Colonial, James I, Vol. II, No. 21.   PRO. [NY]

          Pub: Sainsbury, *Calendar of State Papers, Colonial*, p. 41.

Transcript: New York Public Library, Bancroft Papers, II, folios 9–13.

MARCH 31

432.* **William Capp.** A letter to John Ferrar complaining of George Sandys, approving the governor, and censuring the company. PRO.

    IV.   *Ref:* Manchester Papers, No. 322.

          Pub: Calendar: Hist. MSS. Com., *Eighth Report*, pt. 2, p. 39.

[MARCH OR APRIL (?)]

433.* **William Capps.** A letter to Dr. Wynston, censuring the council. A friend of Captain Butler.

    VI.   *Ref:* Manchester Papers, No. 323.   PRO.

          Pub: Calendar: Hist. MSS. Com., *Eighth Report*, pt. 2, p. 39.

[APRIL?]

434.* [**Nathan. Rich**] Bargrave's charge against Sir Thomas Smyth, with answers in rough draft by [Nathan. Rich.] PRO.

    VI.   *Ref:* Manchester Papers, No. 351.

          Pub: Calendar: Hist. MSS. Com., *Eighth Report*, pt. 2, p. 43.

[APRIL OR MAY?]

435.* **Nathan. Butler.** A letter to Nathaniel Rich. PRO.

    VI.   *Ref:* Manchester Papers, No. 355.

          Pub: Calendar: Hist. MSS. Com., *Eighth Report*, pt. 2, pp. 43–44.

436.* **List** of names of persons fit to be Governor and Deputy Governor of Virginia and Summer Island Companies. PRO.

    VI.   *Ref:* Manchester Papers, Nos. 356, 357, 358, 359.

          Pub: Calendar: Hist. MSS. Com., *Eighth Report*, pt. 2, p. 44.

[APRIL–JUNE]

437.* [**Nathan. Rich**] Notes of the "lres from Virginia; all but Frethorne's, wch must be added out of the Coppy at large." PRO.

    VI.   *Ref:* Manchester Papers, No. 340.

          Pub: Calendar: Hist. MSS. Com., *Eighth Report*, pt. 2, p. 42.

BETWEEN APRIL AND MAY

438.* [**N. Rich**] Rough notes of heads and references to prove charges of mismanagement against the Sandys faction of the Virginia Company. PRO. [LC]

    VI.   *Ref:* Manchester Papers, No. 342.

          Pub: Calendar: Hist. MSS. Com., *Eighth Report*, pt. 2, p. 42.

439.* **Adventurers and Planters.** Complaint from adventurers and planters to His Majesty's commissioners against Sir Ed. Sandys et al. in the last four years of the government.
    III.   *Ref:* Manchester Papers, No. 343.   PRO.
            Pub: Calendar: Hist. MSS. Com., *Eighth Report*, pt. 2, p. 42.

440.* **[Alderman Johnson]** Part of a draft of a statement (under heads numbered 10–39) touching the miserable condition of Virginia and its causes.   PRO.
    VI.   *Ref:* Manchester Papers, Nos. 347, 348.
            Pub: Calendar: Hist. MSS. Com., *Eighth Report*, pt. 2, pp. 42–43.

441.* **Statement** "from attestation of divers sufficient understanding sea men" as to the bad condi tion in Virginia.   PRO-
    IV.   *Ref:* Manchester Papers, No. 349.
            Pub: Calendar: Hist. MSS. Com., *Eighth Report*, pt. 2, p. 43.

442.* **[N. Rich]** Beginning of rough draft of a certificate affirming the truth of statements of Captain Butler.   PRO.
    III.   *Ref:* Manchester Papers, No. 350.
            Pub: Calendar: Hist. MSS. Com., *Eighth Report*, pt. 2, p. 43.

443.* **Note** of the men sent to Virginia in Sir Thomas Smythe's time, over 600 "confessed," with names of ships conveying them.   PRO.
    VI.   *Ref:* Manchester Papers, No. 352.
            Pub: Calendar: Hist. MSS. Com., *Eighth Report*, pt. 2, p. 43.

444.* **Answer** of Adventurers and Planters in Virginia and Summer Islands to a petition exhibited to His Majesty by Lord Cavendish et al. in name of Companies.   PRO.
    III.   *Ref:* Manchester Papers, No. 353.
            Pub: Calendar: Hist. MSS. Com., *Eighth Report*, pt. 2, p. 43.

445. **Alderman Jonnson.** Petition of Adventurers and Planters to the King, praying the appoint ment of a commission to investigate the abuses of the Virginia affairs and propound a reform.   (1) PRO.   (2) LC.
    VI.   *Ref:* (1) Manchester Papers, No. 328.   (2) MS. Court Book of the Virginia Company, II, 270–271.
            Pub: (1) Kingsbury, *Records Virginia Co.*, II.   (2) Neill, *Virginia Company of Lon don*, pp. 387–389.   (3) Brock, *Virginia Company*, II, 169–170.
               The indorsement gives Alderman Johnson as the author. The autograph is quite different from Johnson's. This is recorded in the Court Book under the date of April 18.

446.* **"Names** of Adventurers that dislike yᵉ present proceedings of business in yᵉ Virginia and Somers Islands Companies."   PRO.
    VI.   *Ref:* Manchester Papers, No. 327.
            Pub: Brown, *Genesis*, II, 982.
               Indorsement in autograph of N. Rich.

447.* **"Articles** of Inquirie for the Councᵐ of Virginia" etc.   Addressed to Nath. Rich.   PRO.
    VI.   *Ref:* Manchester Papers, Nos. 331, 332, 333.
            Pub: Calendar: Hist. MSS. Com., *Eighth Report*, pt. 2, p. 40.
               Autograph similar to George Sandys's.

[APRIL?]

448.* Alderman Johnson. "Alderman Johnson's rough draught to a Cõmission & the petiĉon to his Mat͝ᵗ.'' PRO. [LC]
 VI. *Ref:* Manchester Papers, No. 329.
   Pub: Calendar: Hist. MSS. Com., *Eighth Report*, pt. 2, p. 40.
   Photograph of part in Library of Congress.

449.* Heads of inquiries in Virginia by commissioners there. PRO.
 VI. *Ref:* Manchester Papers, No. 334.
   Pub: Calendar: Hist. MSS. Com., *Eighth Report*, pt. 2, pp. 40–41.
   Autograph similar to John Harvey's.

450.* P. Arundle. Extract from letter of P. Arundle, recounting how Spilman was cut off by Indians, and attributing treachery to the example of Europeans. PRO.
 VI. *Ref:* Manchester Papers, No. 341.
   Pub: Calendar: Hist. MSS. Com., *Eighth Report*, pt. 2, p. 42.

451.* Account of a small supply sent to Virginia in the "Bonny Bess," April, 1623. NY.
 VI. *Ref:* Smyth of Nibley Papers, Smyth, 3 (38), p. 155.
   Pub: Catalogue: *N. Y. Pub. Lib. Bull.*, I, 157.
   In John Smith's autograph.

BETWEEN APRIL AND SEPTEMBER

452.* Samuel Moll. Petition to Governor Wyatt to sell and return to England. LC.
 IV. *Ref:* MS. Rec. Virginia Co., III, pt. ii, p. 59ᵃ.
453.* Thomas Passmore. Petition to Governor Wyatt concerning service of indentured servant.
 IV. *Ref:* MS. Rec. Virginia Co., III, pt. ii, p. 59. LC.
454.* Petition to Governor Wyatt by "Margaret and John's" Company, asking freedom from bond to Mr. Douglas. LC.
 IV. *Ref:* MS. Rec. Virginia Co., III, pt. ii, p. 59.

APRIL 2 AND 3

455.* Richard Frethorne. A copy of a letter to his father and mother, concerning suffering from want. PRO.
 VI. *Ref:* Manchester Papers, No. 325.
   Pub: Calendar: Hist. MSS. Com., *Eighth Report*, pt. 2, p. 40.

AFTER APRIL 4

456.* Council in Virginia. Letter from the Council in Virginia to the Virginia Company in London, telling of the recovery of the colony. LC.
 IV. *Ref:* MS. Rec. Virginia Co., III, pt. ii, p. 7.

APRIL 4

457.* Council in Virginia. Letter to Virginia Company of London, describing attempts for sassafras & silke-grass; return of planters to different houses, etc., and treaty with Indians.
 (1) LC. (2) PRO.
 IV. *Ref:* (1) MS. Rec. Virginia Co., III, pt. ii, pp. 6, 6ᵃ. (2) State Papers, Colonial, James I, Vol. II, No. 22.
   Pub: Sainsbury, *Calendar of State Papers, Colonial*, pp. 41–42.

APRIL 12

458. Virginia Company. Petition to the King concerning Alderman Johnson's petition. LC.
 III. *Ref:* MS. Court Book, Virginia Co., II, 263–264.
   Pub: (1) Kingsbury, *Rec. Virginia Co.*, II. (2) Brock, *Virginia Company*, II, 164.

APRIL 7

459.* Sir Francis Wyatt. A letter to John Ferrar, giving particulars of rebuilding of colony and
advising extinction of the Indians and martial law.   PRO. [NY]
  IV.   *Ref:* State Papers, Colonial, James I, Vol. II, No. 26.
         Pub: Sainsbury, *Calendar of State Papers, Colonial,* p. 42.
                Transcript, New York Public Library, Bancroft Papers, II, fos. 33–41.

APRIL 8

460.* George Sandys. A letter to John Ferrar, relating the distressed condition of the colony.
  IV.   *Ref:* State Papers, Colonial, James I, Vol. II, Nos. 27, 35.   PRO. [NY]
         Pub: Sainsbury, *Calendar of State Papers, Colonial,* p. 42.
                No. 35 is an autograph letter and is indorsed Sandys to the Company. Transcript, New York
                Public Library, Bancroft Papers, II, fos. 45–59.

APRIL 11

461.* George Sandys. A letter to John Ferrar.   .   PRO.
  IV.   *Ref:* Manchester Papers, No. 326.
         Pub: Calendar: Hist. MSS. Com., *Eighth Report,* pt. 2, p. 40.

APRIL 12

462. Virginia Company. A relation to the King concerning the proceedings of colonies.
                                                                    (1) LC.   (2) PRO.
  III.   *Ref:* (1) MS. Court Book, Virginia Co., II, 255–263.   (2) Manchester Papers, No. 360.
         Pub: (1) Kingsbury, *Rec. Virginia Co.,* II.   (2) Brock, *Virginia Company,* II, 152–162.
         (3) Calendar: Hist. MSS. Com., *Eighth Report,* pt. 2, p. 44.
463. —— A declaration of the present state of Virginia presented to the King.   LC.
  III.   *Ref:* MS. Court Book, Virginia Co., II, 253.
         Pub: (1) Kingsbury, *Rec. Virginia Co.,* II.   (2) Brock, *Virginia Company,* II, 148–151.

APRIL 14

464.* Christopher Davison. A letter to John Ferrar concerning the arrival of the "Margaret and
John" in distress from an attack by the Spanish.   PRO. [NY]
  IV.   *Ref:* State Papers, Colonial, James I, Vol. II, No. 28.
         Pub: (1) *Virginia Mag. of Hist.,* VI, 243–244.   (2) Sainsbury, *Calendar of State Papers,
         Colonial,* p. 43.
                Transcript, New York Public Library, Bancroft Papers, II, fos. 61–65.

465.* [Nathan. Rich.] Draft of instructions to the commissioners to investigate the Virginia affairs.
  VI.   *Ref:* Manchester Papers, No. 330.   PRO.
         Pub: Calendar: Hist. MSS. Com., *Eighth Report,* pt. 2, p. 40.

APRIL 15

466.* Captain Kendall. A letter from the Summer Islands to Sir Ed. Sandys telling of the blowing
up of the "Seaflower," bound for Virginia.   MC. [LC]
  IV.   *Ref:* Ferrar Papers.
                A. L. S.   Photographic reproduction of part and transcript in the Library of Congress.

APRIL 17

467.* Privy Council. An order that, upon hearing Lord Cavendish and others, representatives, a
commission be appointed to inquire into the true state of Virginia and Somers Island
plantations.   PC.
  I.   *Ref:* Privy Council Register, James I, Vol. V, pp. 668–669.
         Pub: (1) LeFroy, *Memorials of the Bermudas,* I, 289–290.   (2) Sainsbury, *Calendar of
         State Papers, Colonial,* p. 44.

APRIL 18

468. Lord Treasurer Middlesex. A letter to Secretary Conway, concerning proceedings in Privy Council for the King's information respecting the differences of the two companies of Virginia and Somers Islands. PRO.
    I.   *Ref:* State Papers, Domestic, James I, Addenda, Vol. 43.
        Pub: (1) LeFroy, *Memorials of the Bermudas*, I, 290–291. (2) Sainsbury, *Calendar of State Papers, Colonial*, p. 44.

APRIL 19

469. John Chamberlain. A letter to Sir Dudley Carleton concerning the great faction in the Virginia Company. PRO.
    VII.   *Ref:* State Papers, Domestic, James I, Vol. 143, No. 22.
        Pub: Sainsbury, *Calendar of State Papers, Colonial*, p. 44.

APRIL 21

470.* "**Coppie** of the Courte books deliuered by order of the Lords of his Maties Counsell to the Secretary." A Receipt for Court Books from Jan. 28, 1606, to April 2, 1623.
    III.   *Ref:* Ferrar Papers. MC. [LC]
        Photographic Reproduction in the Library of Congress.

471.* "**A Memoriall** of some things wch it may please the lls to insert in their Lo^ps letters to Virginia and the Summer Islands." PRO.
    VI.   *Ref:* Manchester Papers, No. 335.
        Pub: Calendar: Hist. MSS. Com., *Eighth Report*, pt. 2, p. 41.
        Indorsed in Autograph of N. Rich: "deliv. by me to the L. Treas."

APRIL 23, 25

472.* John Wright. A petition to Governor Wyatt demanding that Mr. Douglas deliver certain goods to him which he had had in partnership with Mr. Langley, deceased, master of ship.
    IV.   *Ref:* MS. Rec. Virginia Co., III, pt. ii, p. 59. LC.

APRIL 24 AND MAY 3

473.* Petition to Governor Wyatt and Council in Virginia by passengers in the Margaret and John complaining of evil treatment. LC.
    IV.   *Ref:* MS. Rec. Virginia Co., III, pt. ii, p. 58ª.

APRIL 24

474. Lord Treas. Middlesex. Lord Treas. Middlesex to Secretary Conway, stating that the draft of the Ireland and Virginia commissioners is ready. PRO.
    VII.   *Ref:* State Papers, Domestic, James I, Vol. 143, No. 60.
        Pub: Calendar: *State Papers, Domestic*, Vol. 143.

APRIL 26 AND MAY 3

475.* John Loyde. Petition to Governor and Council in Virginia demanding freedom from apprenticement to Langley. LC.
    IV.   *Ref:* MS. Rec. Virginia Co., III, pt. ii., p. 59.

APRIL 28

476.* Privy Council. Order disallowing the letters of the Virginia Company to the colony and dissolving the tobacco contract. (1) PC. (2) & (3) LC.
    I.   *Ref:* (1) Privy Council Register, James I, Vol. V, p. 674. (2) MS. Rec. Virginia Co., III, pt. i, p. 1ª. (3) Instructions, Commission, and Letters, 1606–1683, pp. 61–62.
        Pub: (1) LeFroy, *Memorials of the Bermudas*, I, 293–294. (2) Sainsbury, *Calendar of State Papers, Colonial*, p. 45.

477.* **Privy Council.** Letter to "Governor, Council and Colony in Virginia," urging care of fortifications, provisions, and habitations.   (1) & (3) LC.   (2) PRO.   (4) PC.   [NY]
    I.   *Ref:* (1) MS. Rec. Virginia Co., III, pt. i, p. 1.   (2) Colonial Entry Book, Vol. 79,
p. 205.   (3) Instructions, Commissions, Letters, 1606–1683, pp. 59–60.   (4) Privy
Council Register, James I, Vol. V, p. 675.
        Pub: Sainsbury, *Calendar of State Papers, Colonial,* p. 45.
        Transcript, New York Public Library, Bancroft Papers, II, fos. 93–95.

478.* ——— Letter to the "Councell in Virginia," announcing Act of Court in London concerning
Tobacco.   LC.   PRO.
    I.   *Ref:* (1) Colonial Entry Book, Vol. 79, p. 204.   (2) Privy Council Register, James I,
Vol. V, p. 674.
        Pub: Sainsbury, *Calendar of State Papers, Colonial,* p. 45.

479.* ——— Copy of a letter to the Governor of Virginia, sent by "Bonny Bess."   MC.
    I.   *Ref:* Ferrar Papers.

480. **Planters.** Answer of Planters to Captain Butler's "Unmasked face of Virginia" as it was
written in 1622.   LC.
    IV.   *Ref:* MS. Court Book, Virginia Co., II, 275–277.
        Pub: (1) Kingsbury, *Rec. Virginia Co.,* II.   (2) Neill, *Virginia Company of London,*
pp. 395–404.   (3) Brock, *Virginia Company,* II, 175–183.

APRIL 29

481.* **Governor in Virginia.** Proclamation calling for labor on the fort at Wariscoyack.   LC.
    IV.   *Ref:* MS. Rec. Virginia Co., III, pt. ii, p. 50ᵃ.

[MAY ?]

482.* **Nicholas Ferrar.** Nicholas Ferrar's computation by which he would prove that to pay but
9ᵈ per pound for Planters' tobacco and bring all in is worse than before to pay 12ᵈ and
be at liberty to bring in what we will.   PRO.
    VI.   *Ref:* Colonial Entry Book, Vol. 74, p. 204.   Manchester Papers, No. 354.
        Pub: Calendar: Hist. MSS. Com., *Eighth Report,* pt. 2, p. 43.
        Indorsed in autograph of Nath. Rich.

483.* **"A Briefe** Answere to a declaraçon made and delivered to his Matie" in Easter week, concerning accusations against the colony.   PRO.
    VI.   *Ref:* Manchester Papers, Nos. 361, 362.
        Pub: Calendar: Hist. MSS. Com., *Eighth Report,* pt. 2, pp. 44, 45.
        No. 361 is in Nathaniel Rich's autograph. No. 362 is in that of Alderman Johnson.

484.* **[Nicholas] Farrar.** "The names of divers Knights, Citizens and Burgesses of Lower House of
Commons that are Adventurers and Free of Virginia Compagny and yet have not
followed the bussiness for sundry yeares."   PRO.
    VI.   *Ref:* Manchester Papers, No. 371.
        Pub: Calendar: Hist. MSS. Com., *Eighth Report,* pt. 2, p. 46.
        Autograph of Nicholas Ferrar. Indorsed in autograph of N. Rich as "by Mr. Farrar."

[MAY]

485.* ⌊**Nath. Rich?**⌋ Heads of two letters to be written to Virginia Company by Mr. Secretary,
declaring His Majesty's pleasure respecting restraint of factious persons, and suggesting
limitation of adventurers.   PRO.
    VI.   *Ref:* Manchester Papers, Nos. 372, 373.
        Pub: Calendar: Hist. MSS. Com., *Eighth Report,* pt. 2, p. 46.

486.* **The Petition** and the heads of suggested answer to an intended petition of the Virginia Company to the King to reconsider his letter respecting constitution of their courts.　　PRO.
　　VI.　*Ref:* Manchester Papers, Nos. 374, 375.
　　　　Pub: Calendar: Hist. MSS. Com., *Eighth Report*, pt. 2, p. 46.

487.* **Alderman Johnson.** Draft of Mr. Johnson's observations on the mode of interpreting his Majesty's letter, adopted by some members of the [Virginia] court.　　PRO.
　　VI.　*Ref:* Manchester Papers, No. 377.
　　　　Pub: Calendar: Hist. MSS. Com., *Eighth Report*, pt. 2, p. 46.

488.* **Adventurers and Planters.** Petition to the Privy Council by sundry adventurers and planters of the Virginia and Summer Islands Companies, concerning unjust accusations, read by Nicholas Ferrar on April 30.　　PRO.
　　III.　*Ref:* Manchester Papers, No. 363.
　　　　Pub: Calendar: Hist. MSS. Com., *Eighth Report*, pt. 2, p. 45.

MAY 2

489.* **Virginia Company.** Letter to the Governor and Council in Virginia, concerning commodities and the tobacco contract. Revised by the Privy Council.　　LC.
　　III.　*Ref:* MS. Rec. Virginia Co., III, pt. ii, p. 27. *a* Instructions, Commissions and Letters, 1606–1683, pp. 110–112.
　　　　Pub: Neill, *Virginia Company of London*, 391–394.

MAY 4

490.* **Anthony Hilton.** A letter to his mother, concerning the colony.　　PRO.
　　VI.　*Ref:* Manchester Papers, No. 364.
　　　　Pub: Calendar: Hist. MSS. Com., *Eighth Report*, pt. 2, p. 45.

MAY 7

491. **Virginia Company.** True answer to Captain Butler's "The Unmasked face of our colonie in Virginia."　　(1) LC.　(2) BM. PRO.
　　III.　*Ref:* (1) MS. Court Book, Virginia Co., II, 286–287.　(2) Sloane, 1039, fo. 92 (part of the document).
　　　　Pub: (1) Kingsbury, *Rec. Virginia Co.*, II.　(2) Brock, *Virginia Company*, II, 191–194.

492. **Virginia Council.** Declaration to his Majesty by the Counsell for Virginia [in London], concerning dissentions in the companies.　　LC.
　　III.　*Ref:* MS. Court Book, Virginia Co., II, 288–298.
　　　　Pub: (1) Kingsbury, *Rec. Virginia Co.*, II.　(2) Brock, *Virginia Company*, II, 195–205.

493. **Planters and Adventurers.** The answer of planters and adventurers to Alderman Johnson's petition.　　LC.
　　III.　*Ref:* MS. Court Book, Virginia Co., II, 283–285.
　　　　Pub: (1) Kingsbury, *Rec. Virginia Co.*, II.　(2) Brock, *Virginia Company*, II, 186–191.

494. **Virginia and Summer Islands Companies.** Petition to King requesting thorough investigation of Virginia affairs and the return of their records, sequestered 14 days since.　　LC.
　　III.　*Ref:* MS. Court Book, Virginia Co., II, 299.
　　　　Pub: (1) Kingsbury, *Rec. Virginia Co.*, II.　(2) Brock, *Virginia Company*, II, 205–207.

MAY [BETWEEN 7 AND 13]

495.* **Adventurers and Planters.** Petition of "sundry adventurers and planters of the Virginia and Summer Islands Companies to Privy Council to command Lord Cavendish, Sr E. Sandys, Mr. John and Nicholas Farrar to appear with certain writings of May 7."　　PRO. [LC]
　　III.　*Ref:* Manchester papers, No. 366.
　　　　Pub: Calendar: Hist. MSS. Com., *Eighth Report*, pt. 2, p. 45.

MAY 8

496.* Secretary Conway. A letter to Sir Ed. Sackville, from Theobalds, concerning the petition
   on behalf of Virginia.   PRO.
  VI. *Ref:* State Papers, Domestic, James I, Vol. 214.
     Pub: Sainsbury, *Calendar of State Papers, Colonial,* p. 45.

497.* ————. A letter to Secretary Calvert, from Theobalds, to hasten the passing of the commission concerning Virginia.
  I. *Ref:* State Papers, Domestic, James I, Vol. 214.
     Pub: Sainsbury, *Calendar of State Papers, Colonial,* p. 45.

[PROBABLY BEFORE MAY 7]

498.* Governor in Virginia. Proclamation of the governor and captain-general of Virginia to be
   careful of the savage treachery.   LC.
    Ref: MS. Records, Virginia Co., III, pt. ii, p. 47ᵃ.

MAY 9

499.* Privy Council. Commission to Sir William Jones, Sir Nicholas Fortescue, Sir Thomas Gofton,
   Sir Richard Sutton, Sir William Pitt, Sir Henry Bourchier, and Sir Henry Spiller to
   investigate the conditions of disputes in Virginia, and report method of procedure.
             (1) BM. (2) PRO. (3) LC.
  I. *Ref:* (1) Additional MSS., 29975, fos. 63–64. (2) Docquet Book, Signet Office, Vol. 7;
    Patent Roll 21, James I, 19th part. (3) Virginia Misc. Records (Bland copy),
    pp. 126–132.

500.* Governor in Virginia. Proclamation by the governor and captain-general of Virginia for
   planting sufficient corn.   LC.
  IV. *Ref:* MS. Rec. Virginia Co., III, pt. ii, p.

MAY 11

501.* Governor in Virginia. Commission by governor and captain-general of Virginia to Captain
   Smith to build a fort at Warosquayak.   LC.
  IV. *Ref:* MS. Rec. Virginia Co., III, pt. ii, p. 40.

MAY 12

502.* Governor in Virginia. Commission by governor and captain-general of Virginia to Gilbert
   Peppet to trade with yᵉ Indians.   LC.
  IV. *Ref:* MS. Rec. Virginia Co., III, pt. ii, p. 40.

503.* ————. Commission by governor of Virginia to Capt. Ralph Tucker to go against the
   Indians.   LC.
  IV. *Ref:* MS. Rec. Virginia Co., III, pt. ii, p. 50ᵃ.

MAY 13

504.* Governor in Virginia. Warrant of governor in Virginia for sending every twentieth man
   to work on the fort at Wariscayack.   LC.
  IV. *Ref:* MS. Rec. Virginia Co., III, pt. ii, p. 51ᵃ.

505.* Privy Council. Order demanding that John and Nicholas Ferrar, of the Virginia Company,
   be confined to houses till further order, as guilty of contempt of Order of Council Table.
                (1) PRO. (2) PC.
  I. *Ref:* (1) Colonial Entry Book, Vol. 79, pp. 205–206. (2) Privy Council Register, James
    I, Vol. V, p. 699.
    Pub: (1) Brown, *First Republic,* 526. (2) Sainsbury, *Calendar of State Papers,*
    Colonial, pp. 45–46.

MAY 14

506.* Secretary Calvert. A letter to the Earl of Southampton, notifying the Virginia Company not to proceed with election of officers until the pleasure of King be known.

I.   *Ref:* State Papers, Colonial, James I, Vol. II, No. 29.   PRO.   [NY]
      Pub: Sainsbury, *Calendar of State Papers, Colonial*, p. 46.
        Transcript: New York Public Library, Bancroft Papers, II, fos. 101-2.

507.* Secretary Sir George Calvert. A letter to Secretary Conway, stating that election of officers of Virginia Company is ordered postponed by King in Council till next court.

VII.   *Ref:* State Papers, Domestic, James I, Vol. 144, No. 45.   PRO.
      Pub: Sainsbury, *Calendar of State Papers, Colonial*, p. 46.

MAY 16

508.* [Nathan Rich.] "Note which I presently took of Captain John Bargrave's discourse to me concerning Sir Edwin Sandys."   PRO.

VI.   *Ref:* Manchester Papers, No. 368.
      Pub: Calendar: Hist. MSS. Com., *Eighth Report*, pt. 2, p. 45.

MAY 18

509. The King. Letter to the Virginia Company concerning the appointment of Commissioners.

I.   *Ref:* MS. Court Book, Virginia Co., II, 317–318.   LC.
      Pub: (1) Kingsbury, *Rec. Virginia Co.*, II.   (2) Brock, *Virginia Company*, II, 217.

MAY 18, 21

510.* Privy Council. Orders releasing Lord Cavendish, Sir Edwin Sandys, and John and Nicholas Ferrar.   PC.

I.   *Ref:* Privy Council Register, James I, Vol. I, p. 709.

[AFTER MAY 18]

511.* Virginia Company. Reasons alleged to persuade the King to reconsider his letter of May 18 not permitting members of Company to meet unless having planters in Virginia.

III.   *Ref:* Manchester Papers, No. 376.   PRO.
      Pub: Calendar: Hist. MSS. Com., *Eighth Report*, pt. 2, p. 46.
       For the petition formulated, see *ante* No. 482.

MAY 20

512.* The King. Copy of a letter to Governor and Company of Summer Islands to keep meetings and place distinct from Virginia Company, and concerning choice of officers.   PRO.

I.   *Ref:* Manchester Papers, No. 369.
      Pub: Calendar: Hist. MSS. Com., *Eighth Report*, pt. 2, p. 45.

MAY 22

513.* Privy Council. Order demanding that all records of Virginia and Somers Islands Companies be delivered to the Commissioners, and that packets from the Colonies be opened by the Commissioners hereafter and be disposed of at will.   (1) PRO.   (2) PC.

I.   *Ref:* (1) Colonial Entry Book, Vol. 79, pp. 206–207.   (2) Privy Council Register, James I, Vol. V, p. 714.
      Pub: (1) Brown, A., *First Republic*, pp. 532–533.   (2) Sainsbury, *Calendar of State Papers, Colonial*, p. 46.

MAY 29

514.* Governor in Virginia. Commission by governor and captain-general of Virginia to Captain Pierce to be captain of ye guard.   LC.

IV.   *Ref:* MS. Rec. Virginia Co., III, pt. ii, p. 40ᵃ.

16455—VOL 1—06——12

515.* Draft of a preliminary report of the commissioners on the condition of the colony of Virginia.
    VI.   *Ref:* Manchester Papers, No. 382.   PRO.
        Pub: Calendar: Hist. MSS. Com., *Eighth Report*, pt. 2, p. 46.

516.* [N. Rich.] Rough draft of a project for the better government of the colony and company.
    VI.   *Ref:* Manchester Papers, No. 381.   PRO. [LC]
        Pub: Calendar: Hist. MSS. Com., *Eighth Report*, pt. 2, p. 46.

517.* Virginia Council. Treasurer and council for Virginia to the Privy Council concerning Capt.
    John Bargrave's Petition.   PRO.
    III.   *Ref:* State Papers, Colonial, James I, Vol. II, No. 7.
        Pub: Sainsbury, *Calendar of State Papers, Colonial*, p. 30.

518.* List of 72 patents granted to several persons named, all of whom have divers partners "whose
    names and several shares we do not know."   PRO.
    III.   *Ref:* State Papers, Colonial, James I, Vol. II, No. 33.
        Pub: (1) Brown, *First Republic*, pp. 628–630. (2) Sainsbury, *Calendar of State Papers, Colonial*, p. 47.

519.* List of shareholders in Virginia Company, with the number of shares and reason for allot-
    ment—by purchase or otherwise, March, 1616–June, 1623.   PRO.
    III.   *Ref:* State Papers, Colonial, James I, Vol. II, No. 33.
        Pub: (1) *Virginia Mag. of Hist*, IV, 299–310. (2) Sainsbury, *Calendar of State Papers, Colonial*, p. 47.

520. The King. Letter to the Virginia Company.   (1) LC. (2) PRO.
    I.   *Ref:* (1) MS. Court Book, Virginia Co., II, 319. (2) Manchester Papers, No. 378.
        Pub: (1) Kingsbury, *Rec. Virginia Co.*, II. (2) Brock, *Virginia Company*, II, 218–219.
        (3) Calendar: Hist. MSS. Com., *Eighth Report*, pt. 2, p. 46.
          The document in Manchester papers is indorsed "Vera Copia" and bears the autograph
          signature of Ed: Collingwood, Secre.

521.* Examination of Captain Isaac and Mary Madison and Serjeant John Harris, taken before Sir
    Francis Wyatt, Governor, and the Council of Virginia, and Christopher Davison,
    Secretary, touching supposed contract of marriage three or four days after husband's
    death; since she has disavowed said contract and formed a new one with William
    Ferrar.   PRO.
    IV.   *Ref:* State Papers, Colonial, James I, Vol. II, No. 30.
        Pub: (1) Brown, *First Republic*, 563–565. (2) Sainsbury, *Calendar of State Papers, Colonial*, p. 46.
          Signed: "Extract," Ed. Sharpless, Cler.

522. Colony in Virginia. Letter to Virginia Company, concerning a settlement about the fort,
    Martin's Hundred, and the seizing of Dutch and French Traders as prizes.   LC.
    IV.   *Ref:* MS. Court Book, Virginia Co., II, 348.
        Pub: (1) Kingsbury, *Rec. Virginia Co.*, II. (2) Brock, *Virginia Company*, II, 238–9.

JUNE 19

523.* "**Notes** Taken out of lres wch came from Virginia in the Abigail and were det the Coffr"'"
    VI.   *Ref:* Manchester Papers, Nos. 338, 339.   PRO.
          Pub: Calendar: Hist. MSS. Com., *Eighth Report*, pt. 2, pp. 41–42.

JUNE 23

524.* [**Sir Nathaniel Rich**]. Draft of a proposition, delivered to the Lord Treasurer, for resettling
    the estate of Virginia.   PRO.
    VI.   *Ref:* Manchester Papers, No. 379.
          Pub: Calendar: Hist. MSS. Com., *Eighth Report*, pt. 2, p. 46.

JUNE 24

525.   **James I.** Letter to Virginia Company, to forbear election of officers.   (1) LC. (2) PRO.
    I.   *Ref:* (1) MS. Court Book, Virginia Co., II, 329. (2) Manchester Papers, No. 380.
        Pub: (1) Kingsbury, *Rec. Virginia Co.*, II. (2) Brock, *Virginia Company*, II, 220–221.
        (3) Calendar: Hist. MSS. Com., *Eighth Report*, pt. 2, p. 46.

JUNE 25

526.   **A quarter** court held for Virginia.   MC.
    II.   *Ref:* Ferrar Papers.
        Pub: Kingsbury, *Rec. Virginia Co.*, II.
         Original of the entry in the MS. Court Book; see date.

JUNE 30

527.* **Secretary Conway.** A letter to Secretary Sir George Calvert, concerning desire of King that
    the Lords of the Privy Council attend promptly to the business of the Virginia Company
    until concluded.   PRO.
    VII.   *Ref:* State Papers, Domestic, James I, Vol. 147, No. 88.
         Pub: Sainsbury, *Calendar of State Papers, Colonial*, p. 47.

[JULY ?]

528.* **Draft** of an answer or notes for an answer to the proposition made by Lord Chichester for
    the better settling of the Plantation in Virginia.   PRO.
    VI.   *Ref:* Manchester Papers, No. 387.
        Pub: Calendar: Hist. MSS. Com., *Eighth Report*, pt. 2, p. 47.

529.* **Captain Baily.** I. Project that the King should make a plantation in Virginia or New Eng-
    land by transportation of poor.
        II. Project concerning Virginia.   PRO.
    VI.   *Ref:* State Papers, Domestic, James I, Vol. 189, Nos. 36, 53.
        Pub: Sainsbury, *Calendar of State Papers, Colonial*, pp. 50, 56.

JULY 2

530.   **Virginia Company.** Answer to the Privy Council stating that they have taken consideration
    as to a supply, and asking until Friday to advise.   (1) LC. (2) PRO. [NY]
    III.   *Ref:* (1) MS. Court Book, Virginia Co., II, 333. (2) State Papers, Colonial, James I,
        Vol. II, No. 34.
        Pub: (1) Kingsbury, *Rec. Virginia Co., post*, II. (2) Brock, *Virginia Company*, II,
        226. (3) Sainsbury, *Calendar of State Papers, Colonial*, p. 47.
         Transcript: New York Public Library, Bancroft papers, Vol. II, fos. 113–115.

531. Lord President Mandeville. A letter to Secretary Conway stating that the Virginia Company have taken measures for the relief of misery in colony, and are considering rules for better government. PRO. [NY]

    VII.   *Ref:* State Papers, Colonial, James I, Vol. II, No. 35.

        Pub: Sainsbury, *Calendar of State Papers, Colonial,* p. 47.

        Transcript: New York Public Library, Bancroft papers, Vol. II, fos. 109-111.

532.* Delphebus Canne. A letter from Virginia to John Delbridge, concerning want in the colony and the hope for a good harvest. PRO. [NY]

    VI.   *Ref:* State Papers, Colonial, James I, Vol. II, No. 36.

        Pub: Calendar: (1) *Virginia Mag. of Hist.,* 373-374. (2) Sainsbury, *Calendar of State Papers, Colonial,* p. 48.

        Transcript: New York Public Library, Bancroft papers, Vol. II, fos. 117-123.

533.* Privy Council. Rules set down for the better government in Virginia. PRO.

    I.   *Ref:* State Papers, Colonial, James I, Vol. II, No. 35.

        Pub: (1) Brown, *First Republic,* 543. (2) Sainsbury, *Calendar of State Papers, Colonial,* p. 48.

JULY 3

534.* Secretary Conway. A letter to Lord Treasurer Middlesex, concerning the refusal of the Virginia Company to comply with the King's request; to be referred to the Attorney-General. PRO.

    VII.   *Ref:* State Papers, Domestic, James I, Vol. 148, No. 19.

        Pub: Sainsbury, *Calendar of State Papers, Colonial,* p. 48.

JULY 4

535.* Privy Council. Order on a representation of Lord Cavendish and others of the Virginia Company, concerning relief to Virginia planters in danger of famine by a general contribution of the whole company. (1) PRO. (2) PC. [NY]

    I.   *Ref:* (1) Colonial Entry Book, Vol. 79, p. 207. (2) Privy Council Register, James I, Vol. VI, p. 55.

        Pub: (1) Brown, *First Republic,* 539. (2) Sainsbury, *Calendar of State Papers, Colonial,* p. 49.

        Transcript, New York Public Library, Bancroft Papers, Vol. II, fos. 129-131.

JULY [4]

536.* List of names of those who will adventure, and amounts subscribed for victuals and provisions to be sent to relief of colony and to particular friends. PRO. [NY]

    III.   *Ref:* State Papers, Colonial, James I, Vol. II, No. 38.

        Pub: Sainsbury, *Calendar of State Papers, Colonial,* p. 49.

        Transcript, New York Public Library, Bancroft Papers, Vol. II, fos. 135-149.

JULY 4

537.* Privy Council. Order to restore Samuel Wrot to his place of counsellor for Virginia and to have session and free vote in courts, notwithstanding deprivation from counsell and suspension from courts. PC.

    I.   *Ref:* Privy Council Register, James I, Vol. VI, p. 57.

538.* List of names who will adventure and amounts to be paid to Richard Caswell, chosen treasurer for the present magazine, for necessary provisions for Virginia. Total, £727.

    III.   *Ref:* State Papers, Colonial, James I, Vol. II, No. 39. PRO. [NY]

        Pub: Sainsbury, *Calendar of State Papers, Colonial,* p. 49.

        Transcript, New York Public Library, Bancroft Papers, Vol. II, fos. 125-127.

539. "**At a Court** held for Virginia on Friday in yᵉ Forenoone yᵉ 4th of July, 1623."   MC.
    II.   *Ref:* Ferrar Papers.
         Pub: Kingsbury, *Rec. Virginia Co.*, II.
           Original of the entry in the MS. Court Book, see date.

JULY 5

540. **Lord President Mandeville.** A letter to Secretary Conway, concerning the measures taken by the Virginia Company for the relief of the colony.   PRO. [NY]
    VII.   *Ref:* State Papers, Colonial, James I, Vol. II, No. 40.
         Pub: Sainsbury, *Calendar of State Papers, Colonial*, p. 49.
           Transcript, New York Public Library, Bancroft Papers, Vol. II, fos. 133–137.

JULY 9

541. **Virginia Court.** "Mʳ Deputy acquaynted yᵉ Compᵃ that according to yᵉ direcčon of yᵉ Last Court he presented to yᵉ LLˢ, of his Maᵗˢ privy Counsell a short Declaračon that was then ordered to be drawne vp, wherein (among other things) was signifyed of yᵉ Companies intent to send a speedy supply to Virginia."   MC.
    II.   *Ref:* Ferrar Papers.
         Pub: Kingsbury, *Rec. Virginia Co.*, *post*, II.
           Original of the entry in the MS. Court Book, see date.

JULY 12

542. [**N. Rich.**] Rough draft of heads of charges against governors of Virginia Company presented to the commissioners.   PRO.
    VI.   *Ref:* Manchester Papers, No. 386.
         Pub: Calendar: Hist. MSS. Com., *Eighth Report*, pt. 2, p. 47.

JULY 15

543.* **Record** of a meeting of the grand committee to answer to the 15 articles prepared against the company at a meeting of the commissioners.   MC.
    III.   *Ref:* Ferrar Papers.

JULY 17, 23

544.* **Governor Wyatt.** Commission to Capt. Pierce to burn yᵉ Indians' Corn; with a minute of the other commissions of that sort and the time when they fell upon the Indians.
    IV.   *Ref:* MS. Rec., Virginia Co., III, pt. ii, p. 41.   LC.

JULY 19

545.* **Privy Council.** Order giving allowance of pay to officers attending on the commissioners to examine the Virginia business.   PC.
    I.   *Ref:* (1) Colonial Entry Book, Vol. 79, p. 207.   (2) Privy Council Register, James I, Vol. VI, p. 72.
         Pub: Sainsbury, *Calendar of State Papers, Colonial*, p. 50.

JULY 21

546.* [**Secretary Conway.**] A letter to Sir Thomas Smythe et al., asking their opinion on Captain Baily's proposition.   PRO.
    VI.   *Ref:* State Papers, Domestic, James I, Vol. 149, No. 16.
         Pub: Sainsbury, *Calendar of State Papers, Colonial*, p. 50.

JULY 22

547.* Privy Council. Order appointing Lords Grandison, Carew, and Chichester to take notes
  hereto adjoined into consideration, and to frame therefrom such orders as are most fit
  for regulating the government of Virginia.   (1) PRO. (2) PC. [NY]
  I.   *Ref:* (1) Colonial Entry Book, Vol. 79, p. 194. (2) Privy Council Register, James I,
          Vol. VI, p. 76.
          Pub: Sainsbury, *Calendar of State Papers, Colonial*, p. 50.
              Transcript, New York Public Library, Bancroft Papers, Vol. II, fo. 141.

JULY 23

548.* An account of sums subscribed and supplies sent since April last for the relief of Virginia,
  with the names of vessels. £3,300.   PRO. [NY]
  III.   *Ref:* State Papers, Colonial, James I, Vol. II, No. 42.
          Pub: Sainsbury, *Calendar of State Papers, Colonial*, p. 50.
              Transcript, New York Public Library, Bancroft Papers, Vol. II, fos. 157-161.

JULY 26

549. John Chamberlain. A letter to Sir Dudley Carleton, concerning the strife between the
  factions of the Earl of Warwick and of Lord Cavendish.   PRO.
  VII.   *Ref:* State Papers, Domestic, James I, Vol. 149, No. 48.
          Pub: (1) Le Froy, *Memorials of the Bermudas*, I, 322-323. (2) Sainsbury, *Calendar of
          State Papers, Colonial*, p. 51.

JULY 28

550.* Lord President Mandeville. A letter to Secretary Conway, stating that the Attorney-
  General is to pass upon the power of the King to issue another patent to the Virginia
  Company.   PRO.
  VII.   *Ref:* State Papers, Domestic, James I, Vol. 149, No. 76.
          Pub: Sainsbury, *Calendar of State Papers, Colonial*, p. 51.

JULY 31

551.* Attorney-General Coventry and Solicitor-General Heath. A letter to the King, giving
  an opinion concerning the resuming of the patent of the Virginia Company.
  I.   *Ref:* State Papers, Colonial, James I, Vol. II, No. 43.   PRO. [NY]
          Pub: (1) Brown, *First Republic*, 547-548. (2) Sainsbury, *Calendar of State Papers,
          Colonial*, p. 51.
              Transcript, New York Public Library, Bancroft Papers, Vol. II, fos. 165-171.

552.* Note of victuals and provision sent by private persons to Virginia in the "George," which is
  to go to Gravesend on Monday next. [Total, £536.]   PRO. [NY]
  III.   *Ref:* State Papers, Colonial, James I, Vol. II, No. 43. I, II.
          Pub: Sainsbury, *Calendar of State Papers, Colonial*, p. 51.
              Transcript, New York Public Library, Bancroft Papers, Vol. II, fos. 153-155. [Gives date
              July 23.]

AUGUST

553.* Protection to Captain John Bargrave.   PRO.
  I.   *Ref:* Docquet Book. Signet Office.

AUGUST 6

554.* Virginia Company. Letter to the governor and council in Virginia, concerning the letter
  of Lords Council in regard to a change in government.   LC.
  III.   *Ref:* (1) MS. Rec. Virginia Co., III, pt. ii, pp. 28-30. (2) Instructions, Commissions,
          and Letters, 1606-1683, pp. 113-124.

AUGUST 12

555.   **Lord Chichester.**   A letter to the Countess of Warwick touching the projected duel between the Earl of Warwick and Lord Cavendish.   PRO.
     VII.   *Ref:* Manchester Papers, No. 160.
          Pub: Calendar: Hist. MSS. Com., *Eighth Report*, pt. 2, p. 29.

AUGUST 31

556.*   **Governor in Virginia.**   Proclamation settling the rates of commodities.   LC.
     IV.   *Ref:* MS. Rec. Virginia Co., III, pt. ii, p. 48ᵃ.
557.*   —— Proclamation about the payment of debts.   LC.
     IV.   *Ref:* MS. Rec. Virginia Co., III, pt. ii, p. 49.

BETWEEN SEPTEMBER AND OCTOBER

558.*   **Stephen Gingby and others.**   Petition to governor of Virginia by Stephen Gingby and the rest of the company belonging to the "Everett" of Midleborough.   LC.
     IV.   *Ref:* MS. Rec. Virginia Co., III, pt. ii, p. 60.
559.*   **William Crakeplace.**   Petition to the governor in Virginia, demanding that the contract with Mr. Langley be fulfilled by Mr. Douglas, his successor as master of the "Margaret and John."   LC.
     IV.   *Ref:* MS. Rec. Virginia Co., III, pt. ii, p. 59ᵃ.

SEPTEMBER 4, 8

560.*   **John Penreis.**   Petition to governor and council in Virginia in regard to rights of trading.
     IV.   *Ref:* MS. Rec. Virginia Co., III, pt. ii, p. 59ᵃ.   LC.

SEPTEMBER 4

561.*   **Governor in Virginia.**   Proclamation about trading with Indians for corn in the bay.   LC.
     IV.   *Ref:* MS. Rec. Virginia Co., III, pt. ii, p. 49.

SEPTEMBER 16

562.*   **Invoice** of goods sent to Virginia by John Harrison in "Marmaduke," John Dennis, master, for use of George Harrison.   PRO.
     VI.   *Ref:* State Papers, Colonial, James I, Vol. II, No. 44.
          Pub: Sainsbury, *Calendar of State Papers, Colonial*, p. 52.

SEPTEMBER 21

563.*   **Governor in Virginia.**   Proclamation about stealing of birds and beasts of domestical and tame nature.   LC.
     IV.   *Ref:* MS. Rec. Virginia Co., III, pt. ii, p. 49.

1623/4

OCTOBER TO FEBRUARY

564.*   **Michael Wilcocks.**   Petition to Governor Wyatt, demanding that at the end of his year's service William Candy pay him 180 pounds of tobacco and build a house, as agreed.
     IV.   *Ref:* MS. Rec. Virginia Co., III, pt. ii, p. 60a.   LC.

BETWEEN OCTOBER AND FEBRUARY

565.*   **Carsten Berksam.**   Petition to governor and council, requesting to be sent home because of the death of his father.   LC.
     IV.   *Ref:* MS. Rec. Virginia Co., III, pt. ii, p. 60.

1623

OCTOBER

566.* Thomas Pasmore.   Petition to governor of Virginia, concerning payment by Valentine Osserly
of money due.   LC.
    IV.   *Ref:* MS. Rec. Virginia Co., III, pt. ii, p. 60.

567.* Governor in Virginia.   Warrant for the levy of taxes.   LC.
    IV.   *Ref:* MS. Rec. Virginia Co., III, pt. ii, p. 52, 52a.

568.* ———.   Order reducing the fine for nonpayment of a tax of 66 pounds of sassafras on each
man from 10 pounds on each 100 pounds of sassafras to 4 pounds of tobacco.   LC.
    IV.   *Ref:* MS. Rec. Virginia Co., pt. ii, pp. 52–52ᵃ.

OCTOBER 3

569.   Lord President Mandeville.   A letter to [Secretary Conway], dispatching a messenger after
the deputy of Virginia Company, as none of the company will take anything upon
themselves in the absence of the governor.   PRO.
    VII.   *Ref:* State Papers, Domestic, James I, Vol. 153, No. 14.
           Pub: Sainsbury, *Calendar of State Papers, Colonial,* p. 52.

OCTOBER 8

570.* Privy Council.   A letter to the governor and council in Virginia, announcing the intention
of the King to change the government of the Colony.   Their Lorpˢ. first Order.
                                   (1)–(3) LC (4) PRO [NY]
    I.   *Ref:* (1) MS. Rec. Virginia Co., III, pt. i, p. 2ᵃ.   (2) MS. Court Book, Virginia Co.,
II, 338–339.   (3) Instructions, Commissions and Letters, 1606–1683 (Vellum Book),
pp. 63–64.   [18th century copy.]   (4) State Papers, Colonial, II, No. 45; Colonial
Entry Book, Vol. 79, pp. 195–196.
        Pub: (1) Kingsbury, *Rec. Virginia Co., post,* II.   (2) Brock, *Virginia Company,* II,
229–230.   (3) Brown, *First Republic,* 550–551.   (4) Sainsbury, *Calendar of State
Papers, Colonial,* p. 52.

        Transcript, New York Public Library, Bancroft Papers, Vol. II, fos. 177–181.

571.* ———.   Order for Sʳ William Jones et al., the commissioners, to examine into the state of Virginia and the Summer Islands, to continue inquiry and report to the board at convenient
time.   (1) PRO.   (2) PC.   [NY]
    I.   *Ref:* (1) Colonial Entry Book, Vol. 79, p. 195.   (2) Privy Council Register, James I
Vol. VI, p. 123.
        Pub: (1) Brown, *First Republic,* 550–552.   (2) Le Froy, *Memorials of the Bermudas,*
I, 323–324.   (3) Sainsbury, *Calendar of State Papers, Colonial,* p. 52.

        Transcript, New York Public Library, Bancroft Papers, Vol. II, fo. 173.

OCTOBER 11

572.* George Jemison and Mr. Undergod.   "To the right Worˡˡ Sʳ Francis Wyatt Knight
Gouernor and Captaine Generall of Virginia.   The humble Petion of George Jemison"
and Mʳ. Undergod of the ship "Everett."   LC
    IV.   *Ref:* MS. Rec. Virginia Co., III, pt. ii, p. 60.

OCTOBER 15

573.* Privy Council.   Order dispensing with attendance of Justice Sir William Jones because of his
other employments; also ordering commission to appoint certain days for meeting so as
to be expeditious.   (1) PC.   (2) PRO.
    I.   *Ref:* (1) Privy Council Register, James I, Vol. VI, p. 125.   (2) Colonial Entry Book,
Vol. 79, p. 196.
        Pub: Sainsbury, *Calendar of State Papers, Colonial,* p. 52.

574. Virginia Company. Answer to an order of the Privy Council of October 8, 1623, begging
respite until November 9. (1) PRO. (2) LC. [NY]
>III. *Ref:* (1) MS. Court Book, Virginia Co., II, 340. (2) State Papers, Colonial, James
>I, Vol. II, No. 46.
>
>*Pub:* (1) Kingsbury, *Rec. Virginia Co.*, II. (2) Brock, *Virginia Company*, II, 231-2.
>(3) Sainsbury, *Calendar of State Papers, Colonial*, p. 52.
>
>Transcript, New York Public Library, Bancroft Papers, Vol. II, fos. 185-187. [Date given
>Nov. 19.]

OCTOBER 17

575. Lord President Mandeville. A letter to Secretary Conway, concerning an alteration in the
frame of government. PRO.
>VII. *Ref:* State Papers, Domestic, James I, Vol. 153, No. 67.
>*Pub:* Sainsbury, *Calendar of State Papers, Colonial*, p. 53.

576. Privy Council. An order to the Virginia Company. Second order in council. Copy.
(1)-(3) LC. (4) PRO [NY]
>I. *Ref:* (1) MS. Rec. Virginia Co., III, pt. i, p. 34. (2) MS. Court Book, Virginia Co.,
>II, 341-342. (3) Instructions, Commissions, and Letters, 1606-1683 (Vellum
>Book), p. 65. (4) Colonial Entry Book, Vol. 79, pp. 197-198.
>
>*Pub:* (1) Kingsbury, *Rec. Virginia Co.*, *post*, II. (2) Brock, *Virginia Company*, II,
>238. (3) Calendar: *Virginia Mag. of Hist.* VI, 382. (4) Sainsbury, *Calendar
>of State Papers, Colonial*, pp. 52-53.
>
>Transcript, New York Public Library, Bancroft Papers, Vol. II, fos. 189-191.

OCTOBER 20

577. Virginia Company. Answer to an order of the Privy Council of October 17, 1623.
(1) LC. (2) PRO. [NY]
>III. *Ref:* (1) MS. Court Book, Virginia Co., II, 342. (2) State Papers, Colonial, James I,
>Vol. II, No. 47.
>
>*Pub:* (1) Kingsbury, *Rec. Virginia Co.*, *post*, II. (2) Brock, *Virginia Company*, II, 234.
>(3) Sainsbury, *Calendar of State Papers, Colonial*, p. 53.
>
>Transcript, New York Public Library, Bancroft Papers, Vol. II, fo. 201. [Ends with "were of
>a contrary opinion."]

OCTOBER 20, 24

578.* Privy Council. Privy Council to the Virginia Company, urging the speedy sending of the
ship to Virginia and that the orders should be published in Virginia.
(1), (2) & (4) LC. (3) PRO. (5) PC. (6) MC. [NY]
>I. *Ref:* (1) MS. Records Virginia Co., III, pt. i, p. 3a. (2) MS. Court Book, Virginia Co.,
>II, 343. (3) Colonial Entry Book, Vol. 79, pp. 199-200. (4) Instructions, Commis-
>sions and Letters, 1606-1683 (vellum book), pp. 66-67. (5) Privy Council Register,
>James I, Vol. VI, p. 131. (6) Ferrar Papers.
>
>*Pub:* (1) Kingsbury, *Rec. Virginia Co.*, *post*, II. (2) Brock, *Virginia Company*, II,
>234-235. (3) Sainsbury, *Calendar of State Papers, Colonial*, p. 53.
>
>Transcript, New York Public Library, Bancroft Papers, Vol. II, fos. 193-195. [Oct. 20.]

OCTOBER 20

579.* Schedule of names of those present at an extraordinary court of the Virginia Company by
appointment of Lords, touching the surrender of the charters, distinguishing those who
were for from those against. PRO.
>III. *Ref:* State Papers, Colonial, James I, Vol. II, No. 48.
>*Pub:* Sainsbury, *Calendar of State Papers, Colonial*, p. 53.
>
>Transcript, New York Public Library, Bancroft Papers, Vol. II, fos. 197-199.

580.* Governor in Virginia. "A Warrant to Capt. Madison to bring 40 souldiers for ye March."
   IV.   *Ref:* MS. Records Virginia Co., III, pt. ii, pp. 52, 52a.   LC.

OCTOBER 22

581.* Robert Byng. A letter to Nicholas Ferrar, concerning the appointment to a position.
   VI.   *Ref:* Ferrar Papers.   MC.   [LC]
            Photographic reproduction and transcript in the Library of Congress.

OCTOBER 24

582.* Privy Council. Order to John Harvey to investigate the conditions of Virginia—plantations,
            fortifications, provisions, boats, public works, and relations with the Indians.   PC.
   I.   *Ref:* Privy Council Register, James I, Vol. VI, p. 137.
            Transcript, New York Public Library, Bancroft Papers, Vol. II, fos. 205-207.

583.* Privy Council. A letter to the Governor and Council in Virginia, instructing Council to assist
            Commissioners appointed to investigate the Colony.   (1) LC.   (4) PRO   [NY]
   I.   *Ref:* (1) MS. Rec. Virginia Co., III, pt. i, p. 2.   (2) Colonial Entry Book, Vol. 79,
            p. 200.   (3) Instructions, comissions, and letters, 1606–1683 (vellum book), p. 62.
            [18th century copy.]   (4) Colonial Entry Book, Vol. 79, p. 200.
            Pub: Sainsbury, *Calendar of State Papers, Colonial,* p. 54.
            Transcript, New York Public Library, Bancroft Papers, II, fo. 209.

NOVEMBER

584.* Sir Thomas Smythe and others. A letter to Secretary Conway, concerning Captain Baily's
            project.   PRO.   [NY]
   III.   *Ref:* State Papers, Colonial, James I, Vol. II, No. 51.
            Pub: Sainsbury, *Calendar of State Papers, Colonial,* p. 54.
            Transcript, New York Public Library, Bancroft Papers, II, fos. 221-223.

1623, NOVEMBER 4 TO 1624, MAY 24

585.* Quo Warranto and Proceedings, by which the Virginia Company was dissolved.
                                                         (1) PRO.   (2) MC.   [LC]
   I.   *Ref:* (1) Coram Rege Roll, James I, 21 year, Michaelmas Term.   Roll No. 1528, mem-
            branes, 39–63.   (2) Ferrar Papers (writ only).
            Photographic reproduction in the Library of Congress.

1623

NOVEMBER 7

586.* Commissioners for Virginia. Warrant concerning sundry petitions referred to them for
            examination.   They require a trunk of writings locked up under custody of clerks of
            Privy Council to be delivered to the bearer.   PRO.
   I.   *Ref:* State Papers, Colonial, James I, Vol. II, No. 49.
            Pub: Sainsbury, *Calendar of State Papers, Colonial,* p. 54.

NOVEMBER 18

587.* Governor in Virginia. A Commission to the Council of State in the Governor's absence.
   IV.   *Ref:* MS. Rec. Virginia Co., III, pt. ii, p. 41.   LC.

NOVEMBER 19

588. Note of shipping, men, and provisions sent and provided for Virginia by the Right Honorable
            Earl of Southampton and the Company since May, 1623, to this 19th November, 1623.
   III.   *Ref:* MS. Court Book, Virginia Co., II.   LC.
            Pub: (1) Kingsbury, *Rec. Virginia Co., post,* II.   (2) Brock, *Virginia Company,* II,
            p. 245.

589.* Governor in Virginia. Order to Captain Maddison and other officers to collect sassafras and
tobacco. LC.
   IV.   *Ref:* MS. Rec. Virginia Co., III, pt. ii, pp. 52, 52a.

590.* ———. Warrant to Captain Pierse to levy 300 lbs. of tobacco for the fort at Wariscoyack.
   IV.   *Ref:* MS. Rec. Virginia Co., III, pt. ii, p. 52. LC.

591.* ———. Order to Captain Pierse to levy the tax of October, 1623. LC.
   IV.   *Ref:* MS. Rec. Virginia Co., III, pt. ii, pp. 52, 52a.

592.* ———. A warrant for Mr. Benet for his meanes. LC.
   IV.   *Ref:* MS. Rec. Virginia Co., III, pp. 53, 53a.

593.* Privy Council. Order for delivering the Virginia Company's books and writings to the Virginia Company, against whom a *quo warranto* has been issued, and for keeping inventory
of the same. PC. [NY]
   I.   *Ref:* Colonial Entry Book, Vol. 79, p. 208.
   Pub: Sainsbury, *Calendar of State Papers, Colonial*, p. 54.
    Transcript, New York Public Library, Bancroft Papers, II, fos. 225–227.

594.* Virginia and Somers Islands Companies. Petition to the King, that a commission
granted on request of Alderman Johnson et al. proceed; that books sequestered 14 days
be restored, and that they be preserved in rights. (1) PRO. (2) KP. [NY]
   III.   *Ref:* (1) State Papers, Colonial, James I, Vol. II, No. 50. (2) De La Warr's collection of MSS.
   Pub: (1) Sainsbury, *Calendar of State Papers, Colonial*, p. 54. (2) Hist. MSS. Com.,
Fourth Report, p. 283.
    Transcript, New York Public Library, Bancroft Papers, II, fos. 245–247.

595.* Governor in Virginia. "A warrant graunted to Mr. Bolton for his meanes." LC.
   IV.   *Ref:* MS. Rec. Virginia Co., III, pt. ii, fo. 53.

596.* Sir Edwin Sandys. A letter to John Ferrar, concerning personal debts, assuring him that
no one will lose by him. MC. [LC]
   VI.   *Ref:* Ferrar Papers.

597.* Governor in Virginia. A warrant to Captain William Tucker to collect 10 pounds of tobacco
for each 1,000 plants at Elizabeth City. LC.
   IV.   *Ref:* MS. Rec. Virginia Co., III, pt. ii, p. 53.

598.* Council in Virginia. Order for preparation of list of all who perished in massacre, as per
order of the company. LC.
   IV.   *Ref:* MS. Rec. Virginia Co., III, pt. ii, fo. 53.

599.* Privy Council. Order touching the costs of a *quo warranto* affecting the charter of the
Virginia Company. (1) PC. (2) & (3) PRO. [NY]
   I.   *Ref:* (1) Privy Council Register, James I, Vol. VI, p. 188. (2) Colonial Entry Book,
Vol. 79, p. 209. (3) Manchester Papers, No. 394.
   Pub: (1) Sainsbury, *Calendar of State Papers, Colonial*, p. 55. (2) Calendar: Hist.
MSS. Com., *Eighth Report*, pt. 2, p. 47.
    Transcript, New York Public Library, Bancroft Papers, II, fo. 229.

600. Privy Council. Order of December 8, 1623.   (1) LC.   (2) PC.
    I.   *Ref:* (1) Court Book, Virginia Co., II, 361.   (2) Colonial Entry Book, Vol. 79, p. 209.
        Pub: (1) Kingsbury, *Rec. Virginia Co.*, II.   (2) Brock, *Virginia Company*, II, 249–250.
        (3) Sainsbury, *Calendar of State Papers, Colonial*, p. 55.

601.* —— Order directing the attorney-general to report on a petition of Nicholas Ferrar, deputy
of Virginia Company, who affirms that commission for examining Virginia Company
and Summer Islands Company had not set course for paying debts of the companies,
which was referred unto them by board.   (1) PC.   (2) & (3) PRO.
    I.   *Ref:* (1) Privy Council Register, James I, Vol. VI, p. 188.   (2) Colonial Entry Book,
        Vol. 79, pp. 209–210.   (3) Manchester Papers, No. 393.
        Pub: (1) Sainsbury, *Calendar of State Papers, Colonial*, p. 55.   (2) Calendar: Hist.
        MSS. Com., *Eighth Report*, pt. 2, p. 47.

602.* —— Order directing the attorney-general to report upon a complaint of William Cannyn
[Canning] *vs.* Thomas Keightly for arresting him on action of £500.
                              (1) PC.   (2) PRO.   [NY]
    I.   *Ref:* (1) Privy Council Register, James I, Vol. VI, p. 187.   (2) Colonial Entry Book,
        Vol. 79, p. 209.
        Pub: Sainsbury, *Calendar of State Papers, Colonial*, p. 55.
        Transcript, New York Public Library, Bancroft Papers, II, fos. 233–235.

603.* Council in Virginia. Order concerning every 20th man to work on the fort of Wariscoyack.
    IV.   *Ref:* MS. Rec. Virginia Co., III, pt. ii, p. 53.   LC.

604.* Mr. Captain Bargrave. "Mr. Captain Bargrave's Proiect touching Virginea." A copy of a
letter to the Lord Treasurer.   (1) BM.   (2) PRO.
    VI.   *Ref:* (1) Additional MSS., 12496, fo. 454.   (Caesar Papers.)   (2) Manchester papers,
        No. 402.
        Pub: Calendar: Hist. MSS. Com., *Eighth Report*, pt. 2, pp. 47–48.

DECEMBER 11 (?)

605. Council in Virginia. Action concerning release of a bond of George Yeardley to Mr. Southern; concerning goods sent home on the "Temperance."   LC.
    IV.   *Ref:* MS. Court Book of the Colony.

DECEMBER 19

606.* Privy Council. A letter to the governor and council in Virginia concerning Captain Martin.
                         (1) LC.   (2) PRO.   (3) PC.   [NY]
    I.   *Ref:* (1) MS. Rec. Virginia Co., III, pt. ii, p. 70[a].   (2) Colonial Entry Book, Vol. 79,
        p. 210.   (3) Privy Council Register, James I, Vol. VI, p. 199.
        Pub: (1) *Va. Mag. of Hist.*, VII, pp. 272–273.   (2) Sainsbury, *Calendar of State Papers,
        Colonial*, p. 55.
        Transcript, New York Public Library, Bancroft Papers, II, fos. 237–239.

DECEMBER 26

607.* Governor in Virginia. Letter to "Capt. Wm. Tucker" concerning his expedition.   LC.
    IV.   *Ref:* MS. Rec. Virginia Co., III, pt. ii, fo. 53.

DECEMBER 30

608. Privy Council. A letter to the deputy governor of the Virginia Company to bring to them
unopened all letters arrived in a ship lately from Virginia.
                 (1) LC.   (2) MC.   (3) PC.   (4) PRO.   [NY]
    I.   *Ref:* (1) Court Book, Virginia Co., II, 358.   (2) Ferrar Papers.   (3) Privy Council
        Register, James I, Vol. VI, p. 215.   (4) Colonial Entry Book, Vol. 79, p. 210.
        Pub: (1) Kingsbury, *Rec. Virginia Co.*, II.   (2) Brock, *Virginia Company*, II, 246.
        (3) *Va. Mag. of Hist.*, X, 132–134.   (4) Sainsbury, *Calendar of State Papers, Colonial*,
        p. 55.
        Transcript, New York Public Library, Bancroft Papers, II, fo. 241.

DECEMBER 31–JANUARY 9

609.* **Council in Virginia.** Proclamation concerning Tucker's collection of tax on tobacco.   LC.
     IV.   *Ref:* MS. Rec. Virginia Co., London, III, pt. ii, fo. 53.

1623/4

JANUARY 7

610.   **Council in Virginia.** Controversy between Thomas Sufram and Clarke and the successors
     of Capt. William Perse and Capt. William Power concerning an agreement for wages
     of a voyage in "Furtherance."   LC.
     IV.   *Ref:* MS. Court Book of the Colony.

611.   **Brief** motives to maintain King's right to River Amazon and coast of Guiana. Note added in
     another hand to point out prejudice to the plantations should King make agreement
     with Virginia and Bermudas companies for tobacco from those places only.
     VII.

612.   **Council in Virginia.** Controversy between George Mynitie for Thomas Hamor and Thomas
     Gibbs concerning a bargain between them.   LC.
     IV.   *Ref:* MS. Court Book of the Colony.

JANUARY 8

613.   **Attorney-General Coventry.** A letter to the Privy Council concerning the case between
     William Canning and Thomas Kightley.   PRO.
     I.   *Ref:* State Papers, Domestic, James I, Vol. 158, No. 12.
         Pub: Sainsbury, *Calendar of State Papers, Colonial*, p. 56.

JANUARY 9

614.   **Council in Virginia.** I. Controversy between Daniel Gookin, through Richard Kensan,
     master of ship "Mary," and Robert Roberts of Bristo, for delivery of commodities.
     II. Controversy between John Chew and William Douglas for goods used on the
     "Margaret."   LC.
     IV.   *Ref:* MS. Court Book of the Colony.

615. ——. Controversy between Weston and James Carter concerning the transportation of goods.
     IV.   *Ref:* MS. Court Book of the Colony.   LC.

JANUARY 14

616.   **Adventurers and Planters in Virginia and others.** Petition to the Privy Council that
     those who oppose the surrender of the charter shall bear the expense of the suit.   LC.
     IV.   *Ref:* MS. Court Book, Virginia Co., II, 362.
         Pub: (1) Kingsbury, *Rec. Virginia Co.*, II.   (2) Brock, *Virginia Company*, II, 250–251.

JANUARY 19

617.* **Governor in Virginia.** A Comission to Captain Hamor given aboard the "Willm and
     John" for trading.   LC.
     IV.   *Ref:* MS. Rec. Virginia Co., III, pt. ii, p. 41.

JANUARY 22

618.* **Governor in Virginia.** A commission to Sr George Yeardley for punishing of swearing and
     drunkenness.   LC.
     IV.   *Ref:* MS. Rec. Virginia Co., III, pt. ii, p. 40.

619.* Governor in Virginia. Warrants for holding elections and summoning the general assembly.
  IV. *Ref:* MS. Rec. Virginia Co., III, pt. ii, fo. 53.   LC.

620.* Council in Virginia. A letter to the Virginia Company of London, describing revenge on
  Indians.   (1) LC. (2) PRO. [NY]
  IV. *Ref:* (1) MS. Rec. Virginia Co., III, pt. i, pp. 7–8. (2) State Papers, Domestic,
     James I, Vol. 156, No. 1.
     Pub: (1) Calendar: *Virginia, Mag. of Hist.*, VI, 374–377. (2) Sainsbury, *Calendar
     of State Papers, Colonial*, pp. 56–57.
       Transcript: New York Public Library, Bancroft Papers, II, fos. 249–269.

621.* General Assembly in Virginia. The Answer to Capt. Butler's vnmasking of Virginia, by
  the General Assembly February, 1623. Directed to the King's most Sacred Matie. LC.
  IV. *Ref:* MS. Rec. Virginia Co., III, pt. i, pp. 9–11.
     Pub: Neill, *Virginia Company of London*, 406–407.

622.* Robert Poole. Petition "To the Right Wor:ll Sr Francis Wyatt Knight," asking for payments
  due.   LC.
  IV. *Ref:* MS. Rec. Virginia Co., III, pt. ii, fo. 60.

623. Virginia Council. Letter to governor and council in Virginia, concerning the complaints of
  Capt. John Martin.   LC.
  III. *Ref:* (1) MS. Rec. Virginia Co., III, pt. ii, p. 71. (2) MS. Court Book Virginia Co.,
     II, 366.
     Pub: Kingsbury, *Records Virginia Co.*, Vol. II.

624.* John Barnett. Petition "To the right Worll: Sr Francis Wyatt Knight Gouernor," for sums
  due from the agent of Mr. Gookin.   LC.
  IV. *Ref:* MS. Rec. Virginia Co., III, pt. ii, p. 60a.

625.* William Paney. Petition "To the right Worll Sr Francis Wyatt Knight" for a claim from
  Captain Nuce.   LC.
  IV. *Ref:* MS. Rec. Virginia Co., III, pt. ii, p. 60a.

626. [Davison?]. A letter to [J. Ferrar?] giving a list of names of the living and dead in Virginia.
  IV. *Ref:* State Papers, Colonial, James I, Vol. III, No. 2.   PRO. [NY]
     Pub: (1) Wynne and Gilman, *Colonial Records of Virginia*, 37–60; 61–66. (2) Sains-
     bury, *Calendar of State Papers, Colonial* p. 57.
       Transcript, New York Public Library, Bancroft Papers, II, pp. 277–327. Secretary Davison
       died before this date.

627. List of 13 letters and papers, including one book received from and sent to Virginia.
  VI. *Ref:* State Papers, Colonial, James I, Vol. III, No. 3.   PRO. [NY]
     Pub: Sainsbury, *Calendar of State Papers, Colonial*, p. 57.
       Transcript: New York Public Library, Bancroft Papers, II, pp. 273–275.

628.* General Assembly in Virginia. "The answere of the generall Assembly in Virginia to a
Declaratione of the State of the Colonie in the 12 years of Sʳ Thomas Smith's Goverment
exhibited by Alderman Johnsone and others."   (1) LC.   (2) PRO.   [NY]

    IV.   *Ref:* (1) MS. Rec. Virginia Co., III, pt. i; p. 4ᵃ.   (2) State Papers, Colonial, James I,
        Vol. II, No. 20.

        Pub: (1) Neill, *Virginia Company of London*, pp. 407–411.   (2) Sainsbury *Calendar of
        State Papers, Colonial*, pp. 39–40.

        D. S.
        Transcript: New York Public Library, Bancroft Papers, II, pp. 349–361.

629.* Governor, Council, and Assembly in Virginia. Letter "To yᵉ right Honoᵇˡᵉ our very good
Lor: the Lors: of his Maᵗⁱᵉˢ most Honoᵇˡᵉ Privie Counsell," requesting the liberty of their
general assemblies and defending the Sandys administration.
                                (1) LC.   (2) PRO.   [NY]

    IV.   *Ref:* (1) MS. Rec. Virginia Co., III, pt. i, p. 5.   (2) State Papers, Colonial, James
        I, Vol. III, No. 4 (vera copia).

        Pub: Sainsbury, *Calendar of State Papers, Colonial*, p. 58.

        Transcript: New York Public Library, Bancroft Papers, II, pp. 365–371.   [Date Feb. 29.]

630.   Ballad concerning the massacre.   "Good News from Virginia."   "To the Tune of All those
that be good fellowes."   Praises the men of the colony.   PRO.

        Ref: Manchester Papers, No. 324.

        Pub: Calendar: Hist. MSS. Com., *Eighth Report*, pt. ii, pp. 39, 40.

631.* John Haruey.   "To the right Worꝗ Sʳ Francis Wyatt &c and to the Counsell of Estate."
Petition concerning disobedience to his orders.   LC.

    IV.   *Ref:* MS. Rec. Virginia Co., III, pt. ii, p. 62ᵃ.

632.* ——.   "To the right Worꝗ Sʳ Francis Wyatt Knight &c and to the Counsell of Estate the
second complaint and peticion of John Haruey Esqʳ."   LC.

    IV.   *Ref:* MS. Rec. Virginia Co., III, pt. ii, p. 62.

633.* Robert Guyer and John White.   "To the Hono:ᵇˡᵉ Sʳ Francis Wyatt knight &c and yᵉ right
Worꝗ the Counsell of State.   The Answer to yᵉ Complaint and Petition of Capᵗ John
Haruey Esquiere."   LC.

    IV.   *Ref:* MS. Rec. Virginia Co., III, pt. ii, p. 62.

634.* ——.   "To the hono:ᵇˡᵉ Sʳ Francis Wyatt knight &c and the right worꝗ the rest of the Counsell of State.   The answer to yᵉ Second Complaint and peticion of Capᵗ John Haruey
Esqʳ."   LC.

    IV.   *Ref:* MS. Rec. Virginia Co., III, pt. ii, p. 62ᵃ.

635.* Haruey and others, commissioners of the King.   A letter to Sir Francis Wyatt, governor,
and to the assembly.   PRO.

    I.   *Ref:* State Papers, Colonial, James I, Vol. III, No. 6 (second paper).

636.* Haruey and others.   Form of subscription presented to the general assembly, agreeing to a
revocation of the letters patent.   PRO. [NY]

    I.   *Ref:* State Papers, Colonial, James I, Vol. III, No. 6 (third paper).

        Transcript: New York Public Library, Bancroft Papers, II, pp. 397–399.

637.* General Assembly in Virginia. A letter to Haruey demanding a commission or an oath as
to his authority.   PRO.

  IV. *Ref:* State Papers, Colonial, James I, Vol. III, No. 6 (fifth paper).

638.* General Assembly in Virginia. "The generall assemblies answere to those fower Propositions made by the commissioners to be presented to the Lors: of his Maties most honor^ble
privie counsell."   (1) LC. (2) PRO. [NY]

  IV. *Ref:* (1) MS. Rec. Virginia Co., III, pt. i, p. 6ᵃ. (2) State Papers, Colonial, James
I, Vol. III, No. 7.

    Pub: Sainsbury, *Calendar of State Papers, Colonial,* p. 58.

      (1) D. S. in Public Record Office. (2) Transcript, New York Public Library, Bancroft Papers,
      II, pp. 381–389.

639.* Governor, Council, and General Assembly in Virginia. "The Answere of Gou^nor, and
Counsell and Generall Assembly to the Letter and wrightinge of Captain John Haruey,"
expressing submissive attitude toward King.   (1) LC. (2) PRO.

  IV. *Ref:* (1) MS. Rec. Virginia Co., III, pt. i, p. 7ᵃ. (2) State Papers, Colonial, James I,
Vol. III, No. 6 (fourth paper).

      Document in State Papers, Colonial, in the autograph of Ed. Sharpless, and certified by him.

[MARCH 2]

640. Commissioners in Virginia. "A briefe declaratione to the Assemblie" (by John Harvy,
John Porey, Abraham Peirsey, and Samuel Mathews.) with a list of four enquiries as to
the state of the colony.   (1) LC. (2) PRO.

  I. *Ref:* (1) MS. Rec. Virginia Co., III, pt. i, p. 6. (2) State Papers, Colonial, James I,
Vol. III, No. 6 (first paper).

    Pub: Sainsbury, *Calendar of State Papers, Colonial,* p. 58.

      Document in State Papers, Colonial, in autograph of Ed. Sharpless, and certified by him.

MARCH 3.

641. John Haruey and others. A letter to Governor Wyatt and the assembly, answering a demand
for authority and acknowledging that they had none to move them to conform to subscription.   PRO. [L. C.]

  I. *Ref:* (1) MS. Rec. Virginia Co., Vol. III, pt. i, p. 7ᵃ. (2) State Papers, Colonial,
James I, Vol. III, No. 6 (sixth paper).

      Document in the State Papers, Colonial, in the autograph of Ed. Sharpless. Photograph in
      the Library of Congress.

MARCH 5

642.* Governor and Council and Assembly in Virginia. Laws and Orders of the Assembly in
Virginia, by the Governor, Council and 2 burgesses elected out of every plantation by
major parts of voices, February 16, 1623/4.   (1) LC. (2) PRO. [NY]

  IV. *Ref:* (1) MS. Rec. Virginia Co., III, pt. i, fo. 8. (2) State Papers, Colonial, James I,
Vol. III, No. 9.

    Pub: (1) Hening, *Statutes,* I, 122f. (2) Sainsbury, *Calendar of State Papers, Colonial,*
p. 59.

      Document in State Paper Office in autograph of Ed. Sharpless. Transcript: New York Public
      Library, Bancroft Papers, II, fos. 329–345.

643.* Governor, Council, and Assembly in Virginia. Order concerning a levy of tobacco. LC.

  IV. *Ref:* MS. Rec. Virginia Co., III, pt. i, p. 9.

MARCH 7

644. Council in Virginia. Action concerning a claim against the company.   LC.

  IV. *Ref:* MS. Court Book of the Colony.

645. Court in Virginia. Transcripts from court records in Virginia, in quarter courts at James-
town, of points relating to the debts of George Thorpe, by Benjamin Harrison.   NY.
    IV.   *Ref:* Smyth of Nibley Papers, Smyth, 38.
        Pub: Calendar: *N. Y. Pub. Lib. Bull.,* I, 189.

1623/4

MARCH 9

646. Council in Virginia. Court Book of the Council in Virginia, concerning a case between Mr.
Horne and Mr. Procter, concerning service.   LC.
    IV.   *Ref:* MS. Court Book of the Colony.

647.* Henry [Horner]. "To the right Worll Sr Francis Wyatt Knight &c and Counsell of Estate
here Assembled," demanding goods due from Procter.   LC.
    IV.   *Ref:* MS. Rec. Virginia Co., III, pt. ii, p. 61.

MARCH 11

648. Council in Virginia. Court Book of the Council in Virginia, concerning degradation of
Richard Quaile from captain to carpenter.   LC.
    IV.   *Ref:* MS. Court Book of the Colony.

649.* Richard Quaile. "The Humble Petition of Richard Quaile to the hono^ble the Gouernor
with the right Worll the Assistant in Counsell," requesting to be released. [Examined
September 9, 1623.]   LC.
    IV.   *Ref:* MS. Rec. Virginia Co., III, pt. ii, p. 61.

MARCH 12

650. Council in Virginia. Court Book of the Council in Virginia, concerning a controversy
between Dr. Pott and Capt. William Holmes for payment of three chests of physic.   LC.
    IV.   *Ref:* MS. Court Book of the Colony.

651. [Edward Nicholas.] A letter to [John Nicholas] concerning the arrival of ships this week
from Virginia and the Somers Islands, certifying the welfare of the people in Virginia
still in enmity with the natives.   PRO.
    VI.   *Ref:* State Papers, Domestic, James I, Vol. 160, No. 70.
        Pub: Sainsbury, *Calendar of State Papers, Colonial,* p. 59.

MARCH 16

652.* Governor in Virginia. A commission to Rawleigh Crashaw to trade with the Indians. LC.
    IV.   *Ref:* MS. Rec. Virginia Co., III, pt. ii, p. 41.*

MARCH 23, 24, 25

653.* John Haruey. "To the right wor:ll Sr Francis Wyatt knight &c and to ye Counsell of Estate
the third petition of John Haruey, Esqr," concerning his admiralty of New England.
    IV.   *Ref:* MS. Rec. Virginia Co., III, pt. ii, p. 63.   LC.

654.* Robert Guyar and John White. "To the right hono:^ble Sr Francis Wyatt knight &c the
right Worll ye Counsell of State." The Humble Petition against Captain Haruey.
    IV.   *Ref:* MS. Rec. Virginia Co., III, pt. ii, p. 63.   LC.

MARCH 30

655.* Jane Dickenson. "To the honol right Worll &c the Gouernor and Counsell of Estate in
Virginia." Petition to be relieved from service.   LC.
    IV.   *Ref:* MS. Rec. Virginia Co., III, pt. ii, p. 61.

1624

[APRIL ?]

656. **[Sir Nathaniel Rich.]**   Heads of a speech in the House of Commons on a petition presented
by the Virginia Company.   PRO.
    VI.   *Ref:* Manchester Papers, No. 410.
        Pub: Calendar: Hist. MSS. Com., *Eighth Report*, pt. 2, p. 48.

APRIL 8

657. **Planters in Virginia.**   Petition to the King, requesting to be relieved of the impost on
tobacco for a time.   LC.
    IV.   *Ref:* MS. Court Book, Virginia Co., II, 373–374.
        Pub: (1) Kingsbury, *Rec. Virginia Co.*, II.   (2) Brock, *Virginia Company*, II, 257–259.

APRIL 8, 14

658. **Privy Council.**   Answers granting the above petition.   LC.
        Ref: MS. Court Book, Virginia Co., II, 374.
        Pub: (1) Kingsbury, *Rec. Virginia Co.*, II.   (2) Brock, *Virginia Company*, II, 259.

APRIL 12, 19

659.* **John Hall.**   "To the right Worll Sʳ Francis Wyatt Knight &c" concerning a claim against
John Hall.   LC.
    IV.   *Ref:* MS. Rec. Virginia Co., III, pt. ii, p. 61.

APRIL 17

660.* **Council in Virginia.**   Letter "to the right Honorbl Henry Earle of Suthampton with the
Lords and others of the Counsell and Compenie of Virginia," concerning acts of the
Assembly sent by John Pountis, and the needs of the colony.   LC.
    IV.   *Ref:* MS. Rec. Virginia Co., III, pt. i, p. 8ª.

[APRIL 22]

661. **Sir Thomas Smythe.**   A letter to Secretary Conway entreating him to attend the Grand Commission of Grievances to-morrow in order to help to stop John Bargrave *vs.* Smythe.
    VII.   *Ref:* State Papers, Domestic, James I, Vol. 163, No. 28.   PRO.
        Pub: Sainsbury, *Calendar of State Papers, Colonial*, p. 60.

662.* **Capt. John Bargrave.**   A letter to the House of Commons on behalf of himself, absent
planters in Virginia, and adventurers against Sir Thomas Smythe.   PRO.
    III.   *Ref:* (1) Manchester Papers, No. 401.   (2) State Papers, Colonial, James I, Vol. III,
No. 11.   (3) State Papers, Domestic, James I, Vol. 163, No. 28.
        Pub: (1) Sainsbury, *Calendar of State Papers, Colonial*, p. 60.   (2) Calendar: Hist.
MSS. Com., *Eighth Report*, pt. 2, p. 47.
        Document in the Colonial State Papers signed by Bargrave.   The date is uncertain.

APRIL 24

663.* **John Harvey.**   A letter to Sir Nathaniel Rich, sending the reply of the Assembly to Capt.
Butler's and Alderman Johnson's accusations.   PRO.
    IV.   *Ref:* Manchester Papers, No. 400.
        Pub: Calendar: Hist. MSS. Com., *Eighth Report*, pt. ii, p. 47.
        Autograph document.

664. House of Commons. "A petition for Virginia read" in the House of Commons, and also a letter from the King. (1) LC. (2) & (3) HL. (4) PRO.
  I. *Ref:* (1) MS. Court Book, Virginia Co., II, 377–379. (2) House of Lords, Supplementary Calendar, C. J., II, 691, 694. (3) Journals of Commons, I. (4) State Papers, Colonial, James I, Vol. III, No. 12.
  Pub: (1) LeFroy, *Memorials of the Bermudas*, I, 336. (2) Calendar: Hist. MSS. Com., *Fourth Report*, pt. 1, p. 122. (3) Brock, *Virginia Company*, II, 263–266. (4) Kingsbury, *Rec. Virginia Co.*, II.

APRIL 28

665.* James I. A letter to the Speaker of the House of Commons not to trouble with the petition, as it would renew the factions of the company, which were in settlement by the King.
  I. *Ref:* State Papers, Domestic, James I, Vol. 163, No. 71. PRO.
  Pub: (1) LeFroy, *Memorials of the Bermudas*, I, 336–337. (2) Sainsbury, *Calendar of State Papers, Colonial*, p. 60.

666.* George Menefie. A letter to John Harrison, telling of the death of his brother George, of his will, and of an inventory of his estate, and asking for instructions. PRO. [NY]
  VI. *Ref:* State Papers, Colonial, James I, Vol. III, No. 15.
  Pub: Sainsbury, *Calendar of State Papers, Colonial*, p. 61.
  Transcript: New York Public Library, Bancroft Papers, II, 473–475.

APRIL 29

667. Sir Isaac Wake. A letter to Secretary Conway, telling that King's letter was received with universal applause and had quieted the great schism caused by the Virginians. PRO.
  VII. *Ref:* Savoy Correspondence, 1624, April 29.
  Pub: Sainsbury, *Calendar of State Papers, Colonial*, p. 60.

APRIL 30

668. John Chamberlain. A letter to Sir Dudley Carleton concerning the King's letter to Lower House yesterday touching Virginia, and reserving the matter likely to have bred dissension. PRO.
  VII. *Ref:* State Papers, Domestic, James I, Vol. 163, No. 74.
  Pub: (1) LeFroy, *Memorials of the Bermudas*, I, 337. (2) Sainsbury, *Calendar of State Papers, Colonial*, p. 61.

MAY

669.* [Nicholas Ferrar.] A rough draft and a copy of a petition to the Commons concerning the loss to England by allowing the importation of tobacco from Spain. MC. [LC]
  VI. *Ref:* Ferrar Papers.
  Rough draft in Nicholas Ferrar's autograph and a copy in Ed. Collingwood's writing.

MAY 4

670. House of Lords. Matters brought from the House of Commons, but no further proceedings.
  I. *Ref:* Lords Journal, III, 340. HL.
  Pub: Calendar: Hist. MSS. Com., *Fourth Report*, p. 123.

MAY 5

671.* Richard Barnes. "To the honoᵇˡᵉ Sʳ Francis Wyatt Knight Governor and Capt. generall of Virginia The Humble Petition" requesting a reinvestigation of censure. LC.
  IV. *Ref:* MS. Rec. Virginia Co., III, pt. ii, p. 61ᵃ.

MAY 6

672. Sir Francis Nethersole. A letter to Sir Dudley Carleton, concerning the discussion of Virginia affairs in the House of Commons.   PRO.
      VII.   *Ref:* State Papers, Domestic, James I, Vol. 164, No. 46.
             Pub: (1) Calendar: *Virginia Mag. of Hist.*, VI, 382–384.   (2) Sainsbury, *Calendar of State Papers, Colonial*, p. 62.

MAY 10

673. Council in Virginia. Action concerning the charge against Edward Sharples, clark to the council of state, of betraying counsels . . . to the King and Lords of the Privy Council and some of the commissioners for reward.   LC.
      IV.   *Ref:* MS. Court Book of the Colony.

674. ——. Action concerning the censure of Richard Barnes for speaking ill of the governor.
      IV.   *Ref:* MS. Court Book of the Colony.   LC.

MAY 12

675.* Council in Virginia. Letter "to the Right Honoble Henry Earle of Suthampton wᵗʰ the Lo: and others of the Counsell and Compenie of Virginia." Complaint concerning Mr. Pory.   LC.
      IV.   *Ref:* MS. Rec. Virginia Co., III, pt. i, p. 9.

MAY 20

676.* Robert Heath. A letter to Sir Robert Harley requesting him to take opinion on a bill proposed in Parliament on the importation of Spanish tobacco.   PRO.
      VII.   *Ref:* State Papers, Domestic, Vol. CLXV, No. 5.
             Pub: Calendar of State Papers, Domestic.   James I, 1623–1625, p. 250.

MAY 28

677.* Sir Robert Heath. "Severall greiuances presented to King James by Sʳ Robert Heath (then Sollicitoʳ geñall) vpon Friday the 28th of May in the name of the Lower House of Parliament in the Banquetting House at Whitehall 1624—concerning Trade" and tobacco.
      VII.   *Ref:* Harleian MSS., 2244, fo. 15.   BM.

MAY 30

678.* Ralph Hamour. "To the honoᵘʳˢ Sʳ Francis Wyatt knight &c and the rest of Counsell of Estate in Virginia. The Humble Petition" concerning the destruction of his patent in the massacre.   LC.
      IV.   *Ref:* MS. Rec. Virginia Co., III, pt. ii, p. 61.

JUNE (?)

679. Henry, Earl of Southampton, and certain other Lords appointed a Council for Virginia.
      I.   *Ref:* Minutes, Colonial Correspondence, 1609, p. 1.   PRO.
             Pub: Sainsbury, *Calendar of State Papers, Colonial*, p. 63.

680. [Nathaniel Rich(?).] An act concerning tobacco. [Proposed bill by Parliament.]   PRO.
      VI.   *Ref:* Manchester Papers, No. 406.

681. Rough draft of a suggestion for preemption of tobacco, and prohibition of planters in England, Ireland, and Wales, and importation of any except from Virginia and Summer Islands.
      VI.   *Ref:* Manchester Papers, Nos. 365, 404, 407.   PRO.
             Pub: Calendar: Hist. MSS. Com., *Eighth Report*, pt. 2, pp. 45, 48.

682. House of Commons. Petition to the King for exclusion of all tobacco not grown in his Majesty's Dominion.   PRO.
      I.   *Ref:* Manchester Papers, No. 405.
             Pub: Calendar: Hist. MSS. Com., *Eighth Report*, pt. 2, p. 48.

JUNE 14

683.* Secretary Conway. A letter to Sir Thomas Merry stating that the King desired letters and papers relating to affairs of Virginia in possession of his late cousin, employed in that business, to be preserved, and any other papers on the business.   PRO.

    I.   *Ref:* State Papers, Domestic, James I, Vol. 167, No. 60.

         Pub: Sainsbury, *Calendar of State Papers, Colonial*, p. 62.

JUNE 15 (?)

684.* Governor Sir Francis Wyatt, Council, and Assembly in Virginia. Petition to the King, expressing fear that the petition sent by John Pountis was not delivered and complaining of the desperate state of the colony.   PRO.

    IV.   *Ref:* State Papers, Colonial, James I, Vol. III, No. 42.

         Pub: Sainsbury, *Calendar of State Papers, Colonial*, p. 74.

           D. S.   Transcript: New York Public Library, Bancroft, II, 585–590.

JUNE 22

685.* Petition concerning Virginia intended for delivery to the King, claiming a desire for revision of affairs only.   PRO.

    VI.   *Ref:* Manchester Papers, No. 403.

         Pub: Calendar: Hist. MSS. Com., *Eighth Report*, pt. 2, p. 48.

JUNE 24

686.* Assembly in Virginia. Law against unlawful implied contracts of marriage.

    IV.   *Ref:* MS. Rec. Virginia Co., III, pt. ii, p. 49.   LC.

687.* Privy Council Order appointing Lord President Mandeville, Lord Paget, Lord Chichester, and others, Commissioners to resolve on the well settling of the colony, to give order therefore, to certify proceedings to the King, and to receive further directions. King determined to give new charter.   (1) PC.   (2) PRO.   [NY]

    I.   *Ref:* (1) Colonial Entry Book, Vol. 79, p. 210.   (2) Privy Council Register, James I, Vol. VI, p. 342.

         Pub: Sainsbury, *Calendar of State Papers, Colonial*, p. 62.

           Transcript: New York Public Library, Bancroft Papers, II, 477–479.

JUNE 26

688.* Commissioners and Adventurers of Virginia Company. Petition to Privy Council that Captain John Bargrave's protection be not renewed till course be taken for the payment of £800 bond for debt of £500.   PRO. [NY]

    III.   *Ref:* State Papers, Colonial, James I, Vol. III, No. 16.

         Pub: Sainsbury, *Calendar of State Papers, Colonial*, p. 62.

           Transcript, New York Public Library, Bancroft Papers, II, 485–487.

689.* Privy Council. Order for Mr. Ferrar, Deputy, to bring to the Council Chamber all patents, books of account, and invoices of the late corporation and lists of people in the Colony, to be retained by the Keeper of the Council Chest till further order.

                                        (1) PC.   (2) PRO.   [NY]

    I.   *Ref:* (1) Privy Council Register, James I, Vol. VI, p. 344.   (2) Colonial Entry Book, Vol. 79, p. 277.

         Pub: Sainsbury, *Calendar of State Papers, Colonial*, p. 62.

           Transcript, New York Public Library, Bancroft Papers, II, 481.

690.* —— Order to the Commissioners for the Virginia business concerning the stock, etc., of the Virginia Company.   PC.

    I.   *Ref:* Privy Council Register, James I, Vol. VI, p. 345.

691.* **Reasons** alleged on behalf of King's Farmers of the custom and impost on tobacco, for redress
of grievances.   PRO. [NY]
    VI.   *Ref:* State Papers, Colonial, James I, Vol. III, No. 22.
          Pub: Sainsbury, *Calendar of State Papers, Colonial*, pp. 68–69.
            Transcript, New York Public Library, Bancroft Papers, II, 573–583.

692.* **Brief** answer to a proposition touching tobacco lately delivered by the King's Farmers of
Customs.   PRO.
    VI.   *Ref:* State Papers, Colonial, James I, Vol. III, No. 23.
          Pub: Sainsbury, *Calendar of State Papers, Colonial*, p. 69.

693.* **Request** to [Privy Council ?] that as King is concluding a contract with divers persons for his
own use, orders should be given to the Governor in Virginia not to suffer trade with the
Hollanders who are now freighting ships for that purpose, since their produce is not
needed there.   PRO.
    VI.   *Ref:* State Papers, Domestic, James I, Vol. 169, No. 7.
          Pub: Sainsbury, *Calendar of State Papers, Colonial*, p. 63.

694.* **"A Briefe** Declaration of the plantation of Virginia during the first twelve years when S[r]
Thomas Smyth was Governor of the Companie [1606–1619] and downe to the present
tyme [1624] by the Ancient Planters now remaining alive in Virginia."
    III.   *Ref:* State Papers, Colonial, James I, Vol. III, p. 21.   PRO. [NY]
          Pub: (1) Wynne and Gilman, *Colonial Records of Virginia* (State Senate Document,
Extra, 1874). (2) Brown, *First Republic*, 572–574. (3) Sainsbury, *Calendar of State
Papers, Colonial*, pp. 66–68.
            Transcript, New York Public Library, Bancroft Papers, I, fos. 529–609.

695. **[Solicitor-General Heath.]** Statement as to a contract ordered by King on July 2/24 as to
tobacco.   PRO.
    I.   *Ref:* State Papers, Domestic, James I, Vol. 169, No. 6.
          Pub: Sainsbury, *Calendar of State Papers, Colonial*, p. 63.

696.* **James I.** A letter to Solicitor-General Heath, concerning a petition of House of Commons
against the importation of foreign tobacco, and a petition of planters and adventurers for
a reasonable price.   PRO.
    I.   *Ref:* State Papers, Domestic, James I, Vol. 169, No. 5.
          Pub: Sainsbury, *Calendar of State Papers, Colonial*, p. 63.

697. **Nethersole.** A letter to Sir Dudley Carleton, concerning the overthrow of the Virginia patent
by the *quo warranto.*   PRO.
    VII.   *Ref:* State Papers, Domestic, James I, Vol. 169, No. 14.
          Pub: (1) Calendar: *Virginia Mag. of Hist.*, VII, 39. (2) Sainsbury, *Calendar of State
Papers, Colonial*, p. 63.

698.* **Governor, Council, and Colony in Virginia.** To the Kings moste Excelent Ma[tie]. "The
Humble Petitione of the Gou[r]nor Counsell and Colony of Virginia in theire generall
Assemblie," praying for a continuation of the present government.   (1) LC.   (2) PRO.
    IV.   *Ref:* (1) MS. Records, Virginia Co., III, pt. i, p. 5[a]. (2) State Papers, Colonial,
James I, Vol. III, No. 21.
          Pub: (1) Calendar: *Virginia Mag. of Hist.*, VII, 45. (2) Sainsbury, *Calendar of State
Papers, Colonial*, p. 65.
            D. S. in the State Papers, Colonial.
            Date uncertain.

699.* **David Sandis.** "To the Hono^ble the Governor wth the rest the worⅱ Counsellors of Estate."
Petition for justice because of defamations by one, Alnut. LC.

    IV.   *Ref:* MS. Records, Virginia Co., III, pt. ii, p. 61^a.

700. **Council in Virginia.** Order that persons remaining at home shall give day's work in place
of those on the march; ordering a commission to be granted to council at home for
dispatch of business until governor's return; also concerning fining Thomas Alnet for
defamation of character of Minister Sandis. LC.

    IV.   *Ref:* MS. Court Book of the Colony.

701.* **James I.** Commission to certain of the Lords of the Privy Council and others for settling a
government in Virginia. (1) BM. (2) PRO.

    I.   *Ref:* (1) Additional MSS., 12496, fos. 464–473. (Caesar Papers.) (2) Patent Roll, 22
James I, pt. 1, No. 4; Chancery Privy Seal, 22 James I, July, 1624.

        Pub: (1) Hazard, *Historical Collection*, I, 183. (2) Rymer, *Foedera*, XVII, 609–613.

702.* **Commissioners for Virginia.** Orders set down at a meeting, July 16, 1624, appointing H.
Fotherby to be in charge of charters, seals, and writings of the company, and providing
for an investigation of the colony. PRO. [LC]

    I.   *Ref:* State Papers, Colonial, James I, Vol. III, No. 17, I.

        Pub: (1) Calendar: *Virginia Mag. of Hist.*, VII, 44–45. (2) Sainsbury, *Calendar of
State Papers, Colonial*, p. 64.

          Transcript: Library of Congress, Bancroft Papers, II, 489–495.

703. **Lord President Mandeville.** A letter to Secretary Conway, giving a brief of the proceedings
of the Commissioners for Virginia, with regard to the free importation of tobacco.

    VII.   *Ref:* State Papers, Colonial, James I, Vol. III, No. 17. PRO. [NY]

        Pub: (1) Calendar: *Virginia Mag. of Hist.*, VII, 43–44. (2) Sainsbury, *Calendar of
State Papers, Colonial*, p. 64.

          Transcript: New York Public Library, Bancroft Papers, II, 513–515.

704.* **Privy Council.** An order for the allowance of £150 to [John] Pory, employed in Virginia
about His Majesty's especial business. (1) PC. (2) PRO.

    I.   *Ref:* (1) Privy Council Register, James I, Vol. VI, p. 376. (2) Colonial Entry Book,
Vol. 79, p. 277.

        Pub: Sainsbury, *Calendar of State Papers, Colonial*, p. 64.

705. **Secretary Conway.** A letter to Lord President Mandeville, stating that the King approves
the proceedings in the Virginia business, and that the restraint as to tobacco is to be
considered. PRO.

    VII.   *Ref:* Minute. Conway's Letter Book, 136.

        Pub: Sainsbury, *Calendar of State Papers, Colonial*, p. 64.

706. ———. A letter to Lord Coventry, concerning putting Mr. Bing in the Commission for Virginia, if there is no cause to the contrary. PRO.

    VII.   *Ref:* Minute. Conway's Letter Book, 137.

        Pub: Sainsbury, *Calendar of State Papers, Colonial*, p. 64.

707.* **Warrant** to pay John Pory £150 in payment of expenditure of £100, and for services in Virginia on King's business.   PRO.
    I.   *Ref:* Sign Manual, James I, Vol. 16, No. 50.
        Pub: Sainsbury, *Calendar of State Papers, Colonial,* p. 65.

708. **Lord Coventry.** A letter to Secretary Conway, stating why Mr. Bing was willingly forgotten from the Commission for Virginia.   PRO. [NY]
    VII. *Ref:* State Papers, Colonial, James I, Vol. III, No. 18.
        Pub: Sainsbury, *Calendar of State Papers, Colonial,* p. 65.
           Transcript: New York Public Library, Bancroft Papers, II, 501–503.

709. **Secretary Conway.** A letter to Lord President Mandeville, concerning John Bargrave.
    VII. *Ref:* State Papers, Domestic, James I, Vol. 170, No. 65.   PRO.
        Pub: Sainsbury, *Calendar of State Papers, Colonial,* p. 65.

710. **Solicitor-General Heath.** A letter to Secretary Conway, stating that the Commission deems it best that the commission from the King be sent to the principal men in Virginia for the present government of the Colony.   PRO. [NY]
    VII. *Ref:* State Papers, Colonial, James I, Vol. III, No. 19.
        Pub: (1) Calendar: *Virginia Mag. of Hist.,* VII, 45.   (2) Sainsbury, *Calendar of State Papers, Colonial,* p. 65.
           Transcript: New York Public Library, Bancroft Papers, II, 505–507.

711. **Sir Thomas Smythe.** A letter to Secretary Conway, stating that the Virginia Company hoped that John Bargrave would pay £500 due before his protection was renewed, and enclosing a petition to the King.   PRO. [NY]
    VII. *Ref:* State Papers, Colonial, James I, Vol. III, No. 20.
        Pub: Sainsbury, *Calendar of State Papers, Colonial,* p. 65.
           A. S. Transcript: New York Public Library, Bancroft Papers, II, 509, 511.

712. **Solicitor-General Heath.** A letter to the Duke of Buckingham, entreating his assistance in settling the contract for Virginia tobacco.   PRO.
    VII. *Ref:* State Papers, Domestic, James I, Vol. 171, No. 7.
        Pub: Sainsbury, *Calendar of State Papers, Colonial,* p. 69.

713. **Sir Thomas Smythe.** A letter to Lord President Mandeville, requesting him to hinder or defer Captain Bargrave's protection, as he hopes to procure a countermand from the King.   PRO. [NY]
    VII. *Ref:* State Papers, Colonial, James I, Vol. III, No. 24.
        Pub: Sainsbury, *Calendar of State Papers, Colonial,* p. 69.
           A. S. Transcript: New York Public Library, Bancroft Papers, II, 517–519.

AUGUST 9

714. Robert, Earl of Warwick. A letter to Secretary Conway, sending Mr. Pory with the commission [for Virginia], to desire him to put out Mr. Pott's name, who was a poisoner of savages there and hence unfit for State business; and asking him to remind the King to write Mr. Attorney to put Mr. Bing on the Commission according to promise.

    VII.   *Ref:* State Papers, Colonial, James I, Vol. III, No. 25.   PRO. [NY]

           Pub: (1) Calendar: *Virginia Mag. of Hist.*, VII, 51.   (2) Sainsbury, *Calendar of State Papers, Colonial,* p. 69.

               Transcript: New York Public Library, Bancroft Papers, II, 521.

AUGUST 13

715. Secretary Conway. A letter to Attorney-General Coventry, concerning conferring with Sir Thos. Smythe and the Earl of Warwick about putting Mr. Bing on the Commission.

    VII   *Ref:* Minute, Conway's Letter Book.   PRO.

           Pub: Sainsbury, *Calendar of State Papers, Colonial,* p. 69.

716. —— A letter to Solicitor-General Heath concerning the returns of the Commission for a Council in Virginia.   PRO

    VII.   *Ref:* State Papers, Domestic, James I, Vol. 171, No. 47.

           Pub: Sainsbury, *Calendar of State Papers, Colonial,* p. 69.

AUGUST 16

717. John Harrison. Power of attorney from John Harrison, of London, to John Carter, master of "Anne."   PRO. [NY]

    VI.   *Ref:* State Papers, Colonial, James I, Vol. III, Nos. 26, 27.

           Pub: Sainsbury, *Calendar of State Papers, Colonial,* p. 69.

               Transcript: New York Public Library, Bancroft Papers, II, 525-529.

718. Council in Virginia. Court Book of the Council in Virginia concerning the complaint of Ensign John Ulie (?) against Tyler for slander.   LC.

    IV.   *Ref:* MS. Court Book of the Colony.

AUGUST 23

719. Council in Virginia. Court Book of the Council in Virginia concerning the sentence of William Tyler for slander.   LC.

    IV.   *Ref:* MS. Court Book of the Colony.

AUGUST 26

720. James I. Commission to Sir Francis Wyatt as governor and to the Council in Virginia.

                                            PRO.

    I.   *Ref:* (1) Patent Roll, 22 James I, pt. 17, No. 2.   (2) Chancery Privy Seal, 22 James I, August.

       Pub: (1) Hazard, *Historical Collection of State Papers*, I, 189-192.   (2) Rymer, *Foedera,* XVIII, 618.

SEPTEMBER 5, 12

721. Council in Virginia. Court Book of the Council in Virginia: list of persons coming to James City, Virginia, in the "Bonny Bess," who took the oath of supremacy.

    IV.   *Ref:* MS. Court Book of the Colony.   LC.

SEPTEMBER 13 OR 15 (?)

722. James I. Commission as governor to Sir George Yeardley in the absence of Sir Francis Wyatt.   (1) PRO. (2) LC.

    I.   *Ref:* (1) Docquet Book, Domestic, James I.   (2) Misc. Records, 1606-1692. (Bland Copy), 122-125.

       Pub: (1) Hazard, *Historical Collection*, I, 235.   (2) Sainsbury, *Calendar of State Papers, Colonial,* p. 69.

723. Council in Virginia. Court Book of the Council in Virginia concerning the fining several
offenders, 20 nobles, toward the repair of the church, for drinking.   LC.

    IV. *Ref:* MS. Court Book of the Colony.

724. Privy Council. An order for an exact account of John Puntis's property to be sent to Thos.
Merry   (1) PC.   (2) PRO.   [NY]

    I. *Ref:* Privy Council Register, James I, Vol. VI, p. 449.
        Pub: Sainsbury, *Calendar of State Papers, Colonial,* p. 70.
           Transcript: New York Public Library, Bancroft Papers, II, 583-585.

725. James I. Proclamation restraining the importation of tobacco except from Virginia and the
Summer Islands. Printed.   JCB.

    I. *Pub:* (1) Hazard, *Historical Collection,* I, 193-198.   (2) Rymer, *Foedera,* XVII, 621.

726. Capt. John Bargrave. A letter to ——, concerning a remodelled project, the only safe and
profitable way to plant Virginia.   PRO.

    VI. *Ref:* State Papers, Domestic, James I, Vol. 173, Nos. 120, 121.
        Pub: Sainsbury, *Calander of State Papers, Colonial,* p. 70.

727. Council in Virginia. Court Book of the Council in Virginia concerning Sybill Royall's will.
                                                                      LC.

    IV. *Ref:* MS. Court Book of the Colony.

728. Council in Virginia. Court Book of the Council in Virginia concerning: I. Accusations
against Captain John Martin for slanderous sayings. II. Claim that Company had
right to appoint ministers. III. Difference as to division of parishes, payment of work-
man's wages for church. IV. Complaints of Elizabeth Abbot's servant—having been
beaten by Mr. Procter, her master.   LC.

    IV. *Ref:* MS. Court Book of the Colony.

729. [Privy Council.] Warrant to prepare a bill for Edward Dichfield and five others on the
recommendation of Virginia Commission, appointing them officers for searching and
sealing tobacco.   PRO.

    I. *Ref:* State Papers, Domestic, James I, Vol. 173, No. 55.
        Pub: Sainsbury, *Calendar of State Papers, Colonial,* p. 71.

730. Council in Virginia. Court Book of the council in Virginia, granting several leases to persons
on governor's and college land for a term of five years from date.   LC.

    IV. *Ref:* MS. Court Book of the Colony.

731. Privy Council. Warrant to Lord Carew, Master of Ordinance, to deliver to the Virginia Commissioner one last of powder.   (1) PC. (2) PRO.

    I. *Ref:* (1) Privy Council Register, James I, Vol. VI, p. 474.   (2) Colonial Entry Book,
Vol. 79, p. 278.
    Pub: Sainsbury, *Calendar of State Papers, Colonial,* p. 70.

732. Council in Virginia. Court Book of the council in Virginia, concerning the complaint of Capt. John Martyn against the master of ship for nine weeks' detention in New England.   LC.

IV.   *Ref:* MS. Court Book of the Colony.

733. "Att the same tyme there was a newe offer made by dyuers honest Men for the good of the Plantation and presented to Mr. Soliciter the :28th of October 1624."   BM. [LC]

VI.   *Ref:* Additional MSS., 12496, fo. 447.   (Caesar Papers.)

734. [Sir Nathaniel Rich.]   Rough notes in criticism of Captain John Bargrave's proposition.

VI.   *Ref:* Manchester Papers, No. 409.   PRO.
   Pub: Calendar: Hist. MSS. Com., *Eighth Report*, pt. 2, p. 48.

735.* Meeting of the adventurers of Martin's Hundred, concerning the land for the East India School.   MC.

VI.   *Ref:* Ferrar Papers.

736. Council in Virginia. Action concerning a will, a complaint, and use of arms by the Indians.   LC.

IV.   *Ref:* MS. Court Book of the Colony.

737. The King. "Proclamation of a concession to Edward Dichfield and others" concerning tobacco.

I.   *Pub:* (1) Hazard, *Historical Collection*, I, 198–202.   (2) Rymer, *Foedera*, XVII, 633.

738. Sirs Thomas Smythe and others. Sirs Thomas Smythe and others, of the council for Virginia, to the Earl of Warwick.   PRO. [NY]

III.   *Ref:* State Papers, Colonial, James I, Vol. III, No. 28.
   Pub: Sainsbury, *Calendar of State Papers, Colonial*, p. 70.
   Transcript: New York Public Library, Bancroft Papers, II, 541-543.

739. Privy Council. A letter to Commissioners for Virginia, to investigate the claims of Lady Wyatt on behalf of her late husband *vs.* the Virginia Company.   PC.

I.   *Ref:* Privy Council Register, James I, Vol. VI, p. 496.

740. [Secretary Conway.] A letter to Solicitor General Heath, stating that the King desires him to prepare grant of denization to Beaumont.   PRO.

VII.   *Ref:* State Papers, Domestic, James I, Vol. 164, No. 85.
   Pub: Sainsbury, *Calendar of State Papers, Colonial*, p. 70.

741. Council in Virginia. Court Book of the Council in Virginia concerning: I. Oath in regard to Captain John Martyn; II. Petition of Alice Boyle, concerning slander of herself by Johane Wilson.   LC.

IV.   *Ref:* MS. Court Book of the Colony.

NOVEMBER 28

742. James I.   A letter to the Commission and Company of Virginia, recommending James Stuart
for fit employment.   PRO.   [NY]
   I.   *Ref:* State Papers, Colonial, James I, Vol. III, No. 29.
        Pub: Sainsbury, *Calendar of State Papers, Colonial*, p. 70.
          Transcript: New York Public Library, Bancroft Papers, II, 545.

DECEMBER 2

743.* Council in Virginia.   Letter "To the right Honobtᵉ Henry Earle of Suthamptone, with the
Lordes and others of the counsell & compeny of Virginia," concerning the victory over
the Indians.   (1) LC.   (2) PRO.
   IV.   *Ref:* (1) MS. Rec. Virginia Co., III, pt. i, p. 11a.   (2) State Papers, Colonial, James I,
        Vol. III, No. 30.
          Pub: (1) Calendar: *Virginia Mag. of Hist.*, VII, 130–131.   (2) Sainsbury, *Calendar
          of State Papers, Colonial*, pp. 70–71.
        D. S.

DECEMBER 18

744. Commissioners for Virginia.   A letter to the King, concerning tobacco.
   I.   *Ref:* State Papers, Colonial, James I, Vol. III, No. 31.   PRO.
        Pub: Sainsbury, *Calendar of State Papers, Colonial*, p. 71.
          D. S. and with seal. 1624 (?).

1624 (?)

DECEMBER 22

745. Colonists in Virginia.   A letter concerning the intolerable rates for commodities.
   IV.   *Pub: Purchas, His. Pilgrimes.*

1624

DECEMBER 27

746.* Council in Virginia.   Orders on the demands of Captain Martin.   PRO.   [NY]
   IV.   *Ref:* State Papers, Colonial, James I, Vol. III, No. 36, II.
        Pub: Virginia Mag. of Hist., VII, 145–146.
          Transcript: New York Public Library, Bancroft Papers, II, 565–571. Series attested by Secre-
          tary Southerne.

DECEMBER 31

747. Grant to Beaumont of denization, confirming lands and liberty in Virginia as granted by the
Commission for Virginia.   PRO.
   I.   *Ref:* Docquet Book, Domestic, James I.
        Pub: Sainsbury, *Calendar of State Papers, Colonial*, p. 71.

1625

748. "**Considerations** Touching the New Contract for Tobacco. As the same Hath beene propounded by Maister Ditchfield, and other vndertakers."   Printed.   (1) BM.   (2) PRO.
   VI.   *Ref:* (1) Additional MSS., 12496, fos. 440–446 (Caesar Papers).   (2) State Papers,
        Colonial, James I, Vol. III, No. 32.
        Pub: Sainsbury, *Calendar of State Papers, Colonial*, p. 71.

1624/5

JANUARY 7

749. Solicitor-General Heath. Motion for release of "Elizabeth of London," Richard Page, Master, bound to Virginia.   PRO.

    VII.   *Ref:* State Papers, Colonial, James I, Vol. III, No. 33.

       Pub: Sainsbury, *Calendar of State Papers, Colonial,* p. 71.

JANUARY 10

750. Sir Francis Wyatt, Governor, and Council in Virginia. A letter to the Earl of Southampton and the Company of Virginia.   PRO. [NY]

    IV.   *Ref:* State Papers, Colonial, James I, Vol. III, No. 34.

       Pub: Sainsbury, *Calendar of State Papers, Colonial,* pp. 71–72.

         (1) Transcript: New York Public Library, Bancroft Papers, III, 141–143.

         (2) D. S. with a seal.

BETWEEN JANUARY 20 AND FEBRUARY 7

751.* Census of 1624.   (1) PRO. [LC] [NY]

    IV.   *Ref:* State Papers, Colonial, James I, Vol. III, No. 35.

       Pub: (1) Neill, in *New England Hist. and Geneal. Register,* Vol. 31, pp. 147, 265, 393. (2) Brown, *First Republic,* 611–627. (3) Summary: *Virginia Mag. of Hist.,* VII, 364–367.

         (1) Transcript: New York Public Library, Bancroft Papers, II, 601–617.

         (2) Document in State Papers, Colonial, in the autograph of Ed. Sharpless.

FEBRUARY

752.* John Harvey. "A Briefe Declaration of the state of Virginia at my cominge from thence in February 1624."   [NY]

    IV.   *Pub:* Mass. Hist. Soc. Collections, fourth series, IX, 60–73.

         Transcript: New York Public Library, Barlow Papers, Virginia, I, No. 27.

FEBRUARY 4

753.* Sir George Yeardley. Answer of defendant to the demand of Capt. John Martin, requiring recompense for wrongs done, and touching his right to cattle left in charge of Lieut. Edmund Saunders.   PRO. [NY]

    IV.   *Ref:* State Papers, Colonial, James I, Vol. III, No. 36.

       Pub: (1) *Virginia Mag. of Hist.,* VII, 136–144. (2) Sainsbury, *Calendar of State Papers, Colonial,* p. 72.

         (1) Transcript: New York Public Library, Bancroft Papers, III, 145–147.

         (2) Autograph of Edward Sharpless, attested by John Southerne.

754.* Examination of witnesses concerning the demands of Capt. John Martin.   PRO.

    IV.   *Ref:* State Papers, Colonial, James I, Vol. III, No. 36.

         Attested by Southerne.

755.* Council in Virginia. Letter from council in Virginia to the Virginia Company of London concerning Capt. John Martin.   (1) LC. (2) PRO. [NY]

    IV.   *Ref:* (1) MS. Rec. Virginia Co., III, pt. ii, p. 12. (2) State Papers, Colonial, James I, Vol. III, No. 36.

       Pub: (1) Calendar: *Virginia Mag. of Hist.,* VII, 131–132. (2) Sainsbury *Calendar of State Papers, Colonial,* p. 72.

         (1) Transcript: New York Public Library, Bancroft Papers, II, 549–555. (2) Photograph in the Library of Congress.

MARCH 2

756. James I. Proclamation for the utter prohibition of the importation and use of all tobacco, which is not of the proper growth of the colonies of Virginia and the Sommer Islands or one of them.   BM.

I   *Ref:* Additional MSS., 12496, fo. 461. (Caesar Papers.)
         Pub: (1) Hazard, *Historical Collection*, I, 224-230. (2) Rymer, *Foedera*, XVII, 668-672.

1625/6

MARCH 4

757. Privy Council. Commission to George Yeardley to exercise government as fully as any governor in the past five years.   PRO.

1.   *Ref:* Colonial Entry Book, Vol. 79, pp. 248-256.
         Pub: (1) Hazard, *Historical Collection*, I, 230-234. (2) Rymer, *Foedera*, XVIII, 311.
         (3) Sainsbury, *Calendar of State Papers, Colonial*, p. 77.

1625

APRIL (?)

758.* Virginia Company. "Discourse of the Old Company." Answer to the Privy Council, requesting a new patent with the old privileges and liberties, and reviewing the history since 1606.   PRO. [N Y]

III.   *Ref:* State Papers, Colonial, James I, Vol. III, No. 40.
         Pub: (1) *Virginia Mag. of Hist.*, I, 155-167; 287-309. (2) Sainsbury, *Calendar of State Papers, Colonial*, p. 73.

         Transcript New York Public Library, Bancroft Papers, III, 1-133.

MAY

759.* "**Extracte** of all yᵉ titles & estates of land" sent home by Sʳ Francis Wyatt (when he returned for England) vnto the Lˢ of his Priuy Councell according vnto their Order in their letter dated at Salsbury. W. Claibourne."   (1) & (2) LC

IV.   *Ref:* (1) MS. Rec. Virginia Co., III, pt. ii, pp. 71-75. (2) Virginia Records, 1606-1692, pp. 84-91.

MAY 13

760. Charles I. A proclamation settling the plantation of Virginia.   PRO.

I.   *Ref:* Proclamation, Charles I, No. 10.
         Pub: (1) Hazard, *Historical Collection*, I, 203-205. (2) Rymer, *Foedera*, XVIII, 72.

JUNE 15

761.* Council in Virginia. Letter to the "Right Honorbˡᵉ the Lord of his Maᵗⁱᵉˢ moste Honorbˡᵉ Priuy Councell," concerning property of John Pountis, punishment of Edward Sharples, and the sole importation of tobacco.   (1) LC.   (2) PRO.

IV.   *Ref:* (1) MS. Rec. Virginia Co., III, pt. 1, pp. 14, 14ᵃ. (2) State Papers, Colonial, James I, Vol. III, No. 41.
         Pub: (1) Calendar: *Virginia Mag. of Hist.*, VII, 134-136. (2) Sainsbury, *Calendar of State Papers, Colonial*, p. 74.

762.* ——. Letter to "the right Honobˡl, the Lords and other his Maᵗⁱᵉˢ Commissioners for yᵉ affayers of Virginia," concerning the establishment of a new government and the condition of the Colony, defending it from evil reports.   LC.

IV.   *Ref:* MS. Rec. Virginia Co., III, pt. i, pp. 12-13a.

1625/6

JANUARY 4

763.* Governor and Council in Virginia. Letter to the Royal Commissioners for the affairs of
Virginia.   (1) LC.   (2) PRO.

    IV.   *Ref:* (1) MS. Rec. Virginia Co., III, pt. ii, pp. 68, 69.   (2) State Papers, Colonial,
        James I, Vol. IV, No. 1.

        Pub: Sainsbury, *Calendar of State Papers, Colonial,* p. 77.

1626

APRIL 6

764.* Governor and Council in Virginia. Letter to "the right Honor^ble the Lo^rds of his Maties most
Honorabl Priuy Counsell."   LC.

    IV.   *Ref:* (1) MS. Rec. Virginia Co., III, pt. ii, pp. 69–70.   (2) State Papers, Colonial,
        James I, Vol. IV, No. 9.

        Pub: (1) Massachusetts Historical Society Collection, fourth series, IX, 74–81.
          (2) Sainsbury, *Calendar of State Papers, Colonial,* p. 79.

            D. 8.

39. Omit: "*Pub: Va. Mag. of Hist.*, IV, 28–29."

40ᵃ. Add, following No. 40 under date of June 9:
Governor Argall. A letter.
> IV. *Ref:* (1) Misc. Papers, 1606–1683, quarto. (Abstract only.) (2) MS. Coll. Va. Hist. Soc., John Randolph MSS., III.
> *Pub: Va. Mag. of Hist.*, IV, 28.

43–48, 50–52, 55–57. *Ref:* Change to: See under No. 39.

64. Change note to: See No. 39, Remarks.

65. *Ref:* Omit: "(Abstract only)". Add: (2) MS. Coll. Va. Hist. Soc., John Randolph MSS., III.
Pub: Add: *Va. Mag. of Hist.*, IV, 29.
Change note to: See No. 39, Remarks.

67, 74, 75. Change note to: See No. 39, Remarks.

78. *Ref:* Change to: See under No. 71.
Pub: Change to: See under No. 71.

108ᵃ. Add, following No. 108 under date of May 25:
James I. Proclamation concerning tobacco.
> *Pub:* Referred to only in Rymer, *Foedera*, 17, 191.

137ᵃ. Add, following No. 137 under date of November 10:
James I. Proclamation concerning tobacco.
> *Pub:* Referred to only in Rymer, *Foedera*, 17, 191.

167. *Ref:* Change to: (1) Privy Council Register, James I, Vol. IV, p. 471.

167ᵃ. Add, following No. 167 under date of April 7:
James I. Proclamation concerning the garbling of tobacco.
> *Pub:* Rymer, *Foedera*, 17, 191.

184. *Pub:* Add, Rymer, *Foedera*, 17, 233.

511. Change to: For the petition formulated, see *ante* No. 481.

Table of Explanations

~ over a word indicates a contraction or an omission of letters.

* * * * * indicate an unintelligible word or part of a word in the manuscript, there being approximately as many asterisks as letters in the word.

[   ] inclose words or letters which are doubtful in the manuscript; also, in a few instances, inclose words or letters reduplicated in the manuscript.

[   ] inclosing words in italics indicate explanations by the editor; also, in a few instances, italics indicate letters supplied by the editor to complete a word.

A line drawn through a word or a part of a word indicates a word or letters canceled in the manuscript.

|| || inclose words interlined in the manuscript by the reviewer.

§   § inclose words interlined in the manuscript by the copyist.

———— indicates words underlined in the manuscript.

SIGNS AND ABBREVIATIONS.

c̃on indicates tion.

Co^{rt} indicates Court.

C^r indicates etc.

l̃re, l̃res indicate letter, letters.

^{li} indicates pound.

l̃l^e, LLs, Lo indicate Lords, Lord.

Lo^{ps}, LL^{ps} indicate Lordships.

M^{ts}, Matie indicate Majesty's, Majesty.

o^r, yor indicate our, your.

p indicates per, par, e. g. pvse (peruse).

p indicates pro.

p̃ indicates pre, pri, e. g. p̃uately (privately).

q̃ indicates que.

Tr̃er, Thr̃er indicate Treasurer.

wᵗᵗ indicates weight.

9 indicates omission of final letters or syllable, e. g. man⁹ (manner).

ꝯ indicates final es or et, e. g. handꝯ (handes).

THE COURT BOOK

VOLUME I, 1619–1622

Records of the

Virginia Company of London

28 APRILL 1619

A QUARTER COURT HELD FOR VIRGINIA
AT Sᴿ THOMAS SMITHS HOWSE IN PHILPOTT
LANE 28 OF APRᵞ 1619 PRESENT
RIGHT HONO:ᵐᵉ

The Earle Southampton.
The Earle of Warwick.
The Lo: Cauendish.
The Lo: Pagett.
Generall Cecill.

Sʳ Thomas Smith knᵗ Thᵉrer.

Sʳ Edwin Sandis.	Sʳ Nath. Rich.	mʳ Wᵐ Bell.
Sʳ Iohn Dāuers.	Sʳ Io: Wolstenholme.	mʳ Humfry Handford.
Sʳ Iohn Merrick.	Sʳ Wᵐ Russell.	mʳ Rich: Rogers.
Sʳ Dudley Diggs.	Sʳ Tho: Wilford.	mʳ Iohn fferrar.
Sʳ Nicholas Tufton.	mʳ Aldᵉan Iohnson.	mʳ Clitheroe.
Sʳ Samuell Sandis.	mʳ Morrice Abott.	mʳ Caning.
Sʳ Henry Rainsford.	mʳ Thomas Gibbs.	mʳ Ditchfeild. Cʳ.
Sʳ Robt Wayneman.	mʳ Thomas Stiles.	
Sʳ Tho: Cheeke.	mʳ Wᵐ Greenwell.	

The last Court referring the duty appertayning to every perticuler
Office to be considered and prepared against the Quarter Court by a
select Comittee, they haue therein taken extraordinary paines: And

according as they were desired haue attended the ħᵉ and receaued their approbaĉon of the orders by them conceiued: Wᶜʰ orders were now presented to the Court; where after they were twice read, (being putt to the question) they were confirmed by a Generall erecĉon of handɛ.[1]

This Quarter Court according to the Lřes Pattents being chiefly ordayned for the elecĉon of Officers: Mʳ Třer desired the Court that before he left his place, he might acquaynt them wᵗʰ two messages Lately reĉ from the King: The one was, that he receaued a ħre from mʳ Secretarie Caluert that his Maᵗᶦᵉ had sent a man vp suspected for Deere stealing, to be transported for Virginia; and vnderstanding that Mʳ Iohn fferrar had a shipp shortly to goe thither, ‖ desired ‖ that his Maᵗᶦᵉ resoluĉon might be fulfilled therein. The other was, that this morning there came a messenger of the Chamber to vnderstand of the welfare of the Plantation, his Maᵗʸ hauing heard that a Shipp was come from thence: And so desired the Court to proceed to the choice of their Officers, signifying that for these Twelue yeares he hath willingly spent his Laboʳs and endeauoᵐ for the support thereof: and being now appointed by the Kinge a Comissioneʳ of his Nauie he could not giue such good attendance as he therein desired. Requesting the Court to shewe him so much fauoʳ as now ‖ to ‖ dispence with him, and to elect [2] some worthy man in his place, for he had resolued to relinquish it, and therefore desired that two requests might be graunted him for all his service done vnto them. ffirst that he ~~may~~ ‖ might ‖ haue their good report according as he hath deserued: And secondly that his account might be wᵗʰ all speed audited, that before he dyes, he might see the same cleered, and receiue his Quietus est vnder the Companies seale. Wᶜʰ the Coʳᵗ finding his resoluĉon to be settled, and that he would not stand in elecĉon; they proceeded according to the Last Standing order now read, to make choice of their Treasuroʳ   Sʳ Edwin Sandis, Sʳ Iohn Wolstenholme and mʳ Aldřan Iohnson being nominated and accordingly ballated, the Lott fell to Sʳ Edwin Sandis to be Třer, he hauing 59 balls, Sir Io: Wolstenholme: 23: and Aldřan Iohnson: 18: wherevpon his oath was administred.[2]

---

[1] For a draft of this report see List of Records, No. 105, page 133 *ante.*
[2] For documents relating to this election see List of Records, Nos. 108 and 170, pages 133 and 140, *ante.*

Proceeding to the elecc̄on of the Deputy, there was nominated mʳ Aldeȓ Iohnson, mʳ Xofer Cletheroe, and mʳ Iohn fferrar, who being balloted mʳ Iohn fferrar was elected Deputy for the ensuing yeare by hauing 52 balls, mʳ Aldȓan Iohnson 29, and mʳ Christopher Cletheroe ten; vpon wch the said mʳ Iohn fferrar had his Oath giuen.

Next the Court proceeded to the elecc̄on of the Comittees, wch was performed according to the Standing order now read, one fourth part being nowe elected, and the rest by erecc̄on of hands confirmed, Their names be these,

mʳ Raphe Gore.	mʳ Edw: Ditchfield.	mʳ Caswell.
mʳ Wm Caninge.	mʳ Geo: Smith.	mʳ Paulson.
mʳ Wm Palmer.	mʳ Dan: Darnelly.	mʳ Keightley.
mʳ Wm Essington.	mʳ Ri: Morer.	mʳ Chambers.
mʳ Tho. Wheatley.	mʳ Berblock.	mʳ Wiseman.
		mʳ Barnard

In like sort for Auditors the Court now haue made choice for the succeeding yeare of Sʳ Io: Dāuers, mʳ Io: Wroth, mʳ Essington, mʳ Io: fferrar, mʳ Briggs, mʳ Wiseman and mʳ Chambers, who taking their Oaths, all saue mʳ Iohn Wroth who was absent, they or any three of them were desired to bestowe some extraordinary paines in the expediting of the Acc° wch they haue promised to performe.

Valentine Markham Bookeeper	Was confirmed in their former places and tooke each of them the same Oath.
William Webb Husband	
ffrancis Carter the Officer Cʳ	
Henry ffotherby Secretary	

Vpon the absence of Sʳ Tho: Smith the Court was moued by Sʳ Edwin Sandis now Treasuror, that in considerac̄on of the greate trouble [3] mixed often with much sorrowe wch Sʳ Thomas Smith had endured, during the terme of Twelue yeares past from the very infancy of the Plantac̄on vnto this present, and had now surrendred vp his place at such time as (by the blessing of God) there was hope that the Action might proceed and prosper if it were followed wth care and industry requisite for soe greate a busines; That therefore in some sort according to their abillities, it were fitting to express their thankfullnes for his good endeauours in conferring Twenty shares vpon him: w[ch] being put to the question, it was agreed he should haue Twenty greate shares and was confirmed vnto him by a Generall erecčon of handes.

This Court was acquaynted, that the Lord of Salisbury desired the admittance of Captaine   [1] Brett into this ffellowshipp, and to that end his Lő[p] hath giuen him Two of his shares in Virginia, requesting that he might be suffered to sitt in the Courtč, and as occasion serueth to sollicite his busines.   W[ch] the Court hath willingly graunted vnto him, so as the same be donne according to the orders of the Company.

Vpon the request of Captaine Daniell Tucker for this Court to conferr 20 shares vpon him for his fiue yeares service spent in Virginia, aswell for his personall Adventure, as for the severall Offices and eminent places w[ch] there he held and executed, as namely, Capemerchant, Prouant M[r], one of the Counsell, Truck M[r] and Viceadmirall, wherein by reason of shortnes of time, was now referred to the Generall Comittee to giue him reward as they shall thinke fitt.

[1] A blank space in the manuscript.

MAY THE 12th 1619

A COURT HELD FOR VIRGINIA AT MR. FERRARS
HOWSE IN ST. SITHES LANE, BEING PRESENT

The Right ho^{ble} The Earle of Southampton.
The Earle of Warwick.

Sr Edwin Sandis Kn^t Trer.

Sr Dudley Diggs.	m^r Io: fferrar Dpty.	m^r Wheatly.
S^r Io: Dauers.	m^r Thorpe.	m^r Swinhowe
Sr Hen: Rainsford.	m^r Tomlins.	m^r Chambers.
Sr Edward Harwood.	m^r Dr Gulston.	m^r Hen. Briggs.
Sr Nath: Rich.	m^r Oxenbrigg.	m^r Berblock.
S^r Io: Wolstenholme.	m^r Tho Gibbs.	m^r Geo: Smith
Sr Tho: Wroth.	m^r Rogers.	m^r Meuerell, etc.
Sr Tho: Wilford.	m^r Nich° fferrar.	
m^r Iohn Wroth.	m^r Gabriell Barbor.	

It was propounded by mr. Trer that for as much as there hath beene
heretofore two seuerall Comittees appointed by the Court; The first
for making of Orders for the Company, & for matter of Graunts and
Pattents of Land; And [4] the other for the setting downe the duty
of euery perticuler Office, that therefore whither they thought it not
expedient, that there should be a third Comittee appointed to take the
labo^{rs} of both the former Comittees into consideraçon, who by adding
them together, and supplying what may seeme defectiue, may reduce
them into one entire body to be presented to the next Quarter Court
for confirmaçon if they shall see cause. W^{ch} Proposiçon the Court
haue condiscended vnto, and to that end haue desired

Sr Dudley Diggs.   Sr Iohn Wolstenholme.
Sr Edward Harwood.   m^r Alder Iohnson &
Sr Nath: Rich.   m^r Iohn Wroth.

to meete vpon ffriday seavenight being the 21th of this instant at S^r
Edwin Sandis howse at seauen of the Clock in the morning.

Mr. Treasurors second Proposicõn was, that there might be another Comittee for the constituting of Lawes and setling of a forme of Governem^t ouer all Virginia, appointing Magistrates and Officers therevnto, and expressing their seuerall dueties: wch the Court generally did very well approue of and haue nominated the former Comittee, and licenced any of the Counsell to repair vnto them, and to haue their voice, and haue added of the Company to be assisting Sr Thomas Wroth, m^r Thomas Gibbs, m^r Dr Gulson, Captaine Bingham, m^r Wm Essington, m^r Edward Ditchfield, m^r Thomas Kightley, m^r Wm Caninge, m^r Henry Briggs and mr. Thomas Wheatley to meet at the same time and place vpon ffriday ffourtenight being the 28th of this instant.

Mr. Thr̃er intimated to the Court, that whereas Sr Thomas Smith at the resigning vp his place should report that there was —4000^{li} for the new Treasuro^r to enter vpon, he now signified that it was true if the Lotteries were dissolued and the account giuen vp: but in the interim there resteth but One thousand poundes in Cash the rest in Stock remayning in the hands of him that hath the managing of the busines, and out of this there is debts to pay, and wch shortly wilbe due to pay the some of—3700^{li}—viz^{tt} old ~~poun~~ debts of Ten yeares old 1800^{li}— and att the returne of the Shipps Sr Geo: Yeardley went in, and the other wherein the Children was transported will amount to—1148^{li}— as also 700^{li}—wch is owing to the Collecċon mony, wch by warrant hath beene yssued out for the vse of the Company; And therefore it was putt to the question whither the Stock remayning should goe or not to the payment of the Companies debts, wch was by erecċon of handℓ allowed that it should.   And further.agreed that the remaynder should be employed either in sending men to the Publique Land to rayse benefitt that wayes or in transporting of Cattle, wch hereafter may seeme fittest.

And forasmuch as there is now remayning in the hands of Gabriell Barbor much old plate wch if the Lottaries were finished, the Company thereby should sustayne great Losse: It was therefore now ordered (vnlesse some can giue iust informacõn of any perticuler abuse) that the same shall continue to be drawne out till the last of Nouember next ensuing & then to cease and determine. [5]

And forasmuch as Sr Thos. Smith is very importunate for the speedy auditing of his Acc° and to that end hath desired some others to be associated vnto the Audito^rs namely, m^r Morris Abbott, m^r Humph: Handford, and m^r Anthony Abdy: It is therefore ordered, that if he so please these three shalbe annexed vnto them, either as Audito^rs or as assistants to see the passage of the busines, that Sr Thomas Smith haue noe wrong: but if it be his pleasure to allowe of them to be Audito^rs, then the next Quarter Court they to take their Oaths for the preventing of all partiallity, and m^r Thomas Keightly is also chosen to be associated to the Audito^rs and to take his oath. And in asmuch as the great paines allready spent by the Audito^rs hath gayned to them selues a more perfect vnderstanding than those wch shall newly enter cann be capable of. Therefore it was moued that Three of the old Audito^rs might be of the Coram, and that nothing should be concluded wth out two at least of their consents; W^ch Proposicōn was well allowed, and mr. Thr̃er, S^r Io: Dãuers and mr. Wroth being thereto nominated, and put to the question, it was by erecc̄on of hand⸗ confirmed.

Captaine Brewster hauing formerly by way of appeale deliuered vnto the Court a certaine writing touching the proceedings of Captaine Samuell Argoll against him at the arriual of the Neptune in Virginia, and the manner of his tryall, and being at this Court ready to mayn-tayne the same, and to obiect other grieuances against him, he was wished rather to forbeare till the said Captaine Argoll were p^rsent: and in the interim haue thought it convenient to deliuer vnto the said Captaine Argoll a coppy of the said writing of Appeale to make answere vnto the same, and haue appointed him to put in his other Articles vpon ffriday morning next to m^r Thr̃er and m^r Deputy to be by them peruused and deliuered into the next Co^rt, and the next Quarter Court to heare the Appeale.

Lieftenant Stokes made request vnto the Court, that they would please in reguard of the Adventure of his person and his Long time spent in Virginia to bestowe some Land vpon him there for the same; wch they found to be now noe convenient time for that purpose; but if at ye next Q^r Court he procure it to be moued for him, that Court will take thereof due consideracōn.

MAY THE   [1]1619

Sr Edwin Sandis Kn^t Thr̃er.

Sr Edward Harwood.	m^r Nich: fferrar.	m^r Geo: Smith.
S^r Io: Dãuers.	m^r Berblock.	m^r Bland.
m^r Io: fferrar Dpt.	m^r Hen: Briggs.	m^r Caswell.
m^r Geo: Thorpe.	m^r Wiseman.	m^r Sparrowe.

A Comission was now sealed to Iohn Iohnson M^r of the Bona Noua for to take his passage from hence in that shipp to Virginia.   [6]

Letters procured from the Lordes of the Counsell to the Company of Grocers and signed by Pembrooke, Southampton, Exeter, Zouch, Carey and Digby was now sealed and referred to mr. Deputy fferrar to deliuer it to the said Company.

Notice being giuen of a new Pattent which one   [1]Sumerscales was about to take about   [1]Tobacco: the Co^{rt} desired m^r Thr̃er to speake wth m^r Atturney generall, and to learne whither the same be any way preiudiciall to the Company or not.

MAY THE 26th 1619

PRESENT

Generall Cæsill.	m^r Tho: Gibbs.	m^r Wm Palmer.
Sr Edw: Sandis.	Capt. N: Butler.	m^r Swinhowe.
S^r Io: Wolstenholme.	m^r Oxenbrigg.	m^r Berblock.
Sr Tho: Wroth.	m^r Rogers.	m^r Conell.
m^r Alder Iohnson.	m^r Tho: Cañon.	m^r Meuerell.
m^r Io: Wroth.	m^r Essington.	m^r Caswell.
m^r Io: fferrar Dp̃t.	m^r H: Briggs.	m^r Roberts etc.

It was made knowne by m^r Treasuror, that the two Comittees appointed by the last Court for the reducing of the Standing orders into one entire body, and for setling a forme of gouernement, and magistracy

---

[1] A blank space in the manuscript.

in Virginia: The first haue mett as they were desired, and at the next
meeting hope to make an end, & present them to the Quarter Court
ensuing: ffor performance thereof haue desired further reference of
the second Comittee till ffriday after this Quarter Court, because
being a busines very waighty, it can not so soone be well digested;
but they will prepare and make them ready for the approbaĉon of a
Quarter Court in Michaelmas terme.

The busines formerly putt to arbitrement, and referred by the Company and the Lady Lawarre vnto mr. Thomas Simonds and m^r
Thomas Westrowe touching the fraight of the Neptune, and the Acc°
of Rich: Beomonnt m^r and Part-Owner being concluded by the Arbi-
trato^{rs}, and the perticulers now read, receiued the confirmaĉon of the
Court: Vpon wch m^r Thŕer paid the mony, and tooke in the Charter
party.

Captaine Brewster hauing deliuered Articles obiected against Captaine
Samuell Argoll touching his governement in Virginia, to m^r Treasuror
and m^r Deputy, as the Last Court required, the same was now presented: Vnto wch order is giuen that Captaine Argoll haue a coppie
of them, as also of the writing of Appeale formerly deliuered in that
he make answere therevnto: And also that the said Captaine Samuell
Argoll (against the next Quarter Court) be warned to bring in his
writt of discharge.

The Last Court wherein m^r Thŕer was desired to repaire to m^r Atturny
Generall to learne the Contents of a Pattent wch should be graunted [7]
to one Sumerscales about Tobacco. He now acquaynted them that he
had performed that trust, and findeth it to be very preiudiciall to this
Company, if the same should passe therefore advised that there might
forthwth be a course taken for to prevent and stopp the proceeding of
it: wch being taken into consideraĉon, the Court haue desired m^r Tŕer
to goe againe to m^r Atturney Generall and to take some more paines
for to hinder the going forward of the same, and haue associated to
goe along wth him Generall Cecill, S^r Io: Wolstenholme, m^r Alder̃
Iohnson and m^r Iohn Wroth to morrowe morning at seauen of the
Clock, and if they faile of doing good therein, it is agreed, that the

Counsell shalbe assembled to take such further course therein as shall seeme requisite m[r] Wm Palmer was desired to write to m[r] Sumerscales to meete them at that hower at m[r] Atturnies.

It was also by m[r] Tᵣer propounded to the Co[rt] as a thing most worthy to be taken into consideracõn both for the glory of God, and hono[r] of the Company, that forasmuch as the King in his most gracious fauo[r] hath graunted his Ɫres to the seuerall Bishops of this Kingdome for the collecting of monies to erect and build a Colledge in Virginia for the trayning and bringing vp of Infidells children to the true knowledge of God & vnderstanding of righteousnes. And considering what publique notice may be taken in foreslowing to sett forward the acčon, especially of all those w[ch] hath contributed to the same, that therefore to begin that pious worke, there is allready towards it —1500[ll],—or thereabouts, whereof remayning in cash 800[ll], the rest is to be answered out of the Stock of the Generall Company for so much wch they borrowed, besides the likelihood of more to come in; ffor m[r] Treasuro[r] hauing some conference wth the Bishop of Lichfield, he hath not heard of any Colleccõn that hath beene for that busines in his Diocese; but promiseth when he hath a warr[t] therevnto he will wth all dilligence further the enterprize; Wherevpon he conceaued it the ~~best~~ fittest; that as yet they should not build the Colledge, but rather forbeare a while; and begin first with the meanes they haue to provide and settle an Annuall revennue, and out of that to begin the erecčon of the said Colledge: And for the performance hereof also moued, that a certaine peece of Land be Laid out at Henrico being the place formerly resolued of w[ch] should be called the Colledge Land, and for the planting of the same send presently ffifty good persons to be seated thereon and to occupy the same according to order, and to ‖haue‖ halfe the benefitt of their Labo[r] and the other halfe to goe in setting forward the worke, and for mayntenance of the Tuto[rs] & Schollers. He therefore propounded that a Shipp might be prouided against the begining of August, to carry those ffifty men wth their prouisions, as also to send ffiftie persons more to the Coɱon Land w[ch] may raise a Stock for the paying of dueties there and defraying the Companies charge here, and to send provision of victualls wth them for a yeare: And for the defraying the charge hereof did also propound the meanes; first for the Colledge there was mony in Cash, and besides it may saue the Ioint stock the sending out a Shipp this yeare, wch for 4^d a pound they will bring from thence all their Tobacco wch may arise to ffive hundreth pound℮ besides mony that may come in otherwise to [8] helpe to beare the charge of the voyage; W^ch Proposiͨon was well liked but the time and season not allowed of all; and by some obiected, that the Generall Plantaͨon should receaue much mony if more men were sent ouer soe sodaynly before those that are allready gone haue procured wherew^th all to subsist; as also being a matter of greate consequence it did more propperly belong to the deciding of a Quarter Co^rt: but the former reasons being answered; and being further alleaged if it were till then prolonged the time would be past for their provisions of beefe, beere, and meate. Wherevpon after Long arguing and disputing thereof it was agreed to be putt to the question; W^ch being propounded whether a shipp should be sett out to carry men for these two good vses and be sett out at the publique charge—(vizt) wth 50 Passengers for the Colledge Land, and 50 for the Coͫon Land, it was by generall consent, and ereͨon of hand℮ allowed and confirmed.

One m^r Weyncop comended to the Company by the Earle of Lincolne intending to goe in person to Virginia, and there to plant himselfe and his Associats presented his Pattent now to the Co^rt; wch was referred to the Comittee that meeteth vpon ffriday morning at m^r Treasuro^rs howse to consider and if need be to correct the same.

IUNE THE VIJth, 1619.

A Preparatiue Court held for the Virginia
Company at Mr. ffERRARS Howse in Sr Sithes Lane.

PRESENT

Sr Edwin Sandis Kn^t Thřer.

Sr Iohn Dăuers.	m^r Ri: Tomlins.	m^r Hen: Briggs.
Sr Nath. Rich.	m^r Hen: Reignoldℓ.	m^r fferrar iunio^r.
m^r Io: Wroth.	Capt Io: Bingham.	m^r Bamford.
m^r fferrar Dpt̃.	Capt Io: Bargraue.	m^r Berblock.
m^r Dr Anthony.	m^r Robt: Smith.	m^r Caswell.
m^r Tho: Gibbs.	m^r Edw: Ditchfield.	m^r Iadwine etc.

The standing lawes and orders formerly allowed and confirmed by
diuers Quarter Courts touching the graunts and Pattents of Land,
and the duty appertayning to euery perticuler Office, being reduced
by a Comittie into one entire body; vnto wch the Counsell being
assembled, haue allowed thereof, and being now presented to this
Court, was red for the preparing them for the confirmačon of the
Quarter Court ensuing.

Whereas the writt of Appeale put in by Captaine Brewster against
Capt. Samuell Argoll is to be answered at the next Quarter Court,
wch depends more vpon matter of Lawe then fact: and being a [9]
question whither Marshall lawe be a iustifiable proceeding in such a
Crime, Order was giuen that the Łres Pattentℓ might be ready at that
time to collect what Light they can touching the same.

And forasmuch as about the time of the Graunt of the first Łres
Pattents, there were also Instrucčons giuen by his Ma^{ty} vnder the
Priuy seale to the Treasuro^r and Company of Virginia, for the gov-
erning of the Plantačon, A coppie of wch m^r Treasuror hauing now

founde in the Ancient Court Rowles wch before he neuer heard of; And inasmuch as they are to be proceeded in wth greate care and advise, Sr Tho: Smith is desired (if it may be) to send in the Originall.

A peticōn was preferred by Capt Bargraue touching his suite comenced in the Chauncery against the Adventure^m of the Ioint stock, was referred to a Comittee, viz to m^r Tomlins, m^r Rogers, m^r Bamford, m^r Briggs m^r fferrar Iunio^r, m^r Berblock or any three of them to meete at this place to morrow at two of the Clock in the Afternoone.

By order of Court, vnder the Seale of the Company m^r Lott Peere receiued his Quietus est for his imployment in the ffiue shillings Lottery, by two seuerall Accountȼ, and had paid Sr Edwin Sandis Thr̄er for the foote of one Acc^o—116—9—11—and for the foote of his other Account—34—15—8—.

That m^r Thr̄er moue the Quarter Court to take order for the paying of prizes in the Lottery.

The Audito^m made allowance of Twelue single shares of Twelue poundȼ ten shillings apeece belonging to sundry Adventurers, all of them being passed ouer to the parties herevnder named

Iohn Hodgson—25^{li} passed to ffrancis Whitney Esqr.
Iohn Tauernor—37^{li}—10^s to Thomas Shepherd Merch^t.
Martine Earle—12—10 to Nicho: Buckeridge Merch^t.

Dr Lawrence Bohun fiue shares of 12:10:a peece.
{ to Richard Boothbie merchant.
to Dr Thomas Winstone.
to Hugh Windham Merch^t.
to Iohn Tucker Merchant.
to Iohn Strange.

Capt Edw: Brewster 1 share to Wm Cranmer Merch^t. [10]

IUNE IXth 1619

A QUARTER COURT HELD FOR VIRGINIA AT
MR FERRARS HOWSE IN S^T SITHES LANE PRESENT

The Right hono^{ble} Henry Earle of Southampton.
Robert Earle of Warwick.

The Lo: Cauendish.	m^r Alder. Iohnson.	Capt: Na: Butler.
The Lo: Pagett.	m^r Io: Wroth.	m^r Hum: Handford.
Generall Cecill.	m^r Geo: Sandis.	m^r Wm Bell.
m^r Treasuror.	m^r Morrice Abbott.	m^r Rich: Rogers.
Sr Tho: Smith.	m^r Io: Ferrar Dept.	m^r Antho: Abdy.
S^r Io: Merrick.	m^r Tho: Gibbs.	m^r Wm Essington.
Sr Dudley Digges.	m^r Hen: Reignolds.	m^r Wm Caninge.
S^r Io: Dāuers.	m^r Rich: Tomlins.	m^r George Swinhowe.
Sr Tho: Gates.	m^r George Thorpe.	m^r Steward.
Sr Wm Thrickmorton.	m^r ‖W^m‖ Oxenbrigg.	m^r fferrar iunio^r.
Sr Nath: Rich.	D^r ffran: Anthony.	m^r Ditchfield.
Sr Antho: Auger.	Dr Gulstone.	m^r Hen: Briggs.
Sr Tho: Cheeke.	D^r ‖F̶r̶ Thomas‖ Win-	m^r Wiseman.
S^r Io: Sams.	stone.	m^r George Chambers.
S^r Io: Wolstenholme.	Capt Samuell Argoll.	m^r Wheatly.
Sr Wm Russell.	Capt Bargraue.	m^r Shepherd.
Sr Tho: Wilford.	Capt Tucker.	m^r Cranmer.
	Capt Io: Bingham.	m^r Boothby.
	Capt Brewster.	m^r Buckeridge.
	Capt Whitner.	m^r Berblock.
		m^r Wm Palmer etc.

The standing lawes and orders for the Company being reduced by the
Comittee into an entire body, and by them presented to the Counsell,
who approuing of them, and hauing beene afterward read to the Preparatiue Co^{rt}, and now to this greate and generall Co^{rt}, not any Lawe
was contradicted saue one, the Chapter of Audito^{rs} concerning the old

Acc° depending in Audite, wch Sr Tho: Smith tooke some excepçons, that three or fower should now contradict that account, whereof 16 worthy and sufficient men allowed, and the party in Court that writt the same, who would be deposed vpon his Oath that it was the same then made and written: And therefore made two requestç; first, that this Account may stand, and the Audito^rs to proceed from thence, if noe iust excepçons can be taken against it. And secondly that by reason of his extraordinary busines, dishabillity in body, and ~~he~~ because he would be ready to answere to any difficulty, requested, that the Audite might be kept at his howse, and to goe forward wth the Acc° of the Cashe, wch he onely is ingaged for and noe other; And what damage appeareth hath beene done to the Company by such Officers as he trusted he will satisfy to the vttmost: But vpon profession that the said lawe was not to preiudice or debarr Sr Thomas Smith from the benefitt of the said old Accompte, they were agreed to be putt to the question: W^ch being done, they were generally confirmed by erecçon of handç.

Afterward vpon the exhibiting of a writing signed by ffower of the Auditors in answere of Sr Thomas Smiths moçon touching the sayd Account; Sir Thomas Smith vpon pervsall of the said writing and to giue all men satisfacçon, gaue his consent that the present Audito^rs should proceed wth his Account from the beginning: And touching the keeping of [11] the Audite at Sir Thomas Smiths howse being disliked by the Audito^rs, and obiected by some of them, that howsoeuer they might haue vse of Sr Thomas Smith, yet they should[1] have more vse of Sr Edwin Sandis by reason of his experience therein, whose busines would not permitt him to come so farr. W^ch was answered by Sr Thomas Smith, that others might be found to haue as much experience in Accounts, as he, and be more fitter in reguard of his greate busines: Yet notw^thstanding to determine this Controuersy, he would referr himselfe to the most voicç of the Audito^rs, whither they would be willing to meete at his house or not. The moçon being well liked, it was ordered, that the seauen Audito^rs chosen by the Quarter Court of elecçon, and fower others by a former Court annexed vnto them, and allowed at this (so that they take their Oaths) namely, m^r Morris Abbott,

---

[1] Written over "would" in the manuscript.

m^r Humphrey Handford, m^r Antho: Abdie and m^r Thomas Kightley doe assemble vpon Munday morning at Sr Edwin Sandis about the Accompt₵, and there to appointe the time and place of meeting, and to adiourne it from time to time as they shall see cause.

A former Act of Court made 26to die Maij, touching the setting out a shipp wth one hundred men for the Colledge and publiq, Land, was now agayne propounded by m^r Thr̃er: W^{ch} being putt to the question, receiued the confirmac̃on of the Court; and agreed that the said shipp should be ready to sett out soone after the middest of July at the fur-thest, that by the blessing of God they may ariue there by the end of October, wch is the fittest and seasonablest time for men to doe some busines.

Captayne Brewsters appeale against Captaine Samuell Argoll touch-ing his condempnac̃on in Virginia being referred to the hearing of this Court; and now questioned by the said Captaine Brewster whither he were Gouerno^r or noe, imagining that at their Landing he had receaued his writt of discharge; and if it were so whether he dealt iustly, proceeding as he did against him in Marshall Lawe, being onely in case of muteny and rebellion that the same should be executed. Touching the point whither he were Gouerno^r or noe, it plainly appeared by a L̃re sent vnto him (wch the said Captaine Argoll now produced) signed by some of the Counsell and Company, that at the Landing of the Lo: Lawarr in Virginia, he should surrender vp his place; W^{ch} seeing it pleased god to take his Lo^{rs} Life from his mortall body before he Landed there, this point stood cleere that he remayned Gouerno^r, in statu quo prius. ffor the other point whether iustice were executed in performing his tryall by Marshall Lawe, because the Court found it more convenient for the busines to be more priuately handled, it was ordered, that the Counsell should be summoned to meete to morrow morning at my Lo: of Warwickes house at eight of the Clock there to decide the business and report to the Court.

This Court taking into consideratc̃on the worthynes of some Noblemen and others now present by giuing their dilligent attendance from time to time to the benefitt and furtherance of the Plantac̃on, as namely

the Right hono^ble Robt Earle of Warwick, Sr Tho: Cheeke, Sr Nath:
Rich, m^r John fferrar deputy and Captaine Nath: Butler haue now [12]
made choice of them to be of his Ma^ts Counsell for Virginia, and each
of them being putt to the question was generally ratified by erecc̃on
of hand℮, and are appointed to ||attend|| my Lo: Chamberlaine for the
taking of their Oaths.

The request of diuers of the Generallity to the T̃rer, Counsell and
Company of Virginia being presented at this Court, touching the
reforming and rectifying of the Magazine busines, was vpon pervsall
allowed of, and being putt to the question ratified by erecc̃on of
hand℮; W^ch points are these that followe,

1. Whereas the Director of the Magazine his Assistants and other
Officers haue vpon the first elecc̃on continued now in their places
two yeares and vpwards, They desire, that according to the vse of
the Officers for the Company they may be chosen anew euery yeare,
or that the former may be continued in their places by a new elecc̃on
yearely.

2. Whereas the Officers of the Magazine haue promised out of the
good℮ returned from Virginia to make a Devision of one Capitall vnto
the Adventurers in Aprill last, and haue not yet performed it, nor
made vp any Accounts to giue the Adventure^rs satisfacc̃on, They desire
that they may be required by the Court to performe their promise
imediately, and to make vp their Account℮ against the next Court day
and then present them to the Court; And that the Adventurers may
then proceed to a new elecc̃on.

3. Thirdly that the Officers of the Magazine as well those that are
now, as those that shalbe hereafter may take their Oaths for their
iust dealing, and trew accompting wch the Company, aswell as the
Officers of the Generall Company who handle not so greate som̃es.

4. That all the letters written from the officers of the Magazine to
the Capemerchant, and from the Capemerchant to them may be
entred in a booke by their Secretary, to the end that all men may
be satisfied of faire dealings and proceedings.

5. That the Assembly for the Magazine may be kept when & where the Courts are to the end the Adventurers may come and speake their mindes more freely, soe farr forth as they shall haue reason.

fforasmuch as it appeared, that there was more busines to be performed then this Afternoone could well determine; It was moued that if mʳ Thᵣer hereafter shall finde the like, that then he may please to giue order for the Company to meete both fforenoone & Afternoone, wᶜʰ was referred to be considered of by the Comittee for the Standing orders.

By reason it grewe late, and the Court ready to breake vp, and as yet mʳ Iohn Whincops Pattent for him and his Associats being to be read, it was ordered that the seale should be annexed vnto it, and haue referred the trust thereof vnto the Auditors to examine that it agree wᵗʰ the Originall; wᶜʰ if it doth not, they haue promised to bring it into the Court & cancell it. **[13]**

A former Comittee appointed concerning Captaine Bargraues busines, the matter being found difficult, and the time short, The Court vpon another petiĉon preferred by Capt Bargraue haue adioyned vnto them Generall Cæsill, Sʳ Dudley Diggs, Sʳ Tho: Cheeke, Sʳ Iohn Dāuers, Sʳ Nath: Rich to meete at Generall Cæsills howse to morrowe Afternoone at two of the Clock; And that mʳ Aldᵣan Iohnson, mʳ Essington & mʳ Ditchfield be warned to be there at that time.

IUNE THE 14ᵗʰ 1619

PRESENT

Sʳ Edwin Sandis Knᵗ Thᵉrer.

Sʳ Dudley Diggs.	Capt. Bingham.	mʳ Chambers.
Sʳ Io: Dãuers.	Capt. Bargraue.	mʳ Wheatley.
Sʳ Tho: Gates.	Capt. Butler.	mʳ Shepherd.
Sʳ Nath: Rich.	Capt. Brewster.	mʳ Kightley.
Sʳ Io: Samms.	mʳ Dʳ Anthony.	mʳ Berblock.
mʳ Iohn Wroth.	mʳ Dʳ Gulson.	mʳ Caswell.
mʳ fferrar Dpᵗʸ.	mʳ Canñon.	mʳ Geo: Smith.
mʳ Hen: Reignoldє.	mʳ Hen: Briggs.	mʳ Sparrowe.
Capt. S. Argoll.	mʳ Wiseman.	mʳ El: Roberts etc.

At this Court mʳ Iohn Wroth, mʳ Morris Abbott, mʳ Humphrey Handford mʳ Anthony Abdie mʳ Wᵐ Essington and mʳ Thomas Keightley were now sworne Auditoʳˢ for the Virginia Company.

The Guift being now returned from Virginia and hauing brought łres from Sʳ George Yeardley directed to Sʳ Edw: Sandis intimating the sore voyage they had; being going thither from the 19ᵗʰ of Ianuary to the 19ᵗʰ of Aprill following, In wᶜʰ time there dyed 14 Landmen and three seamen as also that two children was borne at sea, & dyed, and at his there ariuall finding the Plantaĉon to be in great scarsity for want of Corne, desired the Company to beare wᵗʰ him, if ||for|| this yeare he some thing neglected the planting of Tobacco, and followe the sowing of Corne, where by the next yeare he hopes by the blessing of God to raise such a Cropp thereof, that the said Plantaĉon shall haue noe greate cause to complaine in hast of want. Other priuate busines mʳ Thᵉrer acquaynted the Court was specified in his Łres, wᶜʰ is first to receaue the aduise of the Counsell, and by their direcĉons to reueale it to the Court.[1]

[1] This is probably the letter given in List of Records, No. 93, page 131, *ante*.

It was moued by m^r Thᵲer, that the Generall Comittees should forthwith meete for the setting out this shipp, and furnishing of her wth
good people to be sent to the Colledge and publique Land, wch hitherto
by defect thereof, the Plantaĉon hath beene much wronged: w^{ch} [14]
if the Court would put them in trust for the prouiding of such, they
would intreate the Gentlemen both of Country and Citty to helpe
them therewith.   W^{ch} moĉon the Court comended and haue desired
m^r Thᵲers assistance therein.

The Counsell hauing mett according to order from the Last Court;
touching the appeal of Captaine Brewster against Captaine Samuell
Argoll, the Court hauing cleered one point concerning his Gouerno^r-
shipp, and the Counsell now approuing of the other for his tryall by
Marshall Lawe, holding Captaine Argoll not faulty therein, by reason
he proceeded and followed the example of his Predecesso^{rs}, and the
Custome altogether vsed hetherto in that Plantaĉon, wch is likely to
continue till the standing orders for Virginia be made and enacted;
and he being tryed by a Marshall Court, the Counsell held it to be
the Noblest tryall being iudged by Souldiers and men of worth.   But
forasmuch as it is obiected that the said Captaine Argoll proceeded
vnduely, Capt Brewster comitting noe crime worthy of death, and
being also alleaged that he was first condempned and afterward called
vnto his Answere, wch the Counsell and Court here cann not iudge of,
but is to be tryed there, where the euidence may be giuen; It was
therefore now ordered, that the said Appeale and Captaine Argolls
answere therevnto shalbe sent inclozed wthin a ᵲe of the Companies
to Sr George Yeardley and the Counsell of State, and they to make
examinaĉon of the cause and returne Certificate thereof.   An oath
was also exhibited by Captaine Brewster, wch was administred vnto
him in Virginia, wch is also agreed to be sent for informaĉon of the
truth thereof.

The Comittee by the Court appointed vpon the petiĉon of Captaine
Bargraue, touching the suite depending in Chauncery betwixt him and
some Adventure^{rs} of the Magazine, the same Comittee meeting at the
time and place appointed, and considering thereof hauing both bill

and answere, and the booke of the Orders of Courts, who pervsing the same, and finding that Capt. Bargraue had 14 dayes respite for giuing security to the Adventurers, and wth in six dayes the bargaine was taken of his handes, for wch he was to allowe vnto the Adventurers, —150^li wth a promise that if it were sold for aboue ffiue shillings a pound, he should haue the Ouerplus: but being all sold by some of the Adventurers of the Magazine amongst themselues wth in two dayes after at— iiij^s ix^d it was conceaued by the said Comittee, that the said Capt Bargraue had much wrong offered therein: and therefore did see noe reason why the Company should countenance this busines, but leaue the Defend^ts to followe it; or to take the matter vp amongst themselues. Wherevpon after some debating, being putt to the question whither the Virginia Company should ioyne or noe in suite against Capt Bargraue wth the Defendants, It was agreed by erecčon of hand€ that notw^th standing any order to the contrary, the said Company should neither ioyne nor assist the said Defendants herein. And that vpon Wedensday sevenight, when the said Adventurers of the Magazine doe meete, it be putt vnto them to see likewise if they will vndertake the same.

[15] It was agreed that Mr Aldŕan Iohnson, and the rest of the Adventure^rs and Officers of the Magazine should be warned agaynst Wedensday sevenight to meete at m^r fferrars howse. and to haue the Acc° ready to be deliuered in vpon their Oath.

It was moued by mr. Thŕer that the Court would take into consideračon to appoint a Comittie of choice Gentlemen, and other of his Ma^ts Counsell for Virginia concerning the Colledge; being a waighty busines, and so greate, that an Account of their proceedings therein must be giuen to the State. Vpon §w^ch§ the Co^rt vpon deliberate consideračon haue recoſñended the care thereof vnto the Right wo^r Sr Dudley Diggs, Sr Iohn Dãuers, Sr Nath: Rich, S^r Io: Wolstenholme, m^r Deputy fferrar, m^r Dr Anthony, and m^r Dr Gulson to meete at such time as m^r Treasuror shall giue order therevnto.

fforasmuch as the standing Lawes and orders concerning the governement of Virginia being finished by the Comittee to whome they were recomended, and passed the seuerall Ceremonies according to the

orders of the Company, It was moued that the second Comittee for
the setling of Lawes & Magistracie might be summoned by the
Officer to meete at S[r] Edwin Sandis his howse vpon ffriday morning
next at eight of the Clock, and there to devide the busines amongst
themselues as they shall see cause: W[ch] the Court thought very convenient, and haue allowed thereof.

Also vpon a moc̄on of the Susans voyage to be audited, and the complaint of the Generallity in some abuse offred by the Ioint stock to be
rectified; The ordinary Audito[rs] are warned to meete therevpon vpon
Munday morning at eight of the Clock at m[r] Treasurors howse.

It was agreed vpon the moc̄on of S[r] Dudley Diggs and S[r] Thomas
Gates vnto the Court about a Pattent to be graunted vnto sundry
Kentishmen, who would seate and plant themselues in Virginia, that
they should haue as Large priuiledges and imunities as is graunted to
any other in that kinde.

Vpon the petic̄on of Iohn Woodliefe gentleman (who disbursed
62—10—00 eleauen yeares since, and the like time spent in the Planta-
c̄on in the place of Ensigne[)] to haue a Pattent graunted him and his
Associats whereon to plant the number of 200 persons to be transported into Virginia before the end of Six yeares next Coming, and to
haue the like priviledges to him and his Associats, in lieu aswell of his
said Adventure and personall allowance, as for other his Associats who
haue adventured of old: W[ch] the Court hath now graunted vnto him. [16]

Whereas vpon a former order, it was agreed to pay interest for a some
of mony in the Companies hand℈ during the minority of one Katha-
rine Bath to whome the mony doth belong. The Court vpon better
considerac̄on now finding it not convenient to pay Interest haue agreed
to reverse the said order & to ||pay|| the mony where it is due.

The Court being acquaynted of one m[r] Robert Browne who adventured wth the Lo: Lawarr 25[ll] and went himselfe in person to Virginia,
and there dyed, haue now agreed wth the consent and liking of the

Lady Lawarr that the [said 25ⁱⁱ]¹ shalbe deducted out of the 500ⁱⁱ adventure of my Lordᶜ, and so [that * * * * r]² be giuen to the Bookeeper for the defaulking of it out of the said 500ⁱⁱ adventure, & passing it to the said Robert Browne by a bill [of A]dventure in his owne name. And moreouer haue agreed that for his personall Adventure he shall (according to the orders of the Company) haue 100 Acres of Land.

IUNE THE 24ᵗʰ 1619

PRESENT

The Right honoᵇˡᵉ The Ea. of Warwicke.

Sʳ Edwin Sandis Knᵗ Thᶠer.

Sʳ Io: Dãuers.	mʳ Rich: Tomlins.	mʳ Rich: Morer.
Sʳ Stephen Dowle.	mʳ Anthony Abdy.	mʳ Geo: Smith.
mʳ Io: Wroth.	mʳ Wᵐ Caninge.	mʳ Geo: Chambers.
mʳ Ferrar Dpᵗ.	mʳ Edw: Ditchfield.	mʳ Rich: Berblock.
mʳ Tho: Gibbs.	mʳ Robt Smith.	mʳ: Conell.
mʳ Ferrar Iunioʳ.	mʳ Iadwin.	mʳ Meuerell.
	mʳ Wᵐ Essington.	mʳ Rich: Bull.

The order in the Last Court touching the generall Company not any way to ioyne or countenance the Defendantᶜ against Capt Bargraue, here being some wᶜʰ were absent at the Last Coʳ, and alleadging some reason why the said Company should not altogether relinquish the said Defendants, because the Generallity hauing a stock there, is therein interessed as a perticuler Adventurer of the Magazine; Wᶜʰ point is referred vntill the Adventurers meete; At wᶜʰ time it may be cleered whither the Adventurers shall ioyne in mayntaining that suite; [17]

¹ The manuscript is blotted so as to make this and the two following doubtful passages almost illegible.
² Probably *power* or *order*.

The Comittee by the Last Co^{rt} appoynted for the Colledge hauing mett as they were desired, deliuered now their proceedings, wch the Co^{rt} allowed of being this that followeth,

A note of what kinde of men are most fitt to be sent to Virginia in the next intended voyage of transporting One hundreth men.

A minister to be entertayned at the yearely allowance of fforty pound€ and to §haue§ 50 Acres of Land for him and his heires for euer. To be allowed his transportačon & his mans at the Companies charge, and ten pound€ imprest to furnish himselfe wthall.

A Captaine thought fitt to be considered of to take the charge of such people as are to be planted vpon the Colledge Land.

All the people at this first sending except some few to be sent aswell for planting the Colledge as publiq̨ Land to be single men vnmarryed. A warrant to be made and directed to Sr Thomas Smith for the paym^t of the Collecčon mony to Sr Edwin Sandis Thřer. And that Dr Gulstone should be entreated to present vnto my Lords Grace of Canterbury such Letters to be signed for the speedy paying of the monies from every Diocesse, wch yet remaynes vnpayd.

The seuerall sortes of Tradesmen and others for the Colledge Land.

Smithes.	Potters.
Carpenters.	Husbandmen.
Bricklayers.	Brickmakers.
Turners.	

And whereas according to the standing order seauen were chosen by the Last Court to be of the Comittee for the Colledge the said order allowing noe more. And inasmuch as m^r Iohn Wroth is conceaued by some error to be left out, he is therefore now desired to be an Assistant vnto them and to giue them meeting at such time & place as is agreed of.

The Comittee for ‖the‖ setling of lawes and Magistracie in Virginia haue mett as they were desired and vpon examinačon haue found diuers Lawes in the Łres Pattents and good poynts in the Instrucčons

giuen by his Ma^ty vnder the Privy Seals wch wilbe a greate furtherance for the setling of the busines, purposing to take such paynes
therein as to present them to the next Quarter Court and to that end
(because [18] most in this Vacation time resolueth to goe into the
country) haue devided it amongst them selues for the better preparing
of it against their next meeting.

It was moued by mr. Thr̄er that a Comittee might be appoynted to
call the officers of the Lotteries before them to sett downe a Catta-
logue what prizes remayne yet due and vnpaid that they may be discharged and one to be authorized to pay them to such as shall bring
in their Ticketts, wch the Co^rt hath referred vnto the Auditors.

Also he moued that in reguard of great somes wch is presently to be
issued out vpon this voyage, and the extraordinary busines wch the
Company from time to time imposeth vpon him, that a perticuler
Thr̄er might be appointed vnder him for the issuing out thereof,
wch he [should] not deliuer w^thout a warrant, nor the other should pay
it forth w^thout the like authority of a warrant to be giuen vnto him:
W^ch the Court haue thought fitt, because he stands engaged for it, to
referr it vnto himselfe, who therein hath made choice of m^r Deputy
fferrar.

Stephen Sparrowes request for the personall adventures of ffower
servants wch he sent to Virginia is referred to the Auditors vpon
Munday morning.

William Shackley of London Haberdasher assigned to Oliuer St Iohn
Two shares in Virginia.

Also Mrs Millisent Paulsden assigned to the said Oliuer St Iohn three
shares in Virginia, wch the Co^rt haue now allowed of: Prouided that
shee come into the Co^rt or make her Certificate of her allowance
therein wi^thin this Twelue Moneths.

A controuersy arising amongst the Adventure^rs of the Magazine for
their place of meeting, it being made knowne that m^r Aldr̄an Iohnson
who is the Director thereof, desired it might be at Sr Tho: Smiths, by

reason he was one of the greatest and principall Adventurers and not well able to goe to any other place: but forasmuch as there is a standing order, that so long as the generall Company hath an Adventure in any Ioint stock, their meetings shalbe where the Generall Co^{rts} is kept: m^r Thřer and Deputy insisted strongly for the mayntayning of the said Order, insomuch that it was answered that it were better a little to dispense wth that said order, then a Generall ffaccŏn thereby should be raysed betwixt the Company and adventurers: wch was answered by m^r Thřer that he sawe no reason to feare any such ffaccŏn: but for his part if the Adventurers would repay to the Generall Company their Eight hundreth pounde they haue paid into the Magazine, they might meete in what place they pleased, and that might be done wthout breach of order, till then he was sworne to mayntayne the orders and lawes of the Company vnlesse they shalbe disanulled by the same wayes and meanes that they are [19] confirmed. But much dispute growing herein, and the Counsell all save o[ne] hauing deliuered their opinions to mayntayne the order, It was at length agree[d] that the said Adventure^{rs} of the Magazine should be warned to meete here vpon Munday next in the Afternoone at the Generall Co^{rt} to performe such things as in the Last Quarter Co^{rt} had beene ordered, concerning the Magazine and the officers thereof.

IUNE THE 28ᵗʰ 1619

Present

Right honorable The Earle of Southampton.
The Earle of Warwick.

Sʳ Edwin Sandis Knᵗ. Thřer.

Sʳ Iohn Dāuers.	mʳ Thorpe.	mʳ Morer.
Sʳ Edw: Harwood.	mʳ Tomlins.	mʳ Couell.
Sʳ Nath: Rich.	Capt Argoll.	mʳ Swinhowe.
mʳ Aldřan Iohnson.	mʳ Essington.	mʳ Darnelly.
mʳ Iohn Wroth.	mʳ Antho: Abdy.	mʳ Wiseman.
mʳ Xo Brooke.	mʳ Cartwright.	mʳ Berblock.
mʳ Morrice Abbott.	mʳ Wheatly.	mʳ Iadwine.
mʳ Ferrar Dpt.	mʳ Barber.	With others.
	mʳ Chambers.	

Vpon reading the last order in the last Court, touching the place of meeting of the Magazine Adventurers, mʳ Thřer signified to the Coᵗ, that by reason of such contrary desires to meete a part, they could haue noe meeting wᵗʰ the Adventurers at all, and therefore shewed two reasons that might induce them not to fly from the standing order: One, that the Generall Company hath twice as greate an Adventure therein, as any of the greatest perticuler Adventurers: And the other, that hetherto from time to time, their meetings haue beene at the same time and place, where and when the generall Courtℓ hath beene kept, sauing onely twice: Wᶜʰ was replyed by mʳ Aldřan Iohnson Director of the Magazine, that it could not be soe convenient to meete togethᵉʳ as in meeting a part; because at such meeting ⅓ wilbe of the Generality, but if it be for the mayntayning of the Standing order, that their meetings should be both in one place; it was not unknowne, but that Sʳ Thomas Smith hath offred his howse for them at any time to sitt in, who being a great Adventurer was worthy to haue a voice [*as*] ‖stet‖ occasion serueth amongst them; and the rather that he and some others was engaged to the Chamber of London for one thousand pound€, wch if they pleased to cleare them of that bond, he would consent to meete where they pleased. W^{ch} was answered by m^r Thr̃er, that one reason why they should be vndeuided, was, that from time to time they might receaue their authority from the Generall Co^{rts}: and m^r Aldr̃an well said, they were not tyed to a perticuler place of meeting, therefore he would be willing (if the Court should soe like of it) that they should meet sometimes at Sr Thomas Smiths, at such time as Sr Thomas Smith should haue occasion to desire to be present. And for the 1000^{li} wch Sr Thomas Smith, Sr Iohn Wolstenholme, and m^r Alderman Iohnson standeth bound he held it not convenient to haue any Diuident till that were paid. Wherevpon many in the Court agreeing in opinion wth him, it was desired to be [20] putt to the question; wch being propounded, whither the Thowsand pound€ should be paid, that is at interest at seauen p Cent or that the Vndertakers should remayne in bond€, and a Diuident be made the Adventurers, by erecc̃on of hand€ was concluded, that the said vndertake^{rs} should be released, by repaying the said some of 1000^{li} into the Chamber of London before there should be any Dyvident.

Next was moued by Mr Thr̃er the prosequuting of the Proposic̃on agreed of in the Last Quarter Co^{rt}, wch was, that the Magazine should imitate the order of the Company : ffirst that Officers should be yearely chosen and sworne & that §an§ a true Acc^o should be deliuered in vpon their Oaths. And first taking into consideratc̃on the choice of their Directo^r, it was propounded whither they would haue one or two, wch was agreed to haue but one; and m^r Aldr̃an Iohnson being therevnto nominated and putt to the question, was by erecc̃on of hand€ confirmed. Likewise to be assisting to m^r Director, choice is now made of fiue Comittees, viz^{tt}, m^r Essington, m^r Rich : Morer, m^r Edward Ditchfield, m^r Richard Caswell, and m^r Berblock. And for Auditors m^r Abraham Cartwright, Mr George Chambers, Mr Henry Briggs and m^r Richard Wiseman, who are desired to be at the next Court to take their oaths : and also against that time an exact Account be giuen of the State of the Cash, & what debts is owing, that (if it may be) halfe a Capitall may be deuided amongst the Adventurers.

And it was also by mr Thr̄er desired that the 340ˡˡ wᶜʰ the Magazine
oweth to the Generall stock may be forthwᵗʰ paid, he hauing such
extraordinary occasion to vse mony for the setting out the shipp
agreed to be sent, and what cann be proued either by order of Coʳᵗ, or
otherwise to be due vnto them they shall haue it paid, and therefore
when the Auditors now chosen for the Magazine shall haue seene
into the Accounts, they would repaire to the Generall Auditors at his
howse to conclude the differences vpon Tuesday seauennight at two of
the Clock in the afternoone. And against that time did also request
that they would giue themselues vnderstanding of the first Magazine
sett out in the Susan, that the Generall Stock may receaue the mony
due vnto them vpon that voyage, and that the Account may be cleered
wiᵗʰout further delay.

Mʳ George Chambers in the behalfe of Martins Hundred desired the
Company to make examinac̃on of some abuses offred to their Cor-
porac̃on by the Mʳ and Marriners of the Ship, as also to rectify some
wrong done vnto them by the Capemerchant: Wherevpon the Court
was pleased to call before them the Marriners, administring vnto
them an Oath to answere vnto such Interrogotories as shalbe law-
fully demaunded of them touching Martins Hundred: wᶜʰ done the
examinac̃on thereof was referred to two of the Counsell and two of the
Company, vizᵗᵗ, to mʳ Aldr̄an Iohnson, mʳ Morrice Abbott, & mʳ Abdy
and mʳ Cartwright. And for wrong donne by the Capemerchant, it
being not their case alone that complaynes, It was agreed that a l̄re
should be written from the Counsell to Sʳ George Yeardley, and that
Mʳ Chambers and others [23]¹

findeth none soe fitt and convenient for them as mʳ Deputy fferrars,
if it pleased him to let the Company haue her, there being Cabbins
and euery thing in a readines. But inasmuch as a Publique impu-
tac̃on was Laid vpon him in the disputing of men to be sent to the
Colledge Land, in saying that he had some priuate end€ in solliciting
it soe hard; he therefore desired to be excused, and that they would
prouide some other, Least in performing their desire he should drawe

¹ Pages 21 and 22 are missing from the manuscript. The catch word at the end of page 20 is "deliuer."

some malignity therein vpon himselfe: but being vrged therevnto by the Co^rt, who generally cleering him of that imputaĉon he hath (through the good he wisheth vnto the Company) condiscended to their request, and referred it to the Comittees to allowe him for ffraight what they shall thinke good.

IULY THE VIJ^th 1619

BEING PRESENT

The Right honorable The Earle of Warwick.

Sr Edwin Sandis Kn^t Thr̃er.

Sr Dudley Diggs.	m^r Dr Winstone.	m^r Ed: Scott.
Sr Tho: Gates.	m^r Dr Anthony.	m^r Geo: Swinhowe.
Sr Iohn: Dãuers.	m^r Tho: Gibbs.	m^r Tho: Kightley.
Sr Nath: Rich.	m^r Robt Offley.	m^r Wm Palmer.
Sr Tho: Wroth.	m^r Rich: Rogers.	m^r Wiseman.
m^r Aldr̃an Iohnson.	m^r Wm Caninge.	m^r Lewson.
m^r Iohn Wroth.	m^r fferrar Iunio^r.	m^r Iadwine.
m^r Iohn fferrar Dept.	m^r Essington.	m^r Meuerell.
m^r Geo: Thorpe.	m^r Hen: Briggs.	m^r Roberts.
		wth others.

The Magazine Shipp being returned from Virginia, and a Packett of wrightings receaued from Abraham Persey the Capemerchant, but not any r̃e yet receaued from Sr George Yeardley the Gouerno^r, the same was now presented to this Court, where in the Packett was conteyned a generall r̃e to the Adventurers, an Invoice of the goodⱹ now come home, a bill of Lading, a certificate of the misdemeano^r of one Showell who was sent to assist the Capemerch^t, a note of such goodⱹ as the Country standeth in need of, an Invoice of the goodⱹ wch was Landed by the George 1617, An account of the same goods, two bills of Ex^ch to Sr Iohn Wolstenholme, and a note of mony wch the Marriners oweth to the said Adventurers.

The Generall Ire being now read, It was moued by m^r Thfer, that 2 pointℭ especially therein might be taken into consideracōn;

1. Whither it be convenient that libertie be giuen to the Capemerchant according as he desireth to barter and sell the Comodities as he cann and as is vsuall in free trading: As also liberty to the Inhabitants there to barter and sell their comodities.

2. That as he writeth he is ouercharged wth aboundance of needles Comodities, and wanteth Ploughes and other necessaries, wch he hath often writt for, that it may be thought of how to be remedyed.   **[24]**

To wch purpose, the Court haue now appointed ffower of the Counsell, 2 of Smiths Hundred and 2 of Martins Hundred, viz^{tt} of the Counsell Sr Tho: Gates, m^r Iohn Wroth, m^r Deputy fferrar and Capt Argoll; ffor Smiths Hundred, m^r Thomas Gibbs and m^r Robt Smith; ffor Martins Hundreth, m^r Geo: Chambers, and m^r Wm Caninge, who together wth the Director and Comittees for the Magazine are desired to meete too morrow in the Afternoone at m^r Treasur^{re} howse to consider of these Two points, & to pervse the writings, that care may be taken to redresse what is amisse.

Next according to an order made in the Last Court, m^r Thfer required of the Officers then chosen for the Magazine, such Acc^o as was then comitted to their care to be perfected, and brought in as vpon this day at the furthest: but perceauing that m^r Essington was gone and that noe Account could be presented, being some thing moued that from time to time they should be putt of and could haue neither paid the money wch appeareth to be due to the Company, nor that they would meete to audite the same, addressed himselfe to m^r Alderman Iohnson as Director thereof, saying, he would complaine to the Lordℭ of the Counsell of it, or comence suite against him.   Wherevpon m^r Alderman conceauing as he afterwardℭ said he had threatned him in his owne person, replied, that he durst not, wth some other angry wordℭ he then vttered; wch some of the Counsell tooke excepcōns at, saying, the Court was very much wronged by it, and that if it were suffered to haue the Treasuror so vsed, there would be noe respect given vnto him, to wch the Court consented: And m^r Thfer for his part affirmed, that he did not meane m^r Alderman otherwise then as

||he was|| Director of the Magazine, & when he spoke of himselfe he meant the Virginia Company: Which being putt to the question, whither the Court vnderstood that he spoke perticulerly of his person, or of the Adventurers of the Magazine, it was by most voices affirmed, that they vnderstood in speaking to him, that he ment of the Magazine Company: And because it should not passe w^{th}out some reproofe or acknowledgm^t of his part of an error, for preventing the like hereafter soe neere as may be; It was moued by m^r Wm Caninge, that the Co^{rt} might presently decide it; and afterward vpon putting the question, by generall erec̃con of hand℮ agreed that the Counsell now present being the Ea: of Warwicke, Sr Thomas Gates, Sr Iohn Dãuers, Sr Nath: Riche, m^r Iohn Wroth and m^r Deputy fferrar should meete too morrow morning at my Lo: of Southamptons, and they together wth his Lõ^p to consider of m^r Aldermans words and to censure him accordingly.

And because the Court could not now haue the meanes to end the differences depending betweene the Company and the Magazine Adventurers, it was desired that m^r Thr̃er would please to giue order for an extraordinary Court for the determining (if it may be) [25] of the same: who hath appointed, that vpon Tuesday next in the Afternoone the Company and Officers of the Magazine be warned to meete at Sr Thomas Smithes.

Mr Alderman Iohnson being formerly chosen Director of the Magazine did now disclayme the same; but w^{th}all promising that he would assist the Comittees thereof in any thing he might; but to be the Director he would not.

IULY THE 13th 1619

A Court held for Virginia at Sir Tho:
Smiths howse in Philpott Lane.

Present the Right Hono^{ble} The Earle of Southampton.
The Earle of Warwicke.

Sr Edwin Sandis Kn^t Thr̄er.

Sr Tho: Smith.	m^r Hen: Reignolde.	m^r Hen: Briggs.
Sr Tho: Wainman.	Capt S: Argoll.	m^r Wiseman.
Sr Tho: Gates.	Capt N: Butler.	m^r Couell.
Sr Nath: Rich.	m^r fferrar iunio^r.	m^r Geo: Smith.
S^r Io: Wolstenholme.	m^r Ri: Rogers.	m^r Bereblocke.
Sr Tho: Wroth.	m^r Ro: Bateman.	m^r Roberts.
m^r Aldr̄an Iohnson.	m^r Edw: Scott.	m^r Cranmer.
m^r Iohn Wroth.	m^r Rich: Bull.	m^r Kightley.
m^r Xo Brooke.	m^r Geo: Chambers.	m^r Shepherd.
m^r Geo: Sandis.	m^r Swinhowe.	m^r Melling.
m^r Geo: Thorpe.	m^r Paulson.	m^r Sparrowe. etc.
m^r fferrar Dep̄t.	m^r Rich: Caswell.	
m^r Tho: Gibbs.	m^r Caninge.	
m^r Dr Anthony.	m^r Ri: Moorer.	

The busines by the Last Court referred vnto the Counsell touching
some vnseemely worde giuen by m^r Aldr̄an Iohnson vnto m^r Thr̄er to
be censured by them, they hauing mett as they were desired, and
thereon considered, did now deliuer their conclusion into the Courte,
where after a long disputac̄on and reproofe of the offence comitted by
m^r Alderman, & a generall cleering of m^r Tr̄er by erec̄con of [26] hande
and euery mans testimony of the scandall imputed vnto him by m^r Alderman, that he should wrong any of the Company by vndecent language;
It was agreed that for preventing the Like abuse to the Thr̄er hereafter, the former Comittees, that is to say, the Lord of Southampton,

the Lo: of Warwick, S^r Io: Dãuers, Sr Tho: Gates, Sr Nath: Rich, m^r Io: Wroth, m^r Geo: Thorpe, and m^r Deputy fferrar to whome this busines was formerly referred, now adding vnto their number S^r Io: Wolstenholme, Sr Tho: Wroth, should sett downe in writing to be entred in the Court bookes the iustificaçon wch the Court hath giuen to mr. Tfer; And should wthall propose to the consideraçon of the Court the forme of some strict Lawe for the preventing of the like wrong and abuse in future tyme. [1]

There was also presented to the Court by the Audito^{rs} and there openly read this writing ensuing;

> Whereas it hath appeared plainly that during the time, that m^r Alderman Iohnson was both Deputy of the Company and Director of the Magazine diuers great somes haue beene wrongfully converted from the Cashe of the Company §to§ the vse and Cashe of the Magazine, as namely the some of=341=13=4= of the Companies money was in May—1617—converted to the buying of good^{ds} for the Magazine wch were sent in the George, and receiued by the Capemerchant, and returned in his Acc^o wth the gaine of—85—8—4—And moreouer in October—1618—the Companies Tobacco growing in their Coĩon garden was sold to m^r Abraham Chamberlaine for One hundreth three score and sixteene pound^{ds}; and that soĩe paid into the Cash of the Magazine. And whereas also there are diuers reciprocall demaunds made both by the Company and the Magazine for persons and goodes interchangeably transported by each for other: W^{ch} Account wee the Auditors for the Company haue beene on o^r parts att all times desirous and ready to audite; but haue found noe correspondency nor disposition to the same in the Officers for the Magazine, notwth-standing o^r often requests and diuers orders of Courts, wch they haue neglected and broken and doe soe still persist: fforasmuch as it is very apparent vnto vs, that there is a great some of money of right due to be paid by the Magazine to the Company, wthout wch there is noe meanes for the setting out of this shipp now prepared for the transporting of One hundreth men for Generall service: And wee haue done o^r vtmost endeauo^r therein wch hath proued fruitles: Wee are inforced according to the duty of o^r places to present the consideraçon hereof to yor wisdomes, that some further course may be taken for doing right to the Company, and advancing the Coĩon service thereon depending.
>
> Subscribed: Iohn Dãuers: Io: Wroth:
>
> > Iohn ffErrar. Tho: Keightley.
> >
> > Henry Briggs and Richard Wiseman. [27]

[1] Some papers on this committee are given in the List of Records, Nos. 112, 113, pages 133, 134, *ante*.

This being deliuered by the Audito^{rs}, and wth all the Acc° betweene the Company and Adventurers, which by the helpe of the Courtbooke (hauing examined it thorough) they haue finished; there onely resteth for the Court to decide, that if they will allowe of sundry transportačons of men, by former orders in the said booke not menčoned, that then there wilbe One hundreth poundℓ lesse for the Company to receaue: But it growing late it was agreed, and that the Shipp should be noe longer stayde, that m^r Thřer should make vse of the Three hundreth poundℓ due vnto the Magazine by the Adventurers of Smiths hundred, and that the Account betweene them shalbe forthwth audited: To wch purpose my Lord of Southampton hath promised his assistance vpon ffriday morning next at Sir Thomas Smiths howse, at wch time m^r Alderman, together wth m^r Essington, m^r Abraham Chamberlaine, m^r Richard Moorer and m^r Berblock, are appointed to ioyne wth the Audito^{rs} of the Company and so to decide the Controuersy.

fforasmuch as the Collector for Tobacco refuseth to deliuer the Tobacco now come home, vnlesse the Company will pay twelue pence custome vpon euery pound weight, wch is double aboue the booke of rates, the same being but six pence, and also being freed by his Ma^{ts} lres Pattents of Impost and Custome sauing 5 p Cent: It is now agreed, that a Petičon shalbe drawne to the Lordℓ Comissioners of the Treasury, and haue desired my Lo: of Warwicke, Sr Nath: Riche, m^r Aldřan Iohnson and m^r Brooke to attend their Lo^{ps} vpon ffriday next in the Afternoone for the cleering of the same.

It was moued by m^r Třer, that in reguard the time of the yeare passeth away, and most of the Company retireth themselues into the Country, and as yet a great deale of busines is to be performed before the departure of the Shipp, that a Comittee might be appointed to meete euery day for the dispatch of the same, and that the Generall Courts be dissolued till Michaelmas terme, vnlesse there be an extraordinary occasion, that m^r Thřer or m^r Deputy call an extraordinary Court; Which being approued of by the Court, there were nominated Sr Iohn Dăuers, m^r Deputy, m^r Alderman Iohnson, m^r Iohn Wroth, m^r Tho: Gibbs, m^r Geo: Thorpe, m^r Cranmer and m^r Chambers to meete at m^r Třers for dispatch of those businesses.

M[r] Deputy acquaynting this Court, that the Comittees hauing mett, and devided the busines amongst themselues for the speedier sending away of this shipp; in w[ch] as some of them are to be [28] comended by performing the charge comitted to their trust; so there are some to whome the care of buying apparrell was comitted, whoe part of them being out of Towne, the rest haue failed therein; in whose steede he desires, that some other might be appointed to performe that trust; to w[ch] by the Court is appointed m[r] Cranmer, m[r] Bull and Thomas Mellinge.

All such Bills of Exchange as were now sent from Abraham Persey the Capemerchant concerning the Magazine amounting to Eighte hundreth pounde specified in his Letters, is by the Adventurers thereof this present day accepted to be paid from this present at the determinaçon of the time in the seuerall Bills specified.

The Comittees for the Magazine are intreated by this Court to vndertake for the cleering of these goode now come home in the Wiłłm and Thomas; for the which it is now ordered, that they shalbe saued harmeles.

It was now ordered, vpon the request of S[r] Tho: Wainman, & vpon certificate to the Court from the Lady Lawarr, that shee was content soe farr to satisfy the desire of the said S[r] Tho: Wainman and S[r] Iohn Tasborough, w[th]all desiring the allowance of the Court, that such men as shall appeare to haue beene transported by the Lo: Lawarr for the said Sir Tho: Wainman & S[r] Iohn Tasbrough, & at their proper costs and charge may be free at his or their disposing to be remoued & planted according to their discreçons vpon such shares as shalbe by Pattent graunted vnto them, for the wch her Lāp is content, that there shalbe a ratable deducçon made out of the proporçon of Lande allready graunted and allowed, or hereafter to be graunted & allowed vnto the said Lo Lawarr for his Adventures: And that the Charter pt wch his Lo[p] entred into may not extend to the Losse and preiudice of them.   It being noe part of his Lo[p] or Lads[p] meaning they should suffer for that his Lo[p] stood engaged, and therefore resteth in her Ladishipp to see satisfied; W[ch] was also now confirmed by erecçon of hands.   [29]

IULY THE 21th 1619

A Court held at M^r fferrars howse in
St Sythes Lane, Being present

Right Honor^{ble} Henry Earle of Southampton.
Robert Earle of Warwicke.

Sr Edwin Sandis Kn^t Thřer.

Sr Tho: Smith.	Capt S. Argoll.	m^r　　[1] Shepherd.
Sr Tho: Gates.	Capt D: Tucker.	m^r Edw: Scott.
Sr Edw: Harwood.	Capt N: Butler.	m^r Tho: Couell.
Sr Iohn Wolstenholme.	m^r Ni: Leate.	m^r Dan: Darnelly.
m^r Aldřan Iohnson.	m^r Stiles.	m^r Robt: Smith.
m^r Xō Brooke.	m^r Clitherowe.	m^r Geo: Smith.
m^r Morrice Abbott.	m^r An: Abdy.	m^r fferrar iunio^r
m^r Io: fferrar Dep̄t.	m^r Robt. Offley.	m^r Geo: Chambers.
m^r Tho: Gibbs.	m^r Wm Palmer.	m^r Balmford.
m^r Do^r Gulstone.	m^r Caning.	m^r Paulson.
	m^r Hen: Briggs.	m^r Woodall.
		m^r Meuerell.　etc.

There was at the sitting downe of the Court by an vnknowne person presented to m^r Thřer the Letter following;

To Sr Edwin Sandis Thřer of Virginia.

✠
I H S

Good luck in the name of the Lord, who is dayly magnified by the experiment of your Zeale and Piety in giuinge begining to the foundacōn of the Colledge in Virginia the sacred worke soe due to Heauen and soe "Longed for one earth, Now knowe wee assuredly that the Lord will doe

---

[1] A blank space in the manuscript.

you good, and blesse yo[u] in all your proceeding[s] even as he blessed the howse of Obed Edom and all that pertayned to him because of the Arke of God, Now that yee seeke the kingdome of God, all thinges shalbe ministred vnto yo[u];" This I well see allready, and perceiue that by this your godlie determinaçon, the Lord hath giuen you "fauour in the sight of the people, and I knowe some whose hearts are much enlarged, because of the howse of the Lord our God to procure yor wealth," whose greater [30] designes I haue presumed to outrun with this oblaçon wch I humbly beseech yo[u] may be accepted as the pledge of my Devoçon and as the earnest of the Vowes "wch I haue vowed vnto the Allmighty God of Iacobb concerning this thing," W[ch] till I may in part performe I desire to remayne vnknowne and vnsought after.

The thinges are these

A Communion Cupp wth the Couer and case.
A Trencher plate for the Bread.
A Carpett of Crimson Veluett.
A Linnen Damaske table cloth.

M[r] Alderman Iohnson reported, that according to the trust reposed by the last Court vnto himselfe and some others they had performed, by being wth the Lord[s] Comissioners about the cleering of the Tobacco now come home agreable to the Pattent, whoe referred it to S[r] Lyonell Cranfield and m[r] Attorny Generall, but they being out of Towne, he desired that some other might now be appointed to attend the Lord[s] agayne for the finishing thereof: Wherevpon the Court haue desired, the Lo: of Warwicke, Sr Tho: Gates, Capt Nath: Butler, m[r] Clitherowe and m[r] Wm Caninge to attend them at such time as ffrancis Carter shall giue them notice that they sitt.

Sir Iohn Wolstenholme moued the Court in the behalfe of Martins Hundred, that in consideraçon of the Losse they haue sustayned by the Guift, wch they sett out, that they might haue shares in Virginia for euery—12—10—00 they haue therein spent: wch if the Court would please to graunte, it would encourage them to sett out ffifty men more in convenient time; which he desired might be putt to the question. To the w[ch], reply was made by Sr Edwin Sandis Thr̄er, that hauing beene priuately acquaynted wth this moçon, and hauing throughly waighed it, he could not giue way vnto for ffower reasons;

1. ffirst it was contrary to his Ma^{ts} Lres Pattents;

2. Secondly it was repugnant to ye Standing orders of the ye Company.

3. Thirdly it failed of the very end it aymed at, for it was not any advancem^t to the planting of Martins hundred.

4. ffourthly it was preiudiciall & that in a high degree to the Generall Plantačon, & to ye strength, peace & prosperity of ye Collony.　**[31]**

He began wth the second reason as being fresh in memory, & reading the Orders in the title of Graunts, he shewed, that all Landℰ were to be graunted either to Planters in Virginia by their persons, or to Adventurers by their purses, or by extraordinary merritts of service. That the Adventurers by their purses, were they onely and their Assign - ees, who paid in their seuerall shares of—12—10—to the Cōmon Treas - ure for the charges of transporting men to the priuate Lands of the Adventurers, there was also allowance made to them of 50 Acres the person.　But noe further allowance for any such priuate expences as was now demaunded.

Then he came to the first reason, and shewed that these Orders were not newly deuised, but taken out of the Lres Pattentℰ, namely the second & third; diuers passages of wch he there openly read, importing that the Landℰ in Virginia were to be deuided amongst the Adven - turers by mony, or service and the Planters in person, and that he is to be reputed an Adventurer by money, who payeth it into the Com - panies Treasury, insomuch that if any man be admitted for an Adven - turer, and haue paid in noe mony to the Cōmon Treasury, he is to be compelled thereto by suite of Lawe, yea though he neuer subscribed to any such payment, as is expresly sett downe in the Third Lres Pattentℰ.

Thirdly he shewed, it was not beneficiall to them of Martins hundred in point of advantaging their perticuler Plantačon, for the benefitt grew not by a bare title to Land, but by cultivating & peopling it so to reape proffitt, now of such Land it was in euery Adventurers power to haue asmuch as he pleased w^{th}out any other payment: ffor if an Adventurer (for examples sake) who had but one share of One hun - dreth Acres would send ouer Twenty men to inhabite & occupy it,

fewer at this day will not doe it, he was by the Orders allready established to haue for these 20 an addition of—1000—Acres of Land vpon
a first deuision and as much more vpon a second; And if then he
would also people his—1000—Acres wth Ten score men more, he were
to haue another addition of—10000—Acres more vpon a first deuision
and asmuch vpon a second, & so forward to what extent of Land himselfe should desire.   On the other side to enlarge a mans right vnto
new Land, and not to make vse and proffitt of the Old, were to increase
a matter of opinion, rather then of realty, & a shadowe rather then
a substance.

Lastly he said it was prieiudiciall to the Generall Plantaĉon in many
points of ymportance; first in matter of strength for those titles to
great extent of Land; so to keepe other from it, would be a great
weakning to the Collony by disioyning the parts of it one so farr
from another Vis Vnita Fortior.

Againe it would be a great discouragem^t to new perticule^r Plantaĉons
if either they must sitt downe of bad land, the best being all taken vp
before in titles, or seeke a seate farr of remote from helpe and society :
Besides whereas by the orders now established, men are to encrease
their owne Landℇ there by transporting of people, and so by increasing
the Collony in strength & multitude, the vertue and good intent of
this Order wilbe defeated, if men may haue their Landℇ encreased
wthout such transportaĉon, & onely by fauo^r & plurallity of voicℇ in Co^{rt}.

[32] Nowe as this moĉon is prieiudiciall to ye strength & encrease of
the Plantation, so is it also to the peace thereof, good governmen^t and
iustice :   It is not iust that a man should be paid twice for the same
thing; ffor the men transported they haue allready allowance of Land
—50—Acres the person whither dead or liuing : And the Charges now
spoken of was but in transporting those men.   It is not iust, that
things equall should be vnequally valued; As Martins hundred hath
beene at great charges, so §haue§ diuers other hundreds, so haue
also beene many perticuler persons, Captaine Bargraue alone hath
bought and sett out diuers shipps; if besides the persons transported, he
shall haue allowance of Land oueragaine for all his charges, perhaps
he may take vp a great part of the Riuer : What may my Lo : Lawarr

doe? Sir Tho: Gates, and Sr Tho: Dale, besides a multitude of other who haue spent a Large porčon of their Estates therein and are not thought on; if all these men come in wth their Accounts for all their tyme, what a confusion & disturbance will ensue thereof? shall wee deny that to them wch wee allowe vnto o^r selues? or shall wee admitt of their demaundᵉ and sett them out Land accordingly? how then shall wee ꝑceed in examining their Accountᵉ? how may they be cleered? when would they be ended? this course is a Laborinth and hath noe issue.

He concluded, that he had allwayes fauoured the desires of Martins hundred; but for this perticuler, he would not approue it: Howbeit if men were not satisfied wth these reasons, he would be well content, that the matter might be referred to a Quarter Court, vnto wch it did more properly belong; and that in the meane time, it might be referred to the consideračon of a Graue Comittie to be indifferently chosen out of the Generallity and Counsell.

Vpon this Sr Edward Harwood propounded, that for satisfacčon and encouragement of Martins hundred, there might be some quantity of Land bestowed vpon them by way of gratuity and seruice: wch was generally well liked, and the accomplishment thereof referred to the next Quarter Court, & in the meane time the matter should be prepared by a select Comittee.

And whereas the said Sr Iohn Wolstenholme Long since Lent the Company at one time 300^{li} and at another time—100^{li}, and after a Long time receaued it in agayne by Litle somes; that therefore in consideračon thereof, and that he receiued noe interest for the same, he moued, that the Court would recompence his kindnes by giuing him some Land; wch was now thought reasonable, if the qrter Co^{rt} (as they doe not doubt) shall allow thereof.

Vpon some dispute of the Polonians resident in Virginia, it was now agreed (notwthstanding any former order to the contrary) that they shalbe enfranchized, and made as free as any inhabitant there whatsoeuer: And because their skill in making pitch & tarr and sopeashees shall not dye wth them, it is agreed that some young men, shalbe put vnto them to learne their skill & knowledge therein for the benefitt of the Country hereafter.   [33]

It was ordered vpon consideraĉon that many principall men departeth the Court at or before six of the Clock, whereby the said Court is much weakned, that from henceforward they shall begin at Two, and end at six: after w[ch] time nothing shalbe agreed of, or putt to the question: w[ch] was confirmed by erecĉon of hand℮.

The order of the Last Co[rt] touching the dissoluing of the Courts till Michaelmas terme, being now putt to the question, was ratified by Generall consent.   And for the Magazine Adventurers, it was licenced for them to meete where they pleased till the Generall Co[rts] began againe, and soe often as they shall see cause, or be invited by any occasion.

An Act of the Co[rt] made Decimo quarto die Iunij 1619 concerning a Pattent graunted to Iohn Woodliefe Gent and his Associat℮ is now by the consent of this Court, & liking of the said Iohn Woodliefe altered, & is to goe in the name of S[r] Tho: Wainman & Associat℮: And is agreed vpon the request of the said S[r] Tho: Wainman, that a ĺre of informaĉon there of shalbe written to the Gouernor, inasmuch as it wilbe the qrter Court in Michaelmas terme before it cann passe the seale, and that in the Interim he desireth land to be allotted, wherevpon to plant such men, as shalbe by him & his Associat℮ sent or appoynted therevnto.

OCTOBER THE 20ᵗʰ 1619

PRESENT

Sʳ Tho: Roe Knᵗ.
Sʳ Io: Dãuers.
Sʳ Tho: Gates.
mʳ Mo: Abbott.
mʳ Io: fferrar Dp̃t.
mʳ Tho: Gibbs.
mʳ Geo: Thorpe.
mʳ Dʳ Anthony.
mʳ Dʳ Winstone.

mʳ Dʳ Gulstone.
mʳ Hen: Reignoldᶜ.
Capt S: Argoll.
mʳ Rich: Rogers.
mʳ Hen: Briggs.
mʳ Wᵐ Caninge.
mʳ Geo: Swinhowe.
mʳ Nichᵒ fferrar.
mʳ   ¹ Shepherd.

mʳ Tho: Keightly.
mʳ Rich: Bull.
mʳ Rich: Wiseman.
mʳ Iames Berblock.
mʳ Wᵐ Palmer.
mʳ Rich: Caswell.
mʳ Roberts.
mʳ Tho: Melling.

It was made knowne by mʳ Deputy that the time being expired, wherin during this terme of vacansye, the Generall Courts (according to order) haue discontinued; they are now to proceed againe in their due course every fortnight, this day moneth being a Generall qrter Court: And although mʳ Treasuror be yet absent, the Company will finde at his coming vp next weeke, that he hath not beene wanting to the service of Virginia, but both his minde and time wholly imployed in their busines; contem̃ing² the meanes of sending large supplies of men and Cattle for Virginia this next Spring. **[34]**

A l̃re being sent from his Maᵗⁱᵉ directed to mʳ Tr̃er and Counsell for the sending diuers dissolute persons to Virginia, wᶜʰ Sʳ Edward Zouch knᵗ Marshall will giue informacõn of; after the Counsell had pervsed the same, was brought to the boord and read to the Company, who considering there was noe present meanes of conveying them to Virginia, though fitt to reserue the full answere to his Maᵗˢ l̃re till the next Court, when wᵗʰ the Lordᶜ & mʳ Treasuror it might be agreed how his Maᵗˢ Comaundᶜ might most speedily and conveniently be effected: In the meane while Sʳ Io: Dãuers promised to acquaynt mʳ Secretarie Caluert and Sʳ Edw: Zouch the reason that they gaue not p̃sent answere to his Maᵗˢ gracious L̃re.

---

¹ A blank space in the manuscript.   ² For "contemplating."

Mr. Wiłłm Caninge tooke occasion to expresse some kinde of griefe for the long want of Courts, in wch he had hoped of redresse in the point of what the Co^{rt} had ordered in the busines betweene him and his Associats defendants against Capt Bargraue in Chauncery, intimating that if the Courts had continued or might be kept at Sr Tho: Smiths he would not doubt of the whole Courts satisfaccon otherwise then had beene.   Sir Tho: Smith and others appearing in the behalfe of him, and the defendants against Capt. Bargraue, but Sr Thomas could not & others would not come to this place; and therefore wished that this Court had beene or others might be at Sir Tho: Smiths who had soe freely and courteously offred his howse; and through his Long experience and good will to the Accon, was able to doe the Company very extraordinary service: wch pointℓ concerning the abillities & courtesyes of Sr Tho: Smith were seconded by some others; but Mr Caning farther vrging the reconsideracon of the Acte of Co^{rt} betweene him and his Associatℓ and Captaine Bargraue, and vttering some speeches of discontent, that onely Gentlemen had beene named of the Comittee, desiring a new refference wherein Citizens might also be ioyned; he was told of his wonted manner of seeking to interpose difference betweene Gentlemen and Cittizens, a thing damned heretofore in Court as tending to onely to faction and disturbance of the peace of the Company: But for the matter of his mocon to haue it renewed againe in Co^{rt} where he might presume to produce other testimony, or parties that had not either notice or leasure to be present at the former proceedings, by wch he and his Associatℓ had beene vniustlie preiudiced as he conceiued; Some was of opinion that his mocon was equitable; neuertheles it was held fitt, it should be referred to be moued againe at the next Court, wch should be like to be of a greater presence; Likewise wherein Capt Bargraue might be also heard what he might speake therevnto, least otherwise he might hereafter complaine & so keepe the Court impertinently imployed to order backward and forward, and euen in a matter twice ordered by a selected Comittee chosen by the Court, who had a chiefe reguard vnto the case, as it appeares in the Court Bookes.   [35]

NOUEMBER THE THIRD 1619:

BEING PRESENT

The Right Hono^{ms} The Lo: of Warwick.
Generall Cæsill.

Sr Edwin Sandis Kn^t Thꝰer.

Sr Tho: Roe.	m^r Geo: Sandis.	m^r Tho: Keightley.
S^r Io: Dāuers.	Capt Argoll.	m^r Shepherd.
Sr Harry Rainsford.	Capt Bargraue.	m^r Edw: Ditchfield.
Sr Tho: Wroth.	Capt Tucker.	m^r Rich: Wiseman.
Sr Nath: Rich.	m^r Tho: Gibbs.	m^r [1] Bamford.
Sr Law: Hide.	m^r Rich: Tomlins.	m^r Caswell.
m^r Iohn: fferrar Dpt.	m^r [1] Steward.	m^r Cranmer.
m^r Dr Gulstone.	m^r Geo: Chambers.	m^r Hen: Briggs.
m^r Dr Winstone.	m^r Iohn Delbridge.	m^r Ia: Berblock.
		m^r Lewson, etc.

As in the last Court Mr Deputy acquaynted them of m^r Thꝰer so he being now present it pleased him to relate, that although to the time giuen him by the Companies orders he had beene absent yet he hath not beene idle to Virginia, as he will giue Accompt of: And therefore he had to offer to their consideraĉon a Proposiĉon for the inlarging of the Plantation in the publique. And first touching the Publiq, he shewed how farr the Company had allready proceeded. ffirst in Ianuary last there went ffifty men wth Sr George Yeardley to be Tenant€ of the Gouernors land, whereof there failed by the way two or three, and six were now remayning to him of Capt Argolls guarde. Afterward in Aprill next twenty men should haue beene sent by Xofer Lawne vnto the Coffion Land, but he deliuered but 15 because the Company performed not wth him, touching the Loane of Corne and Cattle as he expected: Then 4 more were sent in the Triall according to the

[1] A blank space in the manuscript.

direcc̄on of his Matie. And in the begining of August Last, one hundreth more sent—50—to the Colledge Land and 50 to the Com̄on: And for one hundreth persons or thereabout wch appeareth to haue beene sent in these 2 or 3 last yeares at the Companies charges, Sr Geo: Yeardley writeth of but three to be found remayning for the Company; So that there is by this Account vpon the Com̄on Land 72 persons, 53 on the Gouernors, and 50 on the Colledges: 175 in the whole. Therefore he proposed now to be considered of against the Quarter Court this day fortnight that there might be sent the next Spring 130 men more, wch will make those allready sent for the Gouerno' Colledge, and Com̄on Land the full nomber of Three hundred, and so the Gouerno^r to haue 100 men wch will not be lesse worth then One thowsand pound€ p Ann̄ as it is esteemed. As for the benefitt of their labors of the Com̄on Land, it standeth otherwise, for their moity is to be deuided betweene the Counsell and Officers there, [36] and for other publique vses, and betweene the Company here. ffor the Counsell who attend€ there, when the Gouernor at all times shall please to call them, cannot neglect their busines w^{th}out reward; soe likewise here, the Company may not expect, that although their Tr̄er for the time past and p̄nte, as also the Deputies of late serue meerely out of their zeale and loue to the Acc̄on, yet those that shall succeede will happily expect a yearely gratificac̄on, when the Company shalbe enabled by their Rents to yeild it. And for the Colledge, there is noe doubt but the benefitt ensuing will build it, and raise a Revennue for the mayntenance. He also thought it fitt to send 100 more to be Prentizes or Servants that the rest may goe on more cheerefully, wherein he hoped the citty would deale as worthily as heretofore. Lastly he wished that a fitt hundreth might be sent of woemen, Maid€ young and vncorrupt to make wifes to the Inhabitn̄nt€ and by that meanes to make the men there more setled & lesse moueable who by defect thereof (as is credibly reported) stay there but to gett something and then to returne for England, wch will breed a dissoluc̄on, and so an ouerthrow of the Plantac̄on. These woemen if they marry to the publiq̄ ffarmors, to be transported at the charges of the Company; If otherwise, then those that takes them to wife to pay the said Company their charges of

transportac̃on, and it was neuer fitter time to send them then nowe.
Corne being here at home soe cheape and plentifull, and great promises there for the Haruest ensuing. Then to euery 100 men, he
aduised there might be sent 20 young Heifers wch wilbe Threescore,
and they wth their breed will soone store the Publique. He also
shewed, that the Inhabitants hauing had great ioy by the Charters of
Graunts and Liberties lately sent by Sr Geo: Yeardley, desired now to
haue choise men sent them from the Lowe Countries to raise ffortifi-
cations, whose charge they will beare, wherein my Lo: Generall
Cesills assistance was perticulerly entreated. Then he spoke of the
way of transporting these persons, wch by reason of the intollerable
charge the Company is at by sending ships, that that course should
be left of and rather send by those that trade to Newfoundland at Six
pound₵ a man, wch wilbe found to be great ease vnto the Company;
but for the Catle a shipp must be sent on purpose, vnlesse a bargayne
may be made for them at 10^li— a peece, as he hath some hope giuen
him that it may be. The totall charge of all this, furnishing the men
reasonably wth all things requisite, will amount (as he hath computed
it) not aboue ffower thowsand pound₵; And one thowsand more will
furnish them in best sort. Then how this mony shall come in, he
shewed how much the Company was bound to giue thankes to God for
all his blessings, who continually rayseth meanes for the supporting
of this worke, making menc̃on of one vnknowne Gentleman that hath
offred to send to him 500^li— for the converting and educac̃on of
Threescore Infidells Children, whensoeuer he shall require the same
& vndertake that worke. And also that vpon his l̃res he had receaued
advertizement from sundry parts and some of them very remote, that
if they goe on wth this busines they shall not want for money. Likewise Gabriell Barbor [37] hath promised of Lottary monies to bring
in before the end of March 35 hundreth pound₵, wch he intend₵ according to the promise made vnto the Lord₵ shall goe to noe other end but
the advancement of the Plantac̃on. And for the Three thowsand
pound₵, wch was spoken of when he entred to be T̃rer he hath not as
yet receaued the whole, but as it cometh in, it shall all goe for the
payment of former debts and dueties, whereof he had discharged
aboue 2000^li allready, promising that he will not leaue the Company

one penny in debt by any Act to be done by him. And for the ratificaĉon hereof, he referred it to the qrter Co^rt, onely now proposing it, that in the interim it might be considered of by the Company.

Next he acquainted, that the Counsell sitting this morning at my Lord of Southamptons, there were some moĉons made for ye busines at home, one was concerning Tobacco in Generall, that the planting of it here would be the destrucĉon of the Plantation, and therefore that the Company might be humble suito^rs for an inhibiĉon thereof; but this was conceaued might be a scandall for Virginia, as that it could not subsist w^thout that weed, intending very shortly to sett in hand with Iron-workes, & the Country affording diuers other good comodities, as Silke, Silkegrasse, Corne, Vines, etc. And therefore it was thought better by the Counsell, forasmuch as the ffarmors of Impost had it on foote allready that they proceed, and the Company as they see occasion to assist them. ffor the perticuler Tobacco of the Adventurers remayning in the Custome howse, he was desired by the Counsell to drawe a ſre in their [names, and to be signed by them, wch he promised forthw^th to performe, to be addressed vnto the Kings Lerned Counsell, shewing the priuiledges of their Pattent, and the Losse they haue sustayned by this extreame delay wth earnest request of present expediĉon. And seeing that m^r Iacobb contrary to the priuiledges of their said Pattent; the Letter of his Ma^ts priuy Counsell in their behalfe, and the Adventurers offer to leaue halfe wth him, that they might obtaine the other halfe to sell away that it might not all perish, had reiected all moĉons and meanes of agreement, and in contempt of their Lo^ps Letter refused to deliuer it vpon those reasonable condiĉons sett downe by their Lps, that therefore he thought it very expedient (the Lordℓ consentℓ being first obtayned) that the Company com̄ence an Acĉon of damages against him, the losse they haue receaued being estimated by many at—2500^li—wch moĉon so suted wth the desire of the Court (sauing that the Lordℓ consent was thought vnnecessary) that for the rest they intreated it might be putt to the question: wch being done, and also propounding whither the suite shall proceed at the Com̄on charge, being for the maynteñnce of the Pattent, and the Magazine to appoint Sollicitors, was ratified by erecčon of handɛ; The Court hauing now chosen for their Counsell, Sⁱ Lawrence Hide and mʳ Xofer Brooke; And to sollicite the cause mʳ Tho: Melling for the Company, mʳ Iames Berblock for the Magazine, and mʳ Richard Caswell is entreated to assist them. [38]

According to the refference in the Last Court his Maⁱˢ Lre was now taken into most dutifull consideračon, and it was agreed wᵗʰ all convenience to fulfill his Maⁱˢ comaund, and to send them ouer to be servants, wᶜʰ wilbe very acceptable vnto the Inhabitantɛ, as mʳ Thřer hath vnderstood from them, and in the meane time till they may be sent, wᶜʰ wilbe about Ianuary, Mʳ Treasuror shewed, that in like case the Lo: Maior had beene sollicited to giue order for the keeping of them in Bridewell, wᶜʰ was answered to be performed allready, and the Court desired mʳ Treasuror to giue his Maᵗʸ an answere by mʳ Secretary Caluert.

Mr Iohn Delbridge močon for a Pattent to be graunted him and his Associats intending to transport—200—men was assented vnto and referred to the Auditors vpon Monday morning to haue his Pattent perfected.

Whereas mʳ Wᵐ Canings complaint the last Court was referred vnto this present to be heard betwixt Captaine Bargraue & him, he being now absent was by diuers now present censured to be a great disturber of the peace of the Company, & molester of the Courts wᵗʰ matter of ffaction: Therefore when the Counsell meetes, that he be warned to attend them to receiue admoničon and if that after he continue in his wonted byas, that then he be disfranchized according to a standing order in that behalfe.

And whereas formerly a seale for the Company called the Legall seale was referred vnto a Comittee to consider ~~it~~ §in§ what manner it should be, and nothing as yet done therein; It was agreed that Mʳ Clarentious be intreated to giue the Auditors sometimes a meeting at Sʳ Edwin Sandis, where they will deuise to take a Cote for Virginia and agree vpon the Seale.

fforasmuch as noe deuision of the Iointstock is yet made to the Adventurers, according long since to promise, nor any acc° hetherto presented (though often called for) whereby they may vnderstand the state of the busines, and other Accounts intermixed wth them be cleered; therefore vpon generall request of the Adventurers now p̃nte, it was agreed that the Counsell be entreated to take the busines into their hand℮, and to call the Officers of the Magazine before them to giue vp their Acc°, as also to heare aswell the obiecc̃ons of the Adventurers, as the answeres of the Officers, that soe right be done, and the differences Long depending may be freindly decided and ended: W^{ch} moc̃on was also extended to such accompts of the former Magazine as remayne yet vncleared. [39]

And although the Company is allready exceedingly behoulding to my Lord of Southampton for his many hono^{ble} fauo^{rs} & nobly countenancing them in all their businesses, and especially such as is of greatest importance; yet notwthstanding the Co^{rt} are most humble suitors vnto his Lõp, that he would please also in these businesses of so great importance, and wch haue beene the onely cause of distracc̃on and discention in the Company, to vouchsafe his presence at that meeting of the Counsell, that by his Lo^{ps} and their authority, those differences might be concluded, the Comp̃ satisfied in their right, and all occasion of continuing iealousies and displeasures be remoued: W^{ch} moc̃on being made by m^r Thr̃er was by Generall erecc̃on of hand℮ confirmed noe one dissenting.

Mr Thr̃er also moued, that Captaine Bargraue should be desired by the Court, that at leastwise after the examinac̃on of his witnesses (vpon wch he resolutely insisted) he would then be content to referr the Controuersy betweene him and some other of the Company, to be heard in like sort and arbitrated by the Counsell, that so all cause of scandall and discord amongst the Company might haue an end: Vnto wch Captaine Bargraue gaue his consent, and the same was generally well approued of by the Court.

NOUEMBER THE 15ᵗʰ 1619

A Preparatiue Court held for Virginia at
Mᴿ ffERRARS HOWSE IN Sᵀ SYTHES LANE. PRESENT

The Right Honoᵇⁱᵉ {
The Lo: of Southampton.
The Lo: Cauendish.
The Lo: Pagett.

mʳ Treasuror.	mʳ Dʳ Winstone.	mʳ Swinhowe.
Sʳ Tho: Roe.	Capt: S. Argoll.	mʳ Wiseman.
Sʳ Io: Dauers.	Capt Bargraue	mʳ Couell.
Sʳ Tho: Wroth.	mʳ Ruggell.	mʳ Cranmer.
Sʳ H: Rainsford.	mʳ Aug: Steward.	mʳ Berblock.
Sʳ Nath: Rich.	mʳ Shepherd.	mʳ Smith.
Sʳ Io: Wolstenholme.	mʳ Bamford.	mʳ Chambers.
Sʳ Anth: Aucher.	mʳ Keightley.	mʳ Boothby.
Sʳ Ro: Winchfeild.	mʳ Briggs.	mʳ Bland.
mʳ Geo: Sandis.	mʳ Meuerell.	mʳ Melling.
mʳ Io: fferrar Dpt.	mʳ Lewson.	mʳ E: Roberts. etc.
mʳ Dʳ Anthony.		

Mʳ Tᵬers proposicõn at the last Court being now read and considered of, Sʳ Iohn Wolstenholme intimated, that for his part [40]
he liked them very well, but wᵗʰall moued that some of the Company
might be appointed by the Court to examine whither the monies to
come in, would be sufficient to doe this, and to leaue some remayning
in the Treasury to defray such charges as either by his Maᵗˢ comaund
for the sending ouer such men as he shall write for, or otherwise may
accidentally happen. Wherevnto was answered, that these Proposi-
cõns had beene formerly proposed to the Counsell at Southampton
howse, where they were generally approued to be beneficiall and

advantagious for the Plantačon, And therefore not fitt they should be reassumed from thence to a priuate Comittie, Esteeming the Counsell the chiefest Comittee could be chosen. Also mr. Tr̃er to the generall satisfaccõn of the whole Court made this answere, that for those nombers to be setled on the Comõn, Gouernors and Colledge Land, he would not leaue the Company indebted one penny: As for former debts he had allready paid aboue 2000ˡⁱ towardɛ discharging of them, and a 1000ˡⁱ he would pay when it came in, wᶜʰ was asmuch as was left vnto him, doubting not but that the yearely comodities coming out of Virginia, would henceforward defray all accidentall charges; it hauing beene truly alleadged before, that the planting and peopling of the Companies Land was the surest way to bring in Revennue. It was alsoe answered by others, that all that was in Cashe was but to be imployed to the advancemᵗ of the Plantačon, and that there could be noe better worke to further that then this, nor nothing more hurt-full then to leaue vnperformed those designes & workes wᶜʰ themselues are certaine and good, for things accidentall and vncertaine; So as noe man further opposing, The former Obieccõn vanished. And it was moued by my Lo: of Southampton, that the Court hauing now heard the Proposičõns read, if they made scruple of any thing, that it might be now debated at full against the Quarter Court. But noe man either seconding the former, or raising any new obieccõn, the Proposičõns rested wᵗʰ generall approbačon of the Court.

Touching the Legall seale spoken of in the last Court, the Auditors at their Assembly haue therein taken some paynes, wᶜʰ they now pre-sented to this Courte: And whereas they had spoken to one for the cutting of it, there is one mʳ Hole who would appropriate that vnto him selfe vnder pretence of hauing a Pattent for the engrauing all seales, wᶜʰ hath the Kings Armes or any part thereof, wᶜʰ he now pre-sented to the Court, and mʳ Tr̃er pervsing the same, found, that it was for the Kinges armes, but not for any part thereof, and therefore appointed them to repaire to mʳ Xofer Brooke of Lincolnes Inne to examine it, and to bring his opinion vnder his hand in writing, & accordingly it should be determined.

Next for the order of the Magazine Acc° referred to the Counsell, My Lord of Southampton was humbly desired to lend his presence for the concluding of it: This and the former Magazine being the cause [41] of all discentions that hath beene amongst the Company, who hath promised his assistance.   And Sʳ Iohn Wolstenholme for the better concluding thereof hath also promised that he will giue order for the meeting of some of the Adventurers, together wᵗʰ mʳ Essington to examine the State of the Magazine, & the Accountℓ against the Counsell meete.

Mʳ Tᵣer also signified, touching the Standing orders that nothing is done, in wᶜʰ time discouereth not some imperfecc͠ons, acquaynting that some § stood in § need of some small explanac͠on, and that there needed to be an addic͠on of Two or three more, wᶜʰ although yet they cannot be soe absolute as the others, wanting the Ceremonies due vnto them, yet till that be performed they stand (if the Company soe please) as orders of a Quarter Court, wᶜʰ to that Court was referred.

Mʳ Tᵣer desired the allowance of this Court of one thing agreed of by the Auditors and Comittees of the Colledge, wᶜʰ was that 1400ˡⁱ—od mony in all being receaued of the Collecc͠on monyes by Sʳ Tho: Smith, of wᶜʰ vpon seuerall occasions, therewas vented by way of Loane for the vse of the Company Eight hundreth poundℓ, the Remainder being 500ˡⁱ odd money was paid vnto mr. Treasuroʳ; Therfore that the said 800ˡⁱ—might be reimbursed out of the Com͠on Cash in to the Colledge mony, wᶜʰ was ratified and allowed of by the Court.

Vpon a petic͠on exhibited by the wife of Abraham Persey, that in lieu of his Long service done the Company, they would gratify him wᵗʰ giuing him some Land in Virginia: wᶜʰ sundry of the Coʳᵗ acknowl-edgin[g] his paynfull endeauoʳ̣, haue agreed for the present to giue him 200 Acres (if the Quarter Court vpon Wedensday next shall allowe thereof; And hereafter as they finde him discharge the busines reposed vpon him, to reward him accordingly.

Also vpon the peticõn of Mathew Cauell Master of the W^m & Thomas, shewing that in consideracõn of a Bote & ship Anchor deliuered to Capt Samuell Argoll for the vse and benefitt of the Plantation, Rec̃d of the said Capt Argoll in Virginia his freedome & 400 w^tt of Tobacco, wch since his coming home, he could not receiue from the Custome howse w^thout putting in caution to pay to m^r Iacobb Two shillings a pound, therefore in reguard of his said freedome, desired he might Copart of the like priuiledges the Company doe.   W^ch was answered, that Capt Argoll could not giue him his freedome, for none can be free but by two wayes, either by money brought in, or by some extraordinary service: Wherein was alleadged, that he did speciall service in the begining of the Plantacõn: Wherevpon he was appointed to make knowne his deserts in writing, & accordingly, he should receaue the Companies fauour.   [42]

At a great and generall Quarter Court
houlden for Virginia on Wedensday
the 17th of Nouemb 1619. Were Present.

The Right hono^{ble} { Henry Earle of Southampton.
Robt Earle of Warwick.
The Lo: Cauendish.
The Lo: Sheffeild.
The Lo: Pagett.

Sr Edw: Sandis Kn^t Threr.

Sr Tho: Roe.	Tho: Gibbs.	m^r Chambers.
Sr Dud: Diggs.	Geo: Sandis.	m^r Palmer.
S^r ffran: Popham.	Arth: Bromfield.	m^r Whitley.
Sr Tho: Gates.	Iohn Bargraue.	m^r Morer.
Sr Ferdinand: Gorges.	Capt. S. Argoll.	m^r Ditchfield.
S^r Io: Dauers.	Hen: Reignoldℓ.	m^r Edwardes.
Sr Hen: Rainsford.	August Steward.	m^r Wiseman.
Sr Tho: Wilford.	Ri: Tomlins.	m^r Shepherd.
S^r Ro: Winchfield.	Tho Wells.	m^r Cranmer.
Sr Tho: Cheeke.	Edw: Brewster.	m^r Berblock.
Sr Nath: Rich.	m^r Io: fferrar Dpt.	m^r Rogers.
Sr Tho: Wroth.	m^r Hanford.	m^r Couell.
S^r Io: Wolstenholme.	m^r Clitherowe.	m^r Boothby.
Dr Math: Sutcliff.	m^r Nich: fferrar.	m^r Caswell.
D^r Fr: Anthony.	m^r Hen: Briggs.	m^r Barnard.
Dr Theod: Gulstone.	m^r Caning.	m^r Roberts.
Dr Tho: Winstone.	m^r Bland.	m^r Geo: Smith.
Dr Law: Bohun.	m^r Bull.	m^r Meuerell.
Phillip Chidley, Esq.	m^r Keightley.	m^r Boulton.
Iohn Wroth.		m^r Mellinge.

Before the reading of the Co^rts there was presented by m^r Trer a list
of all the Counsello^rs names of Virginia, being of Earles, Barons,
Knights, Gentlemen and Citizens about 100 in all, wth this Caution

that if any heard themselues named, and had not taken their Oaths, they were to repair to the Lo: Chauncello^r or the Lo: Chamberlaine to be sworne.

Afterward the writing conteyning an addiĉon & explanaĉon of certaine Lawes and orders for the Company presented in the Preparatiue Court, was now againe read and by generall consent referred to the Comittee formerly chosen for the Lawes & orders of the Company.

The Courtes being read, m^r Treasuror putt the Court in remembrance of his former Proposiĉons propounded in the Co^n iij° Die Nouembris hauing before that propounded them to the Counsell, and lastly to [43] the Preparatiue Court, and desired to haue the iudgment of this Great and Generall Court concerning them: Where, vpon the request of some noble§men§ p͂nte, he related them againe to the Co^n in effect as followeth;

Mr. Thr̄er therefore declared, that his care and duety running ioyntlie for the advancem^t of this noble Plantation, his desire carried him chiefly to the restoring of the Publiq$_1$[1] now lately decayed, and the reforming of some errors, wch had directed their charges and the labo^m of the Collony to a wrong and vnworthy course, and greatly to the disgrace and hurt of the Plantaĉon: ffor whereas not much aboue Three yeares agoe there were returned from Virginia Twelue severall Comodities sold openly in Court to the great hono^r of the Acĉon and encouragem^t of the Adventurers: Since that time there hath beene but litle returned worth the speaking of, saue Tobacco and Sassaphras, which the people there wholy applying, had by this misgouernem^t reduced themselues into an extremity of being ready to starue (vnles the Magazine this last yeare had supplyed them wth Corne and Cattle from hence) to the stopping and great discouragem^t of many hundred℄ of people, who were prouiding to remoue themselues to plant in Virginia. The cause of this erro^r he would not insist vpon, as loth to giue offence by glaunce of speech to any, but for remedy thereof (besides often letters from the Counsell sent lately to the Gouernour

----

[1] This term refers to the Company land or property in Virginia.

for restraint of that imoderate following of Tobacco and to cause the
people to apply themselues to other and better comodities) he had
also by the advice of his Ma^{ts} Counsell here, and according to one of
the new orders now propounded, caused to be drawne a new Covenant
to be incerted in all Pattents of land hereafter to be graunted, that
the Pattentees should not apply themselues wholly or chiefly to
Tobacco, but to other Comodities specified in the said Coueñnt, An
example whereof they should see in the Pattent lying before them to
be passed in this Court to m^{r} Iohn Delbridge and his Associats. Now
touching the Publique, he was first to present to their remembrance
how by the admirable industry of Two worthie knightℰ Sr Tho: Gates
and Sr Tho: Dale, it was sett forward in a way to greate perfecõon,
whereof the former Sr Tho: Gates had the hono^{r} to all posterity to be
the first named in his Ma^{ts} Pattent of graunt of Virginia, and was the
first who by his wisedome, valo^{r} & industry, accompanied wth exceed-
ing paines and patience in the middest of so many difficulties laid a
foundaõon of that prosperous estate of the Collonie, which afterward
in the vertue of those beginings did proceed. The latter, Sr Tho:
Dale building vpon those foundaõons wth great & constant seuerity,
reclaymed almost miraculously those idle and disordered people and
reduced them to labour and an honest fashion of life, and proceeding
wth great zeale to the good of this Company sett vp the Coñmon
Garden to yield them a standing revennue, placed servants vpon
it, as also vpon other Publiq_{s} workes for the Companies vse, Established an Annuall rent of Corne from the ffarmers, Of tribute
Corne from the Barbarians, together wth a great stock of Kine,
Goates, and other Cattle, being the goodℰ of the Companie for the
service of the Publiq_{s}, wch hath since beene the occasion of drawing
so many perticuler Plantaõons to seate in Virginia vpon hope [44]
and promise of plenty of Corne and Catle to be lent them from the
Publiq_{s} for their ease and benefitt vpon their first ariuall. But since
their times all these publiq_{s} prouisions hauing beene vtterly Laid
wast by such meanes as hereafter in due time shall appeare. It hath
beene his principall care in those places wherein it pleased the Company to comaund his service to sett vp the publiq_{s} againe, in as great
or greater hight then heretofore it had: The maintayning of the

publiq, in all estates being of noe lesse importance, euen for the benefitt of the Priuate, then the roote and body of a Tree are to the perticuler branches: And therefore to present vnto them all in one view both what had beene allready done, and what yet remayned to be perfected, he recalled to their remembrance, how by their Comission sent by Sir George Yeardley they had appointed 3000 Acres of Land to be sett out for the Gouernor so to ease the Company henceforward of all charge in mayntayning him: 12000 Acres of Land to be the Comõn Land of the Companie; viz^tt three thowsand in each of the ffower old Burroughes—10000—acres of Land for the vniuersity to be planted at Henrico; of which—1000 for the Colledge for the conuersion of Infidells: The next care was for the placing Tenants vpon these Landč: In Ianuary last there went wth Sr Geo. Yeardley 50 Tenantč for the Gouerno^rs Land transported at the Companies and furnished at his charge, and six he found remayning of Capt Argolls guarde: In the March afterward there were sent §twenty§ to the Companies Land by Mr Lawne, whereof he hath deliuered yet but 15, for want of performance to him of loane of Corne and Cattle: ffower more were sent by the Triall, and Three Sr Geo: Yeardley found in the Country. In the begining of August last in the Bona Noua were sent 100 persons for publiq, service, chosen wth great care, and extraordinarily furnished, whereof 50 for the Companies Land, and 50 for the Colledge Land, So that making deduccõn of some fewe that are dead, there were he hoped at this day 174 persons, placed as Tenants vpon the Publique.

Therefore his first Proposition was, that the Company would be pleased, that these Tenants for the Publiq, might be encreased this next Spring vp to the number of 300, viz^tt one hundreth for the Gouernors Land, 100 for the Companies and 100 for the Colledge Land; w^ch (if he be truly informed by those whoe best should knowe it) being rightly imployed will not yeild lesse in value then Three thowsand poundč yearely revenue for these publiq, vses. And because care both hath beene, and shalbe taken that diuers stayed persons and of good condičons haue beene and shalbe sent amongst them, His second Proposičon was, that for their ease and comodiousnes, there might be 100 young persons sent to be their Apprentices, in the charge whereof he hoped this Hono^bre Citty, would pertake wth the Company as they formerly had done: And because he vnderstood that the people thither transported, though seated there in their persons for some fewe yeares, are not setled in their mindes to make it their place of rest [45] and continuance, but hauing gotten some wealth there, to returne againe into England: ffor the remedying of that mischiefe, and establishing of a perpetuitie to the Plantation, he aduised and made it his Third Proposičon, to send them ouer One hundreth young Maides to become wifes; that wifes, children and familie might make them lesse moueable and settle them, together with their Posteritie in that Soile.

His next Proposičon was, for the manno' of transporting these persons thus to make vp ffiue hundreth for the Publiq Land, wherein he advised, that they should not as heretofore hire Shipping for this purpose, whereof euery Shipp at his returne in bare fraught and wages emptied the Cashe of 800 and sometimes 1000^{li}, but that they should as they had allreadie done this present yeare take the opportunitie of the Ships trading to Newfoundland, and so to transport them at six poundes a person wthout after reckonings.

A ffifte Proposičon for the sending of 20 Heifers vpon eu⁹y 100 of these Tenants, Threescore in the whole, wch he hoped might be done taking the opportunity of Shipping in the Westerne parts at Ten pounde a head 600^{li} in the whole.

Lastly touching the charges he related perticulerly as formerly he had done, diuers great incouragements of supply to come in: he estimated the whole charge at ffoure thousand pounde to be done sparingly & bountifully at 5000^{li}: He promised not to leaue the Company one penny in debt for any thing in his yeare to be performed: And moreouer that he would discharge 3000^{li} of former debts and reckonings according to the Stock left in the Lottaries at his coming to this place: This done he hoped the Publiq would agayne be well restored, A foundačon Laid for a future great state, The Adventurers and Planters well comforted and encouraged, All matter of scandall and reproach remoued, and so he would comend the Acčon to the blessing of God. These Proposičons after some pause, receauing noe opposičon were putt to the question & receaued the generall approbačon of the Court.

Next he acquaynted that at the Court of eleccon, there was choice made of Sixteene Comittees, one third part of them being vnsworne, who since that time haue seldome or neuer mett, or afforded their presence therefore desired that in their steede wch had not taken their oathes, others might be chosen in their Roome, men knowne to be of wisedome and industrie, and whose Zeale to the Accon might appeare by the menaging of the Companies busines, wch now grew great & waighty; Wherevpon there was nominated m^r Doctor Winstone, m^r Shepherd, m^r Rich: Bull, m^r Wiłłm Cranmer, m^r Daniell Darnellie, and m^r Tho: Mellinge, who from time to time have promised their best assistance, & therevpon receaued their oaths.   [46]^1

Mr. Thŕer bin wth my Lord Maior.

Allso hee acquainted thatt in setting forward pt of his proposiconns now confirmed hee had to thatt purpose been wth the Lord Maior who found him as willinge to pleasure the Company as he desyred, wth all desyred to have their myndes in writinge that the Court of Aldermen and the Common Councell may the better vnderstand them, wch being now reddy drawne was read and allowed of, the Coppy of wch ensueth—

To the Ri Honorable Sr William Cockaine kn^t Lord Maior
of the Cittie of London and the Right Woŕp: ye Aldermen his
Brethren and ye Wo^t: the Common Counsell of ye said Citty.

The Companies declaracon to ye Lo: Maior and Courte of Aldermen.

The Thŕer Counsell and Company of Virginia assembled in their great and generall Courte the 17th of Nouember i6i9 have taken into Consideracon the continuall great forwardnes of his honorable Cytty in advancinge the Plantacon of Virginia and pticularly in furnishinge outt one hundred Children this last yeare, wch by the goodnes of God ther saffly Arived, (save such as dyed in the waie) and are well pleased wee doubt not for their benefitt, ffor which yo^ur bountifull assistance, wee in the name of the wholl Plantacon doe yield vnto yo^u due and deserved thanks.

And forasmuch as wee have now resolved to send this next Springe very large supplies for the strength and encreasinge of the Collony, styled by the name of the London Collony, And finde that the sendinge of those Children to be apprentises hath been very grateful ef §to§ the people: Wee pray yor Lo^p:

---

^1 At the top of the following page of the manuscript the handwriting changes to that of Nicholas Ferrar's assistant in supervising the transcription of the records. The corrections are few in number and usually by the copyist rather than by the reviewer. This has been referred to as the autograph of Thomas Collett. See Plates,

and the rest in pursuite of yoʳ former so pyous Acĉons to renew yoʳ like favours and furnish vs againe wᵗʰ one hundreth more for the next springe; Our desire is that wee may have them of Twelue years olde & vpward wᵗʰ allowance of Three pound a peec for their Transportaĉon and fforty shillings a peec for their apparrell as was formerly graunted. They shall be Apprentizes the boyes till they come to 21 years of Age the Girles till the like Age or till they be marryed and afterwardes they shalbe placed as Tennantℭ vppon the publique Land wᵗʰ best Condiĉons wher they shall have houses wᵗʰ Stocke of Corne & Cattle to begin wᵗʰ, and afterward the moytie of all encrease & pfitt what soever. And soe wee leave this moĉon to yoʳ honorable and graue Consideraĉon.

[47] Moreouer that hee had drawne a Publicaĉon wᶜʰ if itt were liked, desyred that itt might be putt in printe beinge for the entertaynment of good and sufficient Laborers and Husbandmen, Artificers and manuall Trades to be sett outt att the time formerly specified vnto the Publique and Colledg Land wᶜʰ beinge read and putt to the question was ratyfied by erecĉon of hands.   *A Publicaĉon ratified*

After this hee signified that accordinge to the desire of the last Courte hee had beene wᵗʰ mʳ Secretary Calvert and delivered the Companies answere touchinge the Transporting of men prest by his Maty wᶜʰ gaue nott full satisfacĉon for that the Kings desyre admitted no delaies butt forthwith to have 50 : of the 100 shipt away with all speed, Notwᵗʰstanding the many inconvenyences wᶜʰ mʳ Thr̃er alleadged would therby accrew vnto the Company that they could not goe in lesse then fower Shipps, for feare they beinge many togeather may drawe more vnto them and so muteny and carry away the Ships, wᶜʰ would stand the Company in fowre thousand poundℭ, and they not suddenly to be gotten att this time of the yeare, butt all not serv-inge the turne hee tolde them what a pinch hee was putt vnto and therfore desyred their Counsell and Advise.

Whervppon divers waise beinge thought on and considered, the Court could finde no fitter nor mor sattisfactory answere then this; That the Company would be att the charge to maynteyne them till ther may be Shippinge provyded, if so be they were commaunded to doe   *The Company to be att the charge to maynteyne till be shippinge provided*

A Comittee to Compass Shipping wᵗʰ all speed.

itt And therfore have apoynted a Comittee of select Marchantts to imploy their wholl endeavours for the Compassinge of Shippinge wᵗʰ all speed possible; Namely, mʳ Deputy Ferrar, mʳ Keightley, mʳ Wiseman, mʳ Cranmore, mʳ Bull, mʳ Sheppard, and mʳ Mellinge and to

800ˡⁱ: to remayne in the Magazine.

that end mʳ Thꝛer was content the Eight hundred poundꝭ Adventured by the generall Stocke in the Magazine should remaine there to be employed to these vses from time to time, whervnto if they pleased

200ˡⁱ more out of the Cash to be Added.

ther should be two hundreth pounds more added outt of the Cash in his Custody, wᶜʰ Thousand poundꝭ to be onely for the sattisfyinge of his Maᵗˢ: desyres from tyme to time.

The Soꝰer Ilands Compⁿ to ioyne for transportinge some of them.

And wheras the Company of the Soꝰer Ilandꝭ doth allwaies reporte of the gracious favour his Maᵗʸ extendeth to Virginia, that therfore the next Quarter Courte for the said Ilands the Company therof be intreated to Ioyne for the Transporte of some of them to be Servauntꝭ

Mʳ Thꝛer to drawe the Answere and deliuer it to mʳ Secrt. Caluerte.

vppon their Land; My Lord of Warwick, Sʳ Edwin Sandys, mʳ Iohn Ferrar and others intendinge to take some of them to that purpose, for prosecutinge of wch itt being putt to yᵉ question was generally agreed of, intreatinge mʳ Thꝛer that to this effect hee would in writinge drawe the answere and deliuer itt to mʳ Secretary Caluert to informe his Maᵗʸ: [48]

The Magazine held to stand Desperate.

Concerning the Magazine wᶜʰ is held to stand in Desperate Tearmes, the goods remayninge in Captivytie; Mʳ Thꝛer fallinge into speech wᵗʰ a greate noble man of the State of Virginia att length Complayned of

Mr. Thꝛers Complaint of yᵉ loss susteynd by mʳ Iacobb

the greate losse they have susteyned by mʳ Iacobbs deteyninge a wholl years harvest, notwithstandinge all the offers that was made, and that other bussines this Tearme being so great this could have noe reso-

The compꝪ: to be exhibited to yᵉ Councell Table

luꝯon from the Kings lear[ne]d Councell; Whervꝑon hee advised him to bringe their Complaynte vnto the Councell Table, and ther they should be sure to receive all the right that might be:

Dispute aboute mayntening or dissoluinge of yᵉ Magazine.

The desperate estate of wᶜʰ and the neglect of the presentinge the Accompts therof caused a suddaine dispute, whither they should proceed forward in the maynteyninge of itt or absolutely to disolve the same, Some beinge of opinion that free Trade might be more benefi-

čall to the Plantačon, vnto wch Sr Iohn Wolstenholme aleaged that Sir Io: Wolstenholmes aleagment to itt
as the settinge vp of that Magazine was the life and cheife support of
that Plantation so hee desyred allthough hee were one of the greatest
Adventurers that itt might no longer subsiste then itt might still so
continue, butt if itt should be dissolued that accordinge to a former
močon well approved of, the Adventurors goods remayninge there in
store estimated att ffiue thousand pounds might be first sould off, before
any other that shall com of the same kinde: Whervpon after much To be argued before ye Counsell.
Debatinge itt was ordered that itt should be argued att full before the
Counsell and they to relate their opynyons to the Courte,

Iohn Delbridge Indentures of Land for him and his Associates beinge Mr Delbridge Indentures ordered to be sealed.
now delivered engrossed into the Courte after beinge read & fyndinge
them Concurre wth the Orders of the Company receaved Confirmation wth allowance of the Seale to be thervnto anexed,

Captaine Brewster desyred to have the hearinge of his cause deferred The hearinge of Capt: Brewsters cause deferred
till the next Preparative Courte wch is agreed then to be heard.

Abraham Peirses allowance of 200 Acres of Land in the last Courte Abraham Peirseys 200: Acres of Land Confirmed.
beinge now putt to the question was Confirmed vnto him,

Sir Iohn Wolstenholme moved that accordinge to an Acte of Courte S^r Io: Wolstenholme močon for some Land to be giuen to ye Corporačon of Martins Hundred
made the 21th die Iulij i6i9 vppon the močon of Sr Edward Harwood[1] for some Land to be given to the Corporačon of Martins Hundred for their further encouragm^t itt was then putt off vnto this great
and generall Courte as proper thervnto by reason itt grew late itt was
referred vnto the Counsell att their meetinge to Consider of. **[49]**

Allso att the same time hee putt the Courte now in remembrance of His proposičon referd to ye Audito^n.
his proposičon then to the Company for some Land to be given him
in consideračon of monney ther in said Courte exprest wch is referred
vnto the Auditors to cast vpp what may be due vnto him by the interest
of itt & accordingly to gratefie him.

Mathew Cauell m^r of the William and Thomas paide now vnto M^r A bill Sealed for 100 Acres of Land to Math: Cauell.
Thr̃er 12^ll:10:00 for wch hee received a bill sealed for one hundred

---

[1] Written over the name "Haywood."

Acres of Land, and admitted into the fellowship of the Company,
And in consideracōn that hee was one of the first finders of the Plantation and had therin merited well, Itt was agreed that hee should

A single Share to
be giuen him have a single Share for the same, wth a note vnder m^r Thr̄ers hand to
the Custome house that hee is a free brother of the ~~same~~ Company.

A r̄e to be writ-
ten to Sr George
Yeardley in y^e be-
halfe of Capt New-
port̄ sonne. Whereas the Company hath formerly graunted to Captaine Newporte
a bill of Adventure of fower hundred pounds, and his sonne now
desyringe orde^r from this Courte for the layinge out some parte of the
[the] same, m^r Treasuror was entreated and Authorized by this generall
Assembly for to write to Sr George Yeardley and the Counsell of State
for the effectinge hereof.

Capt Stallenge
goods to be reserud
for his widdowe. As allso that such things as belonged to Capt: Stallenge slayne ther by
William Epps be reserved for the vse and benefitt of his widdowe.

AN EXTRAORDINARY COURTE HELDE
THE xxij^TH OF NOUEMBER 1619:

PRESENT.

The Ri: Wor^p: Sr Edwin Sandys kn^t Tr̄er.

Sr Nicholas Tufton.	m^r George Sandys.	m^r Bearblock.
Sr Henry Rainsforde.	m^r Thom: Gibbes.	m^r Meverell.
m^r Iohn Wroth.	m^r Nicho: Ferrar.	m^r Blande.
m^r Iohn fferrar, Dep^t.	m^r Tho: Bull.	m^r Casewell.
m^r Dr Anthony.	m^r Keightley.	m^r Eli: Roberts.
m^r Dr Wynstone.	m^r Cranmore.	m^r Couell.
	m^r Hen: Brigḡ.	m^r Mellinge.

A r̄e deliuered
to m^r Secretary
Caluert Mr Treasuror signified that this extraordinary Courte was to acquainte
them that according to the intent of the last great Courte hee had
drawne the r̄e to his Ma^ty in the name of the Tr̄er Counsell and Company
and had delivered itt to m^r Secretary Caluert together wth a Coppie

therof. butt itt beinge thought that ł̄re would not serve his Ma^{ty} hee
was [**50**] to propound his and crave their further advise that if one
nundreth pounds wch should have beene for mayntenance of those men
might be given extraordinary in grosse besides the ordinary allowance
of Six pounds the man to any that may be found to transport them wth
all expediċon, The knight Marshall haveinge promisd Sr Iohn Dauers
that if they may be sent presentlie hee will furnish them wth such
psonns of what quallyty and Condiċon they desire. Vnto wch was
obiected that if some were found to vndertake this, yett itt might be
this moneth before the Ship could be dispeeded and they duringe
such time must be maynteyned at the Companies charge wch was
answered itt could not be helped, his Maties Commaund must be full-
filled, therfore beinge putt to the question was generally allowed of.

100^{ll} to be giuen
extraordinary in
gross besides the
ordinary allow-
ance of six pound
a man.
The Kn^t Marshall€
promise to Sir Iohn
Dauers.

Obiection

Allowed of.

Likewise he acquainted that beinge to goe to the Counsell §table§
aboute the Companies buisines hee purposed to acquainte the Lords
of the Tobacco detayned by m^r Iacobb, notwithstandinge the graunt
of their Pattent their letter from the Lords of the Counsell and the
Companies offer vnto him; Desiringe to vnderstand their further
pleasure, who have agreed to make a further Offer (iff itt may be
accepted) to leave a 20th parte wth him in spetie, as allso an other
xxth pt for ye Kings Custome till they have tryed theire Pattent,
And for the assistinge of m^r Thł̄er theris now entreated, My Lord
of Warwick, Lord Paggett Lord Cauendish, Sr Iohn Dauers, Sr Nath:
Rich, m^r Iohn Wroth and m^r Cranmore.

M^r Tł̄er€: purpose
to Acquaint y^e
Lord€ of the To-
bacco deteyned by
Mr Iacobb

Agreed to mak a
further Offer.

Intelligence beinge given that the Acc^o: of the Magazine beinge made
vpp and redy for the Audite, this Courte have now appoynted
Audito^m for the same viz^d: m^r Bull, m^r Keightley, m^r Briggs, and
m^r Cranmer.

Audito^m to exam-
ine ye Magazine
Accomp^t:

A ł̄re was shewed to m^r Thł̄er by m^r D^r: Wynstone written by a frend
vnto m^r Bland intymatinge a greivous scandall layde vppõ Virginia
by some who hath lived there, of the Barronesse and in fer-
tilytie of the Soyle, wch by reason the reporte of all those that
hath beene there is veryfied to be false, as allso that itt

A ł̄re shewed vnto
m^r Thł̄er written
by a frend to m^r
Bland; touchinge
ye Barroness of y^e
soyle in Virginia

tendeth to the discourragment of sundry Adventurers who purposed
to transport men thither for the settinge vpp of Iron workҀ; Itt
was thought good for the depressinge of such base reports, [( ] a former
Ꞧre to the like effecte beinge formerly diuulged) that itt be showed
to the Counsell, to impose such penalty of the person as may be
held expedient, and to consider of a Publicaꞓon to be sett outt
in printe for the Confutaꞓon therof.   [51]

The Ꞧre to be
shewed to yᵉ Coun-
sell to impose a
penalty vppon yᵉ
person and to con-
sider of a Publi-
caꞓon to be set out
in Printe.

DECEMBER Yᵉ FIRST 1619.

PRESENT.

Right Honoᵇˡᵉ: yᵉ Lord of Southampton.

Sʳ Edwin Sandys Knight ThꞦerr.

Sʳ Thom: Roe.	Nicho: Hide esqʳ.	mʳ Wiseman.
Sʳ Iohn Dauers.	Arth: Bromfield esqʳ.	mʳ Keightley.
Sʳ Ferd: Gorge.	Iohn Bargraue esqʳ.	mʳ Cranmer.
Sʳ Ni: Tufton.	Aug: Stewarde.	mʳ Casewell.
Sʳ Io: Wolstenholme.	mʳ Io: Ferrar Depᵗ.	mʳ Couell.
Sʳ Nath: Rich.	mʳ Kempton.	mʳ Barnarde.
Sʳ Tho: Wroth.	mʳ Nicholas Ferrar.	mʳ Meuerell.
Sʳ Law: Hide.	mʳ Caninge.	mʳ Geor: Smith.
Io: Wroth esquire.	mʳ Blande.	mʳ Leuor.
George Sandys esqʳ.	mʳ Bulle.	mʳ RobertҀ.
Tho: Gibbes esqʳ.	mʳ Ed: Ditchfeilde.	mʳ Mellinge.

Mʳ ThꞦerҀ signifi-
caꞓon of twice at-
tendinge yᵉ LLˢ:
of yᵉ Councell.

Mʳ ThꞦer required
by yᵉ Lords to sett
downe his minde
in Writinge.

Before the readinge of the Courte mʳ TꞦer signified that two seuerall
times hee had attended the Lords of his Maᵗˢ: most honorable Pryvie
Councell, about the Magazine goodҀ butt nothinge was done the first
time because mʳ Iacobb was thought §to§ had been warned but was
not,   Therfore their Loᵖˢ required mʳ ThꞦer to sett downe his minde
in writinge and deliuer itt vnto them vppon this day, against wᶜʰ time
the KingҀ Learned Councell would be present, and Mʳ Iacobb should

be required to attend, wch accordingly Mr. Therrer pformed, and pre- accordingly performed.
sented itt this daie vnto their Lo^ps wch was the first buisines they
tooke into consideracon, notw^thstanding the said m^r Iacobb was nott Mr Iacobb not present.
present, although the messenge^r affirmed that hee warned him, ther-
fore by reason of his absence the Lords would not pceed to a finall
determinacon, Butt m^r Atturny delivered his opinion cleerly for Adiourned.
the right of the Company, whervppo itt was adiourned till to Morrow, vnderstandinge that m^r Iacobb wilbe there w^thout faile.

The last great generall Courte beinge read m^r Threr ~~affirmed~~ acquainted Mr Delbridge desire to fish at Cape Codd
them that m^r Iohn Delbridge purposinge to settle a pticuler Colony in
Virginia desyringe of the Company that for the defrayinge some pt of
his charges, that hee might be admitted to fish att Cape Codd. W^ch
request was opposed by Sir Ferdinando George aleaginge thatt hee His request opposed by Sr Ferdinando Gorges.
allwaies favoured m^r Delbridge butt in this hee thought himselfe
somethinge touched that hee should sue to this Company, and not
rathe^r to him as proplie belonginge to the No^r: Collony to give libertie
for the fishinge in that place, itt lyinge w^thin their latitude, which
was answered by m^r Trer, that the Comp^a: of the S^o: and North Plan- Answered by Mr Threr.
tacons are the one free of the other, And that the lres Pattent is cleer
that each may ffish within the other, the Sea being free for both. [52]
W^ch if the N^o: Colony abridge them of this, they would take away their
means and encourragment of sendinge of men, Vnto which Sr Fer- Sir Ferdinando Georges reply.
dinando Georges replyed that if hee mistake not himselfe both the
Companies were lymitted by the Pattent vnto which hee would sub-
mitt himselfe, ffor the decydinge wherof itt is referred vnto the
Councell who are of both Companies to examine the lres Pattents to The Councell of both Comp^a: to examine ye lres Pattent.
morrow afternoone att my Lord of Southamptons and accordingly to
determine the Dispute.

Mr. Deputy informed the Courte that Capt: Tompson haveinge a good Mr Deputies significacon of ye Comittees agreement wth Capt Tompson.
Ship burthen 320 Tunn, the Comittees att their meetinge have agreed
wth him if the Courte shall allow thereof to give him 1200^li to transport
for them into Virginia Two hundred men; and for 50 Tunn fraight
of goods in the said Ship 100^li more, in all Thirteen hundred pound
and to victuall their men after that proporcon as by a not was shewed

Cap⁺ Tompson to giue Caution for such monneys as hee shall receaue beforehand.
To be redy at Tilbury hope. him, Cap⁺ Tompson promisinge to give Caution to the Company for such monneys as hee shall receive aforehand; And for pformance of the said Voyadge the said Cap⁺: Tompson was demaunded when he would sett outt, who promised to be redy in Tilbury Hope the sixth of ffebruary next, and would stay there fower daies to take in such as should come, and fower daies more att Deale butt if aboue Tenn daies that then itt might be lawfull for him to departe, Demaundinge of the

his demaund of 800ᴵᴵ in hand & 500ᴵᴵ vppon certificate Cʳ.
Mʳ Thrers offer in the behalfe of yᵉ Company. Company Eight hundred pounds in hand and fiue hundred pounds vppon certificate of the men and goods to be landed in Virginia wᶜʰ hee insistinge vppon mʳ Thřer in the behalfe of the Company made offer to give him Seaven hundreth pounds, and Six Hundreth vppon Certificate as aforesaid: He beinge so farr from exactinge of the Company that hee promised that if they would lay into the Ship halfe a Tunn of Aquavitæ for ther Sicke men hee would forbeare the present payment of the 100ᴵᴵ in question wᶜʰ the Courte promised to pforme.

Perticuler Aduenturers.
to Acquaint Mʳ Webb wᵗʰ yᵉ nomber they send. Whervppon mʳ Deputy acquainted the Courte for accomodatinge all men, that if any pticuler Adventurer would send ouer men to Virginia let him give notice of the nomber therof to William Webb the husband and pay vnto him six pounds for their passage   Shippinge should be provided for them wᵗʰ the Companies men.

euery one of yᵉ Company to help for yᵉ furnishing them with good & able men. And because himselfe and the Comittees will have more then enough to provide all things necessary and sufficient against that time of sendinge their people away hee desyred that every one of the Company would give their helpinge hand for the furnishing them wᵗʰ good and able men for this voyadge, and to take such care and paines in itt as if itt were for their owne pryvate prayinge all men to take notice of his request.   [53]

A Table of yᵉ Guiftȼ and names of yᵉ Doners to hang in Court Itt was propounded that in Consideracon of some publique guiftȼ given by sundry Persons to Virginia, divers Presents of Church plate, and other ornaments—200ᴵᴵ already given towards buildinge a Church and ffive Hundreth pounds promised by another towards yᵉ educatinge of Infidles children that for the honour of God and memoriall of such good benefactoᵐ a Table might hange in the Courte wᵗʰ their names and guifts incerted and the Mynisters of Virginia and the Somēr Ilands may have intelligence thereof, that for their pious workꞓ they may comēnd them to God in their prayers, wch gen9ally was held very fitt and expedient.

And forasmuch as by the orders of this Courte the Lotteries are now to dissolve that therfore they would consider of some course for the defrayinge of future charge or else continue them halfe a year longer, Whervppō findinge no other means as yett to accrew vnto the Company, Itt was ordered they should last till midsomer next. and being putt to ye question was confirmed by erecc̄on of hands.

The Lotteries continued till Midsomer next.

ffurther Mr Thr̄er made knowne that hee had received a verie fauourable l̄re from the Lord Arch Bishop of Yorke that if hee will send more breefs ther shalbe new Collecc̄ons, As allso how much the Company was beholdinge to the Dyocess of London, my Lo: Bishopp haveinge sentt in a ffull Thousand pounds, As allso y^t mr Register demaundeth 20^li wch hee saith the Comp^a: promised him for his paynes. wch the Courte thinks him very worthy off, and therfore have agreed that hee shall have the said some of xx^li paid vnto him out of such monneys as shall com to him or is yett remayninge in his Custodie.

Mr Thr̄er signified of a l̄re Receiued from ye Lo: Archbishop of Yorke and how much the Comp^a: is behoulding to ye Dyocess of London.

1000^li sent in by ye Bishop.

20^li to be p^d: to ye Register.

DECEMBER—THE XVth

PRESENT

Ri Hono^{le}: the Lord of Southampton.
The Lord of Warwicke.

The Lo: Pagett.
Sr Edwin Sandys Thr̃e.

Sr Tho: Roe.	m^r Christ: Brooke.	m^r Henry Briggs.
Sr Iohn Dauers.	m^r Tho: Gibbes.	m^r Georg Swinhoe.
Sr Tho: Wroth.	m^r Edw: Harbert.	m^r Aiscough.
Sr Hen: Iones.	m^r Aug: Steward.	m^r Keitley.
m^r Dr Anthony.	m^r Ri: Tomlyne.	m^r Berblock.
m^r Dr Gulstone.	Capt Samu: Argoll.	m^r Nicho: Ferrar.
m^r Dr Winston.	Capt Da: Tucker.	m^r Sheppard.
m^r Io: Wroth.	m^r Nicho: Leate.	m^r Bull.
	m^r Wrote.	m^r Bamforde.
	m^r Io Ferrar Dep^t.	m^r Cranmer.
	m^r W^m: Caninge.	m^r Woodall.
	m^r W^m: Palmer.	m^r Casewell.
		m^r Sparrow.
		m^r Roberte.
		m^r Arundell.
		m^r Wiseman.
		m^r Ditchfield
		and others. [54]

Bills approued of and passed ouer. These seuerall Bills of Aduenture being allowed by the Audito^{rs}, Att their Audite the xiijth of December 1619 were now passed and receaved the Courts Approbacõn.

Iohn Cage esquire turned ouer nine bills six of them to m^r Dr Theodore Gulstone, and Three to m^r Isack Seaward.

Peter Bartes three bills to Dr Theodore Gulstone.

Bills approved of
and passed ouer

The Court Records of Aduenturers being allowed by the
Auditors vpon audit the xv^th of December 1619 were
now questioned and returned the Courte approbacion

John Page squier committed ... L ... Clere as by them to Sr Thomas
Gulston card Thor ... m^r ... Black Seawards

Peter Bartee hath pass to Sr Thomas Gulston ...
John Tayne quit and the Ld Dr Theodor Gulston
Augustine Steward assign 3 ... to Sr Henry Gerrard
Katheren Parke widow owe vnto Edward Herbert esq^r

A petition deliuered by S^r E.
Sandys to y^r M^r touching
m^r Jacobb

The Allegacons of both
partes heard

m^r Jacob to deliuer
the Tobacco

Sr Edwin Sandys ... forward ordered by the last Court
the next day to the Councell Table ... Spottswood to S^r ... hauinge
... ... vpon ... free ... Estate of the Councell and Company
... mad ... the ... State of the Southern m^r Jacob
being here, ... this ... to gue some ... generall ...
... the ... of ... did ... ... general
deliuered the ... ... the 28th ... the Company by them
... ... diuision. And ... it did ...
... ... it ... m^r Jacob ... deliuer the said Tobacco into
his ... at ... that ... apply the ... with ...
... ... L^d ... Exception ... ... the ... petition
together ... give ... order ... the ... in the Court ...
... ... Abbis of ... as follows

To ye Hono^ble the 28th and others of his
Ma^ts most Honorable Priuie Councell
The humble Petition of ye Three
Counsell and Company for Virginia

... ... Humbly shew vnto y^r L^ps Whereas the Plantacon of Virginia by ...
... declaring their
... ... freedome of Navigation
of many great difficulties ... borne and still is a ... it ... fur
... charge to the private Adventurers, And it is nowe ... so that
... Some ... to be brought to perfeccon with ... the Land is now yeeld
... ... at any time ... be will ... a ... not only of ...
... gaines but ... of great profitt to his Ma^t and the people
And by his Ma^t ... in the Colony, into wch the neighbour ...
... ... Virginia will ... and in still some ... agreat
... of groundes by mutuall traffique between the English and
English, ... now yearly ... ... in very great multitudes

Cor ... Collingrood

Iohn Payne gent one bill to Dr Theodor Gulstone.
Augustine Steward esq^r 3 bills to Sr Henry Iones Kn^t.
Katherine Clarke widdow one bill to Edward Harbert esqr.

Sir Edwin Sandys ~~and~~ §as§ itt was ordered in the last Courte repayr- †A peticon deliu9d by Sr Edw: Sandys to ye ħ^s touchinge m^r Iacobb.
inge the next day to the Councell Table presented a Peticon to their
Lo^{ps}: accordinge as itt was referred vnto him in the name of the Councell and Company in wch was conteyned the wholl State of the buisines,
Mr Iacobb beinge there, it pleased their ħ^{ps}: to give them moste honor-
able audience hearinge the allegacons of both sides. Wher m^r Attur- †The Allegacons of both sides heard.
ney generall delivered his cleere opinion to the ḶḶ^s That the Company
by their Pattent were free from Imposicon; And in fine itt was
ordered by their Lo^{ps}: that the said Mr Iacobb should deliver the said †Mr Iacobb to de-liuer the Tobacco
Tobacco vnto them paying all other Duties that might appteyne there-
vnto, wch was submitted to their Lo^{ps}: Iudgments;[1] Therfor he moved
that the Petition togeather wth their Lo^{ps}: order might be entred in
the Courte Booke wch was well liked of: being as followeth.

> To ye Ri: Hono^r: the ḶḶ^s: and others of his Ma^{ie}: most Honorable Priuie
> Councell
> The humble Peticon of ye Threr Counsell and Company for Virginia

> Humbly shew vnto yor Lo^{ps}: Wheras the Plantacon of Virginia by reason of †The Comp^a: Peti-con to ye Lorde de-claringe their free-dome of Imposi-con
> many great difficulties hath beene and still is a matte^r of excessive charge to
> the pticularr Adventurers, And if itt please God to psper the same so as itt be
> brought to pfeccon (wherof the hope is now greate^r then heretofore att any
> time) Itt wilbe a matter not onely of strength and honour butt allso of great
> proffitt to his Ma^{ty}: and his people And to his Ma^{ty} pticulerly in his Customs,
> vnto wch the negotiacon established wth Virginia will raise a cleere and in short
> time a great addicon, as growinge by mutuall Traffique betweene the English
> and English, who now yearly remove thither in very great multitudes: [55]
> In wch and many other important Consideracons itt pleased his most excellent
> Ma^{ty}: of his Princely benegnity by his ł res Pattents bearringe date the 23th of
> May in the Seaventh year of his Raigne of England C^r. To graunt vnto the
> said Company ffreedome from Custome and Subsedie in Virginia for one and
> Twenty years and in England for a certaine numb^r of years now expired, and
> from all other Taxes and Imposicons for ever. "Exceptinge onely the ffiue

[1] See letter from the Privy Council to Abraham Jacobs, List of Records, No. 137, page 136, *ante.*

"pounds p̄ Centū: due for Custome vppon all such goods and Marchandizes
"as shalbe brought or Imported into this Realme of England or any other his
"Ma^ts: Dominions accordinge to the Ancient Trade of Marchants."

And the like graunt hath beene made by his Ma^ty: to ye Comp^a of ye Somer
Ilands by his gracious l̃res Pattents bearinge date the 29th of Ivne in the 13th
yeare of his Raigne of England C^r save that the freedome from Custome and
Subsydie graunted to them is not yett expired. Which Comp^a of the Somer
Ilands are all members of the Virginia Company and for the mutuall strength
of both parties are soe to continue.

All wch notwithstandinge the ffarmo^rs of his Ma^ts: Customs by a generall rate
made of Tobacco att x^s the pound in regard the Spanish Tobacco is worth much
more though the Virginia Tobacco give not halfe so much, demaund of yor
Supplyants vj^d the pound for their Virginia Tobacco wch they humbly desire
may be rated att a iust valew by itt selfe (wch they shall willingly pay) and not
raysed to the double by cooplinge itt wth the Spanish wch is sould ordinaryly
att 18^s the pound and some times att more.

They Complaine allso to your LL^ps: of m^r Iacobb ffarmo^r of ye Impost of
Tobacco who by color of a much latter Graunt from his Ma^ty demaundeth of
them an other vj^d the pound vppon their Tobacco contrary to his Ma^ts most
gracious Graunt, and wch allso itt is not possible that poore Comodity can
beare.

They humbly therfore offer to yor LL^ps: Consideracōn wheras for the support
and increase of that Plantacōn to draw on the Collony more cheerfully to apply
their labour, they have erected here a Society of p̄ticuler Adventure^rs for
Traffique wth them of Virginia in a Ioynt Stocke for dyvers years commonly
called the Magazine, and have contracted with ye people ther, as for other
Comodities so p̄ticularly to give them iij^s a pound for Tobacco, by vertue of
wch Contracts a great multitud of people have lately beene drawne to remove
thither, and not soe fewe as one Thowsand Personns are providinge to goe
and Plant there in the Springe approching, that if to that iij^s be added this
12^d demaunded by the ffarmo^r together wth other charges of ffraight C^r itt will
exceed the vttermost vallew wch att this day the Tobacco can be sould for, and
consequentlie must needs dissolve this Traffique established.

And they further Complaine to yor LL^ps: of m^r Iacobb that wheras this Company for the vphoulding of the said Traffique sett out in September was Twelue
moneth a Ship to Virginia for the bringinge home of the Comodities as itt
were the Harvest of that yeare, wherby the people there are to be maynteyned
wth clothinge and necessary Implements.   [56]

The Company here quickned wth hope of proffite by traffique and by this mutuall negotiaĉon his Ma^{ts} Customs advanced: And accordingly in Iune last their Ship returned and brought home Twenty thousand pound weight of Tobacco for wch besides the Marchandize bartered wth them there they are to discharge here aboue Eight hundred pounds of Bills of Exchange, And vppon returne of their Ship they brought their goods into the Custome house as they were required that they might be weighed and the Custome answered for the same wch they were most willinge and redy to discharge, Mr Iacobb of his owne authority interupted the weyinge of their Tobacco and forbad farther proceeding vnless that impost of vj^d a pound were allso paid vnto him.

Whervppon they flyinge to yor Lo^{ps}: for releife obteyned yor hono^{rs}: Letter to m^r Iacobb to deliver their goods they entringe into bond to pay him whatsoever should appear to be his due, by yor Ħ^{ps} iudgmentĉ vppon certificate from his Ma^{ts}: leirned Councell, and wthin one moneth after itt should be determyned, wch order yor Supplyantĉ did offer him to pforme.

But m^r Iacobb refusinge to pforme yor Ħ^{ps}: order and exactinge of them another bond, vizd to pay him his demaund att a certaine day vnless they pcure in the meane time a discharge from yor Ħ^{ps}: wch they thought vnfitt to vndertake beinge not in their power to effect hath ever since now for the space of fower monneths and vpward Contrary to his Ma^{ts} ĺres Pattents and yor Lo^{ps} honorable ĺres (an example vnheard of) forceably deteyninge their goods to their damage att least of—2500^{li} partly by the impayringe therof in worth through dryinge and other corrupĉon and partly by the Sale of price vppon the Store of English Tobacco wch hath since beene made

They further Complaine of m^r Iacobb that wheras the Soñier Ilandĉ are yett free for two years and an halfe vnexpired of very Custome and Subsedie, m^r Iacobb who standinge by his Officers at Plymouth hath caused 12^d the pound to be exacted for their Tobacco, and bond to be entred for the payment therof on the Sixth of this monneth vnless yor lo^{ps}: shalbe pleased in the meane time to discharge ye same.

In consideraĉon of wch premises these Petiĉoners most humbly beseech your good Ħo^{ps}: that wheras they are now in treaty for the providing & settinge forth of two Ships imeadiately, the one to Virginia expresly for his Ma^{ts} service, and the other to the Somer Ilands for the necessary fortefyinge and securinge of that place, And for as much as they dare not lett them Carry thither soe vnwellcome news, as in the pticulers before sett downe And forasmuch allso as the preparaĉons for the transport of those = 1000 = Persons are now all att a stand waightinge vppon the success of this present buisines that yor Ħ^{ps}: of yor accustomed goodness and fauor toward this Plantaĉon, and to preserve itt from vtter ruine now threatned by those Courses wilbe pleased in vphouldinge of his Ma^{ts}: gracious Graunt vnto them to cause their goods thus deteyned to be att length deliu^9ed vppon payment of such duties as of right ought to be paid.

And they shall allwaies pray for yor lo^{ps}: long Continuance in all prosperity. [57]

Capt Argoll*ę* desire to answer such Crimes as are imputed to him.

Mr Thr̃er*ę* reporte of their proceedings with him.

Captaine Argoll vppon his owne desire to answere to such Crymes as are imputed to him in the time of his Gouerment hath been sundry times summoned to meete the Councell att Southampton house where haveinge sett many daies, Mr Thr̃er now presented the passage of their seuerall ꝑceeding*ę* wth him devydinge his charge into three partes.

1: His Offences in matter of State, 2: The Depredac̃on and spoile of the publique wth other offences to the Company and Councell and 3: his oppression there of the Collony in generall and sundry ꝑticularr men.

To the Two first m^r Thr̃er vppon the desyre of the Counsell was content to collect the falts, and sett downe §in§ Articles the greivances of the Company because the said Capt Argoll desyred to answere every pointe in writinge. Butt the third of the opression of the people haveinge no affinitie wth the two other part*ę* may be answered by themselvs when Certificate shalbe returned from thence of the same hee haveinge answered to the 4 firste Articles of Matter of State, The second parte of depradac̃on was deliu^9d vnto him in Eight Articles by m^r Thr̃er earnestly desyringe the Courte (as the Councell think*ę* itt Convenyent) that the prosecutinge herof might be taken outt of his hands, and referred accordinge to the Councell*ę* order vnto a Lawyer and a Marchaunt to solicite the Companies cause against him: And allso Capt Argoll desyred that in respect hee was no great Scoller that hee might have liberty to entertaine Councell to defend his Cause: Soe the Courte for the Company have now made choyse of m^r Edward Harbert for the Lawyere and mr Tho: Keightley for the Marchant agreeinge that all the writings and evidences shall be putt into their hands, And that the Tr̃er and Councell shall be iudges of the buisines, Mr Deputy promisinge to enforme and ease them as much as hee cann, allowinge allso of Capt Argoll*ę* request.

The buisines to be referrd to a Lawyere & a Marchan^t.

Capt Argoll to entertaine a Councello^r.

The Comp^a choise of their Lawyere and Marchant.

Wher vppon hee made a second that in regard Sir Thomas Smith was Capt Argoll^e second request then Thr̃er, and may say some thinge to some orders wch was given him, that this buisines might be heard att his house, wch m^r Thr̃er said hee would not gainesay, whensoeuer the mattere were handled to the knowledge of Sr Tho: Smith, And the rather for that the firste moveinge against Capt Argoll p̃ceeded from Sr Thomas Smith, and m^r Alderman Iohnson, wth some other as appeareth both by their lette^{rs} to Capt Argoll himselfe of the 3^d of August i6i8, As allso by their other l̃res to the Lord Lawarr att ye same time, wherin they charge him wth all or most of the said Crymes, & that in verie sharpe sorte; Requiringe the Lord Lawarr to send him home to his answere to sequestre his goods there and to restore to the publique all such Cattle as hee had alyenated wthout lawfull warrant:

Wheras the last Court agreed to give vnto my Lord of London^e Reg- My Lo^r: of London^e dislike of xx^{li} to be giuen to his Register. ister for his paines in their Collecc̃ons the some of xx pound^e form9ly p̃mised m^r Thr̃rer informed that his llo^p: hereing therof was not well pleased therewth and would not assent that any p̃t of the 1000^{li} wch hee had sent in should be deminished: As allso that accordinge to the Archbishope of York^e desyre hee had sentt him 200 new breif^e for 200 new briefs sent to ye Archbishop of Yorke. Collecc̃on. [58]

The Councell meetinge accordinge to the referrence in the last Court The Counsells reporte for pvsing ye l̃res Pattents. and pvsinge the l̃res Pattents grew to this Conclusion that by the lycense of the said Councell itt might be lawfull for either of the said Collonies to fish wthin the liberties the one of the other butt since some of the Northerne Collony flyinge from that agreement pretend to Consider better of itt before they will give answere therevnto. Howsover the Councell haveinge occasion to p̃sue itt vppõ the Mõc̃on of m^r Thr̃er have given lycence vnder their seale vnto the Society of Lycense giuen to Smiths Hundred vnder ye seale to Fish in ye N^o Colony Smiths hundred to goe a fishinge wch Seale was this day in open Courte and by the allowance therof affixed to their saide Lycense, as allso to a Duplycate of the same.

Att this Court Mr Thr̃er acquainted the Company that the day before Sir Edw: Sandys mõc̃on for a Publicac̃on to be sett out in printe Sr Tho: Smiths Acc^o had beene brought in to the Audito^{rs} and for the spedyer Auditinge and concludinge of them itt was moved by him in

the name of the Audito^{rs} who by one   ¹ assent had approved therof
that a   ¹ Publicaĉon might be sett outt in printe, In ye firste
parte to sett downe the names in Alphabeticall order of every Adventurer and their seuerall Summs Adventured that therby all may take
notice of their sumes brought in, and be summoned to com in for
their Land proporĉonable thervnto, before the best were possessed by
new Adventuro^{rs} or Planters wch might be allso a means of a speedy

The moĉon ap-
proued of and y^e
drawing of itt re-
ferd to m^r Thɼer
& Dr Winstone.
encrease and   ¹ of the Plantaĉon   And in the second pt to con-
fute such scandalous reports as have beene divulged of Virginia by the
Iustificaĉon of the Inhabitant€ there, wch moĉon was generally approved by the Courte referringe the drawinge of the said Publicaĉon
to m^r Thɼer & D^r: Winstone.²

Mr Keightleys re-
porte touchinge y^e
Magazine Acc^o
Mr Thomas Keightley beinge formerly amongst others chosen an Au-
dito^r for the Magazine Accomp^{ts}, now reported that although ye Court
tooke some distaste att m^r Essington touchinge the same, yett hee
and the rest appoynted wth him haveinge Audited itt never found
books in better order nor Accompts better kept, for not fower peny-
worth of goods is sent butt is orderly sett downe, marvelinge that as
itt appears ther should be 2000 & odd pounds owinge to the Adven-
turo^{rs} and they continue indebted 1000^{li} to the Chamber of London

Mr Thɼer moued
for 3: things to be
considered of
besides—5200 and odd pounds worth of goods remayninge in the
Magazine as itt cost the first penny here: Wthervppon itt was mooved
by m^r Thɼerr that three poynt€ might be considered: 1: The sale of
the Tobacco   2: Concerninge those difficulties that are founde in the
Accomp^{ts} menĉoned by m^r Keightley: 3: wheither to ꝑceed wth the
Magazine or dissolve itt.   ffor the first m^r Bearblock, m^r Caninge,
and m^r Smith are intreated to goe to Sr Iohn Wolstenholme to know
when hee holds itt convenyen^t to make Sale of itt, and accordingly
order shalbe given for the Adventurers meetinge.   [59]

ffor the second itt was agreed accordinge to former order that when
the Accompt€ are prepared they shalbe presented to the Counsell to

---

¹ A blank space in the manuscript.
² Such a list was printed in the *Declaration* of June 22, 1620. There was also a broadside of May
17, 1620, which set forth the condition of the colony and its commodities. See List of Records, Nos.
174 and 183, pages 140 and 141 *ante.*

have those doubtes decyded, And Wheras the Society of Smiths Hundred are indebted to the Adventurers of the Magazine for men transported in the William and Thomas Itt is referred vnto fower to examine what is due and itt shall be paied vizd m^r Caswell and m^r Smith for the Aduenturers, and m^r Iohn Ferrar and m^r Keightley for Smiths hundred; And for the last whether the Magazine shall continue or noe, itt is referred to be disputed of att the Adventuro^{rs} meeting for Sale of the Tobacco.

ffor the fiftie men wch are now to be sent vppõ Cõmaund from his Ma^{ty}: Itt was agreed vppõ the mocõn of m^r Threr for the apparrellinge and furnishinge them wth other necessary expences, one Hundred pounds shall be allowed to be disbursed out of ye Cash and afterward to be reembursd wth the rest by their Maisters.

100^{li} to be disbursed out of Cash for furnishing of ye 50: men.

Mr Threr signifyinge y^t the Lord Maior desyringe some of the Company to be present att their Court att Giuldhall they should vnderstand the Citties pleasure touching the mocõn for the Children, therfore mooved y^t some might be appoynted to attend them to know their resolucõns: Whervppon the Courte ernestly entreated himselfe to take the paines Associatinge vnto him Sr Iohn Dauers, Sr Tho: Wroth, m^r Iohn Wroth, m^r Dr Winstone, m^r Abbott, m^r Gibbs, m^r Bearblock, m^r Caninge and m^r Palmer tomorrow morninge att 10: of the Clocke att Giuldhall wch notwthstandinge the multiplycitie of many other buisinesses for the Company hee hath pmised to pforme.

Some of ye Compa: to be att ye Court at Giulde hall.

Itt is agreed that m^r Batemans bill of Exchange shalbe paide by the Adventurers of the Magazine who are content to disburse the money till itt may be vnderstood who of right shall pay itt.

Mr. Batemans bill of Exchange to be paide by ye Aduenturers of ye Magazine.

Mr Ralph Yeardleys Peticõn in behalfe of his Brother Sr Georg Yeardley was read and approved by the Courte, butt by reason itt grew late itt was referred to the next Court to be pformed.

Mr Ralph Yeardleys peticõn approued of

Elizabeth Barkeleys Peticõn referred to the same time.

Eliza: Berkeleys Peticõn referd.

xvi^{li} to be paide Notice beinge given to Mr. Thřer that Katherine Bath hath chosenn
Frauncis Barra-
dine for ye Vse of Frauncis Barradine of London Chandlor to be her Gardeon, who
Kath: Bath.   beinge present shewed forth an Instrument for the same, Itt was
agreed y^t a warrant should be made for payment of the Sixteene pounds
odd mony to the said ffrauncis Barradine for her vse and so the Company to discharge themselvs of that Debt wch accordinge to a former
order they were to pay vse for appoyntinge him to be vppon Munday
morninge att the generall Audite and hee should receive yt. [60]

DECEMBER, Y^e 23: 1619

PRESENT.

Ri Hono: Lord Cauendish.
Generall Cæcill.

Extr: Courte.

Sr Iohn: Dauers.	m^r Iohn Ferrar Dep^t.	m^r W^m:Cañinge.
Sr Nath: Rich.	m^r Dr Winstone.	m^r Bull.
S^r Io: Wolstenholme.	m^r Ferrar Iunior.	m^r Caswell.
Sr Henry Iones.	m^r Nicholas Leate.	m^r Bearblock.
m^r Iohn Wroth.	m^r Henry Briggs.	m^r Mellinge.
m^r Tho: Gibbes.	m^r Tho Keatley.	m^r Geo. Smith.
m^r Edw: Harbert.	m^r Cranmere.	m^r Robertℯ.
m^r Kempton.	m^r Bamforde.	m^r Sparrow.

A Comission for
In^o Damirŏ or-   A Comission to Iohn Damyron m^r of ye Duety beinge now red &
deredtobesealled. allowed for takinge the first optunytie of winde and weather to sett
Saile for Virginia wth the Passengers the Company shippeth by
Commaund from his Ma^{ty}: was now ordered that the Seale should be
thervnto affixed.

Some of ye Comp^a:
to be at Bridewell Mr Deputy informinge the Court that the knight Marshall havinge
touchinge ye 50: been wth m^r Thřer gave him to vnderstand that vppon Munday morn-
men y^t must be inge, ffiftie of the Persons to be transported for his Ma^{ty}: should be att
transported   Bridewell for the Company to make choyce of such as they thinke for

the present fitt to be sent therfore moved that some might repare thether att 8 of the Clock to meet the kn^t Marshall about that buisines; Whervppon the Courte have desyred Mr Dr Wynstone, m^r Caninge, m^r Cranmore, and m^r Thomas Mellinge to be there att that time.

The Charter party beinge drawne and now psented between Sr Edw: Sandys kn^t Thr̃er and Sr Anthony Aucher, and Capt Thompson expressinge ye Coueñnt℮ betweene the Comp^a: and the said Capt Tompson for fraight of the good Ship called the Ionathan, and Transportaçon of ¹ Passengers; Mr Deputy desyred that Mr Thr̃er beinge to seale yt for the vse of the Company, there might be an order of this Court to save him harmeless. W^{ch} the Courte so willingly assented vnto y^t they confirmed his securitie (beinge putt to ye question) by erecçon of hands.

The Charter party betweene ye Comp^a: and Capt Tompson presented.

Mr Thr̃r. to be saued harmeless.

ffifteen thousand waight of choyce Tobacco beinge sepated from the worst, one third pt of itt was agreed to be putt to Sale by the Candle allowinge Trett 4 in the C: to pay att : 6 : and : 6 : moneths and if any of the Comp^a: buy itt, to have the Custome free if they export itt: Mr Tho: Mellinge biddinge iij^s want a penny att the goinge out of the flame had itt adiudged.

1500: w^{tt} of choyce Tobacco seperated from ye worst

Mr Mellinge had it adiudged.

A warr̃nt accordinge to order in the last Courte was now allowed and signed by the Audito^{rs} to m^r Thr̃er for the paym^t of Sixteen pounds to ffrauncis Barradine Katherine Bath haveinge made choyce of him to be her Guardian.

A warr̃nt sealled to m^r Thr̃r for paym^t of xvj^{ll} to Fra: Barradine for Ka: Bath

Ann other warr̃nt was allowed and signed to m^r Thr̃er for paym^t of 400^{ll}: to Capt: Tompson, in pt of the Comp^a: agreem^t for the fraight of the Ship and Transportaçon of Passenge^{rs} accordinge to order of Courte made primo die xbris 1619.

A warr: sealed to Mr Thr̃r for paym^t of 400^{ll} to Capt Tompson.

Elias Robert℮ haveinge paid in 12^{ll}:10^s:00 to m^r Thr̃er a bill of Adventure was now allowed & sealed vnto him for a single Share of 100 Acres of Land in Virginia. [61]

A bill of Aduenture sealed to m^r Robert℮.

¹ A blank space in the manuscript.

JANUARY Y^e VIIJth 1619

PRESENT.

Sr Edwin Sandys Kn^t Thr̃er.

Sr Iohn Dauers.	m^r Thomas Gibbes.	m^r Edw. Ditchfield.
Sr Frauncis Lee.	m^r Nicholas Ferrar.	m^r Whetley.
S^r Io: Wolstenholme.	m^r Wm Cañinge.	m^r Casewell.
Sr Nath: Rich.	m^r Hen: Briggs.	m^r Bull.
m^r Robert Ofley.	m^r Ri: Wiseman.	m^r Darnelly.
m^r Io: Ferrar Dep^t.	m^r Tho: Keightley.	m^r Bearblock.
m^r Dr Gulstone.	m^r Cranmer.	m^r Georg Smith.
		m^r Robert.
		m^r Mellinge.

The callinge of this Court to consider whether ye Comp^a: wolde farme ye impost of Tobacco — Mr Thr̃er signified that the cause of this extraordinary Courte was to vnderstand their resolucōns, about a matter recomēnded to them frō his Ma^{ty}: by reason of the Maister ||of the|| Wardes, whether the Company would ffarme the impost of Tobacco or any p̃t therof att Eight Thousand pounds p Annū and pay 12^d a pound for Custome of their Tobacco, itt haveinge been thought convenyent to raise the **The Custome thought fitt to be raised.** Custome vppō Tobacco to that Rate for that some Spanish Tobacco hath beene sould att Twenty Shillings p pound of wch 12^d: vj^d: was to be paid to the ffarmers of the Imposte and vj^d to the ffarmers of the Custome.

The resolucōn for paym^t only of y^e: 5:pC. graunted by ye King in his Tres Pattent^c confirmed — After some disputacōn itt was answered that the Kinge had graunted them their Pattent vnder the brode Seale vppon good grounds, to paie onely five p Cent: and no more wch Prevyledge they could not give vp nor betray withoutt great breach of duety, as allso the certaine hazard of the whole Plantacōn, And this poynt was stood so resolutely vppon that being putt to the question itt was confirmed by all the hands noe one dissentinge.

And therfore forasmuch as their Virginia §Tobacco§ was never yett sould in any sale that tooke effect att aboue five shillings the pound but many times vnder they could not give way to pay more for Custome then three pence vppon the pound wch is full five in the hundred yett so that if hereafter itt should rise to a higher price they would willingly encrease their Custome to the highest of that rate.

if ye Virg: Tobacco rise to a higher prise they are content to encreas the Custome to the highest rate.

Yett in regard they vnderstand by m^r Thr̃rer that his Ma^{ty}: out of love and affecc̃on to this Company have given order for ye inhibiting the plantinge of English Tobacco for these five years to begin̄ at Michaellmas next insueinge wch resteth to be proclaymed till the Company have deliuered their Answere wch is expected att ye Counsell Table this afternoone, in Considerac̃on therof itt is now assented [62] to and ordered by the Courte that duringe the said ffive years if ye Proclamac̃on continue so longe and take effect in gratificac̃on ~~of~~ || to || his Ma^{ty} for his most gracious fauour to add nine pence more vppon a pound so to make itt vpp xij^d beinge in full of his Ma^{ts} demaund though not in the same forme.

The Planting of English Tobacco inhibited by his Ma^{ty} for those 5 years.

Nine pence vppon a pound to be Added to sattisfie his Ma^{ts} demaund.

And beinge demaunded by m^r Thr̃er whether they would vndertake the farme or participate therof the Court held itt inconvenyent to medle therwth in their generall for as much as they had neither Stock nor Rente yett wherby to pay itt, Yett because his Ma^{ts}: most gracious offer should nott seeme in any poynt to be neglected or refused, Itt was desyred thatt some pticularr psonns of the Company, and in name of the Company though for their owne pticularr vse should ioyne for some pt therof wch was assented to; And m^r Thomas Keightley wth some other yeilded to accept therof for a third pt wch was Confirmed and so ordered by the Courte.

The Vndertakinge of the farme held inconvenyent.

Some pticular persons of y^{e}Comp^a: to ioyne for some pt therof

And because this their determinac̃on mvst forthwith be presented to the Lords, The Court have desyred mr. Thr̃er to take the paines and have entreated to accompany him, m^r Tho: Gibbℓ m^r Wheatley, m^r Cranmer, m^r Keightley m^r Ditchfielde, m^r Wiseman, m^r Bearblock, m^r Caswell, and m^r Mellinge.

M^{r}Thr̃erand some others to draw ye Comp^a determinac̃on & present it to ye Lord

IANUARY Y^e: 12th: 1619

PRESENT.

Sr Edwin Sandys Kn^t Thr̃er.

Sr Tho: Wroth.	m^r Richard Tomlyn€.	m^r Bamforde
S^r Io: Wolstenholme.	m^r Tho: Keightley.	m^r Caninge.
Sr Nath: Riche.	m^r Harbert.	m^r Briggs.
Sr Henry Iones.	m^r Nicho: Ferrar.	m^r Woodall.
m^r Robt. Offley.	m^r Bearblock.	m^r Couell.
m^r Iohn: Ferrar Dep^t.	m^r Caswell.	m^r George Smith.
m^r Thomas Gibbes.	m^r Meuerell.	m^r Arrundle.
	m^r Swinhow.	m^r Eli: Robert€.
		m^r Tho: Mellinge.

M^r .Thr̃ers report touching ye determinaĉon of that his Ma^ty Comended vnto the.

This Courte was given intelligence by m^r Thr̃er that hee had acquainted the Lords Comissioners for the Treasury as hee and some others ‖were‖ requested touchinge the determinaĉon of that his Ma^ty: recommended vnto them expressed att .large in the Court goinge before wch was y^t notwithstanding they altered the forme of his Ma^ts: demaund yett they agreed in ye substance of giveinge xij^d a pound, vizd 3^d Custome according to ther Pattent and nine pence more for five years in Consideraĉon of the displantinge of English Tobacco. Yett the Lords tooke itt [63]

The Acte to be entred in ye LL^s: Comissioners Records.

acceptably that in substance they had agreed and for matter of forme itt should be accomodated by beinge passed ouer on both sides: Butt for as much as divers of the Courte conceiveth that vnless this offer and the true meaninge therof be entred as an Act in the LL^s: Comissione^rs Records itt wilbe very difficult att the expiraĉon of five

A Comittee to repare to ye Clerk of ye Counsell to take care y^t ye bargaine be entred & to procure a Coppie therof to be entred amongst ye Comp^s orders.

yeares to w^thdraw itt butt that continuinge so longe itt wilbe expected forever as a duty due from the Company to his Ma^ty: ffor preventinge of wch so neere as may be the Courte hath now appoynted a Comittee to repare to the Clark of the Counsell, and to take care that this bargaine be Recorded, and to pcure a Coppy therof to be entred amongst the rest of the Companies orders: And because the said Clarke of the Councell may better vnderstand the Companies true

meaninge they have required their Secretary to Coppy outt their last The Secretary to draw a Coppy of yᵉ last Courte
Courte that the said Comittee may deliver itt vnto him.   The Comit-
tees are Sʳ Iohn Dauers, Sʳ Nathaniell Rich, Mʳ Thomas Keightley,
and Mʳ Berblock, who have promised to goe aboute itt vppon ffryday
Morninge next att eight of yᵉ Clocke.

And wheras some desyred that in handlinge of this buisines they The cleeringe of their garblinge of Tobacco held im-ptinent to this buisines.
would have cleered the garblinge of their Tobacco, wᶜʰ is expected
shortly to be imposed vppon them by the Pattentees thereof: Itt was
answered that itt was not a thinge ptinent to this buisines, as allso that
in the last Court itt was spoken of butt not concluded as thinkinge itt
vnseasonable to goe aboute preventinge of that wᶜʰ as yett was not
demaunded, and in right could not be imposed on the Company whose
goods are free from all imposiĉons and Taxes.

Mʳ Thꝛer and mʳ Deputy beinge yeasterday wᵗʰ the Lo: Maior, Mʳ Thꝛer & Mʳ Deputie their re-port touchinge yᵉ 100 Children to be sent to Virginia
Reported that hee informed them, the Cittie had agreed to provide
one hundreth Children for Virginia, and to allow the Company five
pound apeec three pounds towards their passage and ffortie shillings
for Aparrell, desyringe mr Thꝛer to deliver in writinge the Condiĉons
the Company will pforme wᶜʰ hee hath promised to doe to morrow:
And further did demaund what land they should have in lew of
their Transportaĉon, who answered that they were not to have
any, butt after the expiraĉon of their Apprentishipp, they were
to be Teñntꝰ to the Common Land, butt in regard the Cittie
beareth the halfe charge of their transportaĉon hee thought the
Court would allow them 25 Acres apeec of every each one of them,
wᶜʰ for the p̃sentt his Lorᵖ: seemed to be sattisfied therewith.   [64]

Concerninge the Magazine touchinge the poynt wheither itt should The Magazine dis-solued.
continue or nott, after some reasons given for the maynteyninge of
itt no longer, Itt was generally agreed by the Adventurorꝰ that itt
should be dissolved, wᶜʰ by erecĉon of hands beinge putt to the question was ratefyed, now orderinge that for the 5200: and odd pounds
worth of goods there remayninge rated as they Cost heer first penny
shall first be putt of, before any other of the same kinde wᶜʰ p̃adven-
ture by pryvate men may be sent, and so much to give yᵉ Plantaĉons

informaçon of by letters, as allso that if they will ioyne and take these Magazine Goods remayninge in store, that then itt shalbe lawfull for them to have presently an absolute free Trade, wch may seeme by this restrainte to be in pt debarred from them.

S^r Io: Wolsten-holme freed from ye place of Direc-torr.

And for asmuch as Sr Iohn Wolstenholme by reason of his waightie imployments, can by no means Continue in the place of Director hee is now freed of the same, And by the Adventurors now present agreed that their gouerment shalbe the same, wth the Gouerment of the Courte saveinge that in matters meerly concerninge the Magazine none shall have voyce butt the Adventurers.

for ye Tobacc^o: vn-sould m^r Leate to haue one third of ye whole.

And for the Tobacco remayninge yett to be sould itt was agreed as pt of the Adventurers held itt requisite that Mr Leat for the better Sale of the other should have one third of the whole, vppon such Condiçons as the rest shalbe sould, and to pay for itt att such time and tymes as shalbe for that remayninge concluded vppon; Prouided that itt be good & Marchauntable and for the rest beinge estimated to be about 10000 waight itt was agreed should be devided into ffive parts and have entrusted as well the deliuery of the ⅓ to Mr Leate as the Sale of the rest, vnto Mr Wiseman and Mr Cranmer, for the Company and for the Adventurers, Mr George Smith, Mr Rich: Paulson, Mr Caswell, and Mr Mellinge, wch beinge putt to the question was by hands Confirmed.

Mr Thfer signified y^t ye Alpharbeti-call Publicaçon cannot be pformd because mr Mark-ham deteyneth the Alphabet Bookes.

Mr Markham de-maundeth sattis-facçon for his paines befor he deliu9 ye Alphabet Bookes.

Mr Treasurer declared that for the expeditinge of Sr Thomas Smiths Accomp^ts the Auditors resolved and accordinge as they hadd promised my Lord of Southampton to sett forth an Alphabeticall publicaçon of all the Adventurors wch hee reported now they could not pforme by reason mr. Markham deteyneth the Alphabett Bookes [65] notwithstandinge hee hath often beene required to bringe them either to the said Audito^rs or to the Courte and so had promised, who beinge now present himselfe answered that the keepinge of them could be no hinderance to their proceedings, for asmuch as they had the originall books from whence they were extracted, wch if the Company would give him sattisfacçon for his extraordinary paines, hee would forthwith deliver them: Butt beinge pemptorily warned by m^r Thrrer hee tould him that his Allegacons were false and frivelous, hee promised the next day to bringe in the Companies and for sattis-faccon of his paines, wch were saide by some to have beene greate, itt was not denyed but hee deserved recompence, butt whether from the Company, who for very small service done them had paid him liber-ally or from Sr Thomas Smith the rectyfyinge of whose Accompt had beene the wholl subiect of his Laboure was accordinge to the orders of the Company to be Considered in a Quarter Courte.

Mr Mellinge desyred the allowance of a bill of Adventure dewe vnto m^r Humphrey Tompkins of xij^{li}—x^s: 00: wch hee adventured in the five shilling Lottery: wch the Court now allowed.

Mr Hum: Tomkins bill of Aduenture allowed of

Wheras Mrs Anthony demaundeth some Prizes dew vnto her by the ffiue shillings Lottery the Courte have desyred m^r Iohn Wroth and m^r Cranmer to ripen the buisines of the Lotteries and then present itt to the Audito^{rs} who will take order for the payment of such pryzes as are due.

Mrs. Antho: de-maund for prizes due vnto her by ye 5^s Lotte:

Mr Deputy acquainted this Courte that the Comittees hadd agreed for the transportinge of 200 Personns more wth the owners of a Ship called the London Marchant about 300 Tunns vppon ye same condicons as they did formerly wth Captaine Tompson, namely to pay 700^{li} before the Ship departed and 600^{li} vppon Certificate of the Ships aryvall in Virginia; The Ship to be redy in Tilbury Hope the xxth day of ffeb-ruary next to take in the Passengers: Mr Threr and himselfe beinge demaunded by the said Owners to seale the Charter pty.

The Comittees agreem^t: with ye owners of ye Lo: Marchant for transporting 200 persons approued of

The Court approved of the bargaine and requested them to seale the Charter party, and ordeyned that the Comp^a: should saue them harmelesse. [66]

Mr Threr and m^r Depu: to seale ye Charter party

IANUARY THE 26th: 1619.

PRESENT.

Sr Iohn Dauers.	m^r Edw: Harbert.	m^r Cranmer.
Sr Nath: Riche.	m^r Nicho: Ferrar.	m^r Caswell.
Sr Thomas Wroth.	m^r Sheppard.	m^r Palmer.
m^r Io: Wroth.	m^r Henry Briggs.	m^r Swinhow.
m^r Ferrar Deputy.	m^r Bamforde.	m^r Berblock.
m^r Rich: Tomlyne.	m^r Kempton.	m^r Geo: Smith.
m^r Tho: Gibbes.	m^r Oxenbridge	m^r Chambers.
m^r Dr Winstone.	m^r Swifte.	m^r Couell.
m^r Dr Bohune.	m^r Canninge.	m^r Eli: Roberte.
		m^r Sparrowe.
		m^r Meuerell.
		m^r Arrundell.
		m^r Mellinge.

Mr Thfer pñted a Coppy of ye Offer as itt is entred in the book of ye Acts of ye LL'[1]: Comissi: of ye Treasury. The entringe of itt into ye Comp^a: Court book deferred.

The Comittee appoynted by the last Courte to repaire to ye Clerk of the Counsell for to see wheither their offer to his Ma^{ty}: were rightly entred and accordinge as m^r Thfrer and the Comittee wth him had signyfied and reported, Presented now a Coppie pcured by m^r Thfers help of the Record as itt stands entred in the Booke of Acts of the LL' Comissners of the Thfery; butt the entringe of the Coppie into the Court booke of this Company was deferred vnto the conclusion of a more full and ample Courte, by reason that some of the Company present were of opynyon that not onely the Pattent ought to be preserved from infryngement wch they confessed to be done, butt likewise ought to have beene strengthned, wch they said by this manner of acceptance on the Lords pts was not done.

3 seu9all paire of Inden: for Land allowed of.

Mr Deputy informed the Courte that three seuerall paire of Indentures for Land was demaunded of the Company, one by Robert Heath esquire Recorder of this Citty: The Second by William Tracy of Glocestersheire esqr for Transportacõn of 500 Personns; And the

[1] Written over Accomp^{ts}.

Third to Lawrence Bohune D^r of Phisicke and James Swifte esqr : for the Transportaćon of 300 Personns, wch the Courte graunted and allowed to them, to be pformed accordinge to the orders of the Company and agreeable to former Presidentℇ of the like nature.

Mr Deputy allso signified that wheras accordinge to a former order made xv die Nouembris i6i9 ther is menćon of some explynaćon to be made to some few of the standinge orders and an addićon of two or three more to be anexed vnto them. **[67]**

Mr Thr̃er required y^t the Committee appoynted for them, might for that purpose meet too morrow att Two of the Clock att his howse for the bette^r preparinge of them for the Quarter Courte wch was now accordingly ordered appoyntinge the Officer to Summon them therevnto. The Comittee formerly apoynted for explynaćon to ye Lawes desired to meete.

Next hee acquainted the Courte that the Comittees have agreed for Two Ships (if itt stand wth the likinge of this Courte) for ye transportaćon of Cattle to Virginia for the Company, and those others wch will ioyne wth the Company in the Charges: As allso that m^r Treasurer and himselfe will Seale the Charter ptys if they order their Securitie wch for the first poynt the Court well allowed of, and for the Second of saveinge them harmeless itt was generally assented vnto and confirmed by erection of hands. The Comittees agrem^t for 2 Ships to transporte Cattle to Virginia: allowed of.

The Comittees beinge demaunded what they had done touchinge the Tobacco comended vnto their care, Reported that accordinge to the order in the laste Courte they had taken out one third for m^r Leate butt had not devyded the rest in :5: pts because they could not heere of any thatt would buy itt vpon wch some excepćons was taken about that alredy ordered concerninge Mr Leate, that if the rest were not sould hee paid nothing for his, therfore itt was moved that some of the Adventurers ||that they|| would take out their Dividentℇ att a price, Whervppon m^r William Palmer offered to take outt his att iij^s vj^d the pound and beinge conceived that others would ioyne in the like, itt was againe referred to ye former Comittee to study how to make the best advantage of itt they can; addinge vnto them m^r Keightley, and m^r Palmer and to psent theire opynions to the next Courte. The Comittees report touchinge ye Tobacco comended vnto their Care.

Mr Wm Palmers proffer to take out his att 3^s 6^d a ^{lı}.

notice giuen by M^r
W^m: Caning of sufficient men y^t will
contract wth y^e
Comp^a: for all y^e
Tobacco that
shalbe returned
from Virginia

Mr Cañinge acquainted the Company that ther were dive^{rs} sufficient men that would contract wth them at reasonable pryces for all the Tobacco that shalbe returned from Virginia for a Certaine time wch hee conceived would be highly to the advancement of the Plantaĉon Wheruppõ the Courte desyred him to bring the proposiĉons well disgested and the names of the vndertakers vnto the next Court that there itt might be consydered of.   [68]

A Preparatiue Courte held for Virginia at
Sr Edwin Sandis house ye last of Ianuary } 1619

Present

Ri: hon°: Lord Pagett.

m^r Treasuror.	m^r James Swifte.	m^r Rich: Casewell.
Sr Iohn Dauers.	m^r Tho: Gibbes.	m^r Paulson.
Sr Tho: Wroth.	m^r Iohn Ferrar Dep^t.	m^r Spruson.
Sr Henry Rainsford.	Captain Bargraue.	m^r Meuerell.
m^r Io: Wroth.	m^r Robert Smith.	m^r Berblock.
m^r Dr Anthony.	m^r Brumfeilde.	m^r Leauor.
m^r Dr Gulstone.	m^r Caninge.	m^r George Smith.
m^r Dr Winstone.	m^r Henr: Briggs.	m^r Pe: Arundell.
m^r Ri: Tomlyne.	m^r Nicho Ferrar.	m^r Eli: Roberte.
	m^r Cranmore.	m^r Tho: Mellinge.
		m^r Steph: Sparrow.

The Comittee hau-
ing pused ye standinge orders were
presented and
read.

Mr Treasuror signified that the Comittee appoynted for pursuinge of the standinge orders have looked therinto correctinge some few & explayning others wch hee p̃sented now and red and explayned them to the Courte most of them beinge confirmed in the last § great § generall Courte, and now againe Comendinge them to their consideraĉon, wherby they may receave vppon Wednesday next a fynall ratefycaĉon.

And for asmuch as accordinge to a Law in the standinge orde^{rs} they
are all to be read to the Court once a yeare, vizd in the Quarter Courte
in Hillary Tearme, therfore moved for the fullfillinge of the same that
the Company would be heere wthout faile att two of the Clocke and
the rather Consideringe so much buisines as is then to be dispatched
ffower seuerall paire of Indentures to fower seuerall Personns and
their Associates for graunt of Land in Virginia, three paire menconed
in the last Courte, and one paire since allowed to Sr Iohn Peirce and
his Associates to be red allowed and sealled att that time.

Touchinge the mocon of Mr Caninge deferred from the last vnto this
Courte itt is now so well conceived of the good that may accrew therby
by such a Composicon (if itt be truely ment) that vppon intelligence
of the said Mr Caninge that they desire to converse wth some pticular
men of the Company aboute itt, The Court have now made choyse of
a Comittee to know their resolucons, that is to say Sr Nath: Rich, M^r
Deputy Mr Dr Winstone, Capt Bargraue, Mr Keightley, Mr Wrote, and
m^r Cranmer, and have agreed to meet to morrow afternoone att :2:
of the Clocke in this place Mr Caninge haveinge vndertaken y^t ffower
of those wch ppoundeth this buisines shalbe heere att that time. [69]

*The mocon of m^r
Caninge at ye Last
Court well con-
ceiued of*

*A Comittee ap-
poynted to know
their resolucons*

Wheras his Ma^{ty}: hath graunted to the Lady Lawarr a yearly Pencon
to be paide vnto her by the ffarmo^{rs} of the Custome; The Company
vppon her Ladyships request are content, (consideringe the Custome
for ye Aduenturo^{rs} Tobacco is not yett sattisfied) that the first pcell w^{ch}
is sould if itt amount to 250^{li}: so much beinge due vnto her vppon her
Share shall be paid vnto her or else so much Tobacco presently (if
her Ladyship please to accept thereof) att such price as the rest shalbe
sould or taken off of their hands, And for their discharge to take a
receipt from the ffarmors of the Custome.

*The first parcell of
Tobacco sould if it
amount to 250^{li}: to
be p^d ye La: Lawarr.*

And takinge into Consideracon the losse the Adventurers have susteyned by the Tobacco remayninge vppon their hands, and the daunger
they stand in of a great deall more, if the Ships should com from
Virginia and ye Somer Ilands as they dayly are expected, therfore
itt was propounded to the Adventurors to take out their Capitolle at
iiij^s a pound and soe each make the best of itt hee cann, butt some

*The losse of ye Ad-
uenturers consid-
ered by haueing
their Tobacco ly
vppon their hande.*

*A pposicon for
euery one to take
out their Capitolle.*

thinkinge itt was too much and that rather iij^s vj^d was ennough: itt was agreed to be putt to ye question wch done most voyces allowed of iiij^s, and hee that would be willinge at this price to take out more then his Capitall should have Six and Six monneths for payment, butt entringe into dispute, whether such as tooke outt their Capittall^e in that manner shall Coparte of such proffits as may heer after accrew vnto the rest, itt could not now be agreed vppõ butt was referred to be debated further att the Quarter Courte when more of the Adventurers shalbe present.

The orders from ye LLo^s Comissioners referred.

Touchinge the orders from the LL^s: Comissioners they were referred to the Consideraçon of this Quarter Courte.

The Coppy of ye Citties demaunde touchinge ye 100: Children to be sent to Virginia rectified.

Mr Thr̃er and m^r Deputy haveinge had much Conference with the Lord Maior and Aldermen about the 100 Children intended to be sent found them att the first well adicted and affected vnto theire demaunde. butt since some pticular psonns lesser respectinge (as should seeme) the Companies good have occasioned such straunge demaunds as is not fittinge for them to aske, nor can no wayes by the orders of this Company be graunted, and therfore have determyned to rectifie the Coppy of their demaunds so farr as may stand with the orders of the Company to graunt and so to returne itt to the Courte of Aldermen to morrow att tenn of the clock to accep^t therof or noe [70] to wch purpose is desyred Sr Thomas Wroth, Sr Henry Rainsforde Mr Iohn Wroth, and Mr Deputy.[1]

2 Shares allowed to Iohn Archer.

Itt was ordered in regard sufficient testimony beinge produced that Iohn Archer brother of Captaine Gabriell Archer disceased in Virginia is the next heire vnto him, that the said Iohn Archer shall have two Shares, said to belonge to the said Captaine: vizd one share for xij^{li}—x^s adventured, and the other for the Adventure of his psonn.

Stephen Sparrow: 1: Share to Iohn Hope.

Mr Stephen Sparrow assigned to Iohn Hope Marriner one share of xij^{li}—x^s.00 allowed by the Audito^{rs} and confirmed by this Courte.

[1] An order of the Privy Council, of this date, authorizing the sending of 100 children to Virginia is given in List of Records, No. 161, page 139, *ante.*

ATT A GREATE AND GENERALL QUARTER COURTE
HOLDEN FOR VIRGINIA AT Sᴿ EDWIN SANDYS
HOUSE NEER ALDERSGATE THE SECOND OF FEBRUARY
1619

WERE PRESENT

The Right Honorable: William Earle of Pembrooke.
Henry Earle of Southampton.
Robert Earle of Warwicke.
Iames Vicont Doncaster.
The Lord Cauendish.
The Lord Pagett.

Sʳ Edwin Sandys Knight Thᵉrer.

Sʳ Tho: Roe.	mʳ Iohn Wroth.	mʳ Edwards.
Sʳ Dudley Diggꝭ.	mʳ Ferrar Depᵗʸ.	mʳ Bull.
Sʳ Tho: Gates.	mʳ Tho Gibbꝭ.	mʳ Couell.
Sʳ Iohn Dauers.	mʳ Samu: Wrote.	mʳ Woodall.
Sʳ Henry Rainsforde.	Capᵗ Bargraue.	mʳ Darnelly.
Sʳ Nath: Rich.	mʳ Rogers.	mʳ Casewell.
Sʳ Io: Wolstenholme.	mʳ Bromfeilde.	mʳ Swinhow.
Sʳ Henry Iones.	mʳ Keightley.	mʳ Moorer.
Sʳ Tho: Wrorth.	mʳ Ia Swifte.	mʳ Robertꝭ.
Dʳ Anthony.	mʳ Bamforde.	mʳ Sparrow.
Dʳ Gulstone.	mʳ Wheatley.	mʳ Mellinge.[71]
Dʳ Winstone.	mʳ Berblock.	
Dʳ Bohune.	mʳ Briggs.	
	mʳ Cranmer.	

Accordinge to a standinge Order the Lawes of the Company being **The Lawes red.**
120: in nomber and devided into eighteene Chapters or Tytles were
now red vnto this greate Assembly, wᶜʰ ended mr Thᵉrer related that **mʳ Thᵉrer signified: 4 speciall things reserued to yᵉ 4: Qua:**
the Kinge out of his greate care and wisedome had graunted to the
Company by his most gracious Ɫres Pattents, ffower great and generall **Courtꝭ by Maᵗⁱᵉ: Ɫres Pattentꝭ.**

Courts in the yeare comonly called Quarter Courtes to be held in the 4 Tearms, vnto wch was reserved 4: speciall things.

1: The makinge of Lawes and Orders.   2: Choyse of Officers 3 Graunts of Land.   4: Matter of Trade.

ffor the first hee pceeded as formerly hee had done, that nothing was so pfect wherin time discouereth not some impfeccõns, so in ye Lawes some thinge beinge found defective comended to their Consideracõn some small Addicõn and Correccõn of them formerly allowed in the laste Quarter Courte thence referred to a Comittee by them presented to the Councell, and lastly read in the precedinge Preparative Courte: explayninge what was pformed vnto seuerall Tytles:

To the Tytle of Courtℭ: 3: Laws is added; To the Tytle of Treasuror—2: To the Tytle of Deputy. 1: To the Tytle of Counsell—1: To the Tytle of Grauntℭ of Land—2: in the Tytle of Generallytie an amendm[t] or Addicõn of 2 wordes, in the Sixt order afterward (Court) is added (or Councell) and so in the 13th order of Tytle of Treasuror after the word (quorum) is added (vnderneath or) W[ch] Correccõns

& Addicõns beinge approved off Mr Thr̃rer propounded ye confirmacõn of them in two questions; the one whether they would allow of ye addicõn of these two words in the said Tytles of Treasuror, and Generallyty to be incerted there in the face of the Courte; And whether they would consent that the resydue should be entred by the Secretary amongst the rest (accordinge to their referrences) in the booke of Lawes and standinge Orders both wch by a Generall ereccõn of hands was ratefyed.

To the second poynt of Choosinge Officers he acquainted y[t] accordinge to the said Lres Pattents itt was no Courte vnless five of ye Counsell were present by defect of wch number of the Councell ~~were~~ they are often times att their Courts in tymes of Vacation inforced to stay very longe before that number of the Councell be assembled by reason such as frequents the Court are either in ye Countrie or imployed in other buisines, that they cannott attend, therfore vppon Mocõn from the Councell, hee nominated 2: vnto ye Courte Mr Robert Heath Recorder of this Citty who hath been and is a great Adventurer and favourer of the Acc̃on: And Thomas Gibbs Esquire a gentleman of good sufficiencie, and great zeale [72] to the Acc̃on, who for dive͑ years hath given diligent Attendance at all Courts and is imployed a Comittee allmoste in all buisinesses, w͞ch Two being putt to the question were admitted to be Councello͑ of Virginia by free Consent.

The Third of Graunt₵ of Land hee acquainted them of fower seu⁹all paire of Indentures lyinge all ingrossed before them graunted one to M͑ Robert Heath Recorder of London and his Associates, the s'cond to Doctor Bohune, Iames Swifte and their Associates for Transportinge of 300 Personns: The Third to William Tracy esquire and his Associates for Transportac̃on of 500 Persons, and the ffowerth to Iohn Peeirce and his Associates their heirs and Assignes w͞ch beinge all fowre now red and examined and fyndinge them agree wth the draughts pvsed and allowed by the Audito͑ were all of them allowed and Sealed in veiwe of the Courte w͞th a Totall Approbac̃on

3 Grant₵ of Land:

4 Paire of Indentures allowed of

Itt was ordered allso by generall Consent that such Captaines or lead͑ of Perticulerr Plantac̃ons that shall goe there to inhabite by vertue of their Graunts and Plant themselvs their Teñnt₵ and Serṽ-ñnt₵ in Virginia, shall have liberty till a forme of Gouerment be here settled for them, Associatinge vnto them divers of the gravest & discreetes of their Companies, to make Orders, Ordinances and Constituc̃ons for the better orderinge and dyrectinge of their Servants and buisines Prouided they be not Repugñnt to the Lawes of England.

Captaines or Leaders of Perticuler Plantacons to make orders C͑.

Touchinge the fowerth poynt matter of Trade, M͑ Treasuror acquainted the Courte, that the Magazine had now voluntarylie dissolved ~~her~~ § itt § selfe, w͞th provision graunted for their goods remayning in Virginia so that now matter of Trade was free and open for all men w͞th that provision.

4
Matter of Trade.
The Magazine being dissolued Matter of Trade is free for all men.

Itt was now allso agreed touchinge the Order of y͜e Lords Comissioners that the Company should be humble suto͑ vnto their LL^ps: for some small amendment in the forme therof, M͑ Thr̃er signifyinge that the Counsell of Virginia sittinge w͞thin before the Courte there beinge present all the Noble Lords before sett downe resolved that

The Comp͡ to be suto͞ to y͜e Lords for some amendment in y͜e Order.

nothinge in ye Pattent to be infringed.

they could not yeild to any thinge that might infringe theire [73] Pattent wch resolucõn was wth generall demonstracõn of ioy embraced by the Courte, and therfore desyred to choose a Comittee for that purpose to wch end was nominated the Right Hono^{le}: the Earle of Warwicke, The Lord Cauendish, The Lord Pagett, Mr Treasurer, Sr Dudley Diggs, Sr Iohn Dauers, Sr Henry Rainsford Sr Nathaniell Rich: Sr Lawrence Hide, Mr X^o: Brooke, Mr Nicho Hide, Mr Deputy, Dr Winstone, Mr Gibbs, Mr Keightley, and Mr Cranmer who are desyred to sett downe the Companies meaning in writing and present itt to the LL^s: when Mr Thrẽer shall thinke itt Convenyent to Sũmon them.

A Comittee to sett downe ye Comp^s: meaninge in writinge.

Touchinge the Determinacõn of the Tobacco referred vnto this Courte belonginge to the Adventurers of the Magazine vppon the Mocõn of Sr Iohn Wolstenholme itt is deferred till to morrow afternoone, Att wch time the Adventurers onely are desyred to meete att m^r Ferrars house to consider of the best course and conclude therof accordinglie.

The derminacõn of ye Tobacco referrd.

The Demaunds of the Citty read the last Courte concerninge the hundreth Children beinge much distasted of this Company beinge such as were repugñnt to the standinge Orders w^{ch} ~~w^{ch}~~ Could no way be dispensed wth,[1] therfore the Comittees have rectefyed and Corrected the Coppy so farr forth as may stand wth the Orders to admitt, and have written a fre to the Lord Maior from the Cheife of the Councell agreeinge to send the fre and returne the altered Coppie to morrow morninge to the Courte of Aldermen, requestinge Sr Thomas Wroth, and m^r Gibbes to deliuer them, and require their speedy resoluccõns because the spedy depture of the Ships will suffer no delays this followinge beinge the true Coppie.

The Coppie of ye Citties Demaunds touchinge ye 100 Children Corrected.

A fre written to ye Lord Maior from ye cheife of ye Counsell.

The Letter.

Wheras the number of One hundreth Children whose names are hearafter mencõned were the last Springe sent and transported to the Virginia Company from the Cittie of London vnto Virginia And towards the charge ~~and~~ for the transportacõn and apparrellinge of the same One hundreth Children a Colleccõn of the some of ffive hundreth pounds was made of divers well & godly disposed psons [74] Charitably mynded towards the Plantacõn in Virginia dwellinge wthin the City of London and Subvrbs theirof, and thervppon the same ffive hundreth pounds was paid vnto the saide Company for the pur-

[1]The word "wth" written over "of."

pose aforesaid, And thervppon for the good of the same Children and in Consideraĉon of the premises, Itt is fully concluded ordered & decreed by and Att a generall Quarter Courte this day houlden by yᵉ Treasuroʳ Councell and Company of Virginia that every of the same Children wᶜʰ are now liveing att the charges and by the provision of yᵉ said Virginia Company, shalbe educated and brought vpp in some good Trade and profession wherby they may be enabled to gett their liveinge and maynteyne themselvs when they shall attaine their seuerall ages of flower and twenty years or be outt of their Apprentiships, which shall endure att the least seaven years if they soe longe live.

And further that every of the same Children (that is to say the Boys att their Ages of one and twenty years or vpwards and the maydes or girles att their Age of one and twenty years or day of marriage wᶜʰ shall first happen, shall have freely given and allotted vnto them ffiftie Acres of Land a peec in Virginia aforesaid wᵗʰin the lymi[ts] of the English Plantaĉon the said Acres to be apoynted according to the Statute De terris mesurandis, in England and that in convenyent place or places to hold in ffee simple by Socage tenure to every of them and their heirs for ever freely att the Rent of xijᵈ by yᵉ yeare in full of all rents or other payment or service due vnto the Lord therfore to be rendred or donne.

If the Lord Maior, Aldermen, and Common Councell shall not be sattisfied wᵗʰ the Companies reasons (who desyre that some of themselvs may be admitted to alledge them) that itt is betteʳ for the fformer Children to have the same Condiĉons wᵗʰ these latteʳ the Company wilbe content to lett itt pass for this time yett wᵗʰ this protestaĉon; That as itt is not beneficiall to the Children, so itt is the extreame wrong & preiudice of the wholl Plantaĉon.

And wheras allso itt is intended and fully resolved that this next Springe the nomber of one hundreth Children more whose names are likewise herafter menĉoned, shalbe sent and Transported by yᵉ said Virginia Company out of the Cittie of London vnto Virginia aforesaid and that towards the Charge of transportinge and apparrelling yᵉ same Children the like Colleĉon of ffive hundreth pounds of men godly and Charitably disposed towards the said Plantaĉon wᶜʰ doe reside wᵗʰin the said Citty and Subvrbs therof is to be made, and vppon the Collectinge therof the same shalbe paid to the said Virginia Compʸ: for the purpose aforesaid; Now therfor for the good of the same Children, and in Consideraĉon of the p̃mises, Itt is fully concluded Ordered, and decreed att a great and generall Quarter Courte this day holden by the Treasuror, Counsell, and Company of Virginia that the said hundred Children last menĉoned shalbe sent att the [75] Virginia Companies charge and duringe their Voyadge shall have their provision of victuall sweet and good and well apparrelled and all other things neces-

sary for the Voyage: And that every of the same Children shalbe there
placed Apprentizes wth honest and good Maisters that is to say the boyes for
the tearme of seaven years or more; ~~and~~ so as their Apprentishipps may expire
att their seuerall Ages of one and twenty years or vpwards; And the mayds or
Girles for the tearme of seaven years or vntill they shall attayne their Ages of
one and twenty years or be marryed to be by the same Maisters during that
time educated and brought vpp in some good Craftes, Trades, or Husbandry
wherby they may be enabled to gett their liveinge & mayntennãce for them
selvs when they shall attaine their seuerall ages or be outt of their Apprentiships ‖and during their Apprentiships‖ shall have all things pvided for them
as shalbe fitt and requisite as meate, drinke, Apparrell, and other necessaries.

And further that att the expiracõn of their seuerall Apprentishipps every of
ye said Children shall have freely given vnto them and provided for them at
the said Companies charge, provision of Corne for Victuallꞇ for on wholl yeare
And shall allso have a house redy builded to dwell in, and be placed as a
Tennant in some convenyent place vppon so much land as they can mannage;
And shall have one Cowe and as much Corne as hee or shee will plant, and
forty shillings in monny to Apparrell them, or Apparrell to that value: And
shall allso have Convenyent weapons Municõn and Armo^r for defence, and
necessary implem^{ts} & vtensillꞇ for houshold, and sufficient workinge Tooles
and Instrumentꞇ for their Trades, labor and husbandry in such sort as other
Tennꞇꞇ are pvided for.

Moreover that every of the same Children last menc̃oned wch shall have thus
served their Apprentiships and be placed and provided for as aforesaid shalbe
Tyed to be Tennꞇts or ffarmers in manner & forme afore said for the space of
Seaven years after their Apprentiships ended, and duringe that time of their
labour and paines therein they shall have halfe of all the encrease profitt and
benefitt y^t shall arise grow and encrease by the mannageinge therof aswell y^e
fruites of the earth the increase of the Cattle as otherwise, And the other
moytie therof to goe and remayne to the Owners of the Land, in liew and sat-
tisfacc̃on of a Rent to be payd for the same Lande so by them to be occupied,
And that att the expiracõn of the same last Seaven years every of the same
Children to be att liberty either to Continue Tennꞇꞇ or ffarmo^{rs} to the Company vppõ the same Lands if they will att the same rates and in the manner
aforesaid or else provide for them selvs elsewhere.

And lastly that either of the same Children att the end of the last seaven years shall
have moreouer five and twenty Acres of Land to be given and allotted to them in
some Convenyent place or places wthin the English Plantac̃ons in Virginia aforesaid, to hould in fee ~~Socage~~ simple by Soccage tenure to every of them and their
[76] heirs, for ever freely for the Rent of Six pence for every five & twenty

Acres by way of quitt Rent in leiwe of all services in regard of the tenure; All wch pmises wee the said Treasuror, Counsell, and Company doe order and decree and faithfully promise shalbe iustly and truly pformed towards the said Children accordinge to the true intent & meaning therof.

A Łre from an vnknowne person was read dyrected to m^r Treasuro^r pmisinge five hundred pounds for the educatinge and bringinge vpp Infidellɇ Children in Christianytie wch Mr Treasuror not willinge to meddle therwith alone desyred the Court to apoynt a select Comittee for the mannadginge and imployinge of itt to the best to wch purpose they have made choyse of the

A Łre from an Vn-
kowne pson prom-
ising 500^ll

Lord Pagett.	m^r Tho: Gibbes.
Sr Tho Wroth.	Dr Winstone.
m^r Io: Wroth.	m^r Bamforde &
m^r Deputie.	m^r Keightley.

The Coppy of wch Letter ensueth.

S^r yor Charitable endeavo^rs for Virginia hath made yo^u a ffather wee a favourer of those good workɇ wch although heretofore hath com neer to their birth yett for want of strength could never be delivered, (envy & division dashinge these younglings even in the wombe) vntill yor helpfull hand wth other honorable psonages gave them both birth and beinge, for the better cherishinge of wch good and pious worke seeinge many castinge guiftɇ into the Treasury, I ame encourraged to tender my poore mite and although I cannott wth the Princes of Issaker bringe gould and silver Coveringe yett offer here what I cann, some Goatɇ hayre necessary stuffe for the Lords Tabernacle, protestinge heer in my sinceritie w^thout papisticall merritt or pharasaicall applause wishing from my part as much vnitie in yor honorable vndertakinge as theris sinceritie in my designes, to the furtherance of wch good worke, the Convertinge of Infidles to the fayth of Christe I pmised by my good frends 500^ll for the mayntenance of a Convenyent nomber of younge Indians taken att the age of Seaven years or younger & instructed in the readinge and vnderstandinge the principalls of Xian Religion vnto the Age of 12 years and then as occasion serveth to be trayned and brought vpp in some lawfull Trade wth all humanitie and gentle-ness vntill the Age of one and Twenty years, and then to enioye like liberties and pryveledges wth our native English in that place and for the better pform-ance therof yo^u shall receave 50^ll more to be delivered into the hands to two religious psons wth securitie of payment who shall once every Quarter examine

The Letter

and certifie to the Treasuror herein England the due execuĉon of these premises together wth the names of these Children thus taken, their ffoster ffathers
and ouerseers [77] not doubtinge butt yo^u are all assured that guiftes devoted
to Gods service cannott be diverted to pryvate and ~~singuler~~ §secular§ advantages without sacriledge, if yor graver iudgments can devise a more charitable
course for such younge Children, I beseech yo^u informe my frend wth yor
securitie for true pformance and my benevolence shalbe allwaies redy to be
delivered accordingly, the greatest Courtesie I expect or crave is to conceale
my frends name least importunytie vrge him to betray that trust of secresie
wch hee hath faythfully promised, hee that moved my harte to this good worke,
dyrect yor Charitable endeavours herein, whylest I rest as I ame

Dust and Ashes

Directed   To Sr Edwin Sandys ye faithfull Treasuror for Virginia.

Dr Bohunes request to passe. D^r: Bohunes requests beinge read the Courte have intrusted the Audi-
to^rs to rectefye wch is agreed shall passe (beinge putt to the question)
by erecĉon of hands.

The Petiĉon of Capt Powell and m^r Iohn Smith beinge presented by
their brother Prouest Marshall of Middlesex to have graunt of the
Company 400 Acres of Land for fiftie pounds Adventure betwixt them
vizd, One hundreth lyinge in one pcell between the Sunken Marsh
one the other side the River against Iames Citty Land, and Choapooks
Creek, and one pcell of Marsh Land conteyninge 300 Acres called
To write to ye Gouernor to sett out 400 Acres of Land for Capt Powell & m^r Io: Smith Hogg Iland, The Court held itt inconvenyent to graunt Land in that
kinde, pickt out by the Plante^rs themselvs not knowinge who all-
redie may lay clayme thervnto or otherwise how necessary itt may be
for the publique; Butt m^r Treasuror in regard of the good affecĉon
declared by their brother to the Companies service hath promised to
write to the Gouernor that the said 400 Acres shalbe well sett out for
them and to their Content wth reason.

Frauncis Carter Petiĉon referd to ye Audito^rs. A petiĉon was exhibited, by ffrauncis Carter the Companies Officer
desyringe that forasmuch as hee hath worne himselfe outt in the
Companies service beinge nowe growne lame, that now in his olde age
they would please to take his Case and necessitie into favourable consideraĉon etĉ, wch by reason itt grew late was referred vnto the Audi-
to^rs to psent to the Courte their opinions touchinge the best means
to rewarde him.

Peter Arundles Peticon to have his Shares explayned to be double Shares refered to the Audito[rs] to vew his buisines how itt stand€ and reporte itt to the Courte.   [78]

Pe: Arundles Peticon referrd to y[e] Audito[n].

Captaine Bargraues request to have a Comission for y[e] determyninge of some Controversies betweene him and Cap[t] Martine resydent in Virginia was allso referred vnto the Audito[rs].

Cap[t] Bargraues request referrd to y[e] Audito[n].

The Charter party betweene the Owners of the London Marchant and m[r] Treasuror and Deputy was now Sealled and delivered.

The Charter partie for y[e] Lond: Marchant sealled.

FEBRUARY Y[e] XVJ[th] 1619.

PRESENT

S[r] Edwin Sandys Kn[t] Treasuror.

S[r] Thomas Roe.	m[r] Reignold€.	m[r] Caswell.
S[r] Iohn Dauers.	m[r] Keightley.	m[r] Cranmer.
S[r] Henry Rainsford.	m[r] Sam: Wrote.	m[r] Bull.
S[r] Tho Gates.	m[r] Aug: Steward.	m[r] Eyres.
S[r] Tho: Wroth.	m[r] Bamforde.	m[r] Couell.
S[r] Harry Iones.	m[r] Hen: Briggs.	m[r] Geo: Smith.
m[r] Iohn Wroth.	m[r] Swinhowe.	m[r] Ely: Robert€.
m[r] Deputy.	m[r] Caninge.	m[r] Mellinge.
m[r] Tomlyn€.	m[r] Wiseman.	W[th] others.
Cap[t] Bargraue.	~~m[r] Bearblock.~~	

Vppon the desire of Cap[t] Brewster his buisines was once more deferrd to the next Preparative Courte w[ch] is agreed then to be heard betwixt him and Cap[t] Argoll, and to that end have given order that the said Cap[t] Argoll be acquainted therwith and required then to attend.

Cap[t] Brewsters buisines Deferrd.

Five Shares formerly given by S[r] Thomas Roe kn[t] to Peter Arundell w[ch] were Confirmed vnto him in a Courte held the first of October i6i7   The said Peter Arundell in Consideracon of a Certaine some of

5 Shares ressigned by Peter Arundell to Sr Tho: Roe

monney paid vnto him by the said Sᵣ Tho: Roe hath ressigned the said ffive Shares vnto the said Sᵣ Thomas Roe, wᶜʰ the Auditoᵣˢ haveinge allowed were by this Courte Confirmed.

Mᵣ Thꝼr acquainted the Courte of Łres receiued frõ Virginia
Mᵣ Treasuror acquainted the Courte that hee had receaved Letteʳˢ from Virginia importinge the wellfare of the Plantačon although they have been much distempord by reason of an intemporate heate not onely hapninge vnto them but chiefly amongst the Indians requestinge that the Company would send them some Phisitians and Appothycaries of wᶜʰ they stand much need off: relatinge allso to yᵉ great Comforte of the Compᵃ: and incouragmᵗ of those wᶜʰ shall send the plenty of Corne that God this yeare hath blest them with the like never happened since the English was there planted haveing had two harvestᵉ, the first beinge shaken with the winde p̃duced a second, and the ground beinge so extraordinary ffatt & good yᵗ sowinge Indian Corne vppon that stuble they had likewise a great Cropp therof.¹ [79]

Capᵗ Spillman made a seruant to yᵉ Collony.
Signifyinge allso that one Capᵗ Spillman who thought to deprave yᵉ Gouᵍnor of his Authoritie by his instigačon to Opochankino, of a great man yᵗ should com and putt him out of his place, The said Gouernor and Councell of State have p̃ceeded in due tryall of him butt beinge mercifull in sparinge his life have degraded him from his Capᵗ: Ship and made him a serv̄nnt to the Collony for Seaven years in quallytie of an Interpriter.

Other matter theris to acquainte them wᵗʰ wᶜʰ when hee hath read the rest of the letters hee will the next Courte reporte vnto them.

The Citty yeilded to yᵉ Łre:
The Letter the last Quarter Courte signed by the Lords directed to the Lord Maior of London tooke such effect as mᵣ Thꝛer sayeth the Cittie yeilded to itt:

mᵣ Thꝛeᶜ: reporte of yᵉ 500ˡⁱ giuen for educatinge yᵉ Infidles Children.
Wheras the last Court a speciall Comittee was appoynted for yᵉ managinge of the 500ˡⁱ given by an vnknowne p̃son for educatinge the Infidles Children Mᵣ Thꝛeʳ: signified that they have mett, and taken into consideračon the proposičon of Sᵣ Iohn Wolstenholme, that Iohn

¹ A series of letters, written between January 13 and 21, and received about this time, are mentioned in List of Records, Nos. 156–159, page 138, *ante.*

Peirce and his Associates might have the trayninge and bringinge vpp of some of those Children butt the said Comittee for divers reasons thinks itt inconvenyent, first because they intend not to goe this 2 or :3: monneths and then after there arryvall[1] wilbe longe in settlinge themselves, as allso that the Indians are not acquainted wth them, and so they may stay 4 or 5 years before they have account that any good is donne.

And for to putt itt into the hands of pryvate men to bringe them vpp att x^{li} a Childe as was by some proposed they hould itt not soe fitt by reason of the causualty vnto wch itt is subiect.

Butt forasmuch as divers hundreds and pticularr Plantacõns are allredie there settled and the Indians well acquainted wth them, as namely, Smithɇ Hundred, Martinɇ Hundred, Bartlettɇ Hundred & the like that therfore they receave and take charge of them by wch course they shalbe sure to be well nurtured and have their due so long as these Plantacõns shall hould, and for such of the Children as they find Capable of Learninge shall be putt in the Colledge and brought vpp to be schollers, and such as are not shall be putt to trades, and be brought vp in the feare of God & Christian religion, And beinge demaunded how and by what lawfull means they would procure them and after keep them that they runn not to theire parents or frends, and their said Parrents or frends steale them not away wch naturall affeccõn may inforce in the one and the other, itt was answered and well allowed that a treaty and an agreement be made wth the Kinge of that Country concerninge them wch if itt soe fall out att any time as is exprest they may by his Commaund be returned. [80] Whervppon Sr Thomas Roe promised that Bartley Hundred should take two or three for wch theire well bringinge vpp hee and m^r Smith pmised to be respondents to the Company, and because every Hundred may the better consider hereof they were lycensed till Sunday in the afternoone, att wch time they sitt att m^r Treasurors, to bringe in their answere how manny each will have and bringe those that wilbe respondent for them, & those that others will not take, Mr Treasuror in the behalfe of Smithɇ hundred hath promised to take into their charge.

---

[1] "Arryvall" is written over "arryvinge" by the reviewer.

The proposiĉons
for takinge the
Tobacco att a prize
Confirmed.

The Proposiĉons wᶜʰ were by sundry of the Adventurers allowed of att a meetinge of them att Sʳ Thomas Smiths house the 14ᵗʰ of February aboute takinge off the Tobacco att a price beinge now putt to yᵉ question was confirmed, Comendinge itt to mʳ Caswell to procure others ||to write|| for yᵉ rest.

And fallinge into dispute aboute the Debtℭ what course should be taken for gettinge them in, Mʳ Thrῖer made knowne that of necessitie Officers for man- there must be Officers Chosen for the mannaginge and lookinge to the aginge & lookinge buisines first for the callinge in of the Debtℭ by sendinge their ticketts to yᵉ buisines. vnto them to bringe in their monny, and vppon refusall to putt them in sute 2: to authorize their warrants for payinge of debts, :3: to dispose of their Affaires in Virginia, 4: and lastly in lookinge to the Accompts & pfectinge them, for the last itt was thought good by some yᵗ mʳ Essington should be entreated to pᵉceed wᵗʰ them, and for the mannaginge of the rest vppon nominaĉon ther was made choyce of, mʳ Bull, mʳ Cranmer and mʳ Caswell, and beinge putt to the question was ratefyed by erecĉon of hands.

3 Comissions
sealed.

Three Comissionℭ beinge presented to the Courte was allowed to be sealled one to William Shawe mʳ of the London Marchant the other to Capᵗ Iones mʳ of the Faulcon, and the third to mʳ Edmondℭ mʳ of the Tryall to sett saile wᵗʰ the first fayre winde for Virginia.

Capᵗ Bargraues
Comission to be
sealed.

Captaine Bargraues Comission for the determyninge some Controu⁹sies betweene him and Capᵗ: Iohn Martin in Virginia beinge now presented the Court therof allowed & agreed that the seale should be therevnto affixed.

Mʳ Markham pre-
sented 4 books and
4 Rolls.

Mʳ Markham beinge formerly requyred for the bringinge in the resydue of the bookℭ and Rowles remayninge in his Custodie, presented now to the boorde 4 books, and 4 Rowles of subscripĉons wᶜʰ were Comended to the Care of mʳ Deputy desyringe the Courte to take into Consideraĉon, that for his extraordinary paines hee might have sattisfacĉon, wᶜʰ pointe beinge long disputed betwixt mʳ Thrῖer and him, itt was att length referred to the Auditoʳˢ to consider thereof. [81]

FEBRUARY Y⁰ 22ᵗʰ [1619-20]:

PRESENT.

mʳ Treasurer.	mʳ Rich: Tomlynℓ.	mʳ Ri: Wiseman.
Sʳ Io: Dauers.	mʳ Samu: Wrote.	mʳ Fra: Meuerell.
Sʳ Tho: Gates.	mʳ Keightley.	mʳ George Smith.
Sʳ Nath: Rich.	mʳ Wheatley.	mʳ Abraham Chamberlyn.
mʳ Iohn Wroth.	mʳ Cranmer.	mʳ Henry Briggs.
mʳ Iohn Ferrar.	mʳ Berblock.	mʳ Elias Robertℓ.
mʳ Tho: Gibbes.	mʳ Robert Smith.	mʳ Nicho: Ferrar.
mʳ Dʳ Anthony.	mʳ Richard Wiseman.	mʳ Thomas Mellinge.[1]
mʳ Dʳ Winstone.	mʳ Crowe.	

And forasmuch as the Courte by the Gouernoᵣˢ letter is given to vnderstand that the inhabitants are very desiorus to have Engineers sent vnto them for the raysinge of ffortefycacōns for wᶜʰ they are content amongst themselves to beare the charge therof, vppon wᶜʰ Sʳ Tho: Gates is entreated to write his pryvate letters of dyreccōns both in regard of his skill therin, as allso of his knowledge of the Country, as allso that hee together wᵗʰ Sʳ Nath: Rich conferr wᵗʰ generall Cæsill therin, whose assistance in a former Courte touchinge the same buisines was entreated wᶜʰ they have ꝑmised to doe.   [82]

(margin: Sʳ Tho: Gates devsyred to write pryuate łres of direcōns)

A Box standinge vppon the Table wᵗʰ this direccōn, to Sʳ Edwin Sandis the faithfull Treasurer for Virginia, hee acquainted them that itt was brought vnto him by a man of good fashion who would nether tell him his name nor from whence hee came, butt by the Subscripcōn beinge the same wᵗʰ letter hee coniectured that itt might be the

---

[1] A blank space of one-half page in the manuscript follows.

550ᴸᴵ promised therin. And itt beinge agreed that the Box should be
opened therwas a bagg of new golde conteyninge the said some of
CCCCCLᴸᴵ: whervppŏ Docter Winstone reportinge what the Comittee
held requisite for the mannaginge therof and that itt should be wholly
in yᵉ charge of Smiths hundred itt was desyred by some that the reso-
luc͂on should be p̃sented in writinge to the next Courte wᶜʰ in regard
of the Ashwednesdays sermon was agreed to be vppon thursday after.

Vppon good considerac͂on of the scarcetie of the Mynisters that is
this day remayninge in Virginia haveinge eleaven Burroughs and not
aboue five Mynisters: Mʳ Thr̃er now comended to be considered by
yᵉ Courte the sendinge of one sufficient Deuine to each of those Burroughs, for the Comfort of the soules of the inhabitants, by preachinge
and expoundinge the word of God vnto them: And for the drawinge
and encourragmᵗ of such Preachers herevnto acquainted them of 100
Acres of Land accordinge to former order to be alotted them wᶜʰ
they beinge vnable to mannage alone are vnwillinge to goe ouer,
therfore because itt may be p̃pared for them hee would that there
might be sentt six men as Ten͂ats to each of the 100 Acres of Gleabe
in the saide Burroughs, in doinge of wᶜʰ a yearly maintenance wilbe
raysed vnto them of wᶜʰ the Company to bear the whole charge of them
wᶜʰ shalbe transported to the Colledge Land, the Gouerno͂ʳ, and the
Companies, and for those six that shalbe sent by pticularr hundreths
the Company for their better provocac͂on therevnto shall furnish out
three to each, vppon condic͂on that the pticular Plantac͂on make vp the
other three, wᶜʰ being putt to the question was generally well allowed
of, whervppon itt was thought very expedient that my Lord of London should be solicited for the helping them wᵗʰ sufficient Mynisters,
as allso such of the Company as wᵗʰ out favour or affeccon could
heare of any that were ~~cinccire~~ ||sincere|| and devoute in that callinge
and were desirous to goe, that they would acquainte the Courte therewith that they may be entertayned.

Mʳ Thr̃er allso signifyinge yᵗ all Indentures of Land wᶜʰ yett have
been graunted to pticuler Societies are to come vnder the Seale againe,

therfore moved y^t a new Coveñnt might be incerted for their mayntenance of a sufficient Mynister wch being done the Country wilbe well planted therwth, wch was well approved of.

Hee allso signified vnto them of the Ballatinge Box standinge vppõ the Table how itt was intended att first an other way as might appeare [83] by the Armes vppon itt butt now m^r Holloway had given itt freely to this Company that therfore to gratefie him they would entertaine him into there Societie by giveinge him a single Share of Land in Virginia wch beinge putt to the question was ratefyed vnto him, whervppon m^r Deputy was entreated to provide a Case for the better preservinge of itt.

M^{r}Holloway made free by giueing him a single share.

A Case for ye Ballatinge Box.

Vppon the request of Richard Francke esquire to have 200 Acres of Land layd outt for 4 men wch are to be transported to Virginia and are allredy paied for vnto two of his sonns, W^m: and Arthur Franke there resydinge m^r Thŕer hath promised to write to the Gouernor for the effectinge of his desire.

200 Acres of Land to be layd out for Mr Richard Francks two Sonns.

A Comission beinge now presented for §the§ m^r ~~Richard Francks two Sonnes~~ of the Swan of Barnstaple for takinge the first optunytie of winde and wather for Virginia was allowed to be sealed.

The Comission for ye Swan of Barnstable to be sealed.

Wheras some principall of ye Magazine Aduenturers for the bette^r putting of of the Tobacco had signed to certaine Articles for takinge halfe therof vppon Condiĉon that all the rest should be written for by Certaine time, wch tyme beinge expired and nothinge pformed, the Adventurers now present have agreed, and to that end tyed themselvs that if those wch have subscribed please to stand thervnto they will not sell the rest att lower price wch if they doe then they to pay no more then the rest shalbe so sould for.

Magazine Aduenturers signed to Certaine Articles

MARCH Y^e^ SECOND 1619

PRESENT.

mr Therr̃er.	Dr Winstone.	mr: Augu: Stewarde.
Sr Io: Dauers.	mr Rich: Tomlyne.	mr Swinhowe.
Sr Baptist Hickes.	mr Ro: Smith.	mr Bull.
Sr Io: Wolstenholme.	mr Wm: Caninge.	mr Casswell.
Sr Nath: Rich.	mr Cranmer.	mr George Smith.
mr Io: Wroth.	mr Keightley.	mr Meuerell.
mr Deputy.	mr Briggs.	mr Arundell.
mr Tho: Gibbe.	mr Wm: Essington.	mr Baldwin.
mr Sam: Wrote.	mr Bearblock.	mr Tho Mellinge.

Mr Essington to proceed wth ye Magazine Accompts.

Wheras the last ordynary Court made choyce of three for the managinge the remaynder of the Magazine buisines, and that then itt was agreed that mr Essington should be entreated to ꝓceed wth the Accompts hee being now p̃sent & desyred by the Adventurors to vndertake itt againe assented to ꝑforme itt. [84]

The Couen̄nt made by the Magaz: Adventurers disliked by Alder: Iohnson

And for asmuch as mr Caswell signified that mr Alderman Iohnson did not like the Couen̄nt made by the Aduenturors in the last Courte for the vnderwritters to take off the Tobacco they had vppon Condicõns subscribed for as not beinge effectuall enough for their sattisfaccõn and therfore desyred to have an other meetinge of ye Aduenturos vppon satterday morninge to take itt againe into consideracõn was by the Adventurers present assented vnto and agreed to be att Sr Thomas Smithe house vppon satterday next att ix of the Clocke, att wch time the Courte have intreated mr Cranmer and mr Chambers to be there for the Company.

Ye Aduenturers desired to meete.

Sr Io: Dauers, and Dr Winstone reporte from ye Spanish Agent.

Sir Iohn Dauers and Dr Winstone repayringe to the Spanish Agent as they were intreated and haveinge delivered their message accordinge to the direccõn of the last Courte reported now that itt was very kindely accepted by the said Agent promisinge to write vnto his Maister the kinge of Spaine for to certifie him how Carefull the Company are to holde all due Correspondency wth him, onely desyringe that if therby hereafter they should finde themselves Dampnified and have occasion to renue and prosecute the matter, that then this Company would ioyne wth them for to procure sattisfacčon, which they in the behalfe of the said Company promised to pforme.

And wheras allso in the last Court Sr Thomas Gates, and Sr Nath: Rich were intreated to repaire to Generall Cæsill touchinge the desyre of the Plantačon to be accomodated wth some Enginers att their owne charges for Raysing of fforteficačon Itt pleased Sr Nath: Rich to reporte that accordingly they were wth Generall Cæsill who found him exceedinge redy and willinge to assist them wth his best furtherance although for the present hee knoweth not how to furnish them they beinge so exceedinge deare and hard to be gotten that they will not worke vnder five or six shillings a day, butt acquainted them of a ffrenchman who hath been longe in England very skillfull therin who pmised to agree wth him for a certaine some of monny to goe ouer and live there signefyinge of two sortes of ffortefycačons, one for the induringe of assaults and Battery, which is not as hee Accompts there very needful butt rather the other of chusinge and takinge some place of Advantage, and there to make some Pallysadoes wch hee conceiveth the fittest, and for wch this ffrenchman is singuler good.

Sr Tho: Gates, & Sr Nath: Rich their reporte from Generall Cæsill touchinge Engineers

Mr Thrᵉer signified that accedentally haveinge some Conferrence with ye Right Honble: the Earle of Arrundell itt pleased his Lo^P: to demonstrate the exceedinge much love hee beareth to the Acčon, insomuch that hee could be content to come and sitt amongst them; Hee therfore moved that the Court would admitt his Lo^P: into their Society, wch beinge putt to ye question was ioyfully embraced by generall consent, and referred according to order to a great Courte for electinge of his Lo^P: to be one of the Counsell. [85]

My Lord of Arrundell admitted a fitt brother & referrd to be elected one of ye Counsell

Hee allso acquainted my Lord of London of the Companies intent for the sendinge ouer Mynisters, and their request vnto his Lo^P: for his good furtherance and assistance therin together wth what mainte-

MyLordofLondon made acquainted of ye Comp^s: intent to send Mynisters.

nance they had there ordeyned for them, wch he very well approved of, promisinge to his vttmost ~~of his~~ power to doe what lyeth in him for the good of that Plantacōn.

Smithℓ hundred content to giue 100^{li} to be discharged from ye charge of ye Infidles Children. Sygnifyinge allso that the Corporacōn of Smithℓ Hundred verie well accepted of the Charge of the Infidles Children comended vnto them by the Courte in regard of their good disposicōn to doe good, butt otherwise if the Courte shall please to take itt from them they will willingly give 100^{li}:   And for their resolucōns although they have not yett sett them downe in writinge by reason some things are yett to be considered off. they will so soone as may be pforme the same and present itt.

A Comittee appoynted for ye settlinge of Saltworkes. Wheras duringe the time of Sr Thomas Dales resydence in Virginia therwas by his means sundry Saltworks sett vpp to the great good and benefitt of the Plantacōn, since wch time they are wholly gone to wrack and lett fall in so much that by defect therof the inhabitants are exceedingly distempred by eatinge porke and other ~~things~~ meats fresh & vnseasoned therfore itt was referred to a Comittee to Consider wth all speed for the settinge vpp againe of the said Saltworks, that is to Sr Iohn Dauers Sr Nathaniell Rich, m^r Iohn Wroth, m^r Dr Winstone, & m^r Sam: Wrote to meet to morrow att two of the Clocke att m^r Thr̄ers house—Mr Baldwin is desyred to be there att the same time to further the said Comittee wth his best advise.

The sending of Sr Geo: Yeardly a present referrd to the Comittee. Itt was allso moved by m^r Treasuror that for asmuch as this yeare there hath beene and are in preparinge to be sent to Virginia 1200: personns or their aboute wherof 600: to the publique or for other pious vses wherby a heavy burthen will be vppon Sr George Yeardley for the disposinge of them all accordinge to direcc̄ons and instrucc̄ons sent vnto him, that therfore for his better incoragment the Company would please to send him a Present itt beinge no new thinge butt much vsed by them heretofore whervppon itt was referred to the Committee in ye preceding Order to consider and conclude what shalbe sent vnto him.   [86]

As likewise ‖that in reguard‖ a treaty is to be made wth Opachan- kano touchinge the bette^r keepinge of the Infidells Children wch are to be brought vpp in Christianytie y^t therfore they would authorize Sr George Yeardley to take some such thinge as hee shall like best outt of the Magazine and present itt vnto him for the better attayninge their ends of him wch beinge putt to the question was well allowed.

Sr George Yeardly authorized to take some things out of ye Magazine to present itt to Opachankano.

Sr Thomas Gates, by his bill assigned five Shares of twelve pounds tenn shillings the Share to Samuell Wrote esqr: wch the Audito^{rs} haveinge formerly approved was allowed by this Courte.

Sr Tho: Gates 5 Shares to Sam: Wrote.

Likewise m^r Humphrey Reynolde assigned five Shares to m^r Humphry Slaney wch beinge allso allowed by the Audito^{rs} was ratefyed by this Courte.

Mr Hum: Reighnolde 5: shares to m^r Humfrey Slaney.

MARCH THE 15th 1619

PRESENT.

The Right Honor^{ble}: Robert Earle of Warwick.

Sr Edwin Sandys Thr̃er.

Sr Thomas Roe.	m^r Iohn Wroth.	Capt Dani: Tucker.
Sr Dudley Digge.	m^r Mau: Abbott.	m^r Iohn Smith.
Sr Thomas Gates.	m^r Deputy.	m^r Keightley.
Sr Iohn Dauers.	m^r Tho: Gibbes.	m^r Nicho: Ferrar.
Sr Fard: Gorge.	m^r Robt: Ofley.	m^r Bull.
Sr Tho: Wroth.	m^r Sam: Wrote.	m^r Cranmer.
Sr Iohn: Wolstenholme.	m^r Dr Meddus.	m^r Rogers.
Sr Nath: Rich.	m^r Henry Reighnolde.	m^r Essington.
Sr Tho: Willforde.	m^r Tomlyne.	m^r Ditchfeilde.
m^r Recorder of London.	m^r George Tucker.	m^r Casswell.
m^r Alderm: Iohnson.	m^r Nicho: Leate.	m^r Swifte.
	Capt Sam: Argoll.	m^r George Smith.
		m^r Mellinge, C^r.

The Courte beinge sett m^r Thr̃er made knowne y^t the George beinge returned from Virginia had brought l̃res certefyinge allso of the

The George returned 300: dead

greate mortallytie wch hath beene in Virginia about 300:of the Inhabitants haveinge dyed this last yeare and that Sr George Yeardley comittes the ~~former~~ §same§ error as formerly that hee dyrecteth all his letters to the Counsell and not any to the Company; Butt for y^e

The people sent in ye Bona Noua arriued well.

people sent in the Bona Noua they are aryved in health are all liveinge & p̄sper well applyinge themselvs wth the rest accordinge to direcc̄on to the buildinge of houses tillinge of the ground plantinge Silkgrass: Butt forasmuch as the Courte was wholly ignorant of the State of the Colloney wch by the readinge of these [87] Lette^{rs} now

The readinge of ye L̄res is referd

come they might be enformed of, therfore itt was ernestly moved by divers now present that they might be published to the Courte, butt sundry of the Counsell thinkinge itt inconvenyent, till a full nomber therof hadd first heard itt, wch was accounted seaven to gether, itt was therfore deferred till the next Courte and in the intryme itt was agreed that the Counsell should be desyred to meete vppon ffryday afternoone att m^r Thr̄er̄ house att two of the Clocke, and that Capt

Capt Smith & Capt Maddison to make known their greuances.

Smith, and Capt Maddison then attend to make knowne their greivances wch they pretend done vnto them by Sr George Yeardley.

3 things of mayne consequence Comended by ye Thr̄er̄ to ye Courte. 1:

Then hee Com̄ended to the Considerac̄on and approbac̄on of them three Things of mayne consequence—1: wheras fower shipps are lately dispeeded and another wch wilbe readie to goe by the last of this moneth wth Pasengers & Provisions as itt was delivered and allowed in a Quarter Courte held the 17th of Nouemb^r last that therfore for the better Care of preservinge them att their landinge and nourishinge those wch shalbe sicke for preventinge so neer as may be ye like mortallytie and for the prosicutinge of some well degested orders made

The draught of a Charter for nourishinge those y^t are sicke.

in their Courtes hee had framed the draught of a Charter, wch although this Courte could not give a finall confirmac̄on thervnto, yett if they now approved therof itt might be sent in this Ship to be putt in Execuc̄on, & be confirmed in the next greate generall Courte.

To dispose of ye Ship & good̄c̄ returned. 2:

That wch m^r Alderman Iohnson now proposed that they would take care how to dispose of the Ship and goods now returned for their best advantage.

Of difference betwixt the Northerne and So: Collonys.

ffor the first the Draught of the said Charter beinge extant itt was
agreed should be red wch done was very well approved and allowed
off referringe itt to the Quarter Courte for an example confirmaçon
butt in the meane time agreed that the Coppie therof should be sent
for the Gouernor to putt in practize.

The second beinge m[r] Alderman Iohnson[e] Proposiçon was comitted
to a Comittee to consider of, that is to say

Sr Thomas Smith.	m[r] Alder: Iohnson.	m[r] Cranmore
S[r] Thomas Wroth.	m[r] Io: Wroth.	m[r] Bull &
S[r] Io: Wolstenholme.	m[r] Deputy.	m[r] Caswell or so many
S[r] Nath: Rich.	m[r] Keightley.	el[e] as pleased.

Devidinge the busines into three poyntes.

ffor the plantinge of English Tobacco that notw[th]standinge vppon y[e]
Compa: yeildinge to an imposte, his Ma[ty] by a Proclamaçon hath prohibited the same yett Contrary thervnto itt is pryvately planted.

ffor the procuringe a mitegaçon of the imposiçon w[ch] is conceyved
may be obteyned. [88]

For the Sale of y[e] Goods

All w[ch] is referred as aforesaid, and are entreated to meete att S[r]
Thomas Smith[e] house vppon Satterday morninge next att eight of the
Clocke.

To the third m[r] Thr[e]r signified that the N[o]: Collony intendinge to
replante themselvs in Virginia had petiçoned to the Kinge and to the
Lords for y[e] obteyning a nue Pattent w[ch] the Lords referred vnto
the Lord Duke, & the Lord of Arundell And the Lord of Arundell
delivered itt to him for to call the Counsell, vnderstanding of some
differrences about fishinge betwixt them, and if they could not determine of itt, that then to returne theire opinions to their Lo[ps]: whervppon accordinglie haveinge mett, and as formerly disputed the buisines they could not conclude therof, butt discented the one from the

other, that therfore accordinge to his Lo^{ps} Command the Courte would please to nominate some to give intelligence how the buisines betwixt them doth depend, wch the Courte pceivinge none to vnderstand the cause so well as himselfe most ernestly besought him to take the paines, wch hee beinge very loth and vnwillinge by reason of the exceedinge multitude of the Company℄ buisines depending vppon him desyred to be excused, butt not prevaylinge hee was soe ernestly solicited thervnto that hee could not gainesay itt, whervppon they associated vnto him Sr Iohn Dauers, m^r Harbert, and m^r Keightley to repaire thither to morrow morninge at 8 of the Clocke.

The Articles between m^r Kinge & ye Comp^a: touchinge ye Iron Workes ordered to be sealed. Hee allso signified of one m^r ^{1} Kinge that is to goe wth 50 persons wth him to Virginia there to sett on foote Iron Workes and that there was Articles indented betwixt the Company and him, w^{c}h beinge red was so well liked that they allowed of the same, and agreed that the Seale should be thervnto affixed.

Mr Thr̄er thanked for sealinge ye Charter party for the Bona Venture. And wheras the Ship before exprest to sett forward before the latter of this monneth called the Frauncis Bona Venture, m^r Treasuror haveinge sealed the Charter party betwixt the owners and the Company; The Courte now did render thanks vnto him for the same and have agreed to save him harmeless.

Sr Tho: Gates one Share to m^r Palauicine Sir Thomas Gates assigned one single Share to Edward Palauicine gentleman wch beinge approved by the Auditors and now putt to the question was confirmed vnto him.

The Comission for the Fra: Bona: Venture allowed. A Comission unto ^{1} Maister of ye Frauncis Bona Venture for the takinge optunitie of winde and weather for Virginia was now allowed. [89]

^{1} A blank space in the manuscript.